Encyclopedia of the Zombie

The Walking Dead in Popular Culture and Myth

JUNE MICHELE PULLIAM AND
ANTHONY J. FONSECA, EDITORS

 GREENWOOD

AN IMPRINT OF ABC-CLIO, LLC
Santa Barbara, California • Denver, Colorado • Oxford, England

Library of Congress Cataloging-in-Publication Data

Encyclopedia of the zombie : the walking dead in popular culture and myth / June Michele Pulliam and Anthony J. Fonseca, editors.
    pages cm
Includes index.
ISBN 978-1-4408-0388-8 (hardback) — ISBN 978-1-4408-0389-5 (ebook)
1. Zombies—Encyclopedias.   I. Fonseca, Anthony J., editor of compilation.
II. Pulliam, June Michele, editor of compilation.
  GR581.E53   2014
  398.21—dc23   2014000163

ISBN: 978-1-4408-0388-8
EISBN: 978-1-4408-0389-5

18 17 16 15 14   1 2 3 4 5

This book is also available on the World Wide Web as an eBook.
Visit www.abc-clio.com for details.

Greenwood
An Imprint of ABC-CLIO, LLC

ABC-CLIO, LLC
130 Cremona Drive, P.O. Box 1911
Santa Barbara, California 93116-1911

This book is printed on acid-free paper ∞

Manufactured in the United States of America

For my father, who let me stay up past my bedtime one Friday when I was eight and watch *Night of the Living Dead* all by myself. Ever since, I've never been the same.

—June Michele Pulliam

Contents

Acknowledgments

No book is created in a vacuum. This encyclopedia is the result of the assistance of others, on multiple levels. We would like to acknowledge that assistance here. Thanks go out to the following people: Braden Dauzat and Josh Hamburg, invaluable research assistants during this project, kept a sharp eye out for typos that, would they appear in print, would haunt us to our graves; our friends and colleagues who helped by stopping us in the hallways and bending our ears about various zombie media, or emailed, or Facebooked items to us; S. T. Joshi, who got us interested in the scholarly study of zombies when he first asked for contributions for his *Supernatural Literature of the World: An Encyclopedia.* June sends a shout out to her students, who signed up for her Zombie Literature course and talked about the undead with her, as well as Rick Blackwood, Christopher F. Robertson, Shane Stadler, and Mark R. R. Wilson, who helped in their own ways too by showing her how to shoot zombies on the firing range and in video games, by watching and discussing zombie films with her, and even by alerting her to the existence of special zombie-killing knives that are for sale. And June offers her deepest thanks to the proprietors of Highland Coffees (in Baton Rouge, Louisiana) and The Globe Café (in Prague) for letting her sit for hours in their establishments, nursing a cup of coffee while she pecked away on her laptop, as well as the interlibrary loan staff of Louisiana State University's Middleton Library who continuously procured "yet another zombie book" for her. Tony offers special thanks to the faculty at Elms College and the good folks at The Foundry (in Northampton), who responded to news of the project with genuine enthusiasm and kept his spirits up when his laptop would die and need reanimation.

Introduction

They're Coming to Get You

Zombies are everywhere lately: they are the subject of films, television shows, and epic graphic novel series. People shoot at them in video games and even on the firing range. They can be seen chasing runners in 5K events and shambling around at zombie walks of their own. They teach physicians, veterinarians, and soldiers how to respond to pandemics, natural disasters, and terrorist attacks. And they have been sufficiently domesticated to star in advertisements for Honda and J. C. Penney. Meanwhile, we manage to escape our houses moments before they are overrun with the undead.

Despite their threat, zombies can make us laugh. Because they cannot feel physical pain or even move very quickly, zombies are perfect gory slapstick comedians: when you bash their heads with a cricket bat, their faces barely register the assault; when you hit them in the face with a pie, they are only dimly aware that there is whipped cream clouding their vision.

Most monsters, such as the ghost and the werewolf, have a lengthy pedigree stretching back into antiquity. The zombie, however, is a relatively recent addition to the pantheon of monsters, originating in Haiti in the late 19th century amid islanders' fears that they would soon be recolonized and enslaved by outside corporate interests. During this time, tales of zombies created by Voodoo proliferated, whereby a bokur or zombie priest who practiced dark magic resurrected the dead to use as slave labor. Haitian folklore about the zombie was recounted by Lafcadio Hearn in his essay "The Country of Comers-Back," by William Seabrook in his travelogue *The Magic Island,* and by Zora Neale Hurston in her book *Tell My Horse: Voodoo and Life in Haiti and Jamaica.*

In the early 20th century, the Voodoo zombie soon found its way into American popular culture in films such as *White Zombie, I Walked with a Zombie,* and the comic *Zombies on Broadway,* and it also became a staple in pulp magazines that published fantastic fiction as well as in horror comics. In 1968, director George A. Romero transformed the creature as we know it, crystallizing earlier iterations while adding his own interpretation and elements in his groundbreaking film *Night of the Living Dead.* Following suit, contemporary representations of the zombie explain the creature as hailing from outer space, or as the result of secret government experimentation or a virus gone awry, or as a sign that the apocalypse is at hand. In alternative fictions, zombies were around during the Civil War, when they terrorized Union soldiers (in some accounts), or harassed southerners (in others). Nazi zombies now thrive in a secret level of the video game *Call of Duty,* and they rise from their frozen graves to terrorize humans in films such as *Dead Snow.*

No matter how often they are killed in fictional narratives, zombies will not go away. So we prepare for the impending zombie apocalypse by reading books such as Max Brooks's *Zombie Survival Guide,* while we hone our shooting skills with zombie targets, purchase special products such as zombie killing knives, zombie shooting ammunition, and even a zombie preparedness backpack. As a result, zombies demand justice: fallen soldiers reanimate as zombies to vote out of office the politicians who sent them to their deaths searching for spurious weapons of mass destruction; zombies organize to strike back at those who shoot at them with abandon; zombies demand civil rights.

And now zombies are the sole subject of this encyclopedia.

History of the Zombie

Ethnobotanist Wade Davis traveled to Haiti in the 1980s to report in his book *The Serpent and the Rainbow* that the zombie is real, a victim of a powerful combination of drugs administered by a bokur, a Voodoo priest who uses dark magic, and the victim's own belief in the bokur's supernatural abilities. The bokur slips to the victim a tetrodotoxin derived from the puffer fish, and he or she falls into a catatonic state mimicking death, soon buried by grieving family members. The bokur, then, disinters the victim and revives him or her by administering a paste of zombie cucumber, which produces amnesia, delirium, and suggestibility. In this state, the victim is easily deprived of what little free will he or she possesses to become a zombie slave who can be used to do mindless manual labor. Zora Neale Hurston claimed to have seen one of these zombies approximately 50 years earlier during her travels to Haiti, where the unfortunate victim was found wandering and put into mental hospital. And a decade before Hurston's book was published, one of William Seabrook's Haitian friends showed him men that he claimed were also zombies, blank-eyed men who labored under the broiling sun in the cane fields in conditions that would cause others to collapse from heat exhaustion.

More contemporary narratives build on the idea of the zombie as the living undead. In the *28 Days Later* series, the zombie is someone deprived of all consciousness by the fast-acting rage virus, which transforms victims into fast-moving, red-eyed creatures animated by an insatiable need to tear apart all uninfected humans. These zombies are the living undead, rather than reanimated corpses; they can eventually starve to death.

In other narratives, zombies are the reanimated dead, people whose bodies have actually ceased to function, and who might have also suffered brain death. These dead return and are characterized by a single-mindedness of purpose. This type of zombie is arguably the most recognizable to us today, thanks in part to Romero's iconic 1968 film where an unknown force causes the recently dead to awaken. These undead are hungry and are driven by the desire to feast on the living. However, Romero cannot be credited with transforming the zombie into the living dead. Richard Matheson's 1954 novella *I Am Legend* represents a complicated variety of undead that come into existence in the aftermath of a world nuclear war in 1976, the novel's near future. A virus creates two tiers of undead—one large population of people who have actually suffered brain death, and whose bodies are reanimated, causing them to wander the planet in search of human blood to drink, and a second, smaller population who were infected but who did not suffer brain death. The first tier's mindlessness classifies them as zombies, while the second tier cannot be described as zombies. They have retained their higher brain functions. Both sets of undead have more in common with the vampire than the zombie, however—each is deathly allergic to garlic and cannot tolerate the sunlight (though the second tier of undead have developed medication to permit them to walk in the daylight for short periods of time).

They're All Messed Up

The central horror of zombies who are the reanimated dead is the spectacle of their rotting flesh. In this way, they are a study in abjection. The dreadfulness of the corpse is vividly illustrated in horror comics of the 1930s, 1940s, and 1950s. This spectacle carries over in the 1966 Hammer Studios film *The Plague of the Zombies,* directed by John Gilling. Set in the Victorian era, the film follows a cash-poor aristocrat who attempts to regenerate his family's wealth by mining the tin ore beneath his ancestral lands using cheap labor—zombies he has created from the ranks of the working classes who were no longer willing to participate in this dangerous occupation. Gilling's reanimated dead, with their scabby faces, are visibly decomposing.

Romero builds upon this trope in his *Night of the Living Dead* films, where his zombies are differentiated from the living by their severe bodily injuries. Romero, however, adds another iconic quality to the zombie—his living dead are cannibals. Previously, the living dead only frightened the living but were not an actual threat to them (until Matheson's *I Am Legend,* with his confused, blood-drinking zombies). Romero's zombies, however, gorge themselves on living flesh—on screen, in wet and gory scenes. Romero's cannibal zombies inspired an entire subgenre of Italian horror cinema, the cannibal film, beginning with Lucio Fulci's *Zombi* (1979). So influential is Romero's concept of the zombie that all other zombie fiction after it must give a nod to his flesh-eating zombies, if only to explain why he got the mythology wrong.

Zombies operating by Romero's Rules have been viewed as having their counterpart in humans suffering from rabies or mad cow disease. The rabies virus works on the human limbic system, which is the center of fear and anger in the human brain. The infected are co-opted by the virus to do the work of spreading it to others, and in this way they have lost their own free will. They directly link the rabies virus to the contemporary zombie myth both in how the virus is so rapidly spread and in how it causes the infected to behave as an irrational snarling animal that will attack loved ones and strangers alike.

Shambling Through Life, Metaphorically

A third type of zombie emerges at the end of the 20th century, in part due to the influence of the field of zombie studies in which scholars ponder how the zombie is a fertile metaphor for the hidden workings of the human mind. We hold firm to the belief that we are the captains of our souls, and that our capacity for free and rational will is what differentiates us from other animals. Yet, many of our desires have been programmed at such a deep level that we are not really making conscious choices. This type of zombie can be seen in works such William Sleator's young adult novel *The Boy Who Couldn't Die* (2004).

Alternately, the zombie is a fertile metaphor for exploring the nature of death itself, which, thanks to modern medicine, is no longer as cut and dried as it once was. Modern technology has made it possible to keep the body functioning long after brain death has occurred. David Sutton's short story "Clinically Dead" touches upon this theme, as does Joe R. Lansdale's story "Bubba Ho-Tep." Both examine the lives of the medically frail, kept alive via machines in Sutton's story and warehoused and forgotten in Lansdale's story, lacking the free will to break out of their marginalized existences or even refuse medical treatment that would keep them alive longer without restoring them to health.

In all of its incarnations, the zombie terrifies us because it is a monster, a creature that crosses borders that we have erected in order to provide a comforting illusion of the stability of our social hierarchies. These borders tell us that men are fundamentally different from women, that whites and nonwhites are nearly different species, that the world is made up of good people and terrorists, and even that there is a distinct line between life and death. The monsters is threatening, then, because in crossing these borders, it reveals them as permeable and contrived rather than as natural and solid. Every time we kill a zombie then, or witness one killed in fiction, we are in essence reaffirming these boundaries. We know that these boundaries are illusions, and so we must kill the zombie over and over since it stubbornly refuses to accept our communal lie and stay dead.

Scope of This Book

We have used an expansive definition of the zombie in *The Encyclopedia of the Zombie*. The zombie can either be the enslaved alive or the reanimated dead, and he or she or it may or may not be a cannibal. While these qualities are associated with the zombie, the most essential characteristic of the creature is its lack of free will. The zombie either has its will subordinated by a master, as in the case with zombies created by Voodoo, or its will is effaced by the unquenchable need to consume human flesh (or brains), or even by a crippling rage that drives the creature to tear apart all uninfected humans.

As our work is an encyclopedia, we have not attempted to cite every single representation of the zombie. Rather, we have limited our scope to representations of the creature that are notable in some way—either due to their unique interpretation of the zombie or the influence or popularity of the representation. Since our goal is to make a reference work that gives our readers a broad understanding of the zombie, we have also included entries on stories or mythical creatures that are proto-zombies, monsters that have laid the foundation for the creature we know today.

ABRAHAM LINCOLN VS. ZOMBIES

Abraham Lincoln vs. Zombies is a 2012 straight-to-DVD release directed by Richard Schenkman (born Richard Gerardo Schenkman, 1958–). This dark comedy horror film is a mash-up text derivative of Seth Grahame-Smith's (born Seth Jared Greenberg, 1976–) ground-breaking mash-ups *Pride and Prejudice and Zombies* (2009) and *Abraham Lincoln: Vampire Hunter* (2010). Schenkman combines the larger-than-life folkloric figure of Abraham Lincoln with the trope of the zombie to make the 16th president of the United States into a type of superhero who defeats the Confederacy by killing their zombies.

Like the seeds of succession, the infectious agent that can raise the dead has been present in the United States since Lincoln was 10 years old, and he had to behead his stepmother when she turned into a ravening cannibal. So when the adult Lincoln, now president, gets word of the dead returning to life at Ft. Pulaski, he accompanies his newly formed Secret Service to fight the menace, undead zombies that follow Romero's Rules. *Abraham Lincoln vs. Zombies* was made with cult sensibilities in mind, as those who would appreciate this film would enjoy its qualities that would be lost on a mainstream audience. Critics found that the film was plagued by poor script-writing and historical inaccuracies, though actor Bill Oberst Jr. (born William Oberst Jr., 1965–) was singled out for his excellent portrayal of Lincoln.

Abraham Lincoln vs. Zombies is very similar to Grahame-Smith's *Abraham Lincoln: Vampire Hunter* in its portrayal of Lincoln as a sort of logical extension of the mythic idea of him as a pioneer commander in chief who spent his youth living in a log cabin, splitting rails. While Lincoln did live in a log cabin and split a few rails, this characterization of him was embellished for his 1860 presidential campaign to make him seem more relatable to the voting public. Over time, this representation of Lincoln has combined with other myths about him, where he is positioned as waging the Civil War to free the slaves. In fact, Lincoln was not an abolitionist (though his wife Mary was), and his Emancipation Proclamation only freed the slaves in the 10 states that were still in rebellion against the federal government in 1863—the year it was issued. Such mythologizing made the former president a credible historical figure to be represented as a secret super hero who fights a zombie Confederacy (which in the film is represented much like the Third Reich in various Nazi zombie films, where its leaders are portrayed as supernaturally evil).

See also: Cult Film; Epidemics; Mash-Ups, Literary; Romero's Rules

June Michele Pulliam

ADOLESCENT LITERATURE

See Young Adult Fiction

AFRICA

Africa, or more specifically the western coast of Africa, is technically the birthplace of the zombie. West African Vodun holds that a dead human can be brought back to life by a priest with specific otherworldly powers to commune with the gods. This priest, or bokur, then gains control of the zombified human, who has lost all free will.

A related phenomenon occurs in some parts of South Africa where a witch can turn a person into a zombie much in the same way as a bokur and then use these zombies as slave labor. Often these zombies were impressed into labor on the railways, resulting in stories of trains staffed by zombie workers. Stories of abductions leading to recruitment of more zombies were plentiful. In most of the legends, zombies could be sent back to their graves by giving them salt, which reminded them of their former lives. The West African tradition also created the prototype for the astral zombie. In some modern fictional accounts, this type of zombie occurs when one's soul has been captured. The astral zombie can then be controlled by a bokur during sleep, as in the young adult novel *The Boy Who Couldn't Die* (2004), by William Sleator (1945–2011). In the African tradition, the astral zombie can be used for good luck, since it is a spiritual entity, and kept in a bottle. In such a context, the word zombi, which also refers to the snake loa (lesser or intermediary god, sometimes called a vodun), is similar to the Kikongo word *nzambi*, which means god.

Vodun is practiced by the Ewe, Kabye, Mina, Fon, and Yoruba peoples. It was the enslavement of West Africans that originally brought Vodun to the United States, especially in the area surrounding the Gullah Islands. Enslaved Africans brought to Haiti were primarily from the western and central areas; they created a unique version of the Vodun religion by combining the loas with Roman Catholic saints, in order to comply with the 1685 Code Noir by King Louis XIV of France, a decree that dictated the conditions in slavery in the French colonies, including a prohibition on the practice of any religion other than Roman Catholicism. The African Diaspora also shows its influence in Brazil (Vodum), Cuba (Santería), Puerto Rico (Vudu), Surinam (Winti), and the United States (Louisiana and Gullah Island, Voodoo).

See also: Bokur/Caplata; *Boy Who Couldn't Die, The*; Voodoo

Anthony J. Fonseca

ANGEL, JOANNA

Joanna Angel (born Joanna Mostov, 1980–) is an American pornography actress, producer, director, and webmaster known for popularizing hardcore alt porn. A former model on the Suicide Girl soft-core pornography website, she is the creator of the successful website BurningAngel.com and is regarded as major influence in the mainstreaming of alt porn—pornography that specializes in tattoos and piercings and has a punk rock aesthetic. She has made the genre financially viable. Through BurningAngel.com, she has produced and performed in four popular zombie-themed hardcore films: *Re-Penetrator* (2005), *Dong of the Dead* (2009), *Evil Head* (2012), and *The Walking Dead: A Hardcore Parody* (2013). Related though not technically about zombies, Angel also starred in and directed the 2012 feature, *Fuckenstein*.

Angel grew up in New Jersey, and in her early 20s she dropped out of Rutgers University to pursue working on the website, BurningAngel.com. The site was a self-described "indie-punk-porn site" featuring band interviews, Angel's stories of sex with band members, and nude photography. Eventually, she began to feel that the site was not progressing her feminist ideals and, inspired by a sex show performed by feminist porn star Nina Hartley (born Marie Louise Hartman, 1959–), Angel decided to start making hardcore movies for the site and distributing the content on DVD.

The punk rock origins of BurningAngel and its consistent use of horror tropes exemplify the symbiotic relationship between purveyors of porn and horror, two diverse cultures. BurningAngel is the only company to produce zombie porn—a seldom-seen hardcore subgenre—on a regular basis. Angel's films do not shy away from the grotesque nature of zombies, with performers wearing full zombie make up, staying in character during sex scenes, and suffering gory deaths, a rare sight in mainstream hardcore pornography. She describes her early porn venture as a weird experiment, one that she did not expect to become as popular as it has. Entering the industry with very little knowledge of what was expected of producers and performers, Angel was able to forge her own path in some respects, creating unorthodox punk rock porn that has proved marketable to an existing mainstream porn audience.

See also: Pornography

Laura Helen Marks

APOCALYPSE

The apocalypse is a concept that is not associated with all representations of the zombie but is ubiquitous to those that follow Romero's Rules. However, the idea of a zombie apocalypse predates George Romero's (born George Andrew Romero, 1940–) *Night of the Living Dead* (1968) by 14 years.

The zombie apocalypse is first seen in Richard Matheson's (born Richard Burton Matheson, 1926–2013) novella *I Am Legend* (1954), where in the distant future of 1976, a bacteria that develops in the aftermath of global nuclear warfare causes the dead to reanimate as mindless creatures whose actions have been reduced to a basic need to sleep during the day and find shelter from the sun, since their condition causes them to be allergic to sunlight. As the infected are also allergic to garlic, the living dead, with their diminished intellect, believe that they are vampires, and so

The zombie apocalypse is first seen in Richard Matheson's 1954 novella *I Am Legend,* where in the distant future of 1976, a bacteria develops in the aftermath of a global nuclear exchange, causing the dead to reanimate as mindless creatures who believe that they need the blood of the living to survive. (WireImage)

they come out at night to search for human blood, although they do not require it to live. Robert Neville, Matheson's protagonist, believes that he is the last man on earth, since he has not come into contact with any uninfected, and he must continuously barricade himself in his suburban home if he wants to survive as civilization has toppled worldwide. However, Robert soon learns that there are other living survivors of the pandemic who have not been infected by the bacteria. However, he has not seen these people for over a year because, like the dead infected, they too are severely allergic to sunlight and have only recently developed a drug allowing them to be out during the daytime. Romero names *I Am Legend,* as well as *The Last Man on Earth* (1964), the first film made of Matheson's novella, as influencing his creation of *Night of the Living Dead,* which crystallized earlier representations of the zombie as a mindless ghoul and combined them the idea that the zombie's presence among the living would bring about an apocalypse.

When the dead who behave according to Romero's Rules rise from their graves, the inevitable consequence is the collapse of civilization or the end of the world as humans understand it. This is because zombies who behave according to Romero's Rules transmit a pandemic—the living can be rapidly turned into zombies through a bite, or in some mythologies, through merely coming into contact with a zombie's bodily fluids. Moreover, there is little chance that the dwindling numbers of humans can peacefully coexist with zombies because the creatures are driven to consume human flesh or brains in some mythologies, while in others such as the *28 Days Later* films, those infected by the rage virus are in thrall to a desire to tear apart the living. Thus, the zombie apocalypse is a cataclysmic event after which diminishing numbers of humans must try to survive in a world where they are no longer at the top of the food chain, and where they now lack much of the modern infrastructure that once allowed them to maintain mastery over other species. The other five films in Romero's *Living Dead* series explore how this apocalypse affects the ever decreasing number of human survivors, and indeed, if the human race will survive. Romero, however, never definitively explains why the dead have started returning to life; he offers competing theories that the surviving humans can guess at—ranging from radiation released into the atmosphere from a satellite returning to earth to the biblical end times.

Later notable works of zombie film and fiction and video games explore the causes and/or aftermath of the zombie apocalypse. In Danny Boyle's (born Danniel Boyle, 1956–) *28 Days Later* (2002), the zombie apocalypse is ushered in when the rage virus nearly wipes out the entire population of the United Kingdom in under a month. Max Brooks's (born Maximillian Michael Brooks, 1972–) novel *World War Z* (2006) examines the zombie apocalypse on a global scale and considers what humans would have to do to ultimately return from the brink of extinction. Robert Kirkman's (1978–) epic graphic novel series *The Walking Dead* and the American Movie Classics (AMC) television series based on it follow several characters many years after the initial apocalypse to consider how the dead's returning to life changes the remaining survivors. Video games such as *Left 4 Dead* (L4D) (2008) turn surviving the zombie apocalypse into a game in which players must cooperate with other characters or other players in order to survive the ever-increasing number of zombie hordes. In Cormac McCarthy's (born Charles McCarthy, 1933–) novel *The Road* (2006), the survivors of a worldwide nuclear exchange inhabit a post-apocalyptic landscape and look and behave very much like zombies, a metaphor that all would be familiar when the novel was written.

In fact, while the zombie apocalypse is not a component of all zombie fiction, it is ubiquitous in contemporary zombie fiction to the point that it is often mistakenly thought to be one of the genre's central tropes. The widespread popularity of fiction featuring the zombie apocalypse in the 21st century is something that is particularly illuminating about the creature's appeal. The zombie apocalypse is a secular eschatological narrative, building on very real fears that current events foreshadow a near future apocalypse. Worldwide pandemics, such as AIDS, SARS, and the Avian Flu, global financial meltdowns that have been exacerbated by austerity measures that allow increasing numbers of people to slip into poverty, Hurricane Katrina and other natural disasters whose magnitude killed thousands of people and left a blighted, post-apocalyptic world in their place, and 9/11 are just a few of the events of the 21st century that make it seem, to people in First-World nations, anyway, that it is the end of the world as we know it. Zombies, our former friends, neighbors, and family members, run amok in the blighted landscape of the zombie apocalypse, triumphantly feasting on the flesh of loved ones. So it is no wonder then that the zombie apocalypse has been appropriated as a metaphor for everything from existential angst, as is the case in the comedic film *Shaun of the Dead*

(2004), to fears that governments and corporations have used the excuse of global terrorism to coerce citizens into surrendering their liberties, one of the central themes of the film *Fido* (2006).

Meanwhile, medical schools and schools of veterinary medicine, the Centers for Disease Control, and even the U.S. military have used the metaphor of the zombie apocalypse to teach physicians and veterinarians about pandemics, help citizens understand how to be prepared for life in the aftermath of a major natural disaster such as a hurricane or earthquake, or how to deal with terrorists, respectively. At Michigan State University, "Surviving the Coming Zombie Apocalypse: Catastrophes & Human Behavior" is a course that recently taught students how humans behave during catastrophic events. The zombie apocalypse then has gone from being a freakish and calamitous event that might occur in some distant future to something that is in the process of happening right now.

See also: Epidemics; Existentialism; *Fido*; *I Am Legend* (Novel); *Left 4 Dead*; Matheson, Richard; *Road, The* (Novel); Romero, George; *Shaun of the Dead*; Television; *28 Days Later* Series; *Walking Dead, The* (Graphic Novel); *Walking Dead, The* (Television Series); *World War Z* (Film); *World War Z* (Novel)

June Michele Pulliam

ARMY OF DARKNESS (COMIC)

Army of Darkness is a comic series created in 1992, after Dark Horse Comics achieved great success transforming film characters into comic book stars, producing a miniseries adaptation of the film *Army of Darkness,* following the adventures of Ash Williams, the surviving hero of the *Evil Dead* series. The *Evil Dead* series is an American horror film franchise written and directed by Sam Raimi (born Samuel M. Raimi, 1959–) and produced by Robert G. Tapert (born Robert Gerard Tapert, 1955–). The four feature films, *The Evil Dead* (1981), *The Evil Dead II* (1987), *Army of Darkness* (1992), and the recent remake of *The Evil Dead* (2013), center on *The Necronomicon Ex-Mortis,* an ancient Sumerian text that wreaks havoc on the inhabitants of a rundown cabin in rural Tennessee.

For the original comic book publication, John Bolton (1951–) contributed artwork and adapted the storyline from the script of the third movie, keeping the original ending intact. Dark Horse Comics originally released it as a three-issue miniseries and then revisited the franchise with a four-issue adaptation of *The Evil Dead* in 2008, written by Mark Verheiden (1956–) and illustrated by Bolton. In 2004, Dynamite Entertainment acquired the license to publish titles based on *Army of Darkness,* and in conjunction with Devil's Due Publishing, released *Army of Darkness: Ashes 2 Ashes* miniseries. A second miniseries, *Army of Darkness: Shop till You Drop Dead* followed in 2005. The four issues of *Shop till You Drop Dead* put Ash back in S-Mart and the real world battling the ever-present deadites, undead creatures brought back to life and mutated by *The Necronomicon Ex-Mortis.*

Dynamite Entertainment separated itself from Devil's Due Publishing in 2005 and began focusing entirely on self-published titles featuring the *Army of Darkness* franchise. This included a trade paperback of the original movie comic, published in 2006, and an ongoing series that began in 2005 and saw Ash battling other horror icons, such as Herbert West and Dracula. The series lasted 13 issues before being rebooted with a second volume in 2007 that continued for 27 issues before coming to an end. Also, in 2007, a five-issue miniseries crossover with Marvel Comics began, set in the Marvel Zombies universe and doubling as an origin story for that universe, alongside the interlinked prequel *Marvel Zombies: Dead Days*. In 2008, Dark Horse Comics revisited the *Army of Darkness* franchise with a four-issue adaptation of *The Evil Dead* written by Verheiden and illustrated by Bolton. Over the years, there have also been several one-shot specials as well as crossovers, with a wide variety of characters, including Darkman, Freddy Krueger, Jason Voorhees, Xena the Warrior Princess, Danger Girl, and even Barack Obama. The most recent developments regarding the *Army of Darkness* franchise include a six-issue crossover *Army of Darkness vs. Hack/Slash,* featuring Tim Seeley's character Cassie Hack and a forthcoming overhaul of the series.

See also: Evil Dead, The (Films); Raimi, Sam

Deborah G. Christie

ASIAN CINEMA

Asian cinema has a varied history when it comes to zombie films. Even though over 500 Asian films from 14 countries have utilized the zombie trope or a version of it (some zombie-like creature), zombie films per se are not considered a mature subgenre of Asian horror cinema. China and Japan produce the vast majority of these films. Granted, film franchises such as the *Ringu* series and the *Ju-On* series flirt with the idea of the zombie; however, the creatures in these films are technically either demons or revenging revenants. Despite the fact that there is no *Night of the Living Dead* (1968) equivalent in Asian cinema, one of the most popular noncomedic zombie series in the United States, both in video game and on film, the *Resident Evil* series, was developed in Japan.

Generally, Asian zombie films are low budget and laden with near slapstick farcical humor; this has made it easy for critics to dismiss the subgenre altogether. However, a mythological and cultural subtext exists in even the most inane of these films. Unlike the American zombie film, which borrows from Haitian religious belief and folklore, Asian zombie mythology is rooted in Asian culture. The mythological Asian zombie is also a vampire who can drain the life essence of victims. These creatures, called the *jiang shi* or hopping zombie in China, are referred to as *Kyunshii* in Japan and *Gangshi* in Korea. The Chinese hopping zombie is most often depicted wearing traditional guard uniforms from the Qing dynasty. It is controlled through the use of spell-laden writings stuck to its forehead. This zombie and/or vampire, by its very nature, translates comically to film. Even so, the

Mr. Vampire series from China, begun in the early 1980s, was very successful region-ally and prompted a deluge of low-budget zombie films in the region. Japanese films diverge from Chinese in that they typically adopt the Western zombie and add lots of repetitive gore, along with the gratuitous so-called loli girls, in school-girl pleats and half-buttoned white blouses. They are often staged, reminiscent of live action anime-style video games.

The typical American zombie film hero is the average man, often a loner, strug-gling to survive as an end in itself. The Asian hero, by contrast, is a hidden war-rior waiting to defend life and home in an apocalypse. Such a hero sees zombies as unnatural, since they are created either biologically, out of human abuse of the planet, or supernaturally, by an unholy force. These creatures are reanimated to literally consume the natural world. This hidden warrior is often embroiled in an archetypal conflict. In the farcical *Tokyo Zombie* (2005), a lowly flunky at a fire hydrant warehouse is actually a psychologically broken black belt master who had forsaken his art. In search of salvation, he attempts to mentor a moronic coworker. This fallen hero sinks even lower when he succumbs to the bite of a zombie with false teeth, inducing psychosomatic zombiehood. In *Shaolin Monk vs. Evil Dead* (2004), a holy Chinese white wizard attempts to save the souls of hopping zom-bies, while his counterpart, a black wizard, attempts to use dark arts to absorb their souls, turning himself evil instead. These characters are portrayed as the Western movie heroes of Asia: they reluctantly fight out of necessity, yet they prove them-selves amazingly adept at killing when the need arises.

Even with this nobly overlaid mythos, critically acclaimed films in this subgenre are rare. The one film that is most often included in various top zombie film lists is the Japanese film *Versus* (2000), directed by Ryuhei Kitamura (1969–). This low-budget production aspired to become the Asian breakout zombie film, aban-doning comedy for a mix of ancient legend and automatic weaponry. The main character escapes from prison to meet with thugs who have kidnapped a young woman. Their meeting place is coincidentally the 444th door to a mystical domain. Everything that dies in the area is reanimated as a zombie. These zombies are not slow, clumsy oafs. They retain the martial arts expertise they died with, as well as a healthy knowledge of the use of automatic weapons. The hero escapes with the young woman and dedicates himself to saving her, as he is continually assaulted by ninja-trained zombies with guns. The hero finally meets a character called Boss, who turns out to be an ancient vampire lord; the hero is actually the reincarnation of a samurai warrior who was felled by the vampire centuries before. After a pro-longed martial arts battle, the hero wins and rides off with the girl. The scene then switches to a city in ruins, and we learn that the hero was the cause, for he has been turned. He confronts the reincarnated vampire, now a force for good, and tells him that he wants to be sent to the other side so he can destroy it as well. The movie ends with the two clashing swords. Kitamura admitted that he was inspired by American zombie and horror films directors, such as Sam Raimi, John Carpenter (born John Howard Carpenter, 1948–), and George Miller (born George Miliotis, 1945–).

Another Japanese film given critical praise for sheer outlandishness is *Wild Zero* (2000). The hero, Ace, is a punk rock fan who cannot play an instrument but firmly believes he can become a member of the band Guitar Wolfe (played by a real Japanese Ramones-style punk group of the same name). Alien spaceships invade the earth and cause the dead to become zombies. While the members of the band struggle against these undead, Ace has to single-handedly fend off hordes of zombies, hoping to win the love of and protect the possibly transgendered Tobio. While not as graceful with blunt weapons as the hero in *Versus*, Ace succeeds, as does the band. The movie is like a gory rock video, replete with armed naked girls in showers, leather jackets, and the typical ambling sluggish, American-style zombie.

Other notable Japanese entries in the zombie subgenre include *Door 3* (1996); *Zombie Self-Defense Force* (2006); *Wu long tian shi zhao ji gui* (1982), an early film depicting zombies similar to ghosts in later movies such as *Ringu*; *Stacy* (a.k.a. *Attack of the Schoolgirl Zombies*, 2001); *Battlefield Baseball* (2003), a baseball zombie film; *Junk* (1999); *Bio Zombie* (1998), wherein biological zombies attack a shopping mall; *The Happiness of the Katakuris* (2011), a musical parody featuring claymation zombies; *Tokyo Gore Police* (2008), in which a mad scientist creates zombie and other creatures, while the heroine seeks to avenge her father's downfall; and *High School Girl Zombie* (2010), where school girl ninjas take on the zombie apocalypse. All of these films, many of which are comedies, are low budget, with heavy helpings of sex and gore and martial arts battles.

Quality zombie films from countries other than Japan are rare. The most noted recent film is Thailand's *SARS Wars: The Bangkok Zombie Crisis* (2004). Its hero is another comedic and overly stylized sword-wielding citizen warrior who takes on an apartment block infested by zombies created by the SARS epidemic, in order to rescue a kidnapped girl. Recent Korean films include *The Neighbor Zombie* (2008), in which the AIDS cure causes zombies as a side effect; and *Dark Forest* (2007), wherein a group of friends filming in a forest encounter an evil presence that turns them into zombies, a plot reminiscent of Raimi's *Evil Dead* (1981–). A number of Asian films include a zombie in some form, but the zombie is not the focus of the film. One entry from Singapore, Kelvin Tong's (no date available) *The Maid* (2005), featuring ghosts that appear as zombies, was critically acclaimed and was very successful regionally. From Korea, *G.P. 506* (2008) depicts guards along Korea's demilitarized zone who become infected with a virus that causes a violent madness; infected corpses sometimes reanimate to attack. The film draws from long-standing fears of conflict with North Korea. From Malaysia, banned by that government in 2003 as immoral, *Jembalang Yang Hilang* (1987) featured a ghost/zombie girl. While these films are better overall productions, they are essentially ghost and contagion films.

See also: Ghosts; *Jiang Shi*; Raimi, Sam; *Resident Evil* (Video Game)

David E. Cowen

ASTRO-ZOMBIES, THE

The Astro-Zombies, sometimes known as *Space Zombies* or *The Space Vampires,* is a 1968 science fiction horror film directed by Ted V. Mikels (born Theodore Mikacevich, 1929–), who also serves as cowriter and coproducer along with Wayne Rogers (born William Wayne McMillan Rogers III, 1933–). In this cult B film, John Carradine (born Richmond Reed Carradine, 1906–1988) plays Dr. DeMarco, a mad scientist who was working for the U. S. government to create men filled with electronic parts who can be controlled through electronic thought-wave transmission. The government plans to use these men to venture into space. However, after DeMarco's employers fire him when he begins displaying signs of insanity, he is free to create a different and more sinister experiment, the reanimation of the dead by replacing their organs with electronic ones. DeMarco then electronically strips of all emotion from the brains of the reanimated dead in order to create astro-zombies.

The astro-zombies are humanoid, but have large, skeletal heads with insect-like eyes, and their electronic organs are solar-powered. The astro-zombies are similar to zombies created by Voodoo in that they are raised from the dead and their wills are subsumed to their maker's. Yet the astro-zombies also follow Romero's Rules in that they have no other desire except to commit murder. Because DeMarco's first astro-zombie had the brain of a psychopath which was not properly stripped of emotions, the creature went on a homicidal rampage, which caught the attention of the CIA. The CIA and Satana, an alluring Chinese communist agent who would steal the astro-zombie technology so that her government could create a homicidal army, attempt to stop DeMarco. Eventually, Satana discovers the whereabouts of DeMarco when he is creating his second astro-zombie. Santana breaks into his lab in an attempt to steal his technology, but she and DeMarco are both killed by a newly created second astro-zombie. At the same time, the CIA locates and destroys DeMarco's first astro-zombie.

In this cult B-film, the mad scientist Dr. DeMarco (John Carradine) creates men filled with electronic parts who can then be controlled through thought-wave transmission. (Geneni Film Distributors/Photofest)

The Astro-Zombies is hailed as a cult favorite due to its mostly nonsensical plot and editing, ridiculous dialogue, and exploitative scenes. In 2002, a direct-to-DVD sequel was released, with Satana reprising her original role and Mikels returning to direct, write, and produce the film, titled *Mark of the Astro-Zombies*. Presented as a reinterpretation of the original rather than a sequel, aliens instead of a mad scientist create murderous, mindless zombies to send to earth. Again, foreign spies attempt to capture the technology to create their own army of killer zombies. The astro-zombies in this film resemble those of the original, though this time all are armed with machetes and can be controlled due to microchips implanted in their brains as they are reanimated.

See also: Cult Film; Science Fiction

Braden Dauzat

AUTUMN SERIES

The *Autumn* series is a quartet of post-apocalyptic zombie novels by David Moody (1970–). In the series, 99 percent of the world's population is killed in a single day by an infectious disease that revives humans into flesh-eating zombies.

Moody originally offered his first book in the series, *Autumn,* for free online in 2001. The first novel in the series, *Autumn* (published in 2010) chronicles the attempts of three of the living to survive in a farm house. Although some reviewers complained that plot was derivative and sluggish, the series was, nevertheless, sufficiently popular with fans. *Autumn* quickly became an online phenomenon when half a million people downloaded it, encouraging Moody to write the sequels: *Autumn: The City* (2003, republished in 2011), *Autumn: Purification* (2004, republished in 2011), and *Autumn: The Human Condition* (2005, republished in 2013). He even created his own publishing house, Infected Books, in 2005. While *Autumn* follows protagonists who escaped the city after the initial outbreak, *Autumn: The City* centers on people who were not so fortunate and find themselves trapped in an urban area. The protagonists from *Autumn* and *Autumn: The City* collaborate to survive in *Autumn: Purification*. *Autumn: The Human Condition* is a series of stories including characters from the first three novels.

In 2006, Renegade motion pictures acquired the rights to *Autumn* and made a film by the same name in 2009. It was directed by Steve Rumbelow (born Steven Rumbelow, no date available) and starred David Carradine (born John Arthur Carradine, 1936–2009). Thomas Dunne Books acquired the rights to the series in 2008, prompting Moody to remove the free downloads from his website. Soon after, Moody published two more books: *Autumn: Disintegration* (2011) and *Autumn: Aftermath* (2012). Several months after the initial outbreak, the undead are becoming smarter in *Autumn: Disintegration,* while in *Autumn: Aftermath,* some of the dwindling numbers of the human race attempt to survive their first winter since the apocalypse in a medieval castle.

Although Moody never uses the term zombie to describe his undead, the *Autumn* series is highly derivative of well-known works of post-apocalyptic zombie fiction, particularly in its emphasis in how bands of survivors are as endangered by internal power struggles as they are from the undead.

See also: Apocalypse; Epidemics

June Michele Pulliam

BACTERIA
See Epidemics

BARKER, CLIVE

Clive Barker (1952–) is a British writer, director, producer, and playwright who has shown a consistent, though complicated, interest in the horror genre with his customized and idiosyncratic reimagining of the zombie. In an interview with Douglas E. Winter (1950–), Barker asserted a sociopolitical dimension to the zombie trope, noting that zombies often represent the masses, via reactionary mob mentality. In his novel *Cabal* (1985), Barker twists this cultural anxiety such that the undead are the besieged population. The underground denizens of the necropolis Midian are the shape-shifting, flesh-eating, diabolically reanimated dead referred to mysteriously as nightbreed. These squatters are rousted and nearly exterminated by a fame-hungry local sheriff and a psychotic serial killer masquerading as a therapist. Following the burning of the city at the hands of the deranged sheriff, a suicidal, depressed man is bitten by a nightbreed and becomes one of them, only to violate the code against going topside and interacting with humanity.

Barker supplements this political statement of rising from below with a psychosexual perspective. Zombies stand in for a rich variety of death-driven coping mechanisms. The cautionary message of much horror fiction underlies his explorations of the perennial human fascination with sex and death. In *Clive Barker's A-Z of Horror* (1997), for instance, he claims that the popularity of the zombie trope can be traced to existentialism and a fascination with immortality, demonstrated in the zombie short story "Sex, Death and Starshine," from *Clive Barker's Books of Blood* (1986). The story involves the compromised director of a theater on the verge of closing a swan song performance of *Twelfth Night* who is both saved and damned by a zombified actress, patron, and audience. Barker's sympathy is for the devil, and he suggests that the passionate devotion to a dying theatrical art comes at the high price of sacrificing one's attachment to our living, breathing, mortal coil. The magic of performance can be reanimated, not unlike the zombie in popular culture which, Barker notes, seems to court immortality in its staying power. He reiterates this in his introduction to *The Mammoth Book of Zombies* (1993), where Barker asserts that zombies are an ideal monster because they are impossible to kill.

See also: Existentialism; Reanimation

Jerome Winter

BARON SAMEDI

Baron Samedi is one of the loa of the dead (loosely related to the saints of Catholicism) in Haitian Voodoo. Since most of the loa still follow some of the West-African traditions of Vodun, in which loa are attached to families, Baron Samedi is connected to a family as well. He is considered the head of the Guédé Family of loa, who all embody the powers of death and fertility. Baron Samedi is married to the loa Maman Brigitte (who is connected to the Catholic Saint Brigid). Though he can take corporeal form, Samedi, like all loa, exists in the invisible realm of Voodoo spirits, where he spends most of his time in debauchery and telling dirty jokes, drinking rum, and smoking cigars.

Samedi is normally depicted as a corpse who has been prepared for a proper Haitian burial: he wears a black tuxedo or dinner jacket with a top hat, and has cotton plugs in the nostrils, and his face is often painted white to resemble a skull. Because Samedi is the loa of resurrection, he is often called upon by those near death, as he

A practitioner of Voodoo gestures from the top of Baron Samedi's cross during a ritual to honor him on Day of the Dead, November 1, 2012. Baron Samedi is the loa of the dead, who is normally depicted as a corpse decked out for a traditional Haitian burial. (Associated Press)

has tremendous powers of healing, and he is also the only one who can accept the departed into the realm of the dead. Baron Samedi can also be called upon to make sure that a body rots in the ground so that it cannot be revived and zombified. Fictional depictions of Baron Samedi include the blockbuster James Bond film, *Live and Let Die* (1973), directed by Guy Hamilton (1922–). Hamilton, in fact, used a Trinidadian actor, Geoffrey Holder (born Geoffrey Richard Holder, 1930–), to both play Samedi and choreograph the Voodoo rituals in the film involving the loa. This works well thematically in the film because one of its subplots is zombification. In Lisa Cantrell's novel *Boneman* (1992), the Boneman is another name of the Baron, who is summoned by a local drug kingpin so the loa can reanimate the dead, who can then be used by the criminal to cow his rivals into submission.

See also: Africa; *Boneman*; Haiti; *Live and Let Die*; Voodoo

Anthony J. Fonseca

BIERCE, AMBROSE

Ambrose Bierce (born Ambrose Gwinnett Bierce, 1842–1914?) was an American short-story writer and journalist whose attitudes toward death and reanimation are expressed in "An Inhabitant of Carcosa," published in *The San Francisco Newsletter* and *California Advertiser* in 1886. At its most benign, in Bierce's world, death and sleep are indistinguishable. One finds this in "Bodies of the Dead: Some Authentic Accounts of Their Seeming Caprices" (*San Francisco Examiner*, April 22, 1888), in which the dead have moved in their coffins, probably to become more comfortable. Few of Bierce's works are so benign and readily explicable, and many of his stories convey dark psychological attitudes toward the dead. In "A Tough Tussle: The Facts about Byring's Encounter with an Unknown" (*San Francisco Examiner*, September 30, 1888), Second Lieutenant Brainerd Byring, "a brave and efficient officer," is left by himself, and soon discovers that he is not alone:

American author Ambrose Bierce, who frequently wrote about dead people who rarely lie still and who, at times, may not even be dead. (Bettmann/Corbis)

what he believes to be a moving corpse is nearby. Bierce leaves open issues such as whether there really is a corpse and whether it moves, but the next morning Byring is found dead, stabbed through the heart, though not before he inflicted five wounds on his attacker, who is revealed to be well along in decomposition.

The same open-ended conclusion is found in "The Watcher by the Dead" (*San Francisco Examiner,* December 29, 1888), in which wealthy gambler Jarrette bets two acquaintances, Helberson and Harper, that he can safely spend the night in a dark room with a corpse. Jarrette has not counted on his friends' playing a cruel practical joke, and at the conclusion there is madness, death, and a hint that the dead have displaced the living. A similar problem in recognizing death occurs in "The Boarded Window: An Incident in the Life of an Ohio Pioneer" (*San Francisco Examiner,* April 12, 1891), the tale of pioneer Murlock, whose wife dies. Murlock places her body atop his table in preparation for her burial, then awakens in the night to hear what sounds like bare feet walking along the floor. Murlock shoots into the darkness at the intruder, and sees by the light of the muzzle flash a panther dragging his wife's body toward the window. The next day Murlock finds the clawed and mutilated corpse of his wife, with a piece of the panther's ear in her teeth. Bierce leaves open the issue of whether or not the wife reanimated to fend off the attack on her corpse.

Equally bleak and elliptical is "The Death of Halpin Frayser" (*The Wave,* December 19, 1891): Frayser, after a portentous dream, awakens speaking the name Catharine Larue, a person he has never met. Bierce's description of Frayser's past shows him to be spoiled, dreamy, ineffectual, and, perhaps, incestuously involved with his mother. Frayser is eventually murdered, his strangled body found atop a grave by two manhunters, Holker and Jaralson, who are looking for a killer named Branscom, who had married and then murdered a widow named Frayser. Branscom's real name is revealed to be Larue, and it is Catharine Larue's grave that her unwitting son is found atop when the men hear a strange laugh emerging from the nearby woods. Branscom might have committed the crime against his former wife's son, but Frayser's deceased mother may also be the culprit, strangling her son literally, as she strangled him metaphorically during her life. In the more traditional "Three and One Are One" (*Cosmopolitan,* October 1908), a young soldier who entered the Union Army in opposition to his family's wishes returns to visit and is vouchsafed a silent, but emotionally charged encounter with his relations before learning that all were killed the year previously: has he seen ghosts or the reanimated dead during the reunion? The same question can be asked of "The Other Lodgers" (*Cosmopolitan,* August 1907), in which Colonel Levering discovers his hotel was once a hospital, his room was the morgue of the establishment, and his night-clerk has been dead for a few weeks. Such stories are left open-ended by Bierce and must be resolved by the reader. In Bierce's world, the dead rarely lie still, and at times may not even be dead.

Bierce was born in Horse Cave Creek in Meigs County, Ohio. He was raised in Indiana and fought for the Union in the American Civil War. From about 1867 to 1899, he lived predominantly in California. After 1899, Bierce lived in

Washington, D.C., and in late 1913, he went to Mexico, to cover Pancho Villa's revolution, where he disappeared. Bierce's death date is conjectural, as his body was never found.

See also: Reanimation

Richard Bleiler

BLIND DEAD TETRALOGY

The *Blind Dead* tetralogy is a series of films by Amando de Ossorio (born Amando de Ossorio Rodriguez, 1918–2001), the Spanish director synonymous with the European horror film surge of the 1970s. After beginning his horror film career with *Malenka,* also released as *Fangs of the Living Dead* (1969), he later directed in 1972 the first of the *Blind Dead* movies, an original concept about a cult of blind, undead Templar Knights. When accidentally summoned by a living heartbeat and the scent of blood, the zombie knights come forth on skeletal horses to hack their victims to death with swords, and then drink their blood.

Tombs of the Blind Dead (*La Noche del Terror Ciego,* 1972), the first in the series, is a story about two female friends, ex-lovers who meet by accident at a Portuguese resort. A male friend encourages the two to join him in local exploration. One of the women separates from the trio near the cursed area of Berzano, where she discovers the ruins of a vast stone monastery; there she awakens the undead Templars. The second film, *Return of the Evil Dead* (*El Attaque de los Muertos Sin Ojos,* 1973), is somewhat of a prequel in that its opening explains how Berzano came to be deserted, when the citizens blinded and burned the Templars at the stake. In the present day, Berzano is celebrating the Templars' destruction with pyrotechnics engineered by an American visitor. In this film, it becomes clear that the horses themselves are also zombies. The third film, *The Ghost Galleon* (*El Buque Maldito,* 1974) introduces the zombies as sea-faring undead accompanied by a mysterious fog, as well as adds the consumption of human flesh to their attributes. The final film, *Night of the Seagulls* (*La Noche de los Gaviotas,* 1975), showcases the atmospheric aspects of the tetralogy, opening with a prologue set in the 15th century, where the Templars perform a sacrificial ritual involving blood drinking. The same ritual occurs at various times in the present-day portion of the film, with the difference being that the local villagers chose one of their own, and this person is always a young woman. The villagers then abduct the sacrifice and leave her tied up on the beach for the Templars.

De Ossorio's vengeful corpses are the remains of Crusaders who obtained secret rites to immortality, including drinking the blood of innocent victims. Blinded and killed off by locals who learned of their deeds, they return as zombies, accompanied by demonic or zombified horses. Skeletal creatures, the Templars are extremely slow moving; mechanical skeletons were used to create the special effects. However, they are terrifying, and their would-be victims are often frozen in place with fear. Generally speaking, their victims are not turned into undead, with the exception of their first one in *Tombs of the Blind Dead*. The tetralogy's sound track is as distinctive as its sexploitation, its rape scenes, and its mechanical zombies. The four movies feature a soundtrack filled with moans, screams, and Gregorian chants, as well as character-based themes, created by de Ossorio after he worked with Sergio Leone (1929–1989), Ennio Morricone (1928–), and Alfred Hitchcock (born Alfred Joseph Hitchcock, 1899–1980). De Ossorio was the subject of a 2001 documentary entitled *Amando de Ossorio: The Last Templar* (*Amando de Ossorio: el último Templario*), directed by Jose Zapata (1975–). In his final years, he augmented his income with oil paintings of his Templar Knights.

See also: Italian Cinema

Anthony J. Fonseca

BLOOD CRAZY

Blood Crazy is a 2001 novel by Simon Clark (1958–). It is not typical zombie fare, as the creatures in it are neither the living dead, nor are they bewitched. Rather, they are adults whose higher brain functions are suddenly subordinated to a biological imperative to savagely kill everyone under 20. These afflicted are zombies because they no longer have free will and are animated by a monomaniacal, involuntary drive. This sudden urge to kill the young, however, only applies to the adults introduced at the text's onset; when subsequent teens turn 20, they are not similarly afflicted.

After all of humanity's adults suddenly go from caring for the young to murdering them, civilization rapidly deteriorates into a post-apocalyptic world. Power plants stop functioning, and pumps that keep water out of areas below sea level quit working, returning portions of the land to marsh. Crops are no longer planted, harvested, and distributed, and medical and emergency facilities are left unstaffed. Clark's teen narrator, Nick Aten, recounts how small groups of youngsters in the United Kingdom managed to survive this attack. On an otherwise ordinary day, Nick returns home to discover that his parents have savaged his little brother. Nick leaves home to search for safety, rescuing along the way his love interest, Sarah, and her little sister. As the three seek shelter, they meet Dave Middleton and Martin del Coffey, clean-cut, responsible, church-going types before the great change who have now set up a functioning community.

While the duo is initially effective in organizing their traumatized peers, neither is prepared to deal with bullies such as Tug Slatter, who takes pleasure in hurting people. Soon another such bully with a cache of weapons and a few ruthless henchmen takes over the community, brutalizing members through rape and other forms of violence. Sarah, her sister, and Martin leave the community to live on its outskirts, but a lack of resources such as access to a motor vehicle and fuel prevents them from completely decamping. Before Nick can help his friends escape, he is kidnapped by a group of afflicted adults who for no known reason carry him many miles away in a barge before releasing him. As Nick makes his way back to Sarah, he discovers other communities of survivors. One is run by Bernadette, a charismatic teen who controls the younger members of her group by instilling comforting religious beliefs. Bernadette has been studying what caused the adults to change and surmises that it is some new evolutionary stage akin to what it is believed to have happened with our Neanderthal ancestors, who developed a bicameral consciousness which transmitted group messages that individuals would have experienced as originating from an outside, divine force. As a consequence, Bernadette believes that religious faith is an important tool for helping the young to grow into responsible, caring adults. Nick eventually makes his way back to Sarah in order to dispose the bullies who have terrorized the community and to hopefully help his generation survive this strange evolutionary upheaval.

See also: Apocalypse; Young Adult Fiction

June Michele Pulliam

BLOOD CREEK

Blood Creek is a 2009 film by Joel T. Schumacher (1939–). The movie opens with a simple, quasihistorical statement, informing the audience that Adolf Hitler and his inner circle of advisors were obsessed with achieving immortality through the occult. In an atmospheric black-and-white introduction, Nazi historian Richard Wirth visits the German Wollner family, who has immigrated to a West Virginia farm. The year is 1936. Wirth explains that he uncovered a Nordic rune stone crucial to his studies.

The film transitions to the present, where Evan Marshall is awakened by his brother, Victor, thought dead after vanishing two years previously on a fishing trip. Victor retrieves a gun and asks Evan to return immediately with him to the Wollner farm, where he was confined and tortured. The brothers find the family, who have not aged in over 70 years, and take them captive. They learn that the Wollners kidnap men, on whom Wirth feeds in order to maintain the immortality that he first achieved through the rune stone. Wirth, contained with a spell book stolen by Annaliese Wollner, cannot enter their house himself, but he can convert the dead into zombies with an incantation, invading their home, along with the zombified Wollner father, son, and dog. Annaliese and the brothers escape and plan to poison Wirth with the blood of his ancestors from an ancient skeleton. They crush the bones, grind them into Evan's open wounds, and offer him to Wirth. When Wirth feeds on Evan, he is weakened enough for the Wollners to kill him with a magical knife.

The foundation for a sequel involves the brothers' discovering that the Wollner farm was but one part of a larger Nazi plan, plotting out eight other farms with rune stones that form a swastika when connected on a map. The film draws a correlation between the Nazis who claimed to have just been following orders during the Holocaust and mindless zombies, much like other popular previous works: *Shock Waves* (1977), *Hard Rock Zombies* (1985, with a zombie Hitler), and *Dead*

Snow (2009). These all feature marauding zombie Nazis attacking anyone who unwittingly disturbs them. *Blood Creek* emerges as a surprisingly thoughtful film that incriminates not merely Nazis (here the antithesis of mindlessness) but presumably innocent German families, for their inaction. Immediately upon return, Victor drags the mother to the kitchen window and forces her to acknowledge the outside box where he was held captive while she did nothing to help. The family members have already become zombies, undead servants to the rituals of Wirth, the apotheosis of Nazi occultism blended with zombie mythology.

See also: Dead Snow; Nazi Zombies

Walter Rankin

BOKUR/CAPLATA

A bokur, or caplata, is a Voodoo priest or priestess who specializes in dark magic, such as the type used to create zombies. In Voodoo, houngans and mambos (priests and priestesses) use benevolent magic to heal the sick, perform ceremonies to pacify the loas, or spirits, cast spells for love and protection, and initiate new priests. The bokur, however, uses malefic magic to either reanimate the dead or put the living into a death-like coma and turn them into zombies who can be used as slaves.

The bokur or caplata is often a character in many works of zombie fiction, especially when the creature is created through Voodoo. In the 1932 film *White Zombie,* the character Murder Legendre is a powerful bokur who has raised the dead to use as slave labor in his sugar mill. In the 1943 film *I Walked with a Zombie,* we never know if Mrs. Rand has become a caplata who zombified her daughter-in-law, whose extramarital affair with Mrs. Rand's other son threatened to tear her family apart—or if Mrs. Rand merely believes she has these powers. Squire Hamilton is a distorted version of the bokur in the film *The Plague of the Zombies* (1966). Hamilton is a white, Victorian landowner, the son of a once-wealthy family now in decline; he was sent to the West Indies to make his fortune. The ruthless landowner returns, however, with appropriated knowledge of Voodoo that he uses to enslave the working classes in his ancestral village, after they refuse to work in his tin mines because they had become too dangerous.

These fictional representations of the zombie created through Voodoo (and their makers/masters) have a basis in reality according to folklorist Zora Neale Hurston (1891–1960) and ethnobotanist Wade Davis (born Edmund Wade Davis, 1953–). Hurston claims in her book *Tell My Horse* to have seen an actual reclaimed zombie during her travels in Haiti, when she met a young woman in a hospital who had escaped her masters, but who had permanent brain damage from the potent cocktail of drugs that she was given to first put her into a coma and later, to keep her docile after she was revived. Nearly half a century later, Davis recounts in *The Serpent and the Rainbow* how he was sent to Haiti by pharmaceutical companies to learn the combination of substances used by bokurs and caplatas to create zombies after the story of Clairvius Narcisse (1922–) was publicized. Narcisse was reportedly turned into a zombie in 1962, and his maker brought him to labor on his plantation. Narcisse returned to his incredulous family 18 years later after the bokur who kept him enslaved died, so he was no longer perpetually dosed with zombie cucumber, the substance used to maintain his zombification, and he subsequently regained his earlier memories.

See also: I Walked with a Zombie; Narcisse, Clairvius; Plague of the Zombies, The; Serpent and the Rainbow, The (Book); Tell My Horse; Voodoo; White Zombie; Zombie Cucumber

June Michele Pulliam

BOMBIE THE ZOMBIE

Bombie the Zombie is a Disney character associated with early *Donald Duck* comics. A zombified member of an African tribe, he is commanded by sorcerer Foola Zoola to follow Scrooge McDuck around the world after McDuck uses a mercenary army to drive the tribe off their lands to construct a diamond mine. Represented as inhumanly tall, with blank eyes and no facial expression, Bombie possesses superhuman strength. Much like a Haitian zombie created by Voodoo and under the control of its master, the creature exists solely to deliver a curse on its target. Moreover, the creature is also similar to the Haitian zombie in that it is slow, walking about in a trance, making it easy for Scrooge McDuck to outwit and escape.

The enslaved zombie follows McDuck from 1909 through 1949, tracking him even aboard the Titanic, arriving at Duckburg, where it mistakenly delivers the curse to Donald Duck. However, since the curse has lost most of its efficacy over the decades, Donald Duck does not suffer any ill effects. Having completed its mission, Bombie is stranded, until Huey, Louie, and Dewey travel (with Donald Duck) to Africa in search of Foola Zoola. Bombie the Zombie is first seen in "Voodoo Hoodoo" (*Donald Duck Four Color #238*, 1949), by comic artist Carl Barks (1901– 2000). The character appears in a total of 14 issues, a continuation of Barks's writing and drawing supernatural adventures for the Disney characters in the 1940s, as in "Pirate Gold" and "The Mummy's Ring." Bombie never encounters Scrooge McDuck during the issue. In *The Life and Times of Scrooge McDuck* (1995), comic artist Don Rosa (born Keno Don Hugo Rosa, 1951–) created the prequel to the story in 12 chapters totaling 212 pages. More chapters were later added.

The story arch follows McDuck's life between 1877 and 1947, and most of the chapters were released in the United States and in many Disney publications in Europe, earning Rosa the Will Eisner Award in 1995. The story featuring Bombie is "The Empire-Builder from Calisota" (*Uncle Scrooge #295*), which takes place between 1909 and 1930. In it, McDuck scours the world for business deals, running afoul of Foola Zoola for his colonialist attitude and thievery. Bombie pursues Scrooge to the North Pole and finally to the isle of Ripan Taro, where McDuck makes a deal with a local sorcerer to trap Bombie for 30 years. The zombie makes only cameo appearances throughout the remainder of *The Life and Times of Scrooge McDuck*. In its original incarnation in "Voodoo Hoodoo," Barks had drawn Bombie with open and impassive, blank eyes, but editors had him add pupils and half-closed eyelids to avoid scaring young readers. In later reprints, the ring in the zombie's nose was also removed.

See also: Africa; Graphic Novels and Comics; Voodoo

Anthony J. Fonseca

BONEMAN

Boneman is a novel by Lisa Wright Cantrell (1945–), an American author of four novels and a handful of short stories published during the horror boom of the 1980s and early 1990s. While her first novel, *The Manse* (1987), was the Bram Stoker Award winner for Best First Novel, *Boneman* (1992) is a police procedural, and her only tale about zombies.

Set in Phoenix City, North Carolina, a small town with emerging big city problems involving drugs, the tale begins with rumors that Haitians are behind the recent murders of local drug pushers. The story is related through multiple perspectives, the most important being that of J. J. Spencer, a journalist who is attempting to write a novel and who is friendly with Dallas Reid, inspector in the Phoenix City Police Department's drug task force. It chronicles how Reid, a borderline alcoholic who, nevertheless, gets results in his investigations, partners with Jackie Swann of the State Bureau of Investigation, an attractive mistress of disguise who is investigating the influx of the Haitian gangs. As the reader is aware, and as the investigators gradually discover, the being behind the crimes is the Boneman, an entity summoned by Maurice Martineau, a drug-dealer attempting to muscle into Phoenix City.

The Boneman is another name for Baron Samedi, one of the Loa, or spirits, in Haitian Voodoo. Baron Samedi is the loa of the dead: he accepts individuals into the realm of the dead, and his powers include the ability to resurrect the dead. Like his Voodoo counterpart, Cantrell's Boneman can reanimate corpses, sending them forth to do his bidding. When he is seen, he can be a handsome and eloquent young man, or he can have a skull rather than human facial features, one of the guises of Baron Samedi. The Boneman is likewise amoral and cannot be controlled, as Martineau discovers to his horror; the Boneman is a figure of fear, and he is possessed of a peculiar sense of humor, as Reid and Spencer discover. Cantrell's Boneman's amorality and humor are also typical of Baron Samedi. In a brief afterword to the novel, Cantrell explains that she got the germ of the idea from serving on a panel sponsored by the Carolina Crime Writers Association. *Boneman* as a whole was not particularly successful as a novel. Despite being a figure of fear, the Boneman emerges as a catalyst for personal growth and development. It takes the Boneman to get Reid to mature enough to quit drinking and apply for a position in the State Bureau of Investigation; likewise, following her encounter with the Boneman, Swann saves her marriage by transferring from undercover into training.

See also: Baron Samedi; Haiti; *Live and Let Die*; Voodoo

Richard Blieler

BONESHAKER

Boneshaker is a steampunk zombie novel by Cherie Priest (1975–) set in her Clockwork Century world, which is an alternative 19th-century United States. *Boneshaker*, the first of Priest's Clockwork Century novels, takes place in 1880s Seattle. Sixteen years prior to the novel's beginning, inventor Leviticus Blue was commissioned by the Russians to design a special steam-powered mining machine that can mechanize the mining of gold by tearing up the ground below. But Blue's invention, the boneshaker machine, unleashes disaster on Seattle, causing several city blocks to fall into a chasm and releasing a subterranean pocket of gas that turns all who come into contact with it into the living dead.

In the present day of the novel, Blue has disappeared and is presumably dead, and a wall has been built around the affected area, containing the gas and the living dead inside, and Blue's widow Briar Wilkes just wants to live with her son Ezekiel in peace, without anyone's connecting her to the man who caused the disaster. But when Ezekiel learns who his father is, he ventures into the walled-off city to find the parent that he never knew and now suspects is alive and restore his family's reputation. Briar must hitch a ride on a dirigible in order to be lowered into the dangerous walled city so that she can search for her foolhardy son and make him come home.

Boneshaker won the 2010 Locus Award for Best Science Fiction Novel and was also nominated for a Nebula Award in 2009 and for a Hugo Award 2010. While Priest's zombies are the ravenous undead, they do not completely follow Romero's Rules in that their presence does not usher in an apocalypse. Certainly, the undead are no less dangerous than the pirates, criminals, and desperate poor people who either live in the ruined, walled-off city or venture into it from time to time to loot whatever of value is left. Hammer Studios acquired the rights to *Boneshaker* in 2012 with the intent of turning it into a film.

See also: Cannibalism; Romero's Rules; Science Fiction

June Michele Pulliam

BOOK OF THE DEAD

Book of the Dead: The Complete History of Zombie Cinema is a 2005 fan encyclopedia by Jamie Russell (1974–), published in England. *Book of the Dead* begins with the origin of the zombie in Haitian folklore, through to its commercialization on the Broadway stage, to George Romero's benchmark film *Night of the Living Dead* (1968), to the rebirth of zombie films near the turn of the century. Russell's chapters are as follows: "Caribbean Terrors," "The Zombie Goes to Hollywood," "Down and Out on Poverty Row," "Atomic Interlude," "Bringing It All Back Home," "Dawn of the Dead," "Splatter Horror," and "Twilight of the Dead." Despite its fan appeal, *Book of the Dead* does not shy away from scholarly claims. For example, it traces the first appearance of the word zombie in the English language, attributing it to an article in *Harper's* in 1889 by Lafcadio Hearn (born Patrick Lafcadio Hearn, 1850–1904), and follows the history of the term as it achieved currency in the

1920s due to the exoticism of Voodoo in publications by W. B. Seabrook (born William Buehler Seabrook, 1884–1945), such as his travelogue of Haiti, *The Magic Island* (1929).

Russell's text also chronicles the resurgence of the zombie phenomenon after Romero, of whom he provides an interesting biographical sketch. For example, Russell writes that Romero, who was influenced by his familiarity with the figure of the zombie in EC Comics, created *Night of the Living Dead,* which Russell reports cost $114,000 to make in 1968. Throughout *Book of the Dead,* Russell examines the sociopolitical, spiritual, religious, and psychological undercurrents of zombie cinema. Russell notes that Romero's subsequent films *Dawn of the Dead* (1978), *Day of the Dead* (1985), and *Land of the Dead* (2005) satirized consumer culture, poked fun at paramilitary survivalists, and lambasted profiteering and class warfare, respectively. Russell also spends considerable time examining the ramifications of the fascination with evisceration, death and decay, and gore. Critics generally laud *Book of the Dead* as juxtaposing high-minded philosophical musings against galleries of incredibly gory color stills that remind readers and scholars that the subgenre is defined by viscera, mutilation, eroticism, and raw sexuality.

Although Russell positions Romero as the template for all zombie films, his text is not limited solely to American film, as Russell also discusses Japanese, Hong Kong, and Italian zombie cinema, among others. *Book of the Dead* serves as a comprehensive resource on zombie film, with both individualized discussions of specific movies and a more generalized approach to the trope itself. Russell discusses the conventions of zombie cinema, such as the nature of the monster (the recently deceased return as slow, weak, dumb, disorganized automata whose only desire is to eat the living), the mob mentality and strength-in-numbers metaphor, the motif of the zombie bite always being infectious, the ubiquitous apocalyptic and isolated setting, and the universality of the method of destruction (destroying the brain). *Book of the Dead* includes both black-and-white and full-color photos of film stills, movie posters, book covers, and magazine article photos. The essays are scholarly but accessible, and Russell's emphasis is on history and interpretation of both major and minor films, including cult and B films. Russell's text takes on the task of reminding readers that zombies are grounded in a mundane reality and embody the greatest horror of death: its inescapable sameness.

See also: Asian Cinema; Italian Cinema; Romero, George; Seabrook, W. B.; Universal Studios

Anthony J. Fonseca

BOWERY AT MIDNIGHT

Bowery at Midnight is a 1942 Bela Lugosi (born Béla Ferenc Dezső Blaskó, 1882–1956) horror comedy directed by Wallace Fox (1895–1958). It was distributed by Monogram Pictures on October 30, 1942. In it, Lugosi stars as Dr. Frederick

Brenner, a psychology professor with a double life. He moonlights under the name Karl Wagner as the manager of The Bowery Friendly Mission, a soup kitchen that he has opened as a front for his efforts to organize his own mob of criminals. Using the kitchen as a means of recruiting potential members, he works with an alcoholic and morphine-addicted physician, Doc Brooks, who believes he can raise the dead. Doc Brooks plans to use his discovery to create a mob of slaves consisting of the zombified corpses of Lugosi's criminal enemies.

Though these reanimated dead are never referred to as zombies, their inability to speak and lack of volition and facial expression certainly indicate that they are zombies as the creature is traditionally depicted. Lugosi is finally defeated when, running from the police, he is led into a sub-basement by Brooks, pretending to be his ally, only to discover that the doctor has successfully raised his dead enemies, who attack him. Lugosi had worked with Monogram before on other films: the crime drama *Black Dragons*, earlier that year, also introduced supernatural elements into the script, albeit unsuccessfully. Prior to that, Lugosi played a character with a double life in the Monogram horror film *The Human Monster* (1939). *Bowery at Midnight* was an attempt to more organically incorporate the supernatural into a Lugosi crime film. It begins with a prison break by a safecracker named Fingers Dolan. On the lam, Dolan ends up at The Bowery Friendly Mission, known for its acceptance of all transients, no questions asked. Brenner/Wagner recognizes Dolan and is quick to recruit him, introducing him to two accomplices, Brooks and Trigger Stratton. Brenner/Wagner's plan is for a caper that involves breaking into a jewelry store and raiding its safe. As with all his capers, he then has Stratton execute the new man on the job, in this case Dolan, to eliminate witnesses. Meanwhile, a New York Police Department detective begins to investigate the mission. Brenner/Wagner decides to replace Stratton, so he has him killed in the cellar, and Brooks pretends to dispose of the body in the impromptu graveyard in a room adjacent to the cellar. Brooks, however, takes the body to his own secret chamber, where he conducts secret experiments. In the romantic subplot, one of Brenner/Wagner's psychology students, Richard Dennison, is researching his mentor's activities with the mission because his fiancée works there as a nurse. He is killed and resurrected, becoming one of the reanimated dead who attack Brenner/Wagner. The film concludes with Dennison's marriage but leaves it unclear as to whether he is still a reanimated corpse.

See also: Universal Studios

Anthony J. Fonseca

BOY WHO COULDN'T DIE, THE

The Boy Who Couldn't Die is a 2005 young adult novel by William Sleator, unique for its use of the astral zombie, a living being created when one's soul is removed by a bokur, or a practitioner of Voodoo who uses black magic. Once the bokur turns the appropriated soul into an astral zombie, a physical manifestation of the soul's original owner, this entity can be used to do his or her bidding. The novel is notable in its connection of the astral zombie to the contemporary existential zombie, a philosophical and metaphorical concept that is used to question how and to what degree our actions are shaped by programming that is so deep as to render free will an illusion. In the novel, 16-year-old Ken loses his best friend Roger in a plane crash, and afterward becomes so traumatized by the possibility that someone his age could die that he responds to Cheri Beaumont's ad promising "freedom from death." Thus, Ken allows Cheri, a bokur, to turn him into an astral zombie, not fully appreciating the consequences of his decision.

Ken leaves Cheri's apartment wondering if anything has really happened, aside from his being cozened of $50, when he is nearly hit by a car. As the vehicle should have hit him and killed him instantly, Ken really begins to believe that Cheri has delivered what she promised. Anxious to test his new invulnerability, Ken asks the girlfriend of the school bully on a date, prompting a physical attack, only to discover that the larger boy's powerful blows have no effect whatsoever. Wanting further proof of his invulnerability, Ken convinces his wealthy parents to take him scuba diving on St. Calao, a tiny Caribbean island where, unknown to his family, a tourist was recently killed in a shark attack. Ken learns how to scuba dive on St. Calao and quickly makes his way out to shark-infested waters, in defiance of his teenage scuba instructor Sabine. Sabine comes after Ken, only to witness a shark taking his entire leg in its mouth, but unable to harm him.

However, Ken discovers that invulnerability is not everything that he has hoped for, as with no soul, he finds that food loses its savor, kissing the prettiest girl in school is dull, and people are uncomfortable around him now that he is inexplicably different. Worse still, he is beset by nightmares, such as one where he awakens clutching a butcher knife from which phantom blood disappears. Soon after, Ken learns that on the night of his dream, a man was stabbed to death by an unknown assailant in Cheri Beaumont's neighborhood. Sabine immediately recognizes that Ken is an astral zombie, as Voodoo of this sort is practiced by the island population. She communicates to Ken what was done to him, and eventually comes to the United States to help him in the dangerous undertaking of retrieving his soul, which is hidden in a cave at the bottom of a frozen lake, and which Cheri will not sell back to him for less than $50,000, an amount of money his wealthy parents are unlikely to just hand to him.

See also: Bokur/Caplata; Existentialism; Voodoo; Young Adult Fiction

June Michele Pulliam

BRADBURY, RAY

Ray Bradbury (born Raymond Douglas Bradbury, 1920–2012) is considered a cultural icon, serving as president of the Science-Fantasy Writers of America and as a board member of the Screen Writers Guild of America. Bradbury won the O. Henry Award, the Writers Guild Award, the Nebula Grand Master Award, and the Bram

Stoker Life Achievement Award. His stories are diverse, set either in the American Midwest or on Mars, which in many of his treatments resembles the Midwest. Bradbury's fiction, often considered more akin to fantasy than horror, nonetheless, contains murderers and features numerous instances of corpses, but the trope of the zombie or animated corpse appears mainly in the short stories of his early career. Because of the era's sensibilities and Bradbury's own stylistic approach, those stories featuring animated corpses are usually not explicit or visceral in nature, and the narratives often lack rationales or resolutions. When it comes to the idea of the animated corpse, Bradbury was not an innovator: his use of the trope is relatively traditional.

Particularly noteworthy Bradbury animated corpse tales include "There Was an Old Woman" (*Weird Tales*, July 1944) and "The Dead Man" (*Weird Tales*, July 1945). In the former, aunt Tildy refuses to accept her death and, as a tangible and audible ghost, accompanies her body to the coroner's office, where her protests and threats get her body restored to her, though with a scar from the autopsy. This semi-humorous treatment of the living dead may have inspired "Case of the Stubborns," by Robert Bloch (born Robert Albert Bloch, 1917–1994), first published in *Fantasy and Science Fiction* in 1976. In Bradbury's "The Dead Man," a character named Odd Martin refers to himself as dead, and his neighbors believe him to be speaking metaphorically; however the final scene is one where he and his new wife move into a cemetery. The tale was made into an episode of *The Ray Bradbury Theater* series in 1992. In "The Handler" (*Weird Tales*, January 1947), a perverse and irreverent coroner is visited by the reanimated corpses of his enemies, who return to avenge how their bodies were mistreated. Outstanding in Bradbury's early work is "The Emissary" (*Dark Carnival*, Sauk City, WI: Arkham House, 1947), wherein a young bedridden boy wishes his dead dog back to life; the pet returns smelling of the grave and with company. Bradbury's early tales often incorporated other types of reanimated corpses, such as what he refers to as a vampire, as in "Pillar of Fire" (*Planet Stories*, Summer 1948). Significantly, such characters do not possess the qualities of vampires, having more in common with the reanimated corpse.

See also: Science Fiction

Richard Bleiler

BROOKS, MAX

Max Brooks (born Maximillian Michael Brooks, 1972–), son of comedian and director Mel Brooks (born Melvin James Kaminsky, 1926–), is an American horror author and screenwriter best known for the novel *World War Z* (2006), which was made into a film in 2013, though Brooks had nothing to do with the script or the production of the film. Brooks also authored *The Zombie Survival Guide* (2003) and its graphic novel sequel, *The Zombie Survival Guide: Recorded Attacks* (2009). Brooks's contributions to the zombie subgenre are unique in that they are not novels in the traditional sense, but documentary style narratives with a pretense to reality. Besides the three aforementioned zombie texts, Brooks has also written a *World*

War Z-related short story titled "Closure, LTD," as well as introductions for other texts, including *Raise the Dead* (2007), Dynamite Entertainment's graphic novel zombie miniseries and the Zombie Research Society's *Everything You Ever Wanted to Know about Zombies* (2011), which discusses zombie history, zombie biology, and survival tactics.

Brooks has acted in various television sitcoms, has a second career in voice over animation, and has appeared on both Spike TV and the Discovery Channel as a zombie expert. Brooks has served as guest speaker on college campuses on the challenge of fighting the undead, where he has argued that zombies are an excellent trope for apocalyptic scenarios since they attack in large numbers and in waves, causing the eventual breakdown of society and often existing outside of conventional horror scenarios, as they can walk in both daylight and at night.

Max Brooks, author of *The Zombie Survival Guide* and the novel *World War Z*. (Invision for LG Mobile Phones)

See also: *World War Z* (Novel); *Zombie Survival Guide, The*

Anthony J. Fonseca

BUBBA HO-TEP (FILM)

Bubba Ho-Tep is a 2002 horror-comedy film based on a story of the same name by Joe R. Lansdale (born Joe Richard Lansdale, 1951–). It is directed by Don Coscarelli Jr. (1954–), who is best known for the *Phantasm* series. The film, like Lansdale's story, is deliberately outrageous and open to multiple interpretations. The plot involves Elvis Presley's (born Elvis Aaron Presley, 1935–1977) temporarily trading places with an Elvis impersonator, Sebastian Haff. The real Elvis, played by Bruce Campbell (born Bruce Lorne Campbell, 1958–), enjoys his new life of low-budget freedom but is unable to return to his previous luxurious existence after the document explaining the switch is lost in a fire, after which Haff becomes enamored of prescription drugs and overdoses. Thirty years later, in the present-day time frame

Elvis Presley (Bruce Campbell) moments before he exchanges lives with the Elvis impersonator Sebastian Haff. (Photofest)

of the film, Elvis is now over 70, impoverished, and physically declining. He lives in the Mud Creek Shady Grove Convalescent Home, where he befriends another resident, the elderly African American Jack McLaughlin, played by Ossie Davis (born Raiford Chatman Davis, 1917–2005), who claims to be former president John Fitzgerald Kennedy (1917–1963), dyed black by the enemies who faked his assassination.

The question of whether the two men are who they claim to be is left ambiguous, but in the film's reality, Elvis and Jack are correct in realizing that something lethal is prowling the halls of the Mud Creek Shady Grove Convalescent Home, a creature Jack describes as "an Egyptian soul sucker" that kills the elderly in their sleep. The confirmation of this theory and their final battle to defeat this creature constitutes the rest of the story, which uses the trope of the zombie to question the meaning of life and the place of the elderly in our society. The mummy of the film's title is the most obvious zombie, a reanimated corpse driven by the need to steal souls, as his own was taken from him. However, the residents of the Mud Creek Shady Grove Convalescent Home are existential zombies, deprived of their free will when they were first warehoused in the facility where they live lives so monotonous as to be devoid of meaning. Coscarelli's screenplay largely follows Lansdale's story, and when it takes occasional license, with Elvis's concerns about his impotence, for example, such scenes are presented as voiceover. Though *Bubba Ho-Tep* was completed on a low budget and is a comedy, it offers a serious subtext, the indictment of how the elderly are treated and of nursing homes. It offers as well an exceptional cast: Campbell was at the time best known as a B-film actor in the *Evil Dead* trilogy, but went on to fame, and Davis, a veteran, sought-after actor, brought a profound gravitas to his role. Similar to Anthony Harvey's (1931–) 1971 film adaptation of *They Might Be Giants*, *Bubba Ho-Tep* plays on the audience's acceptance of its principal characters as either icons or demented Everymen; however, the film's ending makes the two aging and diminished characters of Elvis and Jack Kennedy into genuine heroes, offering a positive image of the elderly as possessing a sense of self-sacrifice and bravery not limited to youth. After defeating Bubba Ho-Tep, the dying Elvis consoles himself with the thought that both he and the residents of the home still have their souls.

See also: "Bubba Ho-Tep" (Short Story); Campbell, Bruce; Coscarelli, Don; Existentialism; Lansdale, Joe R.; Mummies; *Phantasm* series

Richard Bleiler

"BUBBA HO-TEP" (SHORT STORY)

"Bubba Ho-Tep" is a 1994 short story by Joe R. Lansdale that first appeared in the anthology *The King Is Dead: Tales of Elvis Post Mortem*. In it, an aging Elvis Presley lives in an East Texas nursing home under an assumed identity. In the present day of the story, Elvis lives a zombie-like existence in the Mud Creek Shady Grove Convalescent Home, where every monotonous day is like the last for the residents, who have been deprived of their free will in order to be warehoused in the facility until they die. Elvis's life begins to have meaning only after he and his friend Jack collaborate to stop a soul gathering mummy/zombie, Bubba Ho-Tep, from preying on the helpless, elderly tenants of the rest home.

Previous to the action set in the nursing home (the 1970s), Elvis had grown bored with fame and with being the pawn of his manager Colonel Parker (born Andreas Cornelis van Kuijk, 1909–1997). Presley hates his life because Parker makes money from encouraging the entertainer to make several ghastly B-movies, and his only meaningful relationship is with his sycophantic entourage now that his wife has left him and taken their daughter. So Lansdale's Elvis changes places with fictional Elvis-impersonator Sebastian Haff. However, Elvis is left with no way to reclaim his former life once Haff overdoses on drugs and leads the world to believe that the King is dead.

The mummy is the story's actual zombie—a reanimated corpse whose will has been subordinated by the need to suck out the souls of the living. However, "Bubba Ho-Tep" is also a metaphorical zombie story: several living characters have lives so devoid of meaning and are so tyrannized by routine that they are existential zombies. The story opens with the aging Elvis cursing his erectile dysfunction as he wonders about a pus-filled boil that has appeared on the head of his penis. Elvis's impotence is a metaphor for his lack of agency in all areas of his life. He wonders how long he has been in the Shady Grove Convalescent Home, whether he is awake or merely dreaming, and how his plans have gone so wrong. He asks himself questions like "When are they going to serve lunch, and considering what they serve, why do I care?" This question also underscore's Elvis's similarity to a zombie in its emphasis on mindless consumption. Elvis's friend Jack is similar to Elvis in his own lack of agency (relative to his younger days). Jack claims to be the former president John F. Kennedy, whose enemies told everyone he was assassinated in Dallas by a sniper's bullet, but secretly put a bag of sand in his head to take the place of his missing brain with all of its memories, and then dyed his skin so that everyone would think he was an African American. The story's scatological imagery reinforces the trope of the existential zombie—while Jack and Elvis recapture some meaning in their lives when they defeat Bubba Ho-Tep, their momentary agency is only temporary, as life itself is about as meaningful and permanent as excrement flushed down the toilet. "Bubba Ho-Tep" was made into a film in 2002 by Don Coscarelli Jr., whose adaptation was remarkably faithful to Lansdale's story, perhaps because the author was one of the screenwriters.

See also: Bubba Ho-Tep (Film); Coscarelli, Don; Cult Film; Existentialism; Lansdale, Joe R.; Mummies

June Michele Pulliam

C.H.U.D. SERIES

The *C.H.U.D.* films are a series of horror movies wherein exposure to toxic chemicals turns a human into a zombie or C.H.U.D. (Cannibalistic Humanoid Underground Dweller) The first film, *C.H.U.D.* (1984), directed by Douglas Cheek (no date available), centers on George Cooper, a photographer with a rapport with the underground homeless of New York. Cooper is asked to bail one of them out of jail. He is then approached by, Bosch, a reporter who convinces him to help investigate the tunnels. At the same time, a police detective has been investigating a series of disappearances in the city, including that of his wife. After Bosch interviews the Reverend, A.J. Shepherd, the two join forces to investigate. They find that the Nuclear Regulatory Commission is covering up the fact that for years it has been

When the populations of homeless people who live in the abandoned subway tunnels beneath New York City come into contact with the toxic waste that is dumped there, they turn into Cannibalistic Humanoid Underground Dwellers (C.H.U.D.s). (New World Pictures/Photofest)

illegally dumping radioactive toxic waste in abandoned subway tunnels. Homeless who come into contact with the waste mutate into grotesque flesh-eating creatures, preying on anyone unlucky enough to roam the city alone at night.

Eventually, the government discovers that asphyxiation kills a C.H.U.D., so it plans to pump gas into the subway tunnels. Since Cooper, Bosch, and the Reverend know about the government's part in creating the disaster, they become targets during the zombie purge. Filled with over-the-top melodrama and unintentionally funny moments, *C.H.U.D.* exemplifies the B-movie. Authorship of the script remains unclear: actors Daniel Stern (born Daniel Jacob Stern, 1957–) and Christopher Curry (born Christopher Root, 1948–), who have major roles in the film, claim credit for half of the script in a long-running dispute. *C.H.U.D.* grossed $4.6 million at the domestic box office.

The sequel, *C.H.U.D. 2: Bud the C.H.U.D.* (1989), was written by Ed Naha (1950–) and directed by David Irving (born David Kenneth Irving, 1949–). In this overtly comic sequel, well-known sit-com actors such as Norman Fell (born Norman Noah Feld, 1924–1998), Larry Linville (born Lawrence Lavon Linville, 1939–2000), Jack Riley (born John A. Riley Jr., 1935–), June Lockhart (1925–), and Rich Hall (born Richard Hall, 1954–) played minor roles. The comic plot begins when three teenagers steal from a military base what turns out to be a C.H.U.D. saved by the government to use in creating a race of super soldiers. The C.H.U.D. (named Bud) is reanimated and immediately escapes. This zombie spends much more time indulging in traditional zombie activities: biting, chomping, and attacking, so the zombie infection spreads much more rapidly. The three teens, who have a solid grasp of science, work to stop Bud, giving the film a campy quality. The film was released directly to DVD. Since its introduction in 1984, the term C.H.U.D. has been widely referenced in popular culture, in everything from the film *Clerks* (1994) to the television series *Futurama* (Season 6, Episode 12) and *Castle* (Season 3, Episode 10), as well as many episodes of *The Simpsons*.

See also: Cannibalism; Science Fiction; Television

Alicia Ahlvers

CABINET OF DR. CALIGARI, THE

The Cabinet of Dr. Caligari (1920) cannot be overestimated for its influence in film. It made German Expressionism a worldwide cinematic phenomenon and is arguably the first feature-length horror film, featuring a title character whose control over another is similar to the control of a Voodoo bokur over the traditional zombie, trapped in a death-like sleep. The victim is transformed via special effects makeup into a pale somnambulist, his pallor highlighted by dark shadows around his eyes, making him seem the prototype for the filmic living corpse. His slow, lumbering walk is a predecessor of that of the zombies in George Romero's *Night of the Living Dead* (1968), which in turn provided the conventions or rules to which future fictional walking dead would conform.

Dr. Caligari (Werner Krauss) and Cesare (Conrad Veidt), the somnambulist whose mind and movements he controls. (Photofest)

The narrative, which protagonist Francis, played by Friedrich Fehér (1889–1950), relates while a patient at an asylum, tells how he and his friend Alan, both suitors to the lovely Jane, become involved with the insidious Dr. Caligari, played by Werner Krauss (born Werner Johann Krauss, 1884–1959). Dr. Caligari comes to Francis's town with a traveling sideshow that reveals Cesare, played by Conrad Veidt (born Hans Walter Conrad Veidt, 1893–1943), a somnambulist whose mind and movements the doctor completely controls. A string of crimes begins, which eventually includes Alan's murder and Jane's kidnapping. Francis and the police trace the crimes back to Cesare and Caligari. A chase ensues in which Cesare at times becomes inseparable from a dummy double and from the backdrop's trees. Jane escapes, and Caligari is discovered to be a madman, modeling his crimes on a legend while posing as a psychiatrist. Then, in a twist, Caligari turns out really to be a psychiatrist who, having discovered Francis's fantasy, can now cure his dementia. Because Cesare is virtually mindless, Caligari is the true villain of the film. Therefore, the zombie-like character is more sympathetic than fearful, comparable to some of the zombies that emerge in both early and recent zombie fiction. Furthermore, by making a human more monstrous than the monster for much of the narrative, a feature seen in the majority of modern zombie tales, *The Cabinet of*

Dr. Caligari raises questions about abuses of power. The abuses critiqued are institutional, in this case of the medical industry.

Amid the economic ruins of World War I, director Robert Wiene (1873–1938) made the decision to build obviously handmade sets. They were both practical and artistic, resulting in towns and country sides with structures and foliage that stand at unreal, often claustrophobic angles that skew perceptions of height, depth, and distance. The settings, thus, appear dreamlike even without the film's frame story, which some historians argue was a producer-enforced addition. This suggests the narrative is the fantasy of a madman.

See also: Cult Film; Voodoo

L. Andrew Cooper

CAMPBELL, BRUCE

Bruce Campbell (born Bruce Lorne Campbell 1958–), has become a horror icon. He is an American actor known for his protruding chin and his portrayal of churlish, easygoing characters, both of which have made him identifiable with modern comic zombie cinema. His characters, most notably Ashley J. "Ash" Williams, are always portrayed as unapologetic for their nonchalant attitudes, even when they are faced with the flesh-eating undead.

A native of Royal Oak, Michigan, Campbell met director Sam Raimi, best known for the *Evil Dead* and *Spider-man* series, while at Wylie E. Groves High School. Together they raised enough money to produce and shoot *The Evil Dead* (1981). Raimi cast Campbell in the lead role, Ash Williams, the hapless member of a group of friends attacked by an unseen evil presence while camping. The presence is a direct homage to *The Thing from Another World* (1951), the classic by Christian Nyby (1913–1993) and Howard Hawks (born Howard Winchester Hawks, 1896–1977). Nyby's and Hawks's film was based on the story "Who Goes There?" by John W. Campbell (born John Wood Campbell Jr., 1910–1971), originally published in *Astounding Science-Fiction* (1938), wherein the creature infests its victims one at a time by possessing their bodies and transforming them into raging, flesh-eating zombies. In *The Evil Dead,* Ash is forced to disembowel and behead his zombified friends and girlfriend to survive. Campbell also worked behind the camera and was credited as coproducer. After a positive review from Stephen King (born Stephen Edwin King, 1947–), Campbell achieved cult status, and the film's success spawned two sequels starring Campbell: *Evil Dead II* (1987) and *Army of Darkness* (1992), both of which opened to favorable critical reviews. Campbell's campy performances made him a fan favorite. In 2013, Campbell produced a remake of *Evil Dead* starring a female rather than a male lead.

Campbell has appeared in virtually every Raimi film, often in cameo roles: an usher in *Spider-man* and a fake French Maître d' in *Spider-man 2*. He has had starring roles in two television series, *Jack of All Trades* (2000) and *The Adventures of Brisco County, Jr.* (1993–1994), and recurring roles in the *Xena* (1995–2001) and

Hercules (1995–1999) series. He currently co-stars in USA Network's *Burn Notice* (2007–2013). Campbell has also starred in many B-movies and has had numerous supporting roles in other movies. In the B-movie *Bubba Ho-Tep* (2002), Campbell plays an aging Elvis Presley confined to a nursing home, where he must fight a mummy before it claims the souls and lives of all of the elderly and marginalized residents. In the metatextual film *My Name Is Bruce* (2007), Campbell plays a parody of himself, a B-movie actor who must live up to the larger-than-life heroes that he plays when a boy comes to him to help protect his town from a newly awakened demon. Campbell's humorous 2002 *New York Times* best-seller autobiography is entitled *If Chins Could Kill: Confessions of a B Movie Actor*.

See also: Bubba Ho-Tep (Film); Comedy; Cult Film; *Evil Dead, The* (Films); Raimi, Sam; Television

David. E. Cowen

CANNIBALISM

Cannibalism, or anthropophagy, is the practice of consuming the flesh of one's own species. Only the human animal, *Homo sapiens*, displays any remorse when committing this act, one which is seen as horrific, monstrous, and emblematic of the disintegration of society by most first and second world nations. Despite this, references to cannibalism are found in a variety of myths, such as that of the Greek titan Cronus's devouring of his sons. In *Agricola*, the Roman historian Tacitus (AD 56–AD 117) refers to a group of Gauls who were forced by starvation to eat one another while hotly pursued by Frisians. A chronicle mentions Christians eating the dead Muslim defenders of the Syrian city of Ma'arra during the First Crusade (AD 1098). In the 16th century, Protestants frequently attacked Catholics for partaking of the Eucharist, which ostensibly incorporated the Real Presence of Christ's body. However, the practice of cannibalism in zombie literature and cinema has little, if any, resemblance to the actual cultural phenomenon, and the zombie's characteristic cannibalism does not have any precedent in the historical or archaeological record.

Indeed, before *Night of the Living Dead* (1968), zombies were not portrayed as cannibals, with one notable exception of pseudo-cannibalism in "Pigeons from Hell" (1938), by Robert E. Howard (born Robert Ervin Howard, 1906–1936). Rather, the original version of the zombie is a person supposedly resurrected from the dead by a Voodoo priest, brought back to perform a variety of tedious labors, presumably for eternity. Although its origins are ancient and can be traced back to Western and Central Africa, the zombie was little known outside of the island nation of Haiti prior to the early 20th century. To be turned into a zombie was to continue one's status as a slave into the afterlife, a belief that had an especially dreadful meaning to Haitians who endured one of the harshest colonial regimes in the New World. In the earliest known film featuring a zombie, *White Zombie* (1932), the zombie is completely bound to the will of the villainous Haitian Voodoo priest who is hell-bent on terrorizing a respectable white couple.

The transformation of the zombie of Haitian lore to the roaming, flesh-eating ghoul of contemporary cinema and television is the influence of the films of Romero, especially *Dawn of the Dead* (1978). In *Dawn,* Romero used the zombie's insatiable hunger as a metaphor for the addictive appeal of consumerism, namely shopping, creating a highly effective horror movie that functioned as a critique of capitalism. Briefly summarized, *Dawn* is about four human survivors who use a shopping mall as an emergency shelter after fleeing the infested city of Philadelphia in a helicopter. After killing all of the zombies in the mall, and securing the exits against an even larger army of undead outside, the group quickly indulges in stealing various goods from the shops and the cash from an ATM. Neither the goods nor the cash has any value in a zombie apocalypse, but the characters cannot help themselves from fulfilling their social roles as mindless consumers. In such an economy, the only valuable asset is human life. But a battle between the protagonists and a motorcycle gang seeking to exploit the mall ends with both groups being devoured by the undead, with a few exceptions to thicken the plot. Romero draws a distinct parallel between our desire to consume everything—including human lives through mass killing—and the zombies' insatiable need for human flesh. Neither human nor zombie is ever nourished by its consumption. Civilization is doomed.

More recently, in the novel *World War Z* (2006), Max Brooks creates a fictional zombie apocalypse aftermath as a lesson in the moral hazards of free market capitalism. The novel is written as a series of survivors' interviews collected by the narrator/author, who provides only introductions to the interviews, and an occasional footnote to clarify the meaning of various acronyms and terminology. At least two of the interviews in *World War Z* suggest a connection between the self-destructiveness of human consumption and the rampaging cannibalism of zombies. The pharmaceutical executive Breckinridge Scott is interviewed about his company's marketing of Phalanx, a placebo disguised as an oral medication that offers protection against the zombie virus. Now snugly protected in his massive bunker in Antarctica, Scott gleefully reveals his manipulation of a naïve public and a cowed regulatory system to make billions in profits. While not a zombie, Scott exhibits the same insatiable hunger, even if the object of his desire is the corpse of humanity itself. In another interview, Fernando Oliveira, a cardiac surgeon, confesses his role in spreading the zombie virus by transplanting into a patient an infected heart that was purchased on China's black market, where human organs are harvested from living so-called donors. Oliveira coolly discloses that all of his requests were made to order and were used to prolong the lives of his rich patrons from North America. He describes a brutally efficient organ and tissue trafficking network that is designed to serve "Yankees" who did not care from where a new kidney or pancreas came. In a free market, the poor are inevitably consumed by the wealthy. Tellingly, the good doctor is now living in the Amazon Rain Forest as a prisoner of the Yanomami, an Indian tribe with a long history of cannibalism.

Cannibalism and zombiism are also associated with anxieties over the control of society's food supply. In *Shaun of the Dead* (2004), the main character walks to a local bodega and glances at a newspaper's headline that reads "GM Crops to Blame." In the background, a lumbering homeless man—and possible zombie—is voraciously devouring a pigeon. A more literal connection is found in *Zombieland* (2009), where the zombie plague's "patient zero" derives the illness from eating what is identified as a hamburger tainted with mad cow, purchased at a fast food chain restaurant. Columbus, the main character and voice-over narrator, describes his own encounters and ultimate deliverance while offering a core set of rules for surviving the zombie apocalypse. As the infection quickly spreads throughout society, a wide variety of victims are dispatched in a gory montage, including an obese (and therefore slow) man who is tackled and eaten on the 35-yard line in a football stadium. Other victims of the undead hordes include a heavy-set patron of a strip club, whose wanton appetite for bare flesh is ironically one-upped by his own hideous death. The reverse of the cannibalism-as-consumption metaphor is likewise applied in *Zombieland*, where the characters visibly eschew the kitschy appeal of consumer culture. When they arrive at an abandoned convenience store, they do not loot the shelves like the central characters in *Dawn of the Dead*: instead, they gleefully vandalize the store and destroy the worthless merchandise.

Apart from the preceding fictional interpretations of the zombie's nature, there are disturbing contemporary cases of psychopathological cannibalism, which is the fetishizing and consumption of a victim's body parts by a serial murderer. Jeffrey Dahmer (born Jeffrey Lionel Dahmer, 1959–1994), the most notorious serial murderer/cannibal in modern memory, killed 17 people between 1978 and 1991. Dahmer not only devoured his victims, but he also attempted to produce a living zombie from two of them who later perished. Dahmer testified at his trial that he frequently engaged in sexual acts with his victims' anatomies as a way of reliving the thrill of their seduction and murder. He even built a shrine composed of his victims' skulls and preserved remains. Dahmer claimed that he was seeking what he called a permanent relationship. In his warped rationale, this left only one option. This macabre evolution from cannibalizing victims to transforming them into private property is also seen in *The Walking Dead* graphic novel series. The governor of the outlaw community of Woodbury shares a close and eerie resemblance to Dahmer in his habits. Prior to the zombie outbreak, the governor, thought to be a man named Philip Blake, is at first a feckless ne'er-do-well hiding in a crawlspace in his parents' house. But in the aftermath of the disaster, he becomes a force to be reckoned with as the leader of a gang of violent psychopaths. Among Woodbury's many horrors, which include a gladiatorial combat arena decorated with impaled bodies, is the governor's private residence that he shares with Penny, his seven-year-old zombified niece. While she is fed the amputated hand of a fresh victim, he opens a package containing two human heads, which are added to a collection of 55, all displayed in transparent case in front of a Lay-Z-Boy recliner. Later, the governor pulls out Penny's teeth with a pair of pliers in order to reduce the likelihood of her infecting him. Bizarrely, he also kisses her deeply on the lips after this procedure. Dahmer and other serial killers/cannibals, such as Dennis Nilsen (born Dennis Andrew Nilsen, 1945–) and Andrei Romanovic Chikatilo (1936–1994), are known to have this compulsion to intimately embrace the dead. The governor's trophy case of severed heads is similar to Dahmer's makeshift shrine, assuring readers that fortunately for humanity, Dahmer's aspirations are only possible in the realm of zombie fiction.

See also: Africa; Haiti; Romero, George; *Shaun of the Dead*; Television; Voodoo; *Walking Dead, The* (Comic); *Walking Dead, The* (Television Series); *White Zombie*; *World War Z* (Film); *World War Z* (Novel); *Zombieland*; Zuvembie

Michael E. Matthews

CARNIVAL OF SOULS

Carnival of Souls is a 1962 independent horror film produced and directed by Herk Harvey (born Harold Arnold Harvey, 1924–1996). The film was distributed by Herts-Lion International Corporation and originally released in Lawrence, Kansas. Harvey, who coauthored the script of this, his sole feature film, used a cast of unknowns, including Candace Hilligoss (1935–) and himself, and incorporated an eerie church organ score to create an atmospheric tale of a haunting by undead ghouls and/or zombies. Harvey managed to finish *Carnival of Souls* in three weeks and keep the budget at an estimated $33,000, and although the film got little attention on release, it has since been reclassified as an atmospheric B-movie cult classic. Prior to this project, Harvey was a director and producer of industrial and educational films; he conceived of the storyline while on vacation in Utah after he saw the abandoned Saltair Pavilion, which serves as the movie's eerie backdrop in the reanimated undead scenes.

In one of the final scenes of *Carnival of Souls*, Mary is confronted by the ghouls who have come to take her from the land of the living. (Herts-Lion Intl / Photofest)

The film begins with Mary Henry (Hilligoss) driving her car with two other young women passengers. The women are represented as being risqué or improper in that they accept a challenge to drag race with some young men. Mary's car wipes out on a bridge, going over the rail and into the river below. While police toil unsuccessfully to find the car hours later, Mary emerges from the river, with no memories of the ordeal. Hired previous to the accident as a church organist, Mary continues to Utah to begin her new job, where she is haunted by discordant organ music on her car's radio; by the sight of a large, abandoned pavilion; and by a mysterious, extremely pale older man (Harvey), whose features are reminiscent of those of the typical cinematic zombie. The man merely stares at Mary, and at times, his pale face takes the place of her reflection. When Mary reaches Utah, she rents a room and again is haunted by the pale older man.

Mary then begins having weird moments where no one else in a room can hear or see her. Soon after Mary starts seeing a doctor about her condition, she discovers that she can no longer play religious music on the organ. Each time Mary attempts to practice, she automatically begins playing the same eerie organ music she heard in her car, causing the church minister to ask her to resign. Finally, Mary returns to the pavilion, which has been beckoning to her, and there other ghouls join the older man, all dancing a waltz to the eerie music. When Mary sees a pale version of herself dancing with the man, she runs away and is chased by the ghouls to a beach where she disappears. In the final scene, the car the girls were driving is located in the river, with Mary's body in the front seat. Although *Carnival of Souls* does not use the typical zombie trope, as either the flesh-eating resurrected undead or the alive/dead Voodoo slave, the makeup for the film emphasized the ghoulish qualities of the walking dead characters.

See also: Cult Film; Ghosts; Ghoul

Anthony J. Fonseca

CELL

Cell (2006), by Stephen King, is a technophobic, apocalyptic novel following Clay Riddell, an aspiring graphic artist, as he attempts to reach his estranged wife and their son Johnny in the wake of something called The Pulse, a mind-altering signal sent through cell phones. The Pulse's effect is to turn cell phone users into so-called phone-crazies, zombies whose wills have been subordinated by the drive to kill anyone who did not initially hear The Pulse. Although they are not the walking dead, the phone-crazies otherwise behave like zombies following Romero's Rules. For example, they primarily use their teeth to attack others: in one scene, Clay watches a woman use her teeth to rip out the throat of another, while a man bites the ear off of a dog. The phone-crazies later exhibit the mindlessness typical of zombies when they move in sync with one another.

Clay teams up with fellow survivors Tom and Alice, traveling through the Northeast in hopes of finding Clay's son. They travel at night because the phone-people move about only during the day (in an inversion of vampire and some zombie narratives). On the grounds of a boarding school, they discover the phone-people's capacity to use portable stereos to broadcast music through their own bodies, an ability the unaffected humans find disturbing, presumably due to the fact that this ability explicitly associates the phone-people and technology. Clay, Tom, and Alice join the former headmaster and his lone remaining student and set off a bomb in the midst of the sleeping zombies. This bombing brings them to the attention of The Raggedy Man, who shows up first in their dreams and then at the phone-people encampment and seems to act as a leader of the phone-people. The Raggedy Man herds the group toward a former county expo site with the promise of "No-Fo," or no phones—yet, as Clay and the others learn in shared dreams, The Raggedy Man sends unaffected humans through a checkpoint requiring them to listen to a version of The Pulse, thus converting everyone into phone-people. Nonetheless, Clay continues toward the expo in hopes of finding his son, and others join him in order to find a way to exterminate the phone-people.

Throughout the novel, characters connect The Pulse to terrorism, particularly drawing upon a post-9/11 fear of U.S. vulnerability. But none of the connections are ever proven. Tom mentions the use of planes early on, also referencing a tower, a link to the 9/11 World Trade Center bombings. This inability to discover the truth behind The Pulse persists through the end of the novel when, after destroying the phone-crazies' main compound and finding his phone-damaged son, Clay finally acts on the group's earlier hypothesis that a second exposure to The Pulse could restore the brain's original functionality. The novel ends as Clay holds an active cell phone up to his son's ear.

Despite *Cell*'s apparent technophobia, King used eBay to auction the opportunity to name a character in the novel. Pam Alexander of Ft. Lauderdale, Florida, won the auction and gave the character her brother's name: Ray Huizenga. In the novel, Ray develops the plan to bomb the phone-crazies' compound but kills himself to keep the knowledge from The Raggedy Man, thus enabling Clay to complete his quest.

See also: Apocalypse; Science Fiction

Margo Collins

CELLAR, THE

The Cellar is a young adult zombie novel by A.J. Whitten, the pseudonym for the writing team of Shirley Jump (1968–) and her daughter Amanda (no date available). It is unusual in its representation of the zombie, as the protagonists Aiden and Marie are turned into zombies by Voodoo, yet they also pass among humans, on whom they must feed to stave off their own decay. Created via a Voodoo spell, Marie retained enough free will to escape the control of her maker, who reanimated the dead to use as mindless labor. Marie then produces her own zombies, who initially travel with her to enjoy the relative immortality and invulnerability the condition imparts.

Whitten's zombies are not necessarily hideous, decaying corpses with poor social skills, but maintain their pre-death appearance for approximately a century provided they periodically ingest human flesh. At first, Marie goes from town to town with her zombies, and the pack hunts discreetly to maintain their youthful appearances. However, most of the pack is hunted down and killed after they take too many victims in one town, thereby alerting humans of their presence. Only Aiden and Marie escape to continue their relationship as lovers. In the present day of the novel, the two have taken up residence in a small town where the relatively youthful-looking Aiden and the now visibly aging Marie pass themselves off as aunt and nephew. Aiden attends high school and quickly becomes the local heart-throb with his 1980s retro style and gothic pallor. Marie, meanwhile, remains confined in the run-down house in which the duo has taken up residence, waiting for Aiden to bring her victims. Because Marie is so much older than Aiden, her body has reached its limit, and she must soon transfer her spirit into a newer body lest she become trapped in the decaying flesh of her present one. Aiden and Marie initially select Heather, a lovely teen, as the vessel for Marie's spirit that will enable to continue her undead existence and her romantic relationship with Aiden. But after Aiden gets to know Heather better, he plans to kill Marie instead while she is in her weakened state and then to turn Heather into his eternal zombie mate.

The Cellar is unusual in how it combines different tropes of the zombie with those of other monsters. While zombies are created in this novel through Voodoo, they partially operate by Romero's Rules in that they must have human flesh in order to survive. Whitten's zombies also deviate from Romero's Rules in ways that make them more similar to the vampire and other supernatural creatures. These zombies can prevent their bodies from decaying by eating human flesh, similar to how vampires are able to prevent their own decay through drinking human blood. Moreover, these zombies are sentient. Finally, Whitten's zombies can possess the bodies of others by transferring their souls into their flesh. *The Cellar* is rather gory and graphic when compared to most young adult works of fiction.

See also: Cannibalism; Sentience; Voodoo; Young Adult Fiction

June Michele Pulliam

CHILDREN SHOULDN'T PLAY WITH DEAD THINGS

Children Shouldn't Play with Dead Things, also known as *Revenge of the Living Dead, Things from the Dead,* and *Zreaks,* is a 1973 comedy-horror film directed by Bob Clark (born Benjamin Clark, 1939–2007). The protagonist, Alan, is a pompous, boorish, and crude director of a group of actors who travel to a secluded and deserted island graveyard to spend the weekend at his request. The actors, who he calls his children, spend the night there inside of an abandoned cabin and discover that the island is a burial place for paupers and criminals of the worst sort. They then watch Alan as he performs a satanic midnight ritual from a grimoire or book of spells to raise and command the dead. Alan pranks the others by having actors painted as zombies pretend to attack the troupe and digs up a real corpse named Orville that he pretends to marry in a farcical ceremony. What starts out as an elaborate prank, however, quickly becomes a real problem as the ritual creates a mass of zombies and ghouls who rise from the dead ravenous for human flesh.

The shuffling and slow-moving horde of zombies claw their way out of the grave and swarm the barricaded cabin with the troupe stuck inside. From this point on, the movie begins to resemble George Romero's *Night of the Living Dead* (1968) quite a bit. The characters, shown to be cruel and insensitive before this point, make an escape attempt and have no qualms about sacrificing others to get away in the dash through the zombie horde. Eventually, all are killed and are eaten by the zombies. The film finishes with the zombies stumbling onto the boat that the actors arrived in as it drifts off, presumably toward the mainland.

The film is noted for its humor and convincing special makeup effects on its low budget. Despite the horrors surrounding them, the actors constantly make jokes and puns and poke fun at various horror movie tropes. The makeup effects hearken to classic zombies. The creatures have white, ghoulish, and putrefying faces, many of them with rotting flesh. Likely due to the lower budget and limited special effects team, most zombies are shown fully clothed in fashion from various eras, with only their white heads and hands seen. Filmed on an estimated $70,000 budget in and around Miami, Florida, the movie received mixed reviews but has since become a cult classic. This was Clark's third film, and he would later go on to direct the classic films *Porky's* (1982) and *A Christmas Story* (1983) as well as cult horror film *Black Christmas* (1984).

See also: Cannibalism; Clark, Bob; Comedy; Cult Film; Ghoul; Romero, George

Braden Dauzat

CHILDREN'S BOOKS

Children's books are normally defined by their eschewal of subject matter and imagery that young readers (and even younger toddlers being read to by parents or teachers) would not find disquieting or disturbing. Despite this, some children's authors have found a small audience who are interested in either the subversive nature, or absurdly comic tone, of a children's book about zombies.

As of 2013, one of the more popular grade-school level (books of about 30–50 pages with a few lines of text per page) children's books is Matt Mogk's (no date available) and Aja Wells's (no date available) *That's Not Your Mommy Anymore* (2011). Fans of the book recommend it as a text for children and adults who are interested in the so-called zombie culture. The text is a nod to Dr. Seuss (born Theodor Seuss Geisel, 1904–1991) in its absurdist rhymed couplet scheme, and it features allusions to various zombie films and their creators. Mogk, the founder of The Zombie Research Society, writes the text as a children's version of the adult zombie survival guide, as it offers advice to a young boy of what to do if he recognizes that his mother has turned into a zombie (and how to recognize the change).

The earliest zombie children's books used zombies as metaphors for the various events in a child's life which he or she might find reprehensible. Scott Nickel (no date available) and Steve Harpster (no date available) teamed up in 2006 for *Night of the Homework Zombies,* a children's graphic novel published by Stone Arch Books. It tells the tale of a Mr. Winklepoof, a new substitute teacher who claims not to be an escaped mad scientist. Winklepoof shows a video that turns school children into zombies by taking away their free will and making them love their homework. The book's protagonist avoids being turned because he has a timely bathroom break, and then he endeavors to escape the zombie fate, even as his friends become zombies. In 2008, Nickel teamed up with Cedric Hohnstadt (no date available), again for Stone Arch Books, to create *Day of the Field Trip Zombies.* Similar to *Night of the Homework Zombies,* the story involves children (this time at an aquarium) being turned into mindless reciters of information, by a character named Dr. Brainium. Eventually the protagonist, Trevor, must face off against Dr. Brainium and an army of zombified penguins.

Other popular zombie children's titles include *Ten Little Zombies: A Love Story* (2010), by Andy Rash (no date available), which basically enumerates the various ways by which zombies die as they chase the protagonists; *Night of the Living Dust Bunnies* (2011), part of the Stone Rabbit series by Erik Craddock (no date available), which follows Stone Rabbit, Andy Wolf, and Henri Tortoise on Halloween, when zombie dust bunnies are unleashed after an atomic lamp is knocked over onto a vacuum; *Jack and Jill Went Up to Kill: A Book of Zombie Nursery Rhymes* (2011), by Michael P. Spradlin (no date available); and *Pat the Zombie: A Cruel (Adult) Spoof* (2011), by Aaron Ximm (no date available) and Kaveh Soofi (no date available), which is characterized by its interactive quality and its over-the-top gore, although it is arguable that the book was never meant for children, as indicated in the title by the insertion of the word "adult."

See also: Comedy; Graphic Novels and Comics; Romero's Rules

Anthony J. Fonseca

CLARK, BOB

Bob Clark (born Benjamin Clark, 1939–2007), was an American actor, director, screenwriter, and producer. Best known for his comedy *A Christmas Story* (1983), he worked in Canada for a decade prior and produced successes in all genres, including the successful slasher film *Black Christmas* (1974), the Sherlock Holmes tale *Murder by Decree* (1979), and the teen comedy *Porky's* (1982). His career was catapulted by the horror genre, however, by his two zombie collaborations with screenwriter and makeup artist Alan Ormsby (1944–). *Deathdream* (also known as *Dead of Night,* 1972), based on the W. W. Jacobs's (born William Wymark Jacobs, 1863–1943) story "The Monkey's Paw," combined the Vietnam War film with the returning undead trope, and *Children Shouldn't Play with Dead Things* (1973), combined horror and black comedy.

While *Deathdream* does not feature a zombie per se, its main character, who had died on a Vietnam battlefield, rejoins the living after his mother wishes his return. However, because he is undead, he needs the blood of human victims at regular intervals in order to replenish his deteriorating body. *Children Shouldn't Play with Dead Things*, also known as *Revenge of the Living Dead, Things from the Dead*, and *Zreaks*, was a low-budget zombie film (made for $70,000) shot in 14 days. Clark offset the lack of funding by working with some of his friends from college, and with special effects by Ormsby, who also stars as the cruel director (Alan) of a theater troupe. In the film, Alan and some friends decide to go on an adventure, taking a boat to a small island where criminals are buried. They desecrate the cemetery, and during what the group believes is a failed séance, they raise the dead using a cursed tome. Afterward, the zombies attack them during the night. For a while, the humans are sheltered in an old house on the island, as these zombies are fairly inept at getting into the dwelling. In addition, the zombies are not able to rapidly swell their ranks as they ingest rather than infect victims, and so it is difficult for them to make more.

The zombies are defined by their facial discolorations (most are blue-tinted, alabaster, or brown), their wild hair, their torn and dirty clothes, and their darkened eye sockets. Moreover, they are slow-moving. They shamble rather than walk, and they have very little coordination, so they are fairly easy to fight, if it were not for the fact that they cannot be killed. The group of humans is killed only when its members venture outside of the house to attempt an escape, and only because the humans are outnumbered by the zombies. In the final scene, the zombies can be seen boarding the boat during the closing credits, headed toward Miami. The 35th anniversary special DVD edition (2007) features the uncut version of the film with a cast commentary. A biographical documentary, *ClarkWorld*, was produced and directed in 2009 by Deren Abram (1966–), who had collaborated with Clark for a decade prior to Clark's accidental death.

See also: Cannibalism; *Children Shouldn't Play with Dead Things*

Anthony J. Fonseca

CLASS

Because the single most defining characteristic of the zombie is its lack of free will, it is a fertile metaphor for class, particularly the plight of the working classes and their lack of control over the means of production relative to the members of the middle and upper classes. Thus, class struggle is an underlying theme is most zombie fiction.

The earliest representations of the zombie grew from the trauma of slavery, first appearing in 19th-century Haiti, approximately 150 years after the slaves who were the majority of inhabitants of the island overthrew their French colonialist oppressors to earn their independence. The Haitian revolution, however, did not lead to permanent freedom for everyone. Afterward, officers in the Haitian military and their cronies were given substantial landholdings, while the majority of the population was forced to continue performing back-breaking agricultural labor on the island's plantations. Meanwhile, Haiti itself was virtually enslaved by France, who demanded an extortionate amount of money from the struggling nation in payment for the land it ceded after the revolution. These forces quickly turned free Haiti into a feudal state where the freed slaves returned to a life of servitude with little opportunity for class mobility. Meanwhile, the island's strategic location, combined with the desperation of its inhabitants, made it attractive to American corporations eager to exploit Haiti's resources, and the American government even assisted these interests during the Wilson (born Thomas Woodrow Wilson, 1856–1924) presidency by sending in the marines to keep order.

Against this backdrop, everyday Haitians feared that actual slavery was not far behind, and the figure of the zombie as the embodiment of these fears proliferated in Haitian folk culture. So the original representations of the zombie, created by Voodoo, is an eternal slave, controlled by its maker who uses it as mindless labor to toil in the fields until its body becomes too broken to function. This sort of slavery is seen when the creature first made its appearance in popular culture, such as the story "Dead Men Working in the Cane Fields" in W. B. Seabrook's travelogue of Haiti published in 1929, and in the 1932 film *White Zombie,* which is loosely based on Seabrook's accounts. In both, the undead are pitiful machines made of flesh, lacking any free will, interchangeable with one another and disposable.

However, later versions of the creature similarly represent it as a wage slave whose filthy and decaying countenance horrifically emphasizes the indignities of poverty. For example, Richard Matheson sets up a class system between the infected living and infected undead in his 1954 novella, *I Am Legend.* The infected undead are slow and mindless. The bacteria responsible for the pandemic makes the victims allergic to sunlight and easily sickened by garlic, and so the infected undead believe themselves to be vampires, which causes them to prey upon the living and attempt to drink their blood, even though ingesting this fluid is not necessary for their survival. The infected living, on the other hand, better understand their condition and are working to both rebuild society, which has been laid to waste due to the pandemic, and destroy the infected undead, who are so mindless as to not even be useful slaves. While the living infected are indistinguishable from Robert Neville, the novel's protagonist who is legend, in part, because he is the last known person on the planet not to succumb to the bacteria, they are fundamentally different from the undead infected, who have ceased to groom themselves and wander around caked with filth in the clothes they died in.

Director George Romero, however, most notably represents the zombie as a member of the proletariat in his *Night of the Living Dead* series of films. Zombies in *Land of the Dead,* the fourth of his six-film oeuvre, are working-class heroes. Many years after the dead have begun returning to life and civilization as we know it has been destroyed, a group of zombies abide in the peaceful hamlet of Uniontown, performing, albeit clumsily, activities that made them happy and gave their lives meaning when they were alive. The peace of this enclave is shattered, however, by a raiding party of humans, who trash the town and gleefully maim and kill zombies while scavenging for supplies. The zombie Big Daddy is outraged at the behavior of the raiding party and visibly mourns one of his numbers who has been decapitated by the raiding party. As Big Daddy euthanizes his still-living maimed zombie comrade, he snarls while looking in the direction of the retreating raiding party. Soon Big Daddy channels his outrage by leading his fellow undead to conduct their own raid on the human's compound, ostensibly as payback for how the living treat the undead. Many years have passed since the zombie apocalypse, yet the undead have not starved to death, so it now seems as if zombies do not eat the living for sustenance but kill them to defend themselves against the living, who have so depersonalized zombies that they rarely have any compunction about killing them, can use them for target practice, and even vivisect them, as we see in the previous film in the series, *Day of the Dead*. We know Big Daddy's name and occupation in life from the gas station attendant's uniform that he still wears with his name emblazoned on the shirt. The raiding party that he organizes consists of workers from diverse walks of life, which is signified to the viewer by the clothes each zombie is attired in, as the undead do not change their clothes after death.

Diana Rowland's (1966–) *White Trash Zombie* series further explores the creature's working-class roots. While the virus that reanimates the dead and gives them an insatiable desire for brains can affect all humans in Rowland's paranormal romance novels, her heroine, Angel Crawford, identifies herself as white trash, and for a time she adheres to all of the negative stereotypes about this social group. Angel, a high school dropout and drug addict, shares a trailer with her abusive, unemployed alcoholic father. She nearly dies in a car accident, and an unknown benefactor, seeing her potential, transforms her into a zombie rather than letting her expire. Ironically, Angel's new need for brains gives her the impetus to straighten up her life. So that Angel can supply her new nutritional need without attracting any unwanted attention toward herself as a supernatural entity, her benefactor has secured her a job with the coroner's office, giving her access to bodies that she can discreetly trepan. As Angel comes to understand that she can improve her life, she struggles to get her GED as well as extricate herself from toxic relationships with people who just drag her down. Angel's transformation from human to zombie, as well as from "white trash" to someone who deserves our sympathy and respect, demonstrates that class is not the result of some immutable inherent characteristics in some that would make it pointless to intervene in their fate. Rather, class is an institution created by humans for the purposes of social control, and so, for example, people denigrated as "white trash" can transcend the limitations placed upon them by this designation if given the chance. In this way, the representation of the zombie calls into question the boundaries between the working classes and others.

See also: Haiti; *I Am Legend* (Novel); *Night of the Living Dead* Series; Race; Romero, George; Seabrook, W. B.; Voodoo; *White Trash Zombie* Series; *White Zombie*

June Michele Pulliam

COLIN

Colin is a 2008 independent movie that is considered the first feature film made entirely from the perspective of the zombie: its titular character spends the entirety of the film as a zombie, having been turned within the first few minutes of the story. Made on a budget of just $70 or £45, *Colin* had a small opening, playing in a limited run on screens in United States in cities such as Albuquerque, Albany, Chicago, Knoxville, Portland, Sacramento, San Antonio, Seattle, and Washington. *Colin* has been positively reviewed in important film magazines like *Sight and Sound*.

Colin, the film's protagonist, is attacked by his zombified flatmate Damien, whom he manages to kill but not before Damien infects him. Afterward, Colin wanders the streets of London when he begins to have cannibalistic cravings that he does not wish to give in to, so he avoids people. Nevertheless, Colin is not left alone: a would-be mugger attempts to rob him of his athletic shoes, when his sister spots him and rescues him from the criminal and brings him to their mother's house. Crazed with the infection that rages throughout his body after he was bitten by Damien, Colin does not recognize his sister, so he bites and infects her. Eventually, zombies attack and kill everyone except for one woman, who escapes into a basement with the undead and a serial killer. Meanwhile, a group of humans bomb a zombie mob and mutilate Colin, who survives; he watches as the humans, led by a sadistic young man with a slingshot, murder three of their own who are bitten during a zombie encounter. He then shambles off to his friend Laura's home, where the film cuts to a flashback to when he was still human.

Writer, director, and editor Marc Price (no date available) began filming *Colin* after hanging out with an actor friend, who introduced him to other actors willing to work on the project for free; he reportedly also placed casting calls on Facebook and Myspace. *Colin* is characterized by harsh lighting and quick editing jumps, as well surprisingly realistic special effects created without computer-generated imagery. Additionally, the characters in the film lack guns or other weapons, something unusual in a movie about a zombie apocalypse. *Colin* was screened at various film festivals, including Cannes, the Málaga Fantastic Film Festival in Spain, and the Abattoir horror festival. During Halloween of 2009, *Colin* was released in cinemas in London and other cities in the United Kingdom, as well as distributed to DVD by Kaleidoscope Home Entertainment. In an interview, director Price cites early films by George Romero, Robert Rodriguez (born Robert Anthony Rodriguez, 1968–), Peter Jackson, and Sam Raimi as inspirations for *Colin,* as well as the book *Digital Film Making* (2007) by director Mike Figgis (born Michael Figgis, 1948–).

See also: Apocalypse; Cult Film; Epidemics; Jackson, Peter; Raimi, Sam; Romero, George; Romero's Rules

Anthony J. Fonseca

COMEDY

Comedy has long been a staple of the horror film industry. In early Universal Studios films, some comic element was usually introduced to lighten the intensity of the suspense. By the 1940s, even the biggest horror stars, Bela Lugosi and Boris Karloff (born William Henry Pratt, 1887–1969), found themselves in comic films (sometimes in comic roles). By the 1950s, writing entire horror comedy scripts for Abbott and Costello (born William Alexander Abbott, 1895–1974 and Louis Francis Cristillo, 1906–1959) was routine. Today, virtually every horror film contains some element of humor, and horror parodies and comedies do well at the box office. Zombie comedies have had a parallel history to that of the larger genre, with zombie comedies existing as early as the 1940s.

Early zombie comedies dealt with Voodoo zombies and were often parodies of individual films as well as of performers and performances. Lugosi was often tapped for his comic potential, not as a comic actor himself but as a parody of his own performances as *Dracula* (1931). In one such film, *Bowery at Midnight* (1942), directed by Wallace Fox, Lugosi stars as a psychology professor who moonlights as the manager of a soup kitchen, which turns out is actually a front for criminal activity. One of his accomplices is meanwhile creating dead mobsters into slaves. Lugosi also stars in *Zombies on Broadway* (1945), directed by Gordon Douglas (1907–1993), was production company RKO's answer to Abbott and Costello. In the parody *I Walked with a Zombie* (1943), the plot involves two Broadway press agents who are in need of a hit show, causing them to create an outlandish scheme of a show about a real zombie. After trying a fake, they are threatened by their ex-gangster boss if they fail to produce a real zombie at the club's opening. The two bumblers travel to San Sebastian, a fictional island, where they encounter a zombie expert and bokur. Ultimately, they return to New York with a zombie serum and turn their boss into the zombie headliner.

Like *Zombies on Broadway,* many zombie comedies fall into the parody category, in that they target for humor either the zombie genre itself or specific zombie films. *Shaun of the Dead* (2004) is a broad parody of the genre directed by Edgar Wright (born Edgar Howard Wright, 1974–), who coauthored the script with lead actor Simon Pegg (born Simon John Beckingham, 1970–). Shaun, a twenty-something manager of an appliance store who is directionless and has a tenuous relationship with his girlfriend, exemplifies the type of the ennui of his generation, young men and women in dead-end jobs where they seldom look up or disengage their iPods, going about the day-to-day existence in a zombie-like stupor. Shaun's teenaged colleagues mock him and disrespect his authority. Shaun's best friend Ed, played by Nick Frost (born Nicholas John Frost, 1972–), spends every night drunk in the local pub. A lot of the humor in the early parts of the film is about how difficult it is to tell zombies from any of these people. Neither Shaun nor Ed seems able to for quite some time. The film also plays up the comic in the characters' reactions to the zombie attacks, in their inability to know anything about survival, and finally in the characters' inability to change their lives significantly, even as zombies. A parody of *Shaun of the Dead, Juan of the Dead* (2011), written and directed by Argentinian Alejandro Brugués (1976–), features a Cuban protagonist who is a 40-year-old slacker. His best friend is a libertine estranged from his children. When the two friends find themselves in the middle of a zombie infestation, the situation is played as a humorous jab at the working conditions in Cuba: at first Juan sees zombies as an opportunity to make money, selling his services as a zombie assassin. Ultimately, when overwhelmed, he and his zombie killers are comically faced with taking a boat off the island. Brugués created the film to have a political subtext, as a commentary on both the zombie-like quality of the citizens of Cuba as well as the 50 years of confrontational posing against the United States characteristic of the Cuban government. *Juan of the Dead* also satirizes what Brugués states on the film's website are the ways Cubans deal with problems: by ignoring them, turning them into business opportunities, or leaving the country.

The term Rom Zom Com is a contraction of Romantic Zombie Comedy and was coined by Pegg and Wright to describe *Shaun of the Dead*. Like the romantic comedy, it involves a couple that either has trouble getting together or find itself parted, only to be reunited in the end, except this time the zombies play a significant role in the kindling or rekindling. Shaun is able to rekindle his girlfriend Liz's love after the two survive a night of fighting the undead. However, as a concept, the Romantic Zombie Comedy predates Wright's film. *My Boyfriend's Back* (1993), directed by Bob Balaban (born Robert Elmer Balaban, 1945–), features an undead, rotting, cannibalistic version of the zombie, who just happens to be the film's love interest. The film tells the story of Johnny Dingle, who returns from the dead as a zombie to fulfill his dream of taking to the prom Missy McCloud, the girl he has loved since he was six years old. As Johnny prepares for his big night, his body parts fall off and decay and he discovers that to stave off decay he must consume human flesh, but each bite will give him only 20 minutes.

A more recent addition to the subgenre was *Zombieland* (2009), a blockbuster directed by Ruben Samuel Fleischer (1974–). The film's narrator, one of the few survivors of a zombie apocalypse, teams up with an older male survivor and two young females. In true romantic comedy fashion, boy meets girl but boy and girl are at odds through half of the film, as it turns out that the women are con artists who do whatever it takes to survive, including robbing the men. The zombie apocalypse makes their eventual romance possible. Their romantic relationship finally flourishes after the film's final standoff against the zombies. *Warm Bodies* (2013), directed by Jonathan A. Levine (1976–), is based on the romantic zombie comedy novel by Isaac Marion (1981–). The film is the story of the zombie R and his love for the human Julie, in a world where the dead reanimate as zombies. R, a sentient zombie who narrates the story, is eventually revitalized by the romantic relationship, causing his heart to beat and making him lose his craving for human flesh, so that he becomes human again. His transformation affects the other zombies as well when their hearts also start to beat, and they no longer desire human flesh.

Some zombie comedies take their humor from the simple absurdity of being faced with an undead foe that cannot be killed. More recent ones actually find their humor in the over-the-top blood splatter that began to define the horror genre after the 1970s. The directors of these films seem to ask the question, what can be funnier than obviously fake deaths, blood, intestines, and severed heads, especially when these body parts continue to do things like chase people (very slowly) down hallways or stop in front of mirrors to view themselves. *Bubba Ho-Tep* (2002), based on a comic story of the same name by Joe R. Lansdale and directed by Don Coscarelli Jr., is deliberately outrageous and absurd. Elvis Presley temporarily trades places with an Elvis impersonator, Sebastian Haff. The real Elvis, played by comic actor Bruce Campbell, is unable to return to his previous existence when the document explaining the switch is lost in a fire and his double overdoses. The film follows the aging Elvis, 30 years later, aged over 70, impoverished, and physically declining, wasting out his days in the Mud Creek Shady Grove Convalescent Home, where he befriends another resident, the elderly African American Jack McLaughlin, played by Ossie Davis, who claims to be former president John Fitzgerald Kennedy, dyed black by the enemies who faked his assassination. The film uses the same trope as *They Might Be Giants* (1961), directed by Joan Littlewood (born Joan Maud Littlewood, 1914–2002), which is that of having protagonists who border between being insane and brilliant, with neither winning out. Ultimately, Elvis and jack must face-off against a mummy/zombie which has been stealing the souls of the elderly, with tragic and comic results.

Re-Animator (1985), directed by Stuart Gordon (1947–) is a cult horror comedy known for its extreme gore. It begins at the University of Zurich Institute of Medicine, where Lovecraftian mad scientist Herbert West gets into trouble for reanimating his mentor, is forced to leave, and comes to the United States, where he attends Lovecraft's fictional Miskatonic University. He rents a room with a basement, but he reanimates his roommate's cat, leading to another reanimation in the local morgue, the death and reanimation of the school's dean, a decapitation and reanimation of the headless body (and the head), more zombies, an eventual showdown among zombies and a headless corpse, and a face-off between West and a mutated zombie. The film ends with a nod to the Rom Zom Com, as West's roommate is forced to reanimate his fiancée, who has been killed by one of the undead corpses. *Dead Alive* (1992), directed by Peter Jackson (born Peter Robert Jackson, 1961–), uses gratuitous gore to humorous effect. The film follows a zombie infestation caused by a bite from the Sumatran Rat-Monkey, where the son of a bite victim tries to care for her, only to end up ushering more zombies into the world. The film tests the limits of the genre and veers off into absurdist comedy. Creatures literally cannot be stopped by anything less than total obliteration, so decapitated heads continue to bite, disembodied legs walk themselves, and severed hands pick noses. An animated pile of entrails moves under its own power, and it ensnares people with intestines; it even preens in front of a mirror. The more recent *Poultrygeist: Night of the Chicken Dead* (2006), directed by Lloyd Kaufman (1945–), is a combination of genres, from horror to comedy to musical, Its gory special effects and a notable cameo by Ron Jeremy (born Ronald Jeremy Hyatt, 1953–), as well as a soundtrack, including punk, punkabilly, and ska bands, made this satire of the fast food industry a cult favorite. The film features a sacred Native American burial ground, zombie chickens, and a parody of Colonel Sanders.

Of a slightly less absurd nature are the black comedies. *Children Shouldn't Play with Dead Things* (1973), directed by Bob Clark, features a pompous director of a group of actors who travel to a secluded and deserted island graveyard to spend the weekend at his request. For a lark, he performs a ridiculous satanic midnight ritual meant to raise and command the dead and even has other actors painted as zombies pretend to attack the troupe; he goes so far as to dig up a corpse. The ritual creates a mass of zombies who rise from the dead ravenous for human flesh. *Zombie Strippers!* (2008), written and directed by Jay Lee (no date available), had star power: porn superstar Jenna Jameson (born Jenna Marie Massoli, 1974–) and *Nightmare on Elm Street* film series star Robert Englund (born Robert Barton Englund, 1947–), and it offered a humorous take on zombies and the striptease industry. Set in a near future in which George W. Bush (born George Walker Bush, 1946–) has been elected for a fourth term, the film centers on an underground strip club where a chemical virus developed by the government to reanimate slain soldiers in order to create a super military force has been accidentally released, spreading the virus to the general population. Once the club's star dancer is bitten, she continues to perform, and her aggressive, bloodthirsty shows are a huge hit with customers, although their subsequent Champagne Room visits prove fatal. Kat's success prompts her fellow dancers to decide whether to become zombies themselves.

The mock documentaries featuring zombies offers a unique possibility for zombie-related humor, in that it plays the seriousness of the film genre, which has a pretense to realism, against the unreality of the zombie. *Rising Up: The Story of the Zombie Rights Movement* (2009), directed by Laura Moss (no date available) features comic moments such as a professor explaining zombie food laws, juxtaposed against documentary style images of zombies eating intestines and disembodied arms. In another scene, a zombie reaches for a child smiling and waving at the camera. *American Zombie* (2007), directed by Grace Lee (no date available), pretends to be a documentary about Los Angeles zombies, all of whom hold jobs like convenience-store clerk, health-food producer, and florist and are represented by ZAG, the Zombie Advocacy Group. Zombie mockumentaries juxtapose horrific and gory images against mundane commentary. *Reel Zombies* (2008), directed by David J. Francis (1970–) is a unique addition to the mockumentary in that it is filmed on a movie set, where the director and writer are looking for real zombies for their horror movie. This metatextual dark comedy follows Francis and his film crew as they deal with the undead invasions of the zombies that were raised in his two previous films.

Finally, the benchmark film text for zombie comedies would have to be *The Evil Dead* series, a critically acclaimed trilogy (recently updated with a fourth, loosely related sequel) of horror films written and directed by Sam Raimi and starring Campbell. *The Evil Dead* series is in a class by itself. *The Evil Dead* (1981), *Evil Dead II* (1987), and *Army of Darkness* (1992) feature the Lovecraftian *Necronomicon,* which raises evil so-called deadites. Possessed humans become rotting corpses that attempt to attack and kill the remaining humans. Each film redefines the mythology of the series, a unique technique, offering alternative versions of previous films in the series. The series is defined by its absurd and farcical scenes, such as when its protagonist battles with his possessed hand for several minutes, or when Campbell approaches the role with a combined seriousness and camp, using silly catchphrases. When the character is sent back in time, he comically uses a Chemistry 101 textbook he left in his car to make weapons to fight against zombies.

See also: Bokur/Caplata; *Bowery at Midnight*; *Bubba Ho-Tep* (Film); *Children Shouldn't Play with Dead Things*; *Dead Alive*; *Evil Dead* Series; Lugosi, Bela; *I Walked with a*

Zombie; *Juan of the Dead*; Mockumentaries; *My Boyfriend's Back*; *Poultrygeist: Night of the Chicken Dead*; *Re-Animator* Series; Rom Zom Com; *Shaun of the Dead*; Voodoo; *Warm Bodies* (Film); *Zombie Strippers*; *Zombieland*; *Zombies on Broadway*

Anthony J. Fonseca

COMICS
See Graphic Novels and Comics

COSCARELLI, DON

Don Coscarelli (1954–) is a film director, screenwriter, and producer born in Tripoli, Libya and raised in southern California. He has been making films since he was 19, with his first feature, the independently produced *Jim, the World's Greatest*

American director Don Coscarelli is noted for his work in the horror genre. His contributions to zombie film include the *Phantasm* series as well as the cult film *Bubba Ho-Tep* (2002) and *John Dies at the End* (2012), both adaptations of literary works. (Christopher Drost/ZUMA Press/Corbis)

(1976) making him the youngest filmmaker to have his work distributed by a major studio, Universal Pictures. He is noted for his work in the horror genre, and often serves as writer, director, and producer for his films and is perhaps best known as the creator of the 1979 award-winning cult film *Phantasm*. There are currently four films in the *Phantasm* series, and Coscarelli holds credit as writer and director on all of them, along with producer credit on the last two in the series, *Phantasm III: Lord of the Dead* (1994) and *Phantasm IV: Oblivion* (1998). The *Phantasm* series has a strong cult following and is noted for its innovative special effects on a low budget, its dream-like imagery, and the figure of The Tall Man. The series deals heavily with zombies and the undead, revolving around the local mortician, an alien known only as The Tall Man, who kills people and steals corpses to reanimate them as grotesque, dwarfish zombies.

Coscarelli's other notable films include *The BeastMaster* series, *Bubba Ho-Tep* (2002) and *John Dies at the End* (2012). *Bubba Ho-Tep* and *John Dies at the End* are both adaptations of literary works: Joe R. Lansdale's short story and David Wong's (born Jason Pargin, no date available) genre-twisting, dark-horror novel of the same names. Both films deal with the undead in a somewhat more comical manner than the *Phantasm* series, and Coscarelli was director and the screen writer for both films. *John Dies at the End* was released in theaters in 2013 and opened to mostly positive reviews. *Bubba Ho-Tep* revolves around an aging Elvis living in a convalescent home when a mummy/zombie is on the loose. The film deals not only with the undead but also with existential zombies in that the aging residents of the Shady Rest Retirement Home where Elvis has found himself are bereft of free will and consequently, their lives are devoid of meaning.

Bubba Ho-Tep is Coscarelli's most award-winning film to date. It was critically successful, being invited to prestigious film festivals, including the Toronto International Film Festival, SXSW, Brussels International Festival, and the Hong Kong International Film Festival. Coscarelli also received praise for his screenplay for *Bubba Ho-Tep,* winning a Bram Stoker Award and Best Screenplay Award at HBO's U.S. Comedy Arts Film Festival. The possibility of a sequel to *Bubba Ho-Tep* titled *Bubba Nosferatu* has been discussed. Coscarelli has also raised the possibility of a fifth film in the *Phantasm* series. He has been inducted into horror magazine *Fangoria's* Hall of Fame.

See also: Bubba Ho-Tep (Film); Cult Film; Lansdale, Joe R.; *Phantasm* Series

Braden Dauzat

"COUNTRY OF COMERS-BACK, THE"

"The Country of Comers-Back" in an 1889 essay published in *Harper's Bazaar* by Lafcadio Hearn. In it he describes a creature which Haitians call a zombie, although it is not the dead reanimated by Voodoo, but a trickster spirit that leads the unwary to their deaths. While W. B. Seabrook's *The Magic Island* (1929) is generally credited with introducing the American public to the trope of the zombie as we know it, Hearn's description predates Seabrook's by 40 years.

Hearn was a foreign correspondent who made a name for himself writing about Japan when few Americans were familiar with that country. He had earlier lived in Haiti, and he wrote about his Haitian travels for *Harper's*. Hearn noted that the zombie's form was fluid. It can range from taking the shape of a beautiful young woman to a hideous wraith, or a child-sized being to someone who is over 14 feet tall. The zombie can appear to humans in the darkness of night or at high noon, and kills its victims by frightening them to death. Hearn relates his description of the zombie in florid prose that eroticizes Haiti as a wild and magical place that would stun Americans: plants are anthropomorphized and the night is never silent, but black and alive with the voices of unseen animals.

In this setting, Hearn relates the folktale of the zombie as told to him by an islander, who described how a young man becomes smitten with a beautiful woman, who leads him through the jungle in pursuit. As sunset draws near, the two come to a high cliff at the top of a ravine, where the woman reveals her hideous zombie form to the young man. Horrified, the young man plunges to his death. While this supernatural Haitian creature described by Hearn is called by a zombie, it bears no similarity to the zombie slave created through Voodoo, which was later described by Seabrook, or to later iterations of the creature as an undead human who follows Romero's Rules.

See also: Haiti; *Magic Island, The*; Race; Seabrook, W. B.

June Michele Pulliam

CRAVEN, WES

Wes Craven (born Wesley Earl Craven, 1939–) is an American director, writer, producer, and actor. Although he is famous for his series of films under the *Nightmare on Elm Street* brand, featuring Freddy Krueger, a revenging revenant who physically resembles a ghoul, two of the director's movies, *The Serpent and the Rainbow* (1988) and *The People under the Stairs* (1991), deal more directly with the zombie trope, featuring Voodoo zombies or zombie-like creatures that live in the dark. Additionally, in George Romero's *Diary of the Dead* (2008), Craven has a voice cameo as a radio announcer.

Though he is most famous for his *Nightmare on Elm Street* series of films, American director Wes Craven made significant contributions to the zombie genre with his films *The Serpent and the Rainbow* (1988) and *The People under the Stairs* (1991). (Associated Press)

After working as an instructor of English and Humanities, Craven decided that he could make more money in film. He started in pornography, where he worked with directing, writing, and editing, including, he claims, on the set of the iconic *Deep Throat* (1972). In his films, one of Craven's major themes is the illusive nature of reality, and the encroachment of dreams into the waking world. *The Serpent and the Rainbow,* one of his best-known films, depicts a world where characters cannot distinguish nightmares as such, perhaps because of the drugs involved with Haitian Voodoo and the creation of the Voodoo zombie. In it, an ethnobotanist based on Wade Davis visits Haiti at the behest of a pharmaceutical company, which wants him to identify the drug used in Haitian Voodoo. After being chased off by authorities, he returns to Haiti where he is buried alive. In a liminal state, he connects with his guiding spirit, a jaguar, to defeat an evil bokur. *The People under the Stairs* features a group of mysterious, albino humanoid creatures who are kept locked up in a dungeon-like basement. These creatures, cannibals who attack in mobs, are simply the starved and abused children of the film's evil brother and sister couple, the film's true monsters.

See also: Bokur/Caplata; Haiti; Romero, George; *Serpent and the Rainbow, The* (Film); Voodoo

Anthony J. Fonseca

CRAZIES, THE

The Crazies is a 1973 science fiction/horror film written and directed by George Romero. Romero is also credited with coauthoring the screenplay. The film is similar to Danny Boyle's *28 Days Later* (2002), a zombie movie in spirit, if not in fact, in that humans are turned into zombies via a viral infection, in this case a government bio-weapon's leaking into the local water supply. While the resulting infected are not the living dead, they are sufficiently zombie-like, making the distinction meaningless.

The plot deals with the government's attempts to contain the disaster and a group of survivors' bid to flee a quarantined town. Probably most interesting as a transitional work for Romero, between the claustrophobic *Night of the Living Dead* (1968) and the more expansive social critique of *Dawn of the Dead* (1978), the film's limited budget is obvious, so much of the movie feels like a sloppy dress rehearsal for the substantially more sophisticated *Dawn*. Nonetheless, *The Crazies* attempts to show the ways that government systems collapse, a favorite theme in Romero's work, and its treatment is fairly complex. Ironically, the military kills citizens much more rapidly than the virus, and there is a breakdown of communications during the crisis. Romero plays with the problem of those in the position of power being unable to discern who is crazy and who is normal. Unfortunately, *The Crazies* has failed to find the large-scale cult following of Romero's *Living Dead* movies. Produced by Pittsburgh Films for $275,000 and distributed by Cambist Films, *The Crazies* had poor distribution and was a financial failure, making roughly $143,000 at the box office.

Consequently, most viewers probably know the story through its 2010 remake. Though the viewer might be inclined to see the remade tale of government mal-feasance and oppression as conservative, the movie was produced by Participant Media, who also made Vice President Al Gore's (born Albert Arnold Gore Jr., 1948–) *An Inconvenient Truth* (2006), as an explicitly liberal movie. Overture's 2010 remake was directed by Breck Eisner (born Michael Breckenridge Eisner, 1970–). It was, by contrast to the original, a moderate box office success, making roughly $55 million worldwide against a production budget of $20 million. Eisner's remake follows the same basic premise, but exclusively from the perspective of the townspeople, leaving the government and military as a vague, brutal existential threat.

See also: Epidemics; Romero, George; Science Fiction

Jason Dupuy

CREEPSHOW

Creepshow is a 1982 film directed by George Romero, from a screenplay by Stephen King, with special effects by Tom Savini (born Thomas Vincent Savini, 1946–). This tribute to the EC horror comics of the 1950s boasted on its theatrical poster the slogan "The Most Fun You'll Ever Have BEING SCARED!" Shot on location in Pittsburgh, the site of nearly all of Romero's work, *Creepshow* is a frame tale in which a young boy is harassed by his father for reading horror comics. The boy is played by Joe King (born Joseph Hillstrom King, 1972–), Stephen King's son, who writes under the pseudonym Joe Hill. These comics provide five stories, two adapted from Stephen King's short stories; two of the tales feature walking dead.

A young boy (played by Joe Hill, son of Stephen King) takes revenge on his abusive father who refuses to let him read horror comics by stabbing a Voodoo doll effigy of his parent. The boy had ordered the doll through an advertisement he found in the forbidden comics. (Warner Bros./Photofest)

Creepshow features two zombie tales: "Father's Day" and "Something to Tide You Over." "Father's Day" begins seven years after Bedelia Grantham killed her abusive father. The patriarch returns from the dead during the family's annual Father's Day celebration, slaughtering his descendants, beginning with Bedelia. The walking dead patriarch is a skeletal creature, covered in unidentifiable sludge; it is similar in nature to the revenging revenants in the film version of *Tales from the Crypt* (1972). The zombie father shambles menacingly with arms outstretched in a way that is reminiscent of creatures in mummy films. But unlike these creatures, he is extremely violent: at the end of the tale he decapitates one of the adult children, placing icing and candles on the severed head, which he carries on a platter. The third vignette in the film, "Something to Tide You Over," features a jealous husband who buries his wife and her paramour up to their necks on a beach, just below the high tide line. The drowning victims later return from the dead, their skin wrinkled and bleached white and covered with seaweed, and they bury the husband in the same manner. The ghoulish seaweed-covered zombies also shamble and are also more concerned with revenge than with attacking random humans. Their attack occurs off-screen, however.

The film also includes the comical "The Lonesome Death of Jordy Verrill," based on King's short story "Weeds." It features King as a farmer who investigates a meteorite, gets infected, begins transforming into a plant-like organism, and then commits suicide, leaving the alien organism to take over the countryside. "The Crate," also adapted from a King story, follows an unopened crate in a university storage area, leading to several brutal deaths, as its savage tenant has not eaten in decades. The last story, "They're Creeping Up on You!" features an aging germaphobe who lives in what he believes to be a hermetically sealed apartment. During a blackout, he discovers, to his horror, a swarm of cockroaches in his residence. He retreats to a panic room, only to realize that he is locked in with literally thousands of the insects. The movie ends with Joe King's taking revenge on his abusive father by means of a novelty Voodoo doll ordered from a vendor advertising in his horror comics.

Creepshow was adapted into a graphic novel, released concurrent with the film. It did well at the box office, reportedly taking in a little over $21 million, and the film spawned sequels. Featuring a Romero screenplay, *Creepshow 2* told three more tales of horror based on Stephen King's concepts and stories. The less successful *Creepshow 3*, produced without involvement of any of the original creative team, was released as a direct-to-video feature in 2007.

See also: Mummies; Romero, George; Savini, Tom; Science Fiction; *Tales from the Crypt* (Film)

Hank Wagner

CRONENBERG, DAVID

David Cronenbreg (born David Paul Cronenberg, 1943–) is a Canadian producer, writer, and director, known primarily for films categorized as body horror or venereal horror. He is also known for the award-garnering dark thrillers and dramas of

Canadian director David Cronenberg's most notable contributions to the zombie genre include the films *Shivers* (1975) and *Rabid* (1977), which were about a parasite and virus, respectively, that hijack their victims' brains, compelling them to harm other humans. (dapd)

his later career. Cronenberg has made two films in the zombie subgenre, both very early in his career: *Shivers* (aka *They Came from Within*, 1975) and *Rabid* (1977). Both films depict a mass infection that produce zombie-like characteristics in humans and is connected to sexuality. The infected are deprived of free will.

In *Shivers*, a man-made, phallic, slug-like parasite intended to be a positive advance in science through its stimulation of sexual desire in its host is released in an apartment complex. This parasite invades human bodies and is transmitted orally, through kissing. The virus in *Rabid* is initially transmitted via a phallic protrusion in a woman's armpit. Rose is brought to a hospital following a motorcycle accident and undergoes experimental plastic surgery. For unexplained reasons, this surgery results in the phallic protrusion, and she develops a hunger for blood. The protrusion impales human bodies during an embrace, and those impaled also develop a bloodlust, leading to mass zombification. As with many zombie films, both *Shivers* and *Rabid* are apocalyptic in vision and urban in setting. They end with no solution in sight. The sexual nature and scientific origin of the zombification in both is noteworthy, reflecting Cronenberg's interest in representing the intersection of sexuality, the body, science, and horror. *Rabid* is particularly notable for Cronenberg's decision to cast Marilyn Chambers (born Marilyn Anne Briggs, 1952–2009) in the lead role. Chambers was at the time a star of pornographic films, appearing in such classics as *Behind the Green Door* (1972) and *The Resurrection of Eve* (1972). She was considered the American sweetheart of the genre, thanks to her classic beauty and prior stint as the Ivory Snow soap model.

Both *Rabid* and *Shivers* were critical and financial successes and remain cult favorites with genre fans. While Cronenberg is considered an influential director, especially in horror and science fiction, he has also been criticized for what some have perceived to be a thinly veiled misogyny in his work. His interest in body/venereal horror has often manifested itself in a scientific and grotesque scrutiny of the female body in particular. Invasion of the female body, and the female body as transmitter of a virus, seen in both films, could be argued to betray a more general gynophobia, yet it is also important to remember that in both the parasite and the protrusion are unquestionably phallic. While Cronenberg did not make any more zombie films, his interest in infection and bodily transformation continued until his later years, at which point his work focused more specifically on psychological horror, in films such as *Spider* (2002), and eventually more mainstream thrillers and dramas such as *A History of Violence* (2005), *Eastern Promises* (2007), and *A Dangerous Method* (2011).

See also: Apocalypse; Cult Film; Epidemics; Pornography

Laura Helen Marks

CULT FILM

The phrase cult film is inconsistently applied by critics and moviegoers; however, most agree that generally, a cult film possesses one or more of three distinguishing factors that set it apart from other: first, a cult film has a cult audience, or a community of viewers whose appreciation of the film differs sufficiently from that of the mainstream reception. Second, a cult film appeals to alternative aesthetic sensibilities. For example, fans of a cult film appreciate specific elements of the work, rather than the film as a whole, even when those elements of the film are unappealing to mainstream viewers. Third, a cult film contains a significant number of elements that typically appeal to cult aesthetic sensibilities. Films about zombies often meet all three criteria.

While the first and second of these factors relate to the film's reception, the third relates to the film text/technique itself. Thus, a filmmaker, critic, or marketer might categorize a film as a cult film before it has even been screened. The clearest examples usually incorporate all three of these factors; Ed Wood's (born Edward Davis Wood, Jr., 1924–1978) *Plan 9 from Outer Space* (1959) is a badly made film, with a story (zombies raised by aliens trying to avert the universe's destruction) that is muddled, shots that are inartistically framed, cuts that are sloppy, and performances that are unbelievably bad, but the film has a sizable following because of these qualities. The community that celebrates the film does so because it finds the film's violation of mainstream standards delightful. Needless to say, it has a non-mainstream audience, it appeals to sensibilities that go against the conventional, and it contains many elements that typically appeal to such sensibilities. Assignation of cult status to a film becomes more debatable when the film and its reception run counter to these three factors. For example, Peter Jackson's *The Lord of the Rings* trilogy (2001–2003) could hardly be more mainstream: in addition to earning mega-blockbuster returns at box offices, the films earned high praise from prominent mainstream critics, even winning Academy Awards. In this case, the third factor is the only one that applies: the films involve fantastic creatures and situations, and these typically appeal to cult sensibilities. Some may still consider the film as cult, given its fanatical following, with fans dressing as characters and/or hosting parties dedicated to rewatching and discussing the films.

The lower production values and gruesome violence that characterize many zombie films can alienate mainstream audiences, while attracting small but devoted followings. Since a large number of zombie films have achieved such followings, filmmakers, critics, and marketers now recognize the zombie as an element that typically appeals to cult sensibilities. The small budgets and ludicrous gore of many Italian zombie films from the 1980s, for example, almost guarantee their rejection by the general public, while assuring their success with a smaller, fanatical community, both in Italy and abroad. The cult status of zombie films and zombie fiction became more visible in the early 21st century, when relatively ample-budgeted zombie films such as Edgar Wright's and Simon Pegg's *Shaun of the Dead* (2004) and Zack Snyder's (born Zachary Edward Snyder, 1966–) remake *Dawn of the Dead* (2004) reached wide audiences. A subset of these audiences gained a broader interest in zombies, fueling further big-budget zombie films such as the blockbuster *Zombieland* (2009). They also swelled the ranks of participants in zombie walks and other public displays of cultish devotion. The growth of the zombie cult fostered rediscovery of many older films, such as *Revolt of the Zombies* (1936), which were once obscure but now have cult status. Fans who take a cult interest in zombie films might also read the various graphic novel series, such as *The Walking Dead* (2003–), or watch the made for television version (2010–). They might read Seth Grahame-Smith's novel *Pride and Prejudice and Zombies* (2009), its sequels, or its graphic novel adaptations. Fostering transmedia multiplicities is a hallmark of the present-day cult audience, and connections to works in other media now help qualify a film as cult.

Zombie films are exemplars of cult film, more generally. Midnight movie extraordinaire *The Rocky Horror Picture Show* (1975) involves a mad scientists' creating a living man from corpses. In *Whatever Happened to Baby Jane?* (1962), actress Bette Davis looks like a zombie, and everyone in *The Room* (2003) behaves like a zombie. Living death is an apparent contradiction, comparable to the camp, a factor central to many cult sensibilities.

See also: Italian Cinema; *Plan 9 from Outer Space*; *Pride and Prejudice and Zombies*; *Shaun of the Dead*; Television; *Walking Dead, The* (Comic); Zombie Walk; *Zombieland*

L. Andrew Cooper

DAVIS, WADE

Wade Davis (born Edmund Wade Davis, 1953–) is a Canadian, Harvard-educated photographer and anthropologist. After earning a doctorate in ethnobotany, he conducted benchmark research in the study of Haitian zombies created by Voodoo ritual. With the 1985 and 1988 publications of *The Serpent and the Rainbow* and *Passage of Darkness: The Ethnobiology of the Haitian Zombie,* Davis became synonymous with zombification theory.

Later in his career, Davis decided to continue the Haitian Voodoo studies of William Seabrook and Zora Neale Hurston. Davis, however, focused not on the cultural and spiritual aspects of Haitian culture but on the traditional uses of and religious associations of psychotropic plants and the chemicals extracted from them. This research was a follow-up to his 1983 hypothesis that tetrodotoxin, known commonly as TTX, also known as Babylonia japonica, fugu poison, maculotoxin, tarichatoxin, and tetrodontoxin, might explain zombification through voodoo. Davis argued that TTX, an aminoperhydroquinazoline poison found mainly in the liver and ovaries of certain fishes, causes paresthesia and paralysis through interference with neuromuscular conduction by blocking sodium channels on the neural membrane. This produces numbness, slurred speech, and paralysis in people who ingested it and would result in a condition that could be misinterpreted or misrepresented as death. Victims could then be buried and later resurrected by the bokur who had given them the drug. The resurrected zombie would then be given regular doses

Ethnobotanist Wade Davis, whose book *The Serpent and the Rainbow* describes the pharmacological and cultural mechanisms in Haiti used by bokurs and caplatas to zombify victims. (Joanna Vestey/Corbis)

of *Datura stramonium,* also known as the zombie cucumber, or more commonly as Jimson weed, part of the nightshade family, which produces amnesia, delirium, and suggestibility. The victims could then be manipulated by a bokur as part of a Voodoo ritual to create the illusion that they are zombies.

Davis's theory was widely challenged by the scientific community, which argued that he manipulated his data, a claim later disputed by other scientists, who also posited that humans could not be kept in a zombified state for years through the use of the drug. Davis was also criticized for his having commissioned a grave robbery to test his theory that tissue from a recently deceased human was routinely used in the chemical mixture created by bokurs. *The Serpent and the Rainbow* became an international best seller. It was later made into a film by Wes Craven in 1988. During his career, Davis has published articles in *National Geographic, Fortune, Newsweek, Scientific American,* and *Condé Nast.* He is an Explorer-in-Residence at the National Geographic Society, having conducted studies in Borneo, Colombia, Greenland, Nepal, Peru, and Tibet, among other areas. Davis's photographs appear in more than 100 magazines and newspapers.

See also: Bokur/Caplata; Craven, Wes; Haiti; Seabrook, W. B.; *Serpent and the Rainbow, The* (Book); *Tell My Horse;* Tetrodotoxin; Voodoo; Zombie Cucumber

Anthony J. Fonseca

DAWN OF THE DEAD

Dawn of the Dead is the 2004 remake of the second film of *The Night of the Living Dead* series by George Romero. Zack Snyder updates the representations of the zombie and the human reaction to the resurrected dead, yet the film is relatively faithful to the original. Tom Savini, who created the horror special effects in Romero's *Dawn of the Dead,* has a cameo in Snyder's remake as a sheriff being interviewed in some news footage about the necessity of shooting zombies in the head and burning the bodies. The scene references one in Romero's *The Night of the Living Dead* where Romero too plays a law enforcement officer who gives similarly worded advice to the reporter filming him for television. Both versions have female protagonists whose professions made them better able to contextualize an unprecedented, rapidly unfolding event, in this case a zombie apocalypse.

While Romero's version began with a television news crew fleeing Pittsburgh in the station's helicopter as the city falls to the zombies, Snyder's opens in a Minneapolis hospital when Ana, a nurse, is ending her shift while most of the world is still unaware that the dead have begun returning to life. Ana and her boyfriend awaken the next day to discover the neighbor's little girl Vivian in their home, catatonic and covered in blood. Vivian attacks Ana's boyfriend, who rapidly becomes infected and chases Ana from the home. Soon Ana meets up with Kenneth, a police officer, as well as Michael, Andre, and his pregnant wife Luda. Luda convinces the small group to head for the mall. The effects of the mass media on 21st-century audiences is apparent in Snyder's version, something evident in the cynical way that many

In Zack Snyder's 2004 remake of George A. Romero's *Dawn of the Dead* (1978), a band of survivors who have taken shelter in a mall gather on the roof, awaiting rescue from a government or civilian force that never materializes. (Universal/Photofest)

survivors, who would have been saturated with footage of looting and rioting after natural disasters, treat one another. In Romero's film, the small band of survivors peacefully coexist in the mall for several months before a group of bikers invades it, allowing the space to become overrun with zombies. However, Snyder updates the reaction of humans to the zombie apocalypse: when Ana and her companions arrive at the mall, they are menaced by a trio of armed security guards, who attempt to evict them from the space because they see the newcomers as threats to their own survival rather than as fellow human beings who should be assisted. This mistrustful attitude is evident a second time when another group of survivors arrives at the mall.

Snyder also updates the representation of the zombie. Snyder's $26 million budget allowed him to create special effects, including gore that is far more graphic and realistic. Also, Snyder's zombies are faster. Finally, Snyder's film ends less hopefully than does Romero's. After zombies overrun the mall in Romero's version, the pregnant reporter Francine is the only survivor. She escapes in the station's helicopter, presumably flying to a safe place where she and her child will help repopulate the planet. In Snyder's version, the pregnant Luda dies in childbirth, and her baby is subsequently zombified, demonstrating that there is no hope for survival of the human race. In fact, zombies have destroyed all domestic spaces where the human family is reproduced and nurtured. We see this in one of the film's opening scenes in Ana's flight from her home, clutching her car keys while running from her infected and seemingly enraged boyfriend. Ana's escape from this once-homely space is reminiscent of a battered partner fleeing her abuser. When Ana and her fellow survivors must escape the once-homely space of the mall, she once again clutches the keys to a vehicle as she runs. More than half of the group dies in the attempt to get away in two fortified buses. While Ana and Kenneth are among the handful of survivors who make it to the marina to board a boat to an island where presumably there are no zombies, the ensuing scenes, interspersed with the film's credits, show a bleak ending: distorted video footage shot by Ana with a found camera shows the craft running out of gas before their eventual landing, stranding them on an island overrun with zombies.

See also: Night of the Living Dead Series; Romero, George; Romero's Rules; Savini, Tom

June Michele Pulliam

DAY OF THE DEAD

Day of the Dead, a 2008 remake by Steve Miner (born Stevan W. Miner, 1951–) of George Romero's film of the same name, is very different from the original. Miner's version opens at the beginning of the zombie apocalypse, when a National Guard unit led by Captain Rhodes, played by Ving Rhames (born Irving Ramses Rhames, 1959–) attempts to keep confined to the small town of Pine Valley, Colorado, what the government believes to be a new and deadly virus. Minern retains some of the character names from Romero's version—Rhodes, Sarah Bowman, Dr. Logan, Bud, and Salazar—but the characters have very different roles. Two main characters from the Romero film become minor ones in Miner's version: Rhodes is killed early in the film, and Dr. Logan is inconsequential. While Sarah Bowman is a principal character in both versions, she is a guardswoman rather than a scientist in Miner's film. Dr. Logan's teachable zombie Bub in the original is in Miner's version-infected guardsman Bud Crane, who is a tame zombie in that his love for Sarah keeps him from harming her or other humans. Miner owes more to *28 Days Later* (2002), by Danny Boyle, than to Romero, as zombiism is caused by a virus originally created as a biological warfare agent by military scientists.

By contrast, Romero's original commences after the governments of the world have collapsed due to the zombie apocalypse. Before its demise, the remaining members of the U.S. government had realized that the undead so greatly outnumbered the living that the only hope for human survival was to domesticate zombies. Scientists who are protected by the sadistic Rhodes attempt to make zombies teachable. However, the group's efforts never come to fruition because struggles between Rhodes and his men and the scientists compromise the group's integrity. Eventually, zombies overrun the compound. In Miner's version, the local National Guard unit is tasked with containing the outbreak to the Pine Valley area, where zombies run riot through the streets to attack the remaining uninfected. The workings of the virus are illustrated in a patient who comes to the emergency room with what at first seems to be the symptoms of an aggressive flu. After the virus rapidly hijacks the central nervous system, the victim's eyes glaze over in typical zombie fashion before his face transforms into a decaying and putrid mass and he leaps across the room to savage his loved ones.

Miner's zombies' celerity is also more characteristic of the infected in Boyle's film rather than the shambling zombies who operate by Romero's Rules, and his zombies are more acrobatic. In one scene, after a zombie is hit by a car and launched into the air, he runs toward his victim on badly broken legs. In another scene, a zombie acrobatically flips into the air to launch himself from the ceiling before falling down on his victim. Miner's *Day of the Dead* also references other zombie films. It is extremely gory, even given the genre. While the special effects are not terribly realistic, they are often gratuitous. For example, a zombified Rhodes pulls out and eats his dangling eyeball before he chases Sarah into the air ducts, dragging himself behind her on the bloody stumps of his legs that have been chewed off by other zombies. Also, Miner's zombies are flammable to the point of being pyrotechnic. When drenched with a Molotov Cocktail, flaming zombies disintegrate within a matter of moments, and some even explode.

See also: Epidemics; *Night of the Living Dead* Series; Romero, George; Romero's Rules; *28 Days Later* Series

June Michele Pulliam

DEAD ALIVE

Dead Alive is the third feature length film by Peter Jackson. A horror-comedy by the New Zealand director best known for his adaptation of *The Lord of the Rings* and his remake of *King Kong,* it was first presented at Cannes in 1992, and released in New Zealand under the title *Braindead.* Jackson and his wife and creative partner Fran Walsh (born Frances Rosemary Walsh, 1959–) helped write the film's screenplay about a zombie infestation.

The film was produced by WingNut Films. Its prologue introduces the Sumatran Rat-Monkey, an animal captured on Skull Island of *King Kong* fame and transported to a zoo in Wellington, New Zealand, in 1957, an event which ultimately leads to the movie's zombie infestation. Lionel Cosgrove, a young man dominated by his social climbing mother Vera ever since his father's mysterious drowning death, is in a relationship with Paquita Sanchez, a grocer's daughter convinced by a Tarot card reading that she and Lionel are destined to be together forever. The two court at the Wellington zoo, where they are spied upon by the jealous Vera, who is bitten by the rat-monkey and infected. Ever the dutiful son, Lionel tries to care for his mother, suffering now from a mysterious illness. Despite his best efforts, Vera's condition deteriorates, and she begins biting people. The infection spreads to other townspeople, all of whom Lionel tries to keep hidden in his home. Eventually Vera, now clearly a zombie, escapes and is hit by a tram. Her funeral introduces Lionel's Uncle Les, who blackmails Lionel into giving him Vera's house. The zombies escape and infect all the guests at Les's well-attended housewarming. The film moves into its final act, an astonishing 30-minute experiment in gore. As the remaining humans struggle to dispatch the rotting horde, it is revealed that Lionel's father did not drown but was murdered by Vera. The zombie massacre enables Lionel, no longer encumbered by Oedipal neurosis, to confront his monstrous mother about this and other issues, and pursue his love with Paquita.

Dead Alive is primarily concerned with testing the limits of the genre, particularly the convention or motif of the zombie's unstoppable nature. The result is not horror but absurdist comedy. Unlike other film zombies, the creatures in *Dead Alive* literally cannot be stopped by anything less than total obliteration. Decapitated heads continue to bite, disembodied legs walk themselves, and severed hands pick noses. An animated pile of entrails moves under its own power, and it ensnares people with intestines; it even preens in front of a mirror. Two zombies copulate and produce a zombie baby. All are fed into a lawnmower. The film's prodigious gore not only ensured its cult status, but it also necessitated heavy editing for international release. Made for reportedly $3,000 between September and October 1991, the film grossed almost $250,000 when released in the United States in 1993. Originally 104 minutes long, *Dead Alive* can also be found in versions as short as 85 minutes (South Korea) and 80 minutes (Germany). The unrated U.S. edition is 97 minutes long.

See also: Cannibalism; Comedy; Epidemics; Jackson, Peter; Romero's Rules

Kevin Dole

DEAD AND BURIED

Dead and Buried is a 1981 American cult horror film directed by Gary Sherman (1945–), with a screenplay co-authored by Dan O'Bannon (born Daniel Thomas O'Bannon, 1946–2009). An atmospheric film, it begins on a picturesque beach, where a visiting photographer is enraptured by a local beauty, who models for his camera. In actuality, she is distracting him so that a group of locals can beat him, then bind him to a post and set him on fire, snapping pictures as they calmly watch him burn. The town's sheriff, Dan Gillis, played by James Farentino (1938–2012), arrives some hours later to discover that the photographer's flame-ravaged body has been placed, upside down, in an overturned vehicle, in a staged accident. The town's coroner and mortician, William G. Dobbs, played by Jack Albertson (1907–1981), arrives to inspect the body. Eventually it is discovered that Dobbs is behind a series of murders, each designed to disfigure the body so that he might practice his art, and that he has discovered a method of reviving the dead so they may serve as his mob of undead assassins.

After the opening death, more attacks follow: A drunken fisherman is killed in a boathouse; a young hitchhiker is murdered after she catches a ride with a resident; and a family is pursued by a group of townspeople in an abandoned house. Gillis then finds out that his schoolteacher wife dabbles in witchcraft, keeps a fetish hidden in their home, and lectures children on Voodoo, specifically on controlling a zombie by keeping the heart of the deceased but still ambulatory creature in a hidden place. It becomes apparent that something akin to Voodoo is at work, as the recently dead, including the photographer, turn up, apparently alive, in various locations around the town. This all leads to a twist in climax, where it is revealed to Gillis that all the townspeople, including his wife and himself, are not living beings but reanimated zombies, controlled by Dobbs.

Dead and Buried is unique in that it combines the trope of the grotesquerie with that of the Haitian Voodoo zombie slave. The former plays into the methods with which characters are killed, since the more their features are destroyed, the more challenging their reconstruction becomes, which appeals to Dobbs. The zombie trope plays in the reanimation angle of the story, except that here the zombies (basically each and every character) are slaves to a bokur (Dobbs); however, they do not walk around in a daze or absentmindedly perform functions. In fact, it is their human qualities that are integral to the story's surprise ending. The original story was overhauled to include these motifs by *Alien* co-creator O'Bannon: the locale, Potters Bluff, a fictional New England town; the mordant black humor of the dialogue; the grotesquely over-the-top special effects created by Stan Winston (born Stanley Winston, 1946–2008), cofounder of the visual effects company Digital Domain; the intricate plot twists, served well by Sherman's able direction. In addition, the performances of the actors, in particular, Albertson as Dobbs, the town's duplicitous coroner/mortician, is often praised by critics.

See also: Bokur/Caplata; Voodoo

Robert Butterfield

DEAD ISLAND

The video game *Dead Island,* developed by Techland and published by Deep Silver in 2011 for the PlayStation 3, Xbox 360, and PC, translated the sandbox zombie game into a first-person action role-playing game set in a tropical resort. It gained advanced buzz due to a nonlinear trailer depicting a young girl becoming a zombie, attacking her father, and being thrown from a hotel window, while her mother is overrun by other zombies. However, while the trailer's bloodiness was typical of the game, the trailer was not as representative of the gameplay or storytelling. The game offers five playable characters, each with a different skill set (e.g., shooting or throwing). Players can upgrade character health and skills over time. Weapon modification (called modding) is emphasized, and players can upgrade and customize these too (e.g., by adding nails to a baseball bat, and later electrifying that bat).

As in the game *Dead Rising,* weapons wear out and break if not repaired. Cutting and blunt-force weapons feature most heavily. Players fight various types of zombies, including fast, slow, large and muscular, and exploding (similar to the classes of enemy in 2008's *Left 4 Dead*), and they can injure these zombies realistically, severing or breaking limbs to slow them down. The film rights to the first game were sold in 2011, and 2013 saw the debut of *Dead Island: Riptide.* This sequel puts the same five characters on a new island in the archipelago and is notable for the controversy that arose from the plastic dismembered bikini-clad female torso that accompanied one edition of the game. Aside from revealing that the series' zombies were created by exposure to chemical weapons, little was introduced or fixed from the first title. In June, 2013, *Dead Rising 3* was announced as an exclusive title for the next-generation Xbox One console.

See also: Dead Rising; Left 4 Dead; Romero's Rules; Video Games

John R. Ziegler

DEAD RISING

The *Dead Island* series introduced variations on open-world gaming to zombie narratives. *Dead Rising,* introduced in 2006,was the first zombie open-world or sandbox game, a genre popularized by the massive success of 2001's *Grand Theft Auto III* and its sequels. This genre allows the player to participate in the missions that make up the game's central narrative, complete side missions, or ignore the mission structure entirely and treat the game world as a giant sandbox. *Dead Island* combined this formula with first-person shooter-style gameplay.

Dead Rising was developed by Capcom (also responsible for the *Resident Evil* series) as an Xbox 360 exclusive title. Like *GTA, Dead Rising* is a third-person action game, and it centers on Frank West, a photojournalist trapped by zombies in a Colorado shopping mall. This sometimes humorous homage to *Dawn of the Dead* (1978) resulted in the MKR group, which holds the rights to the film, suing Capcom in 2008 over the similarities, and losing. The game's zombies arise from secret research to mass-produce cattle, which accidentally resulted in genetically mutated local wasps that inject eggs via their sting. The larvae from those eggs then mature in the brainstem, causing zombification, and West's enemies include both these zombies and human psychopaths. The player must also rescue survivors, and the game's multiple endings derive from player decisions. In a game mechanic reminiscent of *Zombies Ate My Neighbors* (1993), players can use over 200 in-game objects as weapons. Weapons vary in effectiveness and will break with use; they range from traffic cones, acoustic guitars, and potted plants to katanas and machine guns. Players are allotted three days of in-game time/six hours of real-world time to complete the game. *Dead Rising* keeps track of the number of zombies killed during that period, and one of its selling points at release was its ability to render hundreds of enemies onscreen at once. The game was remade both for the Wii (as *Dead Rising: Chop Till You Drop*) and for mobile phones.

Dead Rising 2, released for the Xbox 360, PlayStation 3, and PC in 2010, features a new protagonist, former motocross champion Chuck Greene, and takes place in a resort town in Nevada. It adds the play mechanic of needing to periodically locate and administer anti-zombie medication on Chuck's infected daughter. It also introduces some ability to modify weapons by combining items and increases the number of onscreen zombies to thousands. *Dead Rising 2* was followed by *Dead Rising 2: Case Zero,* a short downloadable Xbox Live Arcade title that takes place between the first two titles: the Xbox 360 downloadable content *Dead Rising 2: Case West,* which features West and Greene together and *Dead Rising 2: Off the Record,* which offers a "reinterpretation" of *Dead Rising 2* with West as the main character.

See also: Dawn of the Dead; Resident Evil (Video Game); *Romero's Rules; Video Games; Zombies Ate My Neighbors*

John R. Ziegler

DEAD SET

Dead Set is a 2008 British miniseries in which the members of the *Big Brother* cast and crew become trapped on the set of the show during the first days of the zombie apocalypse. Because the *Big Brother* house exists in isolation from the outside world, the people on the set do not at first realize that in the space of just one day, civilization as they know it has ceased to exist, that is until after the show's runner, Kelly, breaks the fictional fourth wall and comes into the house to warn contestants. Now with even less contact with the outside world than what the show's rules normally dictate, the housemates must sneak out of the house to get supplies, without being seen by the zombies. The five episode series aired just a week after *Big Brother* concluded and was broadcast on the same channel.

While the members of the cast and crew remain trapped within the house in the first episode, some escape in the second episode and are able to survey the magnitude of the damage, which in one scene is reminiscent of a war zone. Meanwhile, the live feed from the *Big Brother* house continues to broadcast the events inside. The series ends in a way that asks audiences to consider how spectatorship affects the viewer. In the *Big Brother* house, the remaining occupants have been turned into zombies, though no one is left alive to watch the live feed, since presumably everyone without who might view the program has been zombified as well.

The zombies in *Dead Set* operate by a combination of Romero's Rules (in that they are undead cannibals whose presence ushers in the apocalypse and they can infect others through a bite) and the fast, violent zombie created by Danny Boyle in *28 Days Later* (2002). In fact, the filming style of *Dead Set* is quite similar to that of the *28 Days Later* series, with quick editing cuts, harsh bright lighting, lots of loud sound effects to enhance the violence, and a constant intensity in dialogues between characters. While the zombie makeup itself is understated, the scenes of carnage and cannibalism are graphic and realistic. *Dead Set* was nominated for a British Television and Film Arts Award.

See also: Apocalypse; Cannibalism; *In the Flesh*; Romero's Rules, Television; *28 Days Later* Series

June Michele Pulliam

DEAD SNOW

Dead Snow is Tommy Wirkola's (1979–) 2009 comic Nazi zombie film (titled *Dødsnø* in the original Norwegian) that cleverly references the zombie and horror film genres. In a plot that pays homage to Sam Raimi's *The Evil Dead* (1981), seven medical students travel to a cabin in the mountains for a weekend of drinking and playing in the snow. Soon after their arrival, the students are visited by an elderly man who is camping nearby: he warns them of the area's bloody history in the last days of World War II. When the Nazis who had captured the area knew the war was lost, they robbed residents of their gold and silver. The residents eventually collaborated to kill their tormentors, who now continue to haunt the area if they are disturbed.

The students dismiss the old man as a kook, only to spend the weekend fighting the reanimated Nazis in a gory battle. The Nazi zombies are revived after the students find their stash of treasure under the floor boards of the cabin. When the group opens the box of treasure, their faces are illuminated by the contents, a visual reference to Steven Spielberg's (born Steven Allan Spielberg, 1946–) *Raiders of the Lost Ark* (1981). This allusion is reinforced when a character wearing a T-shirt advertising Peter Jackson's gory zombie film *Braindead* (also known as *Dead Alive*, 1992) quips in English "fortune and glory, kid"—a well-known tagline from the *Raiders of the Lost Ark*. *Dead Snow's* bloody battles between zombie and human recreate well-known scenes from *The Evil Dead,* including one where a character cuts off his arm with a chainsaw to keep infection from spreading. More scenes of zombie fighting allude to other well-known zombie films, including George Romero's *Night of the Living Dead* (1968) and the Italian interpretation of it, Lucio Fulci's (1927–1996) *Zombi 2* (1979).

The zombies in *Dead Snow* operate by Romero's Rules in that they are the mindless reanimated dead with an insatiable desire to tear apart humans, as much because they are Nazis as due to their being zombies. The zombies are dead eyed, their mouths set in bloody snarls, and the gray of their undead flesh against the bleak, snowy landscape is a visual indicator of their mercilessness. Only the living are dressed in warm colors, such as blue and red, reminding viewers of the blood that courses through their veins and that will soon be shed. The blood that comes out of the zombies, on the other hand, is a sickening blackish-red rather than scarlet. *Dead Snow* is known for its extreme gore, a characteristic contributing to the film's comic elements. The gore is so over the top that it cannot be taken seriously: bodies are rent asunder, bloody brains plop on the floor, and intestines are ripped from bodies and looped around trees. The snow provides an excellent backdrop to highlight arcs of red blood that jet from humans and zombies, particularly in the film's final melee, when the survivors cut apart the undead with chainsaws, a hammer, and a snowmobile. Other comic elements include a medical student character who is afraid of blood, only to end up covered in the fluid as he fights hordes of the undead, and the film's gleeful metatextuality.

See also: Comedy; *Evil Dead, The* (Films); Fulci, Lucio; Jackson, Peter; Nazi Zombies; Raimi, Sam; Romero, George; Romero's Rules

June Michele Pulliam

DEAD WALK, THE

The Dead Walk (2000), by Andy Black (no date available), writing as J. Anderson Black, examines the history of zombie films. Black claims in the short introduction to use a flexible definition of the word zombie throughout.

The first chapter opens with a discussion of potential historical connections between Haitian Voodoo and zombies, briefly mentioning (but not thoroughly discussing) films such as *White Zombie* (1932), *City of the Living Dead* (1980), and *The Serpent and the Rainbow* (1988). Black's discussion of films begins in chapter two, in which he covers "Monochrome Zombies." These are the early and mid-20th century black-and-white horror films that began to popularize the creature. Black then discusses Hammer Films and the movies of George Romero and Lucio Fulci, then moving to considering zombie films produced in continental Europe, science fiction zombie films, zombie films of the 1980s and 1990s, and finally mummy films.

Black's lack of a clear definition of what constitutes a zombie film makes *The Dead Walk* more useful as a reference text than as a cover-to-cover read. Black includes a filmography of over 200 movies, ranging from *The Mummy* (1912) to *The Dead Hate the Living* (2000) that scholars and aficionados of the genre will appreciate. In 2008, Noir Publishing put out a revised and expanded edition featuring coauthor Steve Earles (no date available). The second edition is 128 pages longer and discusses over 300 movies, drawing upon films produced since 2000 such as the *28 Days Later* series, *Bubba Ho-Tep* (2002), *I Am Legend* (2007), *Land of the Dead* (2005), and the *Resident Evil* series, among others. Though the book does not specify which sections are written by Black and which by Earles, Black claims that Earles's contributions are behind-the-scenes details on key themes and films. These elements appear in sidebars included throughout the book, perhaps indicating that all of the sidebars are by Earles, whereas the primary text is by Black. The second edition's focus on full-color images makes it visually exciting. Both editions of *The Dead Walk* offer an important examination of the history and the continuing popularity of zombie films.

See also: Cult Film; Fulci, Lucio; Hammer Film Productions; Reference Books; Romero, George; Universal Studios

Margo Collins

DEAD WORLD SERIES

The *Dead World* is a series by San Antonio–based author Joe McKinney (1968–). As of 2013, the series consists of three novels and four short stories, with an additional novel and a collection of short stories planned for publication. All of the works in the series take their specific plots from the same basic scenario, and several characters repeat, but each tale can stand alone. The zombies of the *Dead World* are created by the toxic chemical soup resulting from the catastrophic destruction of Houston by five consecutive hurricanes.

McKinney's zombies are not undead but infected with the virus necrosis filovirus, which is spread through bites and gives its victims flu-like symptoms that eventually leave them in a depersonalized, zombie-like state. As the series continues, the zombies change, with those who survive infection becoming more human, able to respond to their names and choosing nonliving, nonhuman foods. The possibility of a cure arises when one character in *Apocalypse of the Dead* (2010) is found to be immune to zombie bites. *Flesh Eaters* (2011), the third book in the series, is a prequel chronicling the spread of necrosis filovirus, focusing on the experiences of Eleanor Norton, a wife, mother, and disaster mitigation officer for the Houston Police Department. Although zombies pose a threat, the biggest danger to the uninfected are those who have not contracted the virus, as the series explores how supposedly civilized humanity reacts to overwhelming disaster.

With the exception of its epilogue, the events of the series' first novel, *Dead City* (2006), occur over the course of one day. McKinney has compared this novel to the medieval play *Everyman*. Protagonist Eddie Hudson is a realistic portrait of an ordinary police officer faced with extraordinary circumstances. This novel is leaner than the others in the series, focusing on the physical challenges of battling a zombie invasion. Crusading elementary teacher Ken Stoler introduces the recurring theme that zombies are simply ill humans who need protection. Stoler forms P.E.T.Z., People for the Ethical Treatment of Zombies, which remains active throughout the series. *Apocalypse of the Dead* moves the action forward and out of the immediate disaster area. Once again, McKinney focuses on different individuals' reactions to the disaster. Several characters, including a porn star, a prisoner, and a slacker Harvard graduate, become heroes. Another reaction to the disaster is a cult formed around a charismatic leader who is reminiscent of Reverend Jim Jones.

The four short stories that round out the *Dead World* series enable McKinney to expand on issues otherwise lost in the course of his longer works. "Survivors" (*Dead Set: a Zombie Anthology,* 2010), set soon after the first two novels, is a study of survivor guilt. "Ethical Solutions," originally published as "People for the Ethical Treatment of Zombies" in 2007 in *The Harrow*, focuses on Stoler's P.E.T.Z. legacy. A group of college students, led by an idealistic professor, try to provide outreach to the zombie community. "Ethical Solutions" also introduces Ben Richardson, a journalist for *The Atlantic* and a major character in *Apocalypse of the Dead*. In "The Crossing" (*Print Is Dead,* 2012), McKinney tackles the subject of illegal border crossings, in this case, uninfected people escaping the quarantine zone. "Dating in Dead World" (*The Living Dead 2,* 2010), is the first actual post-apocalyptic work in the series. Set two decades after the original infestation, it portrays lucky survivors living in protected compounds, while the less fortunate survive as best they can in a devastated, zombie-ridden San Antonio. Andrew Hudson, a baby in Dead City, is now a young man on his first date. Although lighter in tone than other works in the series, the story explores attempts at post-apocalyptic normalcy. *Mutated* (2012) is the first actual sequel in the series, describing the post-apocalyptic world and following characters from previous works. This novel also develops zombie characters and introduces a Stage 4 Zombie, who retains memories of his pre-infected existence.

McKinney received a bachelor's in American history from Trinity University (1991) and a master's in English from the University of Texas at San Antonio (1994) and went on to become a sergeant in the San Antonio Police Department. He worked as a homicide detective and a disaster mitigation specialist. His insider's knowledge of disaster response informs his *Dead World* series. *Apocalypse of the Dead* and his non-zombie novel *Quarantined* (2009) were both Bram Stoker Award finalists. *Flesh Eaters* won the Bram Stoker Best Novel of 2011 Award. As the award nominations attest, McKinney is a brilliant voice in zombie literature. In the *Dead World* series, he has created a complex world which is both a philosophical examination of the nature of humanity and an action-packed adventure.

See also: Apocalypse; Epidemics; Sentience

Leah Larson

DEMENTIA

Dementia is nearly synonymous with representations of the zombie, which brings to mind an image of slowly shuffling, often groaning creatures who are no more than a shell of their former selves. Much of this imagery is often used to characterize patients affected by dementia, a debilitating mental disease that is often associated with aging. Dementia is a disease that is characterized by a significant loss of brain function, usually in the form of decreased memory, judgment, and cognitive function. This disorder is often connected to aging, as it is present in much higher levels in the elderly. Alzheimer's disease, a form of dementia, affects nearly 6 million elderly Americans. What is truly interesting about dementia is the fact that its onset is usually as a result of some other form of brain trauma, whether it be disease or injury. Huntington's disease, multiple sclerosis, and Parkinson's are just a few examples of neurological disorders that can eventually lead to dementia. Dementia is first diagnosed at the onset of chronic forgetfulness, with impairment of cognitive functions, including issues with speaking and calculating, following soon after. In the end, dementia results in a decreased quality of life not only for patients but also for the family members who care for them.

The zombie in its two primary forms is an apt metaphor for dementia. The Voodoo zombie, the reanimated dead brought back to life to serve as slaves, has much in common with people suffering from dementia. The zombies in W. B. Seabrook's "Dead Men Working in the Cane Fields" and the film *I Walked with a Zombie* (1943) are examples of the parallels between the zombie and people with degenerative neurological disease, in that their higher brain functions have been permanently destroyed. Voodoo zombies lack the ability to recognize or react to things that were once important, such as family and friends, offering the truest comparison to patients affected by dementia. As the self begins to break down in Alzheimer's and dementia patients, they find it increasingly harder to relate to the world in which they had previously functioned. Similarly, the zombie created by Voodoo cannot think, react, remember, or even speak.

Zombies that operate by Romero's Rules are a more horrific departure from the merely vacant Voodoo zombies that preceded them. The modern version of the zombie, popularized in George Romero's *Night of the Living Dead* (1968) is a lifeless body that has returned from death to feed upon the living. Therefore, the modern zombie is a metaphorical or figurative parallel to human beings with dementia. It is a walking corpse returned to life, and as such it has usually begun to decompose: the physical degeneration of the body serves as a metaphor for the neurological degeneration of dementia. Another correlation between the undead creatures of modern zombie fiction and humans with dementia is the dread they raise in other humans, as both represent the idea that control has been lost. Survivors of a zombie apocalypse are often represented as fearful that society has lost the order maintained through government and codes of civility. Moreover, survivors in zombie fiction fear contagion, that they have the potential to become zombies themselves. This is why many characters fear the "reliving," as they are called, in John Ajvide Lindqvist's 2005 novel *Handling the Undead*. This same fear is often present in family members who find themselves witnessing their relations with Alzheimer's and dementia: they become genuinely afraid of potentially suffering from dementia themselves someday almost as if the condition is communicable. In fact, many scholars have argued that the reason so many people fear those with mental disorders has to do with the stigma placed on the afflicted as real-life zombies. The anxiety felt by those left behind to deal with both zombies and people suffering from dementia is often derived from the fear of proximity and contagion, whether it occurs genetically or through a bite (or other type of physical interaction).

See also: Handling the Undead; I Walked with a Zombie; Night of the Living Dead Series; Romero, George; Seabrook, W. B.

Jacob Peoples

DRAUGAR

The draugar, also known as the aptrgangr (after-goer or after-walker), is a creature of Scandinavian mythology that is a malicious proto-zombie. In Old Norse, it is called the draugur, and in Icelandic it is called the draug. This powerful, reanimated corpse fiercely guards its treasure with the violence of a zombie and the mindless dedication of an Egyptian mummy. Draugar are featured in a variety of folktales and sagas from the Middle Ages, as supernatural undead monsters that inhabit and guard grave mounds from thieves. Draugar may also be restless corpses that rise from the dead on the way to their burial.

Philologist Rudolf Simek (1954–) describes them as ghosts or wraiths that not only fight grave robbers but may also menace innocent humans and livestock, especially during midwinter. Historian Claude Lecouteux (1943–) presents draugar as corporeal revenants, dead humans that retain any wounds or scars they suffered in life but with bodies that never decay or rot. Draugar may be large, black in color, and possess the ability to change their size, shape, and weight. These juggernauts retain something of their original intelligence, and they both know what they are and delight in their condition. Lecouteux claims that draugar possess the ability to disappear into the ground, and antiquarian Hilda Roderick Ellis-Davidson (born Hilda Roderick Ellis, 1914–2006) ascribes even more supernatural attributes to the monsters, including the ability to control the weather and see into the future. Draugar are possessed of superhuman strength and malice, and they assault their victims physically, breaking their bones and tearing them to pieces. Lecouteux says draugar bodies are particularly resilient and can be destroyed only by fire; Simek proposes an even hardier creature, one that can be defeated only by cutting off the monster's head, placing it on its own buttocks, and then burning the body to ashes.

Beyond the Norse and Icelandic legends discussed by Ellis-Davidson and Lecouteux, the draugar has rarely appeared in modern popular culture. However, with the increased popularity of the American zombie, draugar have been rediscovered, appearing in *The Sword and the Satchel* (1980) by Elizabeth Boyer (1913–2002) and *The Morganville Vampires* series (2006–) by Rachel Caine (born Roxanne Longstreet Conrad, 1962–). They are also the featured foes in Tommy Wirkola's Nazi-zombie film *Dead Snow* (originally *Dødsnø*, 2009), the Finnish movie *Rare Exports: A Christmas Tale* (2010) by Jalmari Helander, and in the videogame *Skyrim*, the fifth iteration of *The Elder Scrolls* series (Bethesda Game Studios, 2011).

See also: Dead Snow; Mummies

Kyle William Bishop

ED AND HIS DEAD MOTHER

Ed and His Dead Mother is comedic 1993 zombie film, set in 1950s suburban America. In it, Ed Chilton, played by Steve Buscemi (born Steven Vincent Buscemi, 1957–) really loves his mother, and when she dies, his grief is boundless. When Ed is unable to contact his mother via séances, he gives some of his mother's insurance money to Happy People, Ltd so they can have her reanimated. Because she was an organ donor and has been dead for over a year, salesman A. J. Pattle asks for just a bit more money in order to get the job done with a corpse that is not fully intact. When Pattle shows up the next day with Ed's recently reanimated mother in tow, Ed welcomes her with open arms.

Uncle Benny, played by Ned Beatty (born Ned Thomas Beatty, 1937–) is not convinced reanimating Ed's mother is a good idea and is soon proven correct as Mother Chilton collapses. Ed rushes to find a doctor, but A. J. just happens to be standing by and informs Ed his mother can only be kept alive by feeding her live roaches. Ed reluctantly agrees to pay the small fee for the roaches to feed to her, which allows Mother Chilton to quickly reanimate. Everything is wonderful for Ed until Mother overdoses on roaches and begins to exhibit odd behavior. At first, she says things she would not have said when alive and chases pets around the neighborhood. When Mother chops up the neighbor with a chainsaw, Ed seeks help from A. J., who has the solution for a price. When he has to rescue his girlfriend Storm from his mother, he acknowledges he must do something more drastic to control her. By the end of the movie, Ed is arrested in a graveyard after dismembering his already dead mother; he has spent the insurance money his mother left him. Nonetheless, he and Storm live happily ever after.

Ed and His Dead Mother keeps the gore to a minimum and relies on a slightly gray facial makeup to emphasize Mother Chilton's undead state. The movie explores the difficulty of letting go of loved ones after death and how disastrous it can be to continue to hold on. Released shortly after Peter Jackson's film *Dead Alive* (1992), *Ed and His Dead Mother*, directed by Jonathan Wacks (no date available) featured more deadpan acting and much mess gore. Fans, however, responded to its comedic cast and understated, sly humor. Overall, the film succeeds as comic horror and enjoys cult movie status. In the United Kingdom, it was renamed *Bon Appetit, Mother* or *Motherhood*.

See also: Cannibalism; Comedy; *Dead Alive*; Jackson, Peter

Alicia Ahlvers

EPIDEMICS

Epidemics are practically synonymous with recent zombie fiction. Prior to 1954, the zombie was most frequently represented in fiction and film as someone deprived of free will, and perhaps even brought back from the dead by a bokur, a Voodoo priest who practices dark magic. These zombies then served the will of the bokur. Anthropologist Zora Neale Hurston, in *Tell My Horse: Voodoo and Life in Haiti and Jamaica* (1938), postulated that zombies were not the living dead as was popularly believed, but living people who were drugged into a coma resembling death, then buried alive, only to be disinterred by their maker and given a partial antidote to the first drug so that they were rendered completely docile and subject to their maker's will. This process created the illusion of resurrection. Hurston's concept was further explored decades later by anthropologist and scientist Wade Davis, who traveled to Haiti to discover the actual chemical agents used.

In 1954, the novella *I Am Legend,* by Richard Matheson, introduced the correlation between the advent of the walking dead and the outbreak of an epidemic (that becomes a pandemic). Protagonist Robert Neville believes himself to be quite literally the last man on earth, a state of affairs that necessitates he barricade himself in his home at night when the undead infected, who erroneously believe that they are vampires, seek to drink his blood. The undead infected, however, are more similar to zombies than vampires in that they are relatively unintelligent and their wills are subordinated to an overwhelming desire to drink blood that they do not even require to sustain them. In 1968, filmmaker George Romero introduced the modern, iconic undead zombie in *Night of the Living Dead,* using Matheson's concept of worldwide and apocalyptic pandemic in his film. While we never know definitively in any of Romero's six *Night of the Living Dead* films why the dead initially began returning to life, they are markedly different from their predecessors who could only be created intentionally through Voodoo. Instead, the living dead can transmit their condition to humans through a bite, creating an actual epidemic, though people also reanimate upon death if they are not bitten. Romero's vision has been the model for most zombie fiction since 1968.

The popularity of the zombie since 1968 may have its roots in humanity's real fear of epidemics and pandemics. The *Yersinia pestis* bacterium was the cause of The Black Death, a plague that is estimated to have killed 30–60 percent of Europe's population in the 14th century. The plague reappeared in Europe periodically, killing thousands of people in the 17th and 18th centuries. In 1842, Edgar Allan Poe (1809–1849) used the plague as fodder for his literary creation, "The Masque of the Red Death," a story readily embraced by a public still ill at ease with concept of outbreaks. In 1918, the Spanish flu was the cause of a worldwide pandemic that took the lives of between 50 and 100 million people in two years, more than who were killed during World War I. To this day, popular fictional works such as the 2011 film, *Contagion,* explore what might occur if a flu epidemic of such virulence were to reoccur. Taking this into account, it is reasonable to suggest that fictional treatments of such devastating outbreaks may serve a cathartic function; experiencing an illusory epidemic may serve to ease anxieties about having to ride out such an event in real life. A zombie epidemic may, hence, be a fictional stand-in for the apocalypse. Scientists have predicted climate change will transform the planet during this century in ways that threaten our species' survival. Many people now interpret *The Bible,* the predictions of Nostradamus, the Mayan calendar, and various other sources as predicting the imminent near end of the world. Not since the height of the Cold War has the possibility of an "Eve of Destruction" been so loudly and publicly proclaimed.

One real-life epidemic which bears a particularly eerie resemblance to the fictional zombie apocalypse was documented in *Deadly Feasts* (1997), by Richard Rhode (1937–). In fact, the comparison is so strong that the agent of the disease was adopted by the filmmakers of *Zombieland* as the cause of a fictional zombie invasion. The disease itself is called Kuru, related to Creutzfeldt-Jakob disease, popularly known as Mad Cow Disease. Several key elements of the disease bring to mind the post-Romero concept of the zombie: the disease attacks and eats the human brain, the organ which had evolved in the zombie mythos as the food of choice for the creature. The victims evidence an unsteady gait and loss of motor function in the initial stages of the disease; and the disease agent can survive just about anything, including the death of its host.

Other films also ground their concept of the zombie in an epidemic. *Shivers* (1975) and *Rabid* (1977), two films by Canadian director David Cronenberg, depict a mass infection of humans producing zombie-like characteristics, depriving the infected characters of free will; this is connected to sexual activity. The 2008 film *Pontypool* depicts an epidemic that erupts in a small francophone Canadian town. The disease, spread via the English language, puts the infected suddenly in thrall to the drive to destroy other humans, and try to bite through their mouths, the source of the infection. The British film *28 Days Later* (2002) represents the zombie apocalypse as the result the rage virus, synthesized by scientists in a lab in the United Kingdom by exposing chimpanzees to hours of violent video footage depicting real and staged carnage that humans are bombarded with every day via the mass media. The virus is released into the human population when some well-meaning animal rights activists break into the lab and release the chimps. One activist is bitten and is transformed immediately from a compassionate human being to a red-eyed infected creature whose will is subordinated by the desire to tear apart her fellow humans. Twenty-eight days after this event, nearly all of the United Kingdom has succumbed to the virus.

Literary works similarly represent the zombie apocalypse as being precipitated by an epidemic. Robert Neville, the last man on earth in Richard Matheson's novella *I Am Legend,* is the remaining human not to succumb to a bacterial infection borne by dust in the aftermath of a worldwide nuclear exchange. David Moody's *Autumn* trilogy, Jonathan Maberry's (1958–) Joe Ledger novels, and Joe McKinney's *Dead World* series all use an epidemic to explain the existence of zombies in their fictional universes. In Moody's *Autumn* series, a disease kills 99 percent of the planet's population in under 24 hours. In *Patient Zero,* the first novel in Maberry's Joe Ledger novels, the zombie apocalypse is ushered in by a virus that has been bioengineered by terrorists. A toxic chemical soup resulting from the catastrophic destruction of Houston by five consecutive hurricanes turns humans into zombies in McKinney's

Dead World series. The trope of the zombie created by an epidemic is so ubiquitous that texts offer no explanation for its origins.

Because the zombie apocalypse is so commonly represented as either due to an epidemic or at least capable of spreading as quickly as an epidemic can, the zombie has become a fertile trope for explaining infection in medical schools and colleges of veterinary medicine. The Centers for Disease Control and Prevention (CDC) has appropriated this trope with their ongoing Zombie Preparedness Campaign. Inaugurated in 2011 by the CDC's Office of Public Health Preparedness and Response, the campaign seems to have taken a cue from the best seller of author Max Brooks, *The Zombie Survival Guide,* published in 2003. The campaign enacted an epidemic which turns humans into zombies, overwhelming existing social services and leading to a collapse of societal infrastructure. The program, replete with a zombie blog, zombie posters, a zombie YouTube video contest and a zombie novella, was not intended to authenticate the existence of zombies but to serve as an entertaining way of educating the general public on reacting to actual emergencies. The CDC official website explains that the campaign originally was tongue-in-cheek and has proven very effective. The absurdist aspect of the CDC's message is, perhaps, lost on a portion of the public, who are convinced that an actual zombie apocalypse is imminent. In 2012, following a rash of violent incidents in which the cannibalistic behavior of the perpetrators caused the events to be labeled as zombie attacks by the press, the CDC was forced to quell public concerns in regard to the existence of zombies.

See also: Bokur/Caplata; Brooks, Max; Cronenberg, David; Free Will; Hurston, Zora Neale; *I Am Legend* (Novel); Matheson, Richard; *Night of the Living Dead* Series; *Pontypool*; Romero, George; *28 Days Later* Series; Voodoo; *Zombie Survival Guide, The*; *Zombieland*

Robert Butterfield

EVIL DEAD, THE (FILMS)

The Evil Dead series is a critically acclaimed trilogy of horror films written and directed by Sam Raimi and starring Bruce Campbell. The series consists of three films: *The Evil Dead* (1981), *Evil Dead II* (1987), *Army of Darkness* (1992). The plot of each revolves around *The Necronomicon,* a fictional ancient Sumerian book that raises evil spirits, who appear in the form of so-called deadites when they possess a human body, either living or dead.

The evil spirits are never shown in the films, only appearing through point-of-view shots, usually when they are flying through the woods. The deadites appear in alternate forms in each film. In *The Evil Dead,* the deadites are simply humans possessed by demonic spirits. The possessed take on the form of rotting corpses that attempt to attack and kill the remaining humans. In *Evil Dead II,* the deadites can also turn the dead humans that they possess into alternate beast-like forms. In *Army of Darkness,* the deadites are mainly the undead raised from the grave to attack the living. While the deadites are not strictly zombies, they, along with the films themselves, possess many zombie elements.

The Evil Dead seems to have drawn much from George Romero's *Night of the Living Dead* (1968), as both films center on a group barricaded in a cabin in the woods, desperately listening to recordings for instructions that might save them from the undead human forces who are attacking them. The deadites generally behave like zombies in that most lack free will and all desire to harm the living. The demons controlling the bodies are sometimes intelligent, having the ability to speak and use tools and weapons. The deadites' appearance as pale, decaying corpses is also inspired by Romero's zombies. Each film describes the mythology of the

Ash Williams (Bruce Campbell) uses his chainsaw to fight off hordes of the undead in *The Evil Dead* (1981). (New Line Cinema)

series differently, with *Evil Dead II* and *Army of Darkness* opening with a prologue showing an alternative version of the previous film in the series, making it unnecessary to watch the films in order to understand the events. *The Evil Dead* trilogy has also been expanded into stage musical, video game, and comic book forms. The original films along with the protagonist Ashley "Ash" J. Williams (Campbell) have since achieved financial success as well as a strong following.

The Evil Dead opens with a group of college students who travel to a cabin in the woods for the weekend. While there, they discover the recordings of a professor reading from *The Necronomicon,* along with many other strange things in the basement of the cabin. When the students play the recordings, the professor's readings of the Sumerian incantations raise evil spirits, who surround the cabin. One of the women in the group, Cheryl, senses the spirits and goes outside to investigate, leading to an infamous scene where the forest itself becomes possessed by the spirits and rapes her. This scene caused the film to be banned in several European countries. Cheryl runs screaming back to the cabin, where none believe her story. Soon after, Cheryl is possessed by the spirits and attacks her friends, until everyone but Ash is possessed. Ash is forced to kill his girlfriend, Linda, using a ceremonial dagger, only to have her reanimate and attack him again as a zombie before he beheads her. Ash's friend Scotty also reanimates. Ash, timid and queasy at the sight of blood at the beginning of the movie, must fight both Scotty and Cheryl in a gory final battle that he wins by throwing *The Necronomicon* into the fireplace, causing the deadites to melt in a gruesome fashion. The film ends in a twist as we are shown a point-of-view shot of an evil spirit descending upon Ash as he screams in the final frame.

The Evil Dead was filmed on a rumored budget of $375,000, which Raimi, Campbell, and Robert Tapert, friends at the time, raised themselves after shooting a 30-minute horror short *Within the Woods* (1978), to convince investors that they were capable of making the movie. Tapert and Campbell also produced the other two films in the series. The low budget is apparent in the effects of the movie, for which it is now famed. Creamed corn, 2 percent milk, and red syrup are used liberally for guts and blood throughout the film. The scenes shot from the evil spirits' perspective as they fly through the woods were created by Raimi's and Campbell's attaching the camera to a board, which both grasped on either side as they ran through the trees while filming. *The Evil Dead* is famous for its gratuitous violence, especially in the finale when Ash defeats the deadites in a gory battle and begins to see visions where his reflection is talking to him and blood is running down the walls.

The Evil Dead is different from the later two films in the series in a number of ways. In *The Evil Dead,* the viewer only knows that *The Necronomicon* can raise spirits. However, the terms deadite and *The Necronomicon* are not standardized until the second and third movies. Also, *The Evil Dead* is a serious horror film, though the ridiculous blood and gore achieve a kitschy effect. *Evil Dead II* and *Army of Darkness,* on the other hand, embrace the ridiculousness of the story so that they are campy reinterpretations of *The Evil Dead.* Nonetheless, *The Evil Dead* was influential. *Evil Dead II* picks up where the first film left off, portraying the events of *The Evil Dead* as only happening to Ash and his girlfriend Linda and omitting in a brief prologue the destruction of *The Necronomicon.* Ash becomes a deadite until the sun rises and the spirit dissipates. After the financial success of the first film (with an estimated $2.4 million domestic gross in box office during its initial run, and to date making nearly $30 million), *Evil Dead II* was given a much larger budget of an estimated $3.6 million, making just under $6 million in its initial box office run. The higher budget is immediately apparent in the improved special effects, especially in the early scene where Ash's hand is still possessed after the sun rises and he begins to have surreal experiences. Ash battles with his possessed hand for several minutes in a farcical scene culminating in his severing this appendage from his body while laughing maniacally. Ash later attaches a chainsaw to the stump in a ludicrous attempt to defend himself and destroy the other deadites. Meanwhile, the professor's daughter, Annie, and three others come to the cabin in an attempt to learn of her father's fate. When night falls, the evil spirits attack; they possess the newcomers and leave Annie and Ash to battle the swelling number of deadites.

Ash's whole body is possessed yet again, and he takes on a zombie-like form and menaces Annie. However, Ash's zombification is eventually reversed through the force of his will after he sees his girlfriend's necklace that he gave her in the prologue. The ability of deadites to take other forms is revealed when one of them transforms into a long-necked monster. Annie, having found a missing page to *The Necronomicon,* discovers the chant that will send the evil spirits back to their realm, thereby releasing those they have possessed. As Annie reads the chant aloud, she is stabbed by Ash's still-possessed dismembered hand, opening a portal that transports Ash and his car back in time to the 14th-century Middle East. Ash's cheesy seriousness and his campy, over-the-top antics in this film are a large part of Campbell's cult status as a celebrated B movie actor. Ash's sanity and seeming lack of fear is a recurring theme throughout the trilogy.

Army of Darkness centers around Ash's quest to get *The Necronomicon* back and return to his own time, while also preventing an undead army, who locate Ash soon after he has exited the portal, from destroying Lord Arthur's castle. *Army of Darkness* builds on the comical and campy elements in *Evil Dead II*: Ash behaves like a cheesy action hero, using catch phrases such as "groovy" and "Hail to the King, baby." The signature gore is present, with literal geysers of blood bursting out of wells and bloody battles between undead and living, but it is more toned down from the previous two installments, making *Army of Darkness* more like an action movie than a horror film. Also, in *Army of Darkness, The Necronomicon* can raise the dead, not just evil spirits. Ash accidentally uses it to summon an undead army in a scene where animatronic skeletons burst from their graves to form an army of skeletons led by the undead, "Bad" version of Ash. Bad Ash appears after miniature versions of Ash tie him down in a farcical scene reminiscent of Jonathan Swift's (1667–1745) *Gulliver's Travels* (1726). One of the small Ashes jumps down Ash's throat, attacking him from the inside. In a scene recalling the ridiculousness of Ash's hand attacking him in *Evil Dead II*, Ash laughs while he swallows boiling water to kill the creature within his stomach. Afterward, Ash shoots and buries Bad Ash, after he sprouts from his shoulder. However, Bad Ash is later resurrected to lead the skeletal army.

Army of Darkness has more humor than either of the first two films in the trilogy, mainly stemming from Ash's ridiculous demeanor and quotes. Ash learns from his Chemistry 101 textbook that he left in his car how to make gunpowder that he can use to fight the zombies and creates a mechanical handout of armor to replace his chainsaw in scenes that recall the creation of his chainsaw hand in the second film. After Ash successfully fights off the army and converts his new love interest, Sheila, from deadite back to human, he returns to his own time, where he is an employee in a discount hardware store. *Army of Darkness* also ends on a cliffhanger, as one of the patrons in the store transforms into a deadite and is shot by Ash.

Raimi, Tapert, and Campbell produced a reboot of *The Evil Dead,* which is intended to start a new series loosely based on the original trilogy. The film, titled *Evil Dead,* premiered in 2013 and was directed by Fede Alvarez (1978–), who coauthored the script. The dialogue of the film was spruced up by writer Diablo Cody (born Brook Busey-Maurio, 1978–), who remained uncredited. The storyline of Alvarez's *Evil Dead* is similar to that of Raimi's but features all new characters and is not intended to follow the same path. The story revolves around Mia, a heroin addict, her brother David, and their friends. They have decided to bring Mia to the cabin in the woods for the weekend in a last ditch attempt to get her clean after her recent near-fatal overdose. The group releases the evil spirit from *The Book of the Dead* (this time called the *Naturo Demento*) in the basement of the cabin as before, and afterward Mia is possessed by the demon in an updated version of the infamous forest rape scene. The book contains prophetic signs of the coming demonic possession and states that the demon must possess five souls before it can unleash the Abomination from Hell.

Mia, who is experiencing signs of demonic possession, is not believed by the others, who merely think she is experiencing withdrawal and making up excuses to leave. The group learns from *The Book of the Dead* that the only ways to drive out the possession are by fire, beheading, or live burial, mirroring the different ways that Ash used to dispose of the possessed in the original trilogy. The demon can only fully possess one person at a time, and this is Mia for most of the movie. This possession turns the victim into a sort of zombie whose body takes on the appearance of a rotting corpse, and whose free will has been replaced by violent behavior and crude language. However, the possession is also similar to an infection in that its effects can travel through wounds and blood, causing a secondary possession that reanimates the dead and as well as anyone wounded by Mia. These secondary possessed likewise have the appearance of rotting corpses, but they are even more similar to zombies operating under Romero's Rules than is Mia because they move in a stilted manner and lack the power of intelligent speech. David, who has not been attacked or possessed, decides he cannot kill his sister. Instead, he captures Mia and buries her and the demon inside her alive. He then digs up Mia's body and revives her through a homemade defibrillator, mirroring her revival during her earlier overdose. After this, the demon leaves Mia's body and possesses the remaining member of the group, who then wounds David before being killed. David, who knows that his wound will cause him to be possessed soon, sends Mia off in the car to escape and then sets the cabin ablaze with himself and the demon inside. However, since the demon has possessed five souls on this night, the Abomination has now been raised amid a torrent of blood from the sky and Mia must defeat the creature.

Alvarez's *Evil Dead* contains many references to the original trilogy. For instance, when the possessed Mia bites another character on the hand, it begins to rot and decay and she must amputate her possessed appendage the way Ash had to in *Evil Dead II*. Alvarez also opted for mostly makeup-oriented special effects over computer-generated ones in homage to the low-budget original, and employed the fast-cut sequences characteristic of the trilogy. The Abomination raised at the end is also reminiscent of Bad Ash from *Army of Darkness* in that the creature is a bloody and undead version of Mia, who also loses a hand in the battle but ultimately defeats the creature with the help of a red chainsaw found in the shed, a reference to Ash's chainsaw hand in *Evil Dead II*. Alvarez's *Evil Dead* ends with a shot of the *Naturo Demento* as Mia walks away, and contains a brief after the credits scene of Bruce Campbell saying "groovy" as an older Ash. The film was a box office success, making an estimated $97 million. Alvarez is returning to write and direct a sequel, and he and Campbell have also raised the possibility of making a direct sequel to 1993's *Army of Darkness*, as well as a seventh and final film that will merge the storylines of Ash and Mia.

See also: Army of Darkness (Comics); Campbell, Bruce; Comedy; *Evil Dead: The Musical; Evil Dead, The* (Video Game); Raimi, Sam; Romero, George

Braden Dauzat

EVIL DEAD: THE MUSICAL

Evil Dead: The Musical is a musical stage show based on the *Evil Dead* trilogy of horror films, directed by Sam Raimi and starring Bruce Campbell. Opening in Toronto, Canada, in August 2003, the musical quickly became a hit, and in 2004, the production moved to Montreal before making its 2006 off-Broadway debut in New York. The musical has since won several awards, and productions have popped up in numerous cities around the world, such as Las Vegas, Seoul, Tokyo, Phoenix, and Madrid.

The musical combines elements, characters, and plot points from all three movies of the *Evil Dead* trilogy, as well as adding original elements to create a unique storyline. The musical begins when a group of college students spending the weekend in a cabin in the woods find *The Necronomicon,* a fictional ancient Sumerian book that has the capability of raising the dead and evil spirits to create what are called deadites, zombie-like creatures that attack the living. The campy and over-the-top gore and blood for which the trilogy is famed is also present in the musical. The first three rows of the production are covered in clear plastic and are designated as the splatter zone, where audience members are sure to get drenched in fake blood, guts, and gore. *Evil Dead: The Musical* was also a critical success, being compared favorably to *The Rocky Horror Picture Show* by such publications as *The New York Times, The Las Vegas Review Journal,* and *Maxim Magazine.* The songs are also given particular praise as zany, campy fun. The cast album from the off-Broadway New York production was released in 2007 and went on to reach number 4 on the Billboard Top Cast Albums chart, in the top five along with other musical juggernauts such as *Wicked, Monty Python's Spamalot,* and *Mama Mia!* and is available on iTunes and Amazon.com.

Such songs as "Cabin in the Woods," "What the F—- Was That?," and "All the Men in My Life Keep Getting Killed by Candarian Demons" have received special praise as well, from publications such as *Broadway World.* The musical was written and created by George Reinblatt (1977–). Campbell and Raimi are both fans of the musical, with Campbell making a surprise question and answer appearance after the August 11, 2007 performance in Toronto. Reinblatt has denied rumors that there will be a movie version of the musical but has stated that he would like do the musical as an ice show.

See also: Campbell, Bruce; Comedy; *Evil Dead, The* (Films); Raimi, Sam

Braden Dauzat

EVIL DEAD, THE (VIDEO GAME)

The Evil Dead video games are based on the *Evil Dead* films directed by Sam Raimi and starring Bruce Campbell, and have been through six iterations by 2013. The first game, *The Evil Dead*, was released in 1984, three years after the first movie in the *Evil Dead* series.

The Evil Dead was released on the Commodore 64 platform and produced by Palace Software. Players in *The Evil Dead* run around as Ash, the protagonist of most of Raimi's films, who closes windows to keep the spirits out of the cabin where he is trapped while fighting deadites, undead zombie-like creatures, with various weapons. The next game, *Evil Dead: Hail to the King,* was produced by THQ studios, developed by Heavy Iron studios, and released on the PlayStation, Dreamcast, and PC platforms in 2000. *Hail to the King* received mixed reviews. The gameplay involves Ash's returning to the cabin where the *Evil Dead* trilogy of films began, where he fights "Bad Ash," his evil deadite doppelgänger, while his possessed hand raises deadites. *Evil Dead: A Fistful of Boomstick,* released in 2003 on the PlayStation 2 and Xbox platforms, received marginally better reviews. It was also produced by THQ but was developed by VIS entertainment. Its gameplay consists of Ash's fighting deadites, which are multiplying in traditional zombie fashion throughout the town, as Ash tries to win back *The Necronomicon* to defeat them. *A Fistful of Boomstick* takes place in Michigan 11 years after the events of *Army of Darkness* (1992), the third film in Raimi's series. The next game in the series, *Evil Dead: Regeneration,* produced by THQ and developed by Crazy Pants Games, holds the highest ratings of the series for its mix of hack-and-slash gameplay and puzzles. It was released on PlayStation 2, Xbox, and PC platforms in 2005. This time, the story takes place in an alternate reality where Ash was not transported back in time at the end of *Evil Dead II* (1987) but is instead locked in a mental institution at the behest of a mad scientist wishing to study *The Necronomicon* to raise an undead army and conquer the planet. Ash and a half-deadite partner, Sam, an experiment of the doctor's, must team up to stop him.

Critics have praised Campbell's voice acting as Ash in the games. Ted Raimi (born Theodore Raimi, 1965–) voices the new character Sam in *Evil Dead: Regeneration.* The games were also praised for attempting to capture the feel of the movies by using copious amounts of humor, gore, and zombie hordes, along with signature quotes from the films. The last two *Evil Dead* games moved away from consoles and were released on Apple's iOS platform in the App Store for the iPhone, iPad, and iPod Touch. *Evil Dead: The Game* was released in July 2011 by Trigger Apps on the iOS platform. The game has the player as Ash as he defends the cabin from deadites with various weapons. *Army of Darkness Defense* is an army wave-based defense game released in December 2011 for the iOS platform, created by Backflip Studios. Campbell again voices Ash in this game, which is based on the third film, *Army of Darkness,* where the player attempts to defend Lord Arthur's castle from the incoming Army of Darkness. Ash was the playable character in all of the games in the franchise, and the story for each was only very loosely based on the films. The video games, like each of the movies, interpret *The Necronomicon* and its powers differently in every entry. They also take a cue from the movies and do not have a linear storyline, instead rewriting past events from the series in each new iteration. Each game, like the films, adds to the lore and mythology of the *Evil Dead* franchise in different and sometimes contradictory ways, creating a motley collection of zombies and undead creatures that inhabit the *Evil Dead* world.

See also: Campbell, Bruce; *Evil Dead, The* (Films); Raimi, Sam; Video Games

Braden Dauzat

EXISTENTIALISM

Existentialism is integral to zombie fiction. Zombies perform an important function in the modern world—they enable humans to make meaning of their own lives. This is a theme in post-apocalyptic zombie narratives as diverse as Richard Matheson's novella *I Am Legend,* Max Brooks's novel *World War Z* and the films *28 Days Later* (2002) and *Shaun of the Dead* (2004).

Existentialism can be loosely defined as the idea that human beings rather than some outside force or institution create meaning for their lives. Consequently, humans have difficulty functioning effectively when they lack a stable narrative about the meaning of their lives. The zombie that operates by Romero's Rules is itself the antithesis of existentialism. With few exceptions, it is a creature with an essence, whose sole purpose is to consume human flesh for no ostensible reason. Still, the zombie lacks the intellect to be aware of this purpose, let alone to formulate another purpose for its existence. Ironically, the zombie can only be fully disabled by destroying the brain, although this organ is incapable of creating meaning for itself.

The trope of the zombie apocalypse is usually set against the backdrop of a modern world, where people are in existential crisis because they lack a sense of community that might give their lives meaning and are instead increasingly dependent on the caprices of consumer culture to give them a sense of purpose. Director George Romero plumbs this theme in his film *Dawn of the Dead* (1978), where a group of survivors take shelter in a mall, the cathedral of modern American culture where people go to find fleeting fulfillment. In the face of the zombie apocalypse, which has rapidly toppled human civilization, a small band of survivors regroup in this mall where, surrounded by the familiar paraphernalia of modern consumer life, they hope to reestablish a sense of normalcy. Cocooned in the mall, the group lives for a while as if little has changed, but they are unable to sustain this pretense. Even before a second group of people raids the mall, enabling the zombies outside to pour in and breach the security of the compound, small group of survivors are discovering that unlimited access to all of the products that they believed would give them rich and meaningful lives is ultimately unfulfilling. The film ends with the zombies reoccupying the mall, the place where they were happy in life, and where they now behave as contented shoppers, while remains of film's original group of survivors search for a new place where they can be safe and eventually recreate meaning for themselves. Francine, one of the survivors who is pregnant, will presumably find that meaning in a more traditional way, as a mother.

The survivors in later zombie narratives more obviously experience their pre-apocalypse lives as lacking meaning. For example, in the romantic zombie comedy *Shaun of the Dead,* the titular protagonist as well as his fellow British citizens lead rote existences that are so devoid of meaning that when the dead first begin returning to life, Shaun and his friends do not notice since they themselves are so similar to the undead. This similarity is underscored in the film's opening scene, a close-up of Shaun's seeming to moan as if he were a zombie, when in fact he is only yawning as a prelude to beginning another uninspiring day as a manager of a big box appliance store. Shaun realizes that his life is at a crisis point when his girlfriend Liz dumps him because he has relatively little direction. The zombie apocalypse gives Shaun this opportunity as it forces him to develop a life plan, albeit a short-term one, in order to survive the crisis. His mantra becomes "take Pete's car, . . . grab mum, . . . go over to Liz's place, hole up, have a nice cup of tea and wait for all this to blow over." The rest of the film involves Shaun's trying to implement this plan until the zombies are subdued by the military, and Shaun and Liz are reunited. Afterward, it seems if no one has succeeded in forming new meaning in their lives. While Shaun and Liz now cohabitate in his cleaner flat, Shaun's life has changed little—he still works at the same unfulfilling job, managing an appliance store. He still plays video games with his best friend Ed, now a zombie, during his time off.

Robert Neville believes himself to be the last man on earth in *I Am Legend,* in that he is surrounded by infected undead who lack the cognitive ability to do more than come out at night and surround his barricaded home in an attempt to take his blood, as they believe themselves to be vampires. Because he is constantly in a state of siege, Neville redefines himself as a survivor, though he is often uncertain about what his existence means in the absence of others like him who could perpetuate civilization as he knew it. But as the last man on earth, Neville unwittingly engages in a sort of moral relativism when he kills both the infected undead and the infected living because he does not fully appreciate the difference and believes that all infected are necessarily a threat to his survival. Neville's moral relativism is pointed out to him in the novella's penultimate chapters, when he is finally captured by the infected living, who put him on trial for his crimes against their kind. While in Neville's mind he is just a man trying to survive in a post-apocalyptic world, to the infected living who are trying to establish a new civilization after the human race has been decimated, he is legend in that he is a blood-thirsty serial killer who must be eliminated if they are to thrive. The novella's shifting perspective of Robert emphasizes its existentialist point of view.

The survivors on the British Isles in the film *28 Days Later* have lost meaning in their lives after the rage virus pandemic has so reduced the population that only a handful of uninfected survive, cowering from the infected, who are slavering cannibals that tear apart all uninfected that they come into contact with. The apocalypse has taken a great psychological toll on the uninfected as well. Major West describes the infected as the embodiment of people who are without meaning in their lives because they are futureless: they will "never bake bread, plant crops, raise livestock," activities all associated with civilization and a hope for the future. Yet, West's men are similar to the infected in that they too fear that they will never perform these activities, or any others related to civilization that give their lives meaning, and so many of them have taken their own lives during the brief 28 days that the rage virus has spread throughout the United Kingdom. West's answer to infection, for his men anyway, is women, because they mean a future; he sees them as possessions that can be sexually dominated and will enable men to reproduce a patriarchal civilization in which everyone plays previously familiar roles that would presumably give hope to men, if not to the women. Jim and Selena, the film's protagonists, find meaning in their lives through affinity with others, though not in relationships in which women are coerced into playing their roles. Selena is slightly envious of the relationship that their fellow survivors Frank and Hannah, father and daughter, have. At the beginning of the film, Selena quips that "plans are pointless" and "staying alive's as good as it gets." But Selena notices that the events of the past 28 days do not affect Frank and Hannah the way they have affected Jim and her because Hannah and her dad have each other. But Frank is killed by West's soldiers soon after he becomes infected, and at the end of the film, Jim helps Selena and Hannah escape the commander's men, who are planning to rape the women as part of their plan to return meaning to their lives. Selena revises her opinion of what makes her life worth living after the three form a makeshift family and are relatively safe from the infected. She tells Jim that she was wrong about staying alive being the point of existence.

The presence of zombies gives more lasting meaning to people's lives in Max Brooks's epic novel *World War Z*. Zombies in Romero's films have the potential for reversing an isolating American rugged individualism because the collapse of civilization forces them to collaborate in order to survive. Sadly, in Romero's films, individualism ultimately prevails when people cannot work together for the common good, something that permits the zombies to swarm their protected enclaves. Brooks's novel is set approximately 10 years in the future after the human race has come back from the brink of extinction and triumphed over the living dead because the zombie apocalypse has forced people to work together for the common good. *World War Z* is loosely based on Studs Terkel's (born Louis Terkel, 1912–2008) *The Good War: An Oral History of World War II,* in which Terkel similarly reflects on how individuals from all walks of life collaborated to defeat fascism. A notable theme in Brooks's novel is how people develop a sense of purpose in their lives that was lacking before the arrival of the zombies. For example, Kondo Tatsumi goes from being someone who spends all of his waking hours trolling cyberspace, finding supposedly secret information such as the tax receipts of Japanese ministers or "the location and condition of all the shin-gunto swords of the Pacific War," to living by his ancestors' bushido code in order to destroy zombies for the good of humanity. Arthur Sinclair Jr., the former minister of the American wartime Department of Strategic Resources, describes how people who had been executives, representatives, analysts, and consultants in the old world were trained by their first-generation immigrant cleaning ladies and handymen to perform manual labor in a world where gunsmiths, carpenters, masons, and machinists were desperately needed. After much initial complaining, these former pampered members of the middle and upper classes eventually "admitted that they got more emotional satisfaction from their new jobs than anything closely resembling their old ones." These were survivors who had so much doubt about their purpose in the world that they almost did not attempt to rebuild civilization at all. The president stressed the danger of individual nations retreating into isolationism after they had conquered the zombie problem within their borders. Rather, it was crucial that people from all nations collaborate to reclaim the planet for the benefit of the species, collectively moving forward.

See also: Brooks, Max; *Dawn of the Dead*; *I Am Legend* (Novel); Matheson, Richard; Romero, George; *Shaun of the Dead*; *28 Days Later* Series; *World War Z* (Novel); Zombie Studies

June Michele Pulliam

"FACTS IN THE CASE OF M. VALDEMAR, THE"

"The Facts in the Case of M. Valdemar" is an Edgar Allan Poe short story that appeared simultaneously in the December 1845 issues of *The American Review* and *Broadway Journal*. Fascinated with hypnosis, Poe made it the focal point of an earlier story, "Mesmeric Revelation" (1844), where a physician mesmerizes his dying patient, Vankirk. As Vankirk falls into a hypnotic trance, the physician interrogates the patient on matters related to the soul's immortality. Vankirk, so entranced by whatever it is that he experiences, chooses to die, leaving the physician without answers. "The Facts in the Case of M. Valdemar," which Poe wrote after attending an 1845 lecture series given by mesmerist Andrew Jackson Davis (1826–1910) in New York City, reads like a sequel to "Mesmeric Revelation," with the addition of the introduction of an undead character.

In it, an unnamed narrator relates how he conducted a hypnotic experiment on the dying M. Ernest Valdemar in order to determine if hypnosis can halt death. Valdemar volunteers for the experiment and, on learning that he has 24 hours to live, summons the narrator. In the waning seconds before Valdemar's death, the narrator places Valdemar under a mesmeric trance. Returning hours later, the narrator finds Valdemar barely breathing, his eyes shut, his body "rigid and cold as marble." Further into the night, the narrator accepts that Valdemar is indeed dying but queries the patient. Valdemar responds that he is dead. The narrator determines that death has been arrested by hypnosis, yet he fears that awakening the patient would ensure instant dissolution. Valdemar remains under suspended hypnosis for seven months, after which the narrator resolves to awaken the patient from the trance, no matter the consequences. When questioned, Valdemar's jaws and lips remain rigid, yet his tongue rolls violently in his mouth. Unnerved, the narrator summons Valdemar out of the trance. Valdemar awakens, and his cadaver, within a single minute, rots into a nearly liquid mass.

Thematically, both Poe stories of hypnosis at the moment of death address death anxiety. Also, both, like Poe's "The Masque of the Red Death" (1842), remind readers of the futility of attempting to escape death. The instantaneous and horrific decomposition of Valdemar functions as commentary on human attempts to sidestep mortality. "The Facts in the Case of M. Valdemar" is more of a proto-zombie story than zombie narrative per se. While Valdemar is not the walking dead, hypnosis has made him similar to a zombie in two important ways. First, he is undead, suspended between life and death. Second, Valdemar's will has been subordinated to that of the narrator's in that he cannot permit his body to decompose and release his soul.

See also: "Malthusian's Zombie"; Poe, Edgar Allan

Matthew McEver

FIDO

Fido is a 2006 Canadian comic zombie film directed by Andrew Currie (1973–). The film features a parallel 1940s universe where radiation reanimates the dead, leading to a worldwide zombie war instead of World War II. A newsreel in the film's opening explains that the human race had nearly become extinct until Dr. Hrothgar Geiger invents a collar that, once placed around a zombie's neck, renders it docile. Zombies are then kept as slave labor, pets, and sex slaves.

Zomcom, a Haliburton-esque corporation that promises "better living through containment" in the film's alternative 1950s postwar era, markets zombie slaves to clean municipal grounds, deliver milk and newspapers, and work as personal servants for well-to-do middle-class families. In the small town of Willard, the corporate headquarters of Zomcom, everything is precisely contained. Yards are kept within well-maintained borders; women and children are subordinate to men; and people do not ask questions, except for young Timmy Robinson. When Mr. Bottoms, a Zomcom executive, visits Timmy's class, Timmy quizzes him about whether or not zombies can feel pain. Timmy's question sets up the film's premise: are zombies deserving of the same dignity afforded to the living?

Quick thinking on the part of Cindy Bottoms prevents Timmy Robinson from getting into trouble for having his zombie off of a leash when the girl lends him her jump rope as a makeshift restraint. (Lions Gate Films/Photofest)

When Timmy's family gets its own zombie, played by comedian Billy Connolly (born William Connolly Jr., 1942–), the boy becomes friendly with the creature, naming him Fido. This causes others to question their relationships with their zombies, as well as their own subordinate status in this highly stratified society. The Robinsons' creepy neighbor Mr. Theopolis, whose zombie Tammy is his sex slave, eventually learns to treat her with respect. Timmy's mother Helen begins to care for Fido, despite the objections of her husband Bill. Dylan Baker (1959–), who plays Bill, bears a striking resemblance to William H. Macy (born William Hall Macy Jr., 1950–) as the traditionalist husband George Parker in *Pleasantville* (1998). Dylan is terrified of zombies and worried that the family cannot afford this expensive luxury, so his wife's actions amount to her stepping outside of her subordinate status. Although set in a parallel 1950s America, *Fido* is also about contemporary American fears of terrorism and outsized corporate influence. Under a legal system that parallels the Patriot Act, citizens of Willard can be seized by Zomcom security personnel without due process. An elderly neighbor is whisked away by Zomcom security personnel, accused of giving his wife an illegal burial, which not only endangers the citizens of Willard with a loose zombie but also deprives Zomcom of the profits it makes enslaving the undead. Offenders are exiled to the Wild Zone, a place full of uncollared zombies whose clothing and relatively long and unkempt hair is reminiscent of the 1960s, emphasizing the creature's connection to social change.

Fido does eventually bring about social change in Willard. After Mr. Bottoms arranges for Fido to be seized and returned to Zomcom headquarters, Timmy, Helen, and Mr. Theopolis rescue him, causing a momentary melee in which some zombies escape, killing Mr. Bottoms and Mr. Robinson, who dies defending his family from Zomcom. The film ends in a way that is atypical of horror films in that boundaries have been muddied rather than solidified. Although Zomcom is still in power, family structures are radically reorganized. Fido now seems to be Helen's love interest, yet Timmy still calls him Fido, indicating that the zombie is still a pet. Cindy Bottoms walks her now-zombie father on a leash. She tells Timmy that she calls her zombie "Daddy," indicating to what degree this new familial relationship is blurred. As a comic zombie film, *Fido* parodies earlier well-known works in the genre, specifically paying homage to *Night of the Living Dead* (1968) in that these zombies are created by cosmic radiation. George Romero hints at this possibility himself in his 1968 film. Even *Fido*'s setting, Willard, references Romero, as this is the same name as the town that *Night* is set in. Like many recent comic zombie films, *Fido* includes existential zombies, or the living who might as well be the living dead. In many ways, live humans are more dead than the zombies, as their lives are full of stultifying routine. Currie made this low-budget film for an estimated $8 million. *Fido* was not widely released: it was shown in a mere 67 theaters for 5 weeks, and only grossed $426,224. Nevertheless, it has a cult following and is widely referenced in scholarship about zombies.

See also: Comedy; Cult Film; Existentialism; *Night of the Living Dead* Series; Romero, George; Romero's Rules

June Michele Pulliam

FOG, THE

The Fog (1980) is the second feature film made by well-known horror director and co-written by John Carpenter, with an all-star cast: his then-wife Adrienne Barbeau (born Adrienne Jo Barbeau, 1945–), Jamie Lee Curtis (1958–) and her mother Janet Leigh (born Jeanette Helen Morrison, 1927–2004), Hal Holbrook (born Harold Rowe Holbrook Jr., 1925–), and John Houseman (born Jacques Haussmann, 1902–1988). The film is more ghost story than zombie film. However, the reanimated dead, the film's monsters, are corporeal rather than ethereal, and like many zombies, they are animated by a single purpose, in this case, revenge on the ancestors of those who have wronged them.

At midnight, on the centennial of Antonio Bay, California, residents learn the truth about their sleepy little town's founding after the hamlet is enshrouded in a mysterious fog, appliances begin to turn themselves on and off, phones ring for no apparent reason, and a large stone falls from the wall of Father Malone's church, revealing a diary from 1880. The diary recounts how Antonio Bay was founded by six people, including Malone's grandfather, who committed murder to acquire the necessary gold: The six learned that a ship in the bay sailing toward them was piloted by a wealthy leper hoping to found a leper colony in the area. The six conspire to steal the ship's gold and keep the lepers away by lighting a fire on the beach near some dangerous rocks, creating a false beacon that causes the clipper to run aground, killing all aboard and allowing the six to plunder. Now, a century after their deaths, the crew return for revenge, intent on killing six residents, including Father Malone, before they leave.

The revenging revenants are a cross between ghosts and zombies. Like ghosts, they have unfinished business, revenge. However, their corporeality makes them reanimated dead, and as such, they are able to exact a grisly revenge that is unavailable to a disembodied spirit. Moreover, the revenging revenants reanimate the corpse of one of their victims, a fisherman who is found washed ashore with his eyes gouged out. When the coroner autopsies the body, he is perplexed by its advanced state of decomposition, and the body reanimates, rising from the autopsy table and scratching the number three on the autopsy room with a scalpel, as he was the third victim of crew. The revenants are also mindless in a way similar to the typical zombie in that they have a single purpose. Once they kill six residents of Antonio Bay, they will disappear. They even travel as a shambling mob, as do zombies. Rupurt Wainwright (1961–) remade *The Fog* in 2005, but the film received uniformly negative reviews.

See also: Ghosts

June Michele Pulliam

FOREST OF HANDS AND TEETH **TRILOGY, THE**

The Forest of Hands and Teeth trilogy, by Carrie Ryan (1978–), is a series of young adult novels considered some of the first texts to successfully blend romance with the horror of a zombie apocalypse. Its novels are less concerned with the mechanics of a zombie apocalypse than the struggle young people face to break free of restrictive rules as they find their way in a hostile world. Ryan does not disclose the cause of the apocalypse, instead focusing on how knowledge, history, and culture can erode, and how they can be changed into something unrecognizable to the reader. The forest represents the unknown, full of the danger and hope that all teens face when striking out on their own for the first time.

The first novel, *The Forest of Hands and Teeth* (2009), tells of a village that has existed for seven generations. Mary has never known life beyond the village's gates, apart from the stories her mother passes down, and does not know if there are other survivors of The Return, the name given to the zombie apocalypse. Mary's mother's stories comfort her during the years defined by the harsh rules of the Sisterhood, rules designed to keep all humans safe from the Unconsecrated, the trilogy's undead. The rules also keep humans safe from each other. When she sees a mysterious stranger being held captive by the Sisterhood, Mary begins to question her beliefs. To keep her quiet, the Sisterhood betroths Mary to a young man, and Mary' struggles with the Sisterhood begin in earnest. When the Unconsecrated break through the gates, Mary and a few other teens flee through the forest, hoping there is refuge beyond.

In *The Dead-Tossed Waves* (2010), Mary finds refuge near the ocean in a place protected from the Unconsecrated. Here, Mary's daughter Gabrielle grows up, but unlike her mother, she has no desire to step outside its gates. When a group of friends convince Gabrielle to indulge in a little teenage rebellion, they are attacked by zombies. Gabrielle and her friend Catcher escape, but he is bitten. Miraculously, though Catcher has been infected in the attack, he does not turn into one of the Unconsecrated. Better still, zombies also do not target Catcher because he no longer appears human to them. Realizing Catcher will be killed by humans if they remain, they brave the forest with a mysterious stranger, Elias. When the Militia Recruiters find out that Catcher is immune, they pursue the teens, hoping to use Catcher in their war against the Unconsecrated. Catcher and Gabrielle escape. The final novel, *The Dark and Hollow Places* (2011), opens as Gabrielle and Catcher enter the Dark City ahead of a zombie horde. While searching for Gabrielle's sister Annah, they are captured by renegade Recruiters, who have taken control of the Militia. After their capture, Catcher is forced to go into the city to scavenge for supplies. If Catcher refuses, his friends will be killed. While Catcher is scavenging, the others seek a way to escape the increasingly brutal Recruiters and find a place of safety in a dangerous world.

See also: Apocalypse; Young Adult Fiction

Alicia Ahlvers

FRANCO, JESS

Jess Franco (born Jesús Franco Manera, 1930–2013) was arguably one of the most influential purveyors of sexual horror. Franco was a Spanish director who also had experience as a cinematographer and actor, appearing in virtually all of his 150 plus films. In 1982, he directed *Oasis of the Zombies,* also known by its variant title *The Treasure of the Living Dead,* as well as its variant, titled *La Tumba de los Muertos Vivientes* (1982). Both versions are arguably the earliest films featuring Nazi zombies.

In 1973, Franco directed *A Virgin among the Living Dead,* also released as *Christine, Princess of Eroticism* or *Christina, Princesse de L'érotisme,* and he was originally slated to direct *Lake of the Living Dead* (*Zombie Lake*), a Nazi-related zombie film, in 1980. However, Franco had other commitments, so producer Daniel Lesouer hired director Jean Rollin, who later directed zombie footage to be added to *A Virgin among the Living Dead* for its re-release. Franco was signed for *Oasis of the Zombies,* which had a plot similar to *Zombie Lake.* He simultaneously shot his variant version, *La Tumba de los Muertos Vivientes,* to be released in Spain. Franco's zombies are slow-moving, often taking more than one scene to come out of the ground. They resemble corpses at various stages of decomposition, and their facial features are often covered in dirt. They can easily be dispatched by burning. Franco has directed films under various pseudonyms taken from famous jazz musicians, such as Clifford Brown and James P. Johnson. His films are best known for their sexploitation, often featuring lesbianism, especially among vampires, as well as imprisoned women, surgical horror, and sadomasochism. He is also known for his use of handheld camera and zoom shots.

Franco began composing music at six, and started in film as a composer in 1954. He then worked as an assistant director, as well as a production manager and screenwriter, as he had earlier publishing experience, writing novels under the pseudonym David Khume. As a director, Franco broke into the business slowly, with industrial and cultural short films. After some cult success with *The Awful Dr. Orloff* (*Gritos en la Noche,* 1962), he started receiving critical attention, as his film *Succubus* (*Necronomicon: Geträumte Sünden,* 1968) was nominated for the Festival of Berlin and was a box office success, as were *Ninety-Nine Women* (*Der Heiße Tod,* 1968), *The Bloody Judge* (*Il Trono di Fuoco,* 1970), and *Count Dracula* (*Nachts Wenn Dracula Erwacht,* 1970). After this success, Franco moved to France because the industry there was more friendly to sex and violence in film, but he ended up directing low-budget and X-rated soft and hardcore pornographic films, usually starring his long-time partner Lina Romay (born Rosa María Almirall Martínez, 1954–2012). When Franco lost the respect of his peers, who considered him a porn director, he revisited the idea of the low-budget horror film, directing *Bloody Moon* (*Die Säge des Todes,* 1981).

See also: Cult Film; Nazi Zombies

Anthony J. Fonseca

FREE WILL

Free will, one of the primary philosophical and religious doctrines related to the essence of humanity, is often presented as a gift from various gods, as well as the defining characteristic of what it means to be human. Therefore, it is not surprising that the defining characteristic of nearly all zombies is a lack of free will. It is evident in the Voodoo zombie, which is controlled by a bokur, or zombie master, and it is obvious in the zombie's, operating by Romero's Rules, complete sublimation to a drive to consume flesh. Because the zombie lacks free will, it is viewed by extension as devoid of humanity—something wholly Other and therefore monstrous. But it is a third and most modern iteration of the creature, the existential or philosophical zombie, that causes us to question whether or not human free will is an illusion.

The zombie as supernatural slave represents fears of complete subservience, literally, having little to no self-control. In Haiti, where the figure of the zombie originated, the creature is regarded with fear, perhaps because of its association with colonial slave culture. Stories describing resurrection for the purpose of enslavement involve those in the upper echelons of the religious or spiritual system misappropriating power. This is the case in the 1932 film *White Zombie*, where planter and bokur Murder Legendre has used black magic to enslave those who were more powerful than him, including the magistrate, another bokur, and the high executioner. The 1988 film *The Serpent and the Rainbow* views this type of zombie as a product of rational as much as supernatural causes. Loosely based on ethnobotanist Wade Davis's work of nonfiction of the same name, *The Serpent and the Rainbow* follows a research scientist who journeys to Haiti in order to investigate claims that zombies are real in that they are made by bokurs who give poisons to their victims. Tetrodotoxin partially paralyzes the victim in a way that mimics death. Then, after the victim is presumed to be dead and buried, he or she is unearthed by the bokur and revived with zombie cucumber, which undoes the paralysis robs the victim of free will, turning him or her into an ideal slave who can be used to perform menial labor. Craven's zombies are created by those who, according to our first-world perspective, have misappropriated power. However, in Craven's version, instead of an upstart bokur such as Murder Legendre victimizing those more powerful than himself, political leaders maintain their power through their ability to zombify those who challenge their authority. The zombies described by anthropologist Zora Neale Hurston in her ethnography of Haiti *Tell My Horse* also fit into this category.

Zombies operating by Romero's Rules also lack free will. However, these zombies are not controlled by a more powerful zombie master; instead, they have their free will subordinated to one uncontrollable drive. Romero's Rules are based upon the representation of the creature in George Romero's 1968 film *Night of the Living Dead*, which crystallized earlier representations of the creature, transforming it from a glassy-eyed victim of ensorcellment who was to be pitied for its lack of free will (or perhaps even lack of a soul, depending on the narrative) to a shuffling undead cannibal driven by the insatiable desire to feast on the flesh of the living and transform others into zombies. Other representations of the creature to follow this pattern include those in Robert Kirkman's graphic novel series *The Walking Dead* and the television series made of it; Lucio Fulci's film *Zombie* (1996), and the zombies in the *Evil Dead* films. The zombies in *The Return of the Living Dead* (1985), a parody of Romero's *Night of the Living Dead*, are credited as the first representation of the zombie as a creature craving human brains, not just general human flesh. In *Return*, director Dan O'Bannon's zombies are sentient—something learned when one of them is hooked up to a device that permits the rotting creature to articulate its thoughts—yet their monomaniacal desire for brains still classifies them as lacking free will. *Return's* "talking" zombie tells the audience that being dead is painful but consuming brains momentarily dulls this pain. Nevertheless, the ability of these zombies to articulate their condition does not endow them with free will. The infected of the *28 Days Later* series similarly lack free will. The *28 Days Later* series does not feature creatures that can be considered zombies in the traditional sense—they are alive but infected by the rage virus, are fast rather than slow-moving, and are not so much led to consume human flesh as attack and bite (and otherwise tear asunder their victims). Also, they are never called zombies in the film. Nevertheless, their highly infectious malady, combined with their drive to savage all humans, a drive that has wiped out all other facets of their personality, qualifies them as zombies. In the BBC series *In the Flesh,* zombies suffer from a condition that turns them into ravening cannibals. However, because the condition can be controlled, they are rounded up by the government and given treatment, and are encouraged to think of themselves as being similar to people who suffer from a particularly severe form of mental illness that makes them not fully responsible for their actions before they were given help.

The third type of zombie, the philosophical or existential zombies, also lacks free will. The philosophical zombie, or p-zombie, was conceptualized by Rene Descartes (1596–1650). It adheres to the belief that a robotic or otherwise crafted faux human's existence results in a monstrous creature that may act according to a pre-asserted objectives. In other words, the theory posits that the appearance of humanity, minus actual humanity, is possible. The p-zombie has no free will and possesses only the human façade. Descartes's positing of the p-zombie's existence exemplifies the import of free will for humanity and the role its absence plays in creation of the zombie as monster. Examples of the philosophical zombie can be seen in the films *Shaun of the Dead* (2004) and *Fido* (2006). The philosophical zombie is not at first recognized as a zombie per se since it is not controlled by a Voodoo master nor does it operate by Romero's Rules. Rather, in these films, the viewer comes to understand certain characters as philosophical zombies when they are compared to the other zombies in the film who operate by Romero's Rules.

In *Shaun of the Dead* and *Fido,* humans must fight the living dead in order to survive. However, it soon becomes apparent that these humans have lives that are devoid of free will, in spite of the dizzying array of choices they apparently believe they have. Shaun and his friends live in a world where they can choose from over 100 television channels and stores filled with seemingly limitless consumer products, where they have a wide range of careers and a limitless possibility of romantic partners and lifestyles available to them. Nevertheless, Shaun and his best friend Ed spend nearly every night drinking pints at the Winchester or playing video games. Raymond Smullyan's (born Raymond Merrill Smullyan, 1919–) paradox regarding the existence of a p-zombie questions the role that free will plays in determining humanity. He posits that if a man intended to drink a potion that would transform him into a being that performed all of his basic functions but was separate from his self (or soul), then the free will of that man caused him to intend the taking of the draught. This certainly describes Shaun at the end of the film. After the zombie threat has been minimized, his life has not been transformed, in spite of the death of his best friend Ed nor that of his roommate or his parents. Rather, he continues nearly the same routine existence as before, even playing video games with undead Ed, who has reanimated into a zombie and is kept chained in the tool shed. The humans in *Fido* eventually realize that they are philosophical zombies. In an alternative universe, the world did not engage in World War II but worked together to fight the undead in the 1940s. Thanks to the invention of Dr. Geiger, the undead are controlled through a special collar that renders them docile and useful for domestic service, thereby transforming them from zombies operating by Romero's Rules into ones that more closely resemble those enslaved through Voodoo. The living in this 1950s world also exist in a consumer paradise that offers them unlimited buying choices, but little way of breaking out of narrowly prescribed gender and social roles, which have rendered their existences as rote and devoid of meaning as those of the living dead against whom they must be constantly vigilant. *Fido* ends with the film's protagonists realizing their own zombified state and rebelling against their rigid social hierarchy in order to break free of this condition.

While the lack of free will is a defining characteristic of most zombies, some zombies notably have free will. In Daryl Gregory's (1965–) novel *Raising Stony Mayhall* (2011), the undead are as capable of the living as making rational and informed choices. The premise of Gregory's novel is that in 1968, the dead in a rural Pennsylvania area suddenly come back to life, and they have a desire to consume human flesh, just as Romero depicts in what the novel represents as a documentary representation of an historical event. The condition is rapidly spread when the undead bite the living without killing them. However, what is not depicted in Romero's film is that the zombie's desire to consume human flesh abates after the first 72 hours when the brain fever accompanying their new condition passes. After the dead reanimate on this first night in 1968, other humans can become zombies only if they are bitten by one. The government, wishing to give the appearance of containing the threat, exterminates all of the undead that it can find, in spite of the fact that zombies are only temporarily in thrall to their cannibalism, who control this desire and live normal lives if given the chance. Stony Mayhall, the novel's protagonist, is one of many of the undead who are in hiding from the government, while working with others of his kind to gain acceptance and even legal rights.

In the film *White Zombie* (1932), some zombies are morally stronger than others. Madeline Short, the white zombie of the title (the others are either black or Creole), is able to occasionally defy her maker when he commands her to do something that is morally repugnant to her, such as kill her husband. Finally, Romero himself questions whether or not zombies have free will in later installments of his *Night of the Living Dead* series of film. In *Land of the Dead* (2005), the undead collaborate to fight back against the living after their peaceful enclave is raided by humans scavenging supplies. The raiding party gleefully mutilates and kills zombies, outraging *Land's* zombie protagonist Big Daddy, who is seen sadly euthanizing a fellow zombie who has been too badly injured to survive comfortably. Afterward, Big Daddy exhibits enough free will and intelligence to formulate a plan to go after the humans who have harmed them. His fellow zombies likewise demonstrate free will in following him. Big Daddy is not represented as a zombie master able to control others of his kind, but rather, a member of the undead with leadership qualities who persuades others that his ideas are worth following. As the other zombies follow Big Daddy into the humans' compound, they demonstrate their own critical thinking skills in their ability to make tools to aid them in destroying barriers to their entry. Moreover, we see in *Land* that zombies are not necessarily in thrall to their desire to consume human flesh. While they will attack humans in the vicinity, they have no need to leave their enclave to seek out more human flesh. Thus, we can posit that perhaps zombies attack humans as a method of self-defense against those who treat them as abject Others and would dispatch them on sight. As a consequence, it begs the question as to whether these zombies lack free will.

The philosophical zombie and zombies who have free will then cause us to reconsider what we think we know about the creature as well as whether or not our own free will is perhaps an illusion.

See also: Bokur/Caplata; Class; Existentialism; *Fido*; Haiti; *In the Flesh*; *Night of the Living Dead* Series; *Raising Stony Mayhall*; Romero's Rules; *Serpent and the Rainbow, The* (Book); *Shaun of the Dead*; Tetrodotoxin; *28 Days Later* Series; Voodoo; *Walking Dead, The* (Comic); *Walking Dead, The* (Television Series); *White Zombie*; Zombie Cucumber

Celise A. Reech-Harper

FULCI, LUCIO

Lucio Fulci (1927–1996) is one of Italy's most prolific directors of horror films. In the zombie subgenre, he is best known for *Zombi 2* (1979), also known as *Zombie*, and for *The Beyond* (1981), which features ghosts, demons, murdered parents who become zombies, and a malevolent, indestructible corpse. *Zombi 2* combines the undead zombie motif with that of the traditional Voodoo zombie. Fulci's *Gates of Hell* trilogy garnered a significant cult following.

The trilogy begins with *City of the Living Dead* (released in the U.S. as *The Gates of Hell*), in which a curse brought on by a priest's suicide raises the dead. The film combines the American gothic of Edgar Allan Poe, especially the Poe-esque live burial, and the settings of H. P. Lovecraft (born Howard Phillips Lovecraft, 1890–1937), particularly Dunwich, with the trope of the Catholic Church, and of course, zombies. Even more emphasis on the Lovecraftian can be seen in the second film, *The Beyond*, which veers further away from rational narrative. *The Beyond* features a cursed or haunted modern hotel where previously a warlock, such as the one in Lovecraft's *The Case of Charles Dexter Ward*, uses the fictional *Book of Eibon*, which is similar to the *Necronomicon*. This opens a gate to a realm of evil. Zombies show up in the final scenes. The trilogy concludes with *The House by the Cemetery* (1981), about a New England house haunted by Dr. Freudstein (Freud meets Frankenstein) a serial killer who is part mad scientist and part zombie. Fulci's zombie-infused trilogy is generally underappreciated, but its cult following has ensured lasting admiration.

Fulci's work also includes spy films, comedies, thrillers, and erotica. During the 1970s, he made several noteworthy *gialli*, violent murder mysteries popularized by Mario Bava (1914–1980) and Dario Argento (1940–). Fulci modeled *Lizard in a Woman's Skin* (1971) on Argento's successful *The Bird with the Crystal Plumage* (1970), amplifying the earlier film's sexual themes. *Don't Torture a Duckling* (1972), the best-known of Fulci's films from this period, follows the same model but provides a controversial view of the Catholic Church that is rare in the *giallo* genre. *The New York Ripper* (1982), a slasher-like *giallo* featuring a killer who quacks like a duck, takes the earlier films' mixture of sex and violence to extremes, earning critical denunciations for misogyny and sadism. It cemented Fulci's reputation as the Godfather of Gore: known particularly for mutilating eyeballs, Fulci created unforgettable images of abjection, such as a woman vomiting her own intestines, in *City of the Living Dead* (1980). Although many critics dismiss Fulci's films as thoughtless, commercial spectacles, the metatextual *A Cat in the Brain* (1990) provides a different perspective, delivering signature gore alongside a self-reflective story about a film director named Lucio Fulci, played by Fulci. The character gets mixed up with a killer who acts out violence from fictional universes, Fulci's earlier films to be exact.

See also: Gates of Hell Trilogy; Italian Cinema; Lovecraft, H. P.; Poe, Edgar Allan; *Zombi* Series

L. Andrew Cooper

GATES OF HELL TRILOGY

The *Gates of Hell* trilogy, by Italian director Lucio Fulci, began in 1980 with *City of the Living Dead* (*Paura nella città dei morti viventi*), released as *The Gates of Hell* in the United States in 1983. Two later films, *The Beyond* (1981) and *The House by the Cemetery* (1981), make up the remainder of series, which tells the loosely connected story of various acts of murder and suicide that open portals to hell, releasing undead monsters into the world.

City of the Living Dead tells how a priest's suicide in a cemetery opens up the gates of Hell, ushering in supernaturally strong zombies who have magical powers like the ability to levitate and teleport themselves. In a nod to H. P. Lovecraft, the film's two protagonists, psychic Mary Woodhouse and reporter Peter Bell, go to Dunwich, New England, before All Saints Day to close the gates. *The Beyond* (*L'aldilà*, aka, *Seven Doors of Death*) upped the ante as far as gore was concerned. When it was released in the United States in 1983, many of its scenes had to be cut. This second film in the trilogy moves the action from present-day New England to Louisiana in 1927, where in the prequel, an artist residing at the Seven Doors Hotel is murdered. The artist is believed to be a warlock, and his murder opens one of the seven doors of death. Years later, the Seven Doors is reopened when it is inherited by a new owner, bringing to life the portal to hell and ushering in an army of living dead, ghosts, impossibly large tarantulas, and the zombie/ghost of the warlock, who is now indestructible.

The House by the Cemetery (*Quella villa accanto al cimitero*) was, like its immediate predecessor, released in Italy in 1981. It moves the action back to New England, where Fulci returned to the haunted house theme he toyed with in *The Beyond* (which was originally intended to be a haunted house movie). In *The House by the Cemetery*, a series of murders occur when a woman is murdered after entering an abandoned house. Back in New York, a young man and his parents move to a house whose last owner murdered his mistress there and afterward committed suicide. The film also includes a mysterious, ghostly girl. While this, the third film in the trilogy, does not contain zombies, it does introduce a walking, rotting corpse, which is more of a revenging revenant or a ghoul. This creature is the reanimated remains of Dr. Freudstein, a Victorian surgeon known for his cruel experiments, who has discovered how to use body parts from others to regenerate his own blood cells. All three films end with the protagonists being dragged into the portals.

See also: Fulci, Lucio; Ghosts; Ghoul; Italian Cinema; Lovecraft, H. P.

Anthony J. Fonseca

GENDER

Gender, a social term, not to be confused with sex, a biological distinction, is represented in zombie fiction in ways typical of the horror genre: men and women are monstrous to the degree that they deviate from stereotypical notions of masculinity or femininity. While sex refers to biological differences between sexes in a species, such as genitalia, chromosomes, and hormonal profiles, gender describes what characteristics a given culture designates as masculine or feminine. As well, gender may describe the consequences attending that designation. Stereotypical femininity is associated with passivity and the faculty for having one's will subordinated to male authority, whereas stereotypical masculinity is associated with the need to control others, as well as a capacity for violence and the open expression of anger. Deeply held cultural beliefs often represent these qualities as biologically rooted in sex, rather than as the consequence of culturally proscribed gender roles. In the zombie narrative, both zombies and humans deviate from stereotypical masculine and feminine behaviors in ways that are unsettling. However, these representations ultimately prompt the reader or viewer to challenge deeply held convictions about the alleged nature of men and women.

In narratives where zombies are created through magical means such as Voodoo, the resulting creature is an iteration of stereotypical femininity in its extreme passivity—it is subordinated to the will of its maker. Thus, male zombies of this variety are unsettling because they are in effect emasculated when their maker deprives them of free will. For example, in the film *The Plague of the Zombies* (1966), Squire Hamilton in a sense emasculates the working-class men of his Cornish village by turning them into undead slaves to labor in his tin mines that are so dangerous that the living refuse employment in them. Some zombified women created through magical means are frightening because their wills cannot be fully subordinated, revealing in them qualities that are more typically associated with masculinity. For instance, in the films *White Zombie* (1932) and *I Walked with a Zombie* (1943), the zombified Madeline and Jessica, respectively, should be ideal women as they lack any will of their own. Yet, neither can be fully controlled by others. Madeline retains enough free will to resist her maker's directive to murder her husband. Jessica, meanwhile, remains stubbornly desirable and, therefore, uncontrollable in her undead state, causing her husband and brother-in-law to feud for possession of her body as they battled for her affections before she was zombified.

Undead zombies following Romero's Rules are stereotypically masculine in that they are not controlled by a master. Moreover, their desire to bite and even tear apart humans seems to be born of anger, an emotion that is associated with hegemonic masculinity. For example, the zombies in the film *28 Days Later* (2002) have been infected by the rage virus, which takes only seconds to transform victims into fast-moving, red-eyed fiends intent on tearing apart anyone who crosses their paths. While the rage virus infects men and women alike, the majority of infected presented on screen in *28 Days Later* are adult males. Romero's zombies too seem angry, particularly in *Land of the Dead* (2005), where a group of them led by the zombie Big Daddy attack a fortified human settlement in Pittsburgh in response to a foraging party's gleeful maiming and killing of several zombies during a supply scavenging mission.

In post-apocalyptic zombie narratives, the presence of zombies affects gender for the human characters. The human male hero in so much post-apocalyptic zombie fiction is frightening. His position of authority is an extreme example of hegemonic masculinity. If, as psychoanalytic theorist Nancy Chodorow (born Nancy Julia Chodorow, 1944–) holds, the typical masculine subject position is to be separated from the world rather than connected to it, then characters such as Robert Neville of the novella *I Am Legend* (1954) are extremely masculine in their isolation from all other humans on earth. Yet, the collapse of civilization in these narratives reveals that gender is not just an immutable aspect of sex, but a performance determined by cultural factors that are often so firmly established that they are invisible, as Judith Butler (1956–) describes in *Gender Trouble*. This tendency is apparent in films such as the 1990 remake of George Romero's *Night of the Living Dead* and *28 Days Later*. Jim and Selena, the protagonists of *28 Days Later,* have switched gender roles. When Jim first meets Selena, she demonstrates a masculine individualism after her travelling companion suddenly becomes infected. Selena ignores his pleas for mercy and immediately hacks him to death with a machete before he is a danger to her. Afterward, Selena coldly informs Jim that she would do the same to him in a heartbeat should he become infected, revealing that she will not permit feminine sentimentality to be a detriment to her own survival. Jim, on the other hand, has a more feminine attitude toward his fellow survivors—he tells Selena that he would not be so quick to execute them. Selena begins to question her own survival strategy, however, when she and Jim meet Frank and his pre-teen daughter Hannah, and the four venture to an army battalion headquartered outside of Manchester, whose emergency radio broadcast promises that they have the answer to infection. Yet, when the four finally locate the battalion, the commander reveals that his answer to infection is to violently re-establish patriarchy for his men, who have lost hope in the face of a plague that has wiped out most of the population of the British Isles. Soldiers immediately gun down Frank, the oldest male in the group, after he is infected by a freak accident, and then escort the remaining three into their compound.

That evening their commander, West, confides to Jim that women will offer his soldiers hope, since their submission will allow them to feel as if they are men. When Jim objects to this plan, West has him locked up, and then confines Hannah and Selena so that they can be raped by the soldiers. Jim and Selena are only able to ensure the survival of all three of their group by reverting to traditional gender roles. Selena takes a motherly interest in Hannah, protecting her from the soldiers by offering herself to them. Jim, meanwhile, escapes confinement to rescue Hannah and Selena, and his resulting outrage makes him nearly indistinguishable from one of the infected. When Jim bursts through a skylight to rescue Hannah and Selena, Selena demonstrates her own femininity when she does not do as she promised—instead, believing for the moment that Jim has become infected, she hesitates to attack Jim. The hesitation proves to be long enough for Selena to ascertain that Jim is uninfected, and the trio escapes as the soldiers are killed by more infected who have now swarmed their encampment. The trio again begins to defy gender stereotypes, something that allows them to survive. Hannah shows her automotive prowess by starting the vehicle they arrived in and using it to trap West with a zombie before rescuing Jim and Hannah. Jim is badly injured when the three must crash through the fortified gates in order to complete their escape, which we learn in a scene where Selena is using her medical prowess gleaned through her pharmacy training in order to restart his heart with adrenaline. Selena's skill is a combination of conventionally masculine and feminine behaviors in her use of advanced technology and caring. The film ends almost as it begins, with shots of Jim as the unconscious, and by implication, helpless, patient, but this time cared for by Selena and Hannah.

We also start to see that groups of humans who have the best long-term chances of survival are the ones whose members have flexible ideas about gender as well as race. In a world where everyone's talents are necessary, and one can never be sure about what sort of skill might be needed next, sexism and racism are archaic ways of thinking that prevent women and nonwhites from fully contributing to the survival of the group. For example, in Season Three of American Movie Classics's television series *The Walking Dead* (2010–), the group led by Rick at the prison is better able to survive than the Woodbury enclave, which is a familiar version of patriarchy where women defer to men because that is what they have done pre-apocalypse. When Andrea joins the Woodbury group, she is a skilled markswoman and also an experienced zombie fighter, as she has been surviving outside of the protective walls of this compound for nearly a year. Yet, the Governor, the Woodbury group's leader, constantly attempts to put Andrea in traditionally feminine caretaking roles rather than take advantage of her fighting prowess. Rick's group, on the other hand, is more open to letting others contribute more fully. Rick accepts women as his equals, using their fighting skills to help defend the group, and the muscular and dreadlocked Michonne, who is deadly with her katana, is one of their most effective fighters.

The 1990 remake of Romero's 1968 film is notable because it does more than represent men and women switching gender roles. Rather, it questions the assumptions about the inherent superiority of masculine leadership strategies. Romero's Barbara is transformed from a catatonic damsel in distress whose inability to even care for herself makes her a liability to the other would-be survivors into the smartest and most flexible person in the group. Romero's human characters in *Night of the Living Dead* (1968) all adhere to their appropriate gender roles: the women defer to male authority, and Barbara's complete helplessness is merely a demonstration of her extreme femininity. Romero's characters are artifacts of their time, a few years before Second Wave Feminism transformed how women thought about themselves, and how they would be represented in horror as sometimes better suited to fighting the monster than their male counterparts, as is the case in 1974's *The Texas Chainsaw Massacre*. Barbara in the 1990 remake of *Night of the Living Dead*, however, quickly overcomes her initial trauma at witnessing the reanimating dead kill her brother in order to become the most rational person in the group. Barbara is able to survive the night because she does not adhere to a script of gendered behavior. Rather, she combines the best and most useful characteristics of masculinity and femininity in order to figure out how to escape the farm house that is surrounded by the undead. As Ben and Cooper engage in masculine posturing about who controls access to parts of the house and who has the right to tell others what to do, Barbara learns how to fire a rifle and observes the undead, discovering that they are slow and stupid. Eventually, Ben and Cooper's disagreement about the best survival strategy boils over into violence, which allows the house's security to be breached: the two men exchange gunshots before sealing themselves off in the basement and attic, respectively, while zombies swarm the building. Barbara, meanwhile, strikes out on her own after thoughtfully listening to what each member of the household has to tell her about the zombies. Barbara recognizes that as zombies are a new phenomenon, no one person in the house is more authoritative about how to best combat them, and so she respectfully listens to the experience of each, regardless of sex or age, in order to synthesize her own strategy for dealing with the undead. As a result, Barbara survives the night and is able to return (too late) to rescue Ben and Cooper. However, in the new world that she has inherited, she must continue to figure out appropriate responses based on masculine and feminine strategies. The others who have survived the night include a camp of armed rednecks whose skill with firearms is commensurate with hegemonic masculinity, and the new civilization that they are in the process of establishing seems to re-create the same racist and sexist hierarchies from the old world.

Many monsters are gendered, even though they come in both sexes. The werewolf, for example, with its outsized desires for food, sex, and violence, is an extreme iteration of hegemonic masculinity. The witch, on the other hand, is more closely affiliated with stereotypical femininity in that her magical ability is most typically associated with the natural world. The zombie, by comparison, is a sexless monster whose different varieties are linked to typical masculinity or typical femininity. As a consequence, the zombie cannot be easily categorized as masculine or feminine, a situation that causes unease for the humans who encounter it and who are accustomed to understanding the world through binaries. The human characters (and sometimes the viewers and readers as well) are forced to question the validity of their own assumptions about gender and other binaries that they have used to make sense of their world.

See also: I Am Legend (Novel); *I Walked with a Zombie*; *Night of the Living Dead* (1990); *Plague of the Zombies, The*; Romero's Rules; Television; *28 Days Later* Series; *Walking Dead, The* (Television Series); *White Zombie*

June Michele Pulliam

GHOSTS

Ghosts, like zombies, represent the returned dead. Where the zombie is corporeal, the ghost traditionally ranges from being an invisible presence to a barely visible, unidentifiable shape. However, in some versions, particularly in film, the ghost can take a physical form. When it does so, this stretches the fine line between ghosts and zombies, especially if the ghost suffers from the same type of physical deterioration as the zombie. The Old English root of the word does not indicate any essential malevolence of the ghost or spirit as it refers to any spirit, good or evil.

The form of the ghost which most resembles the zombie is the revenant, sometimes referred to as the revenging revenant. This reanimated creature is typically the corpse of a deceased person who returns from the dead to haunt the living, usually the individual(s) who wronged the person while in life. Sometimes, the revenant, or a mob of revenants in some cases, will return to seek revenge not on the wrongdoer but on his or her descendants. For example, *The Fog* (1980) features a ghost mob of lepers who were killed for their gold; they return a century later as desiccated zombie-like ghosts who exact physical revenge. *A Nightmare on Elm Street* (1984) features Fred Krueger, covered in scars after he was burned to death, who seeks revenge against the children of his killers. Both the 1998 Japanese film *Ringu* and the American version *The Ring* (2002) tell the story of a demonic ghost which takes a physical form, moving very much like a zombie in the American version. In literature, revenging revenants who have zombie-like characteristics exist in Peter Straub's (born Peter Francis Straub, 1943–) *Ghost Story* (1979), which was made into a film in 1981. Dealing with these types of revenants is similar to ancestor worship, a practice normally used to prevent revenants, by offering sacrifices or using magic to banish the deceased so that they cannot return. Stephen King's novel *Pet Sematary* includes a ghost that resembles the zombie: when the ghost of Victor Pascow appears, his body takes the hideous shape it acquired at the moment of his death when he was hit by a car, his mangled flesh representing that of the zombie from director George Romero's *Night of the Living Dead* series of films. Another version of the ghost, the fetch, resembles the astral zombie of *The Boy Who Couldn't Die* (2005) in that it is the visible ghost or spirit (related to the doppelgänger) of a person who is still alive.

The difference between ghosts and zombies can likely be traced back to medieval Europe, where ghosts were viewed as more substantial or corporeal and were divided into two distinct categories. The souls of the dead were those ghosts that returned for a specific purpose, while demons or demonic ghosts were the returned dead who had no specific reason to be resurrected but existed only to torment the living. The zombie, if seen as a returned living person, would fall squarely into the second category.

See also: Asian Cinema; *Boy Who Couldn't Die, The*; *Night of the Living Dead* Series; *Fog, The*

Anthony J. Fonseca

GHOUL

The ghoul is of particular interest to the study of the modern zombie, as it represents one of the most influential sources for George Romero's flesh-eating monsters. While the ghoul has usually been presented as a living demon or monster that feasts on the flesh of dead humans, Romero merged the creature's characteristics with the undead existence of the vampire; the result is a walking-dead monster that eats both the blood and flesh of living humans, while communicating its condition in the process. The characters of *Night of the Living Dead* (1968) call the invasive monsters *ghouls* throughout the film.

The ghoul (*ghul* in Arabic, from *ghala*, "to seize") is a malevolent demon from Arabian folklore that likely first appeared in *The Thousand and One Nights,* particularly "The Story of Sidi Nouman" and "The History of Gherib and His Brother Agib." In early translations of the stories, Shehrazade tells the sultan that ghouls are demons that wander about the fields and surprise passengers, whom they kill and devour. She adds that if a ghoul fails to meet a traveler, it will dig up dead bodies and feed upon them. This depiction, based on the French translation by Antoine Galland (1646–1715), clearly influenced the conception of the ghoul in Western literature, including William Beckford's (born William Thomas Beckford, 1760–1844) Orientalist Gothic novel *Vathek* (1786); the 1813 poem "The Giaour" by Lord Byron (born George Gordon Byron, 1788–1824); and the fairy tale "The Wild Swans" (1838) by Hans Christian Andersen (1805–1875). In the United States, Edgar Allan Poe refers to ghouls in his poems "Ulalume" (1847) and "The Bells" (1848), and H.P. Lovecraft features types of ghouls in both "Pickman's Model" (1926) and the novella *The Dream-Quest of Unknown Kadath* (1926).

More recently, versions of the ghoul can be found in the *Ringworld* series (1970–2004) of Larry Niven (born Laurence van Cott Niven, 1938–), Chelsea Quinn Yarbro's (1942–) Saint-Germain cycle (1978–), Laurell K. Hamilton's (born Laurell Kaye Klein, 1963–) *Anita Blake* series (1993–), as well as *The Dresden Files* series (2000–) by Jim Butcher (1971–), and Neil Gaiman's (born Neil Richard Gaiman, 1960–) 2008 novel *The Graveyard Book,* to name just a few. An innocuous version of the ghoul can even be found in J.K. Rowling's (born Joanne Rowling, 1965–) *Harry Potter* novels, in which the creatures are treated like pests. While ghouls are surprisingly limited in cinema, except in *The Ghoul* (1975) and perhaps *Ghoulies* (1985) and its numerous sequels, they do appear in the television series *Supernatural* (2005–) and the made-for-TV movie *Ghoul* (2012), based on Brian Keene's (1967–) novel of the same name (2007). The term *ghoul* remains an acceptable designation for many zombies as well.

See also: "History of Gherib and His Brother Agib, The"; Lovecraft, H. P.; *Night of the Living Dead* Series; Poe, Edgar Allan; Romero, George; Television

Kyle William Bishop

GIL'S ALL FRIGHT DINER

Gil's All Fright Diner is A. Lee Martinez's (1973–) debut novel, published in 2005. When Duke, the werewolf, and Earl, the vampire, stop at the eatery of the title, all they want is a sandwich and a break from the petty annoyance of road trip togetherness. Of course, they barely have a chance to order when who should appear but the zombies. Not that they were not expecting it. They are supernatural beings after all. Loretta is not surprised by the appearance of zombies in her diner, but she is surprised when the burly-looking customer named Duke turns into a werewolf and quickly dispatches them. In desperation, she offers Duke and his friend Earl $100 if they will stay and help her with her little zombie problem.

Meanwhile, she also enlists them to install a new gas line for the diner. Having nothing better to do, the two take up Loretta on her offer and move into the storage room. After getting settled, Duke sends Earl out to investigate the graveyard while he gets started. Meanwhile, teen bombshell Tammy, or Mistress Lilith, Queen of Night, as her followers (consisting of one hormone-riddled teenage boy named Jimmy) like to call her, cannot understand why Loretta would not flee in terror from her zombies the way any normal person would. Loretta cannot unleash the apocalypse if she cannot get access to The Gate, inconveniently located in the middle of Gil's Diner. Grudgingly, Earl goes to the graveyard where he talks with Cathy, the guardian of the graveyard. She informs him that not only has the graveyard been emptied by the zombie uprising, but, in fact, far more zombies have appeared than she can account for. There are simply more zombies than there were graves. Alarmed, Earl consults with Duke, and they conclude there is a malevolent force at work that seems to be focused on Loretta and the diner. Soon the small Southern town of Rockwood is awash in ghosts, bovine zombies, ghouls, tentacles, and ancient gods. To add to the fun, Earl and Cathy fall head over heels for each other and experience love among the headstones.

Mistress Lilith becomes more and more frustrated; Duke and Earl find a way to fight back. In addition, when raising the dead does not drive off Loretta and her new employees, Tammy has to resort to drastic measures. Her new diabolical plan includes trapping the undead Gil's spirit, forcing him to help her with her diabolical plan. As she conspires to rain down terror on the world, the fearless heroes, heroine, and Cathy's ghostly terrier race to save the day from the forces of evil. As the novel ends, Earl and Cathy ride off into the sunset, accompanied by her beloved dog and Duke. Things are not so pleasant for Mistress Lilith, who is now the guardian of the graveyard, trapped with her loyal minion, Jimmy.

This humorous urban fantasy novel published by Tor was a 2006 American Library Association's Alex Award winner. It was optioned to be made into a movie in 2009. In 2010, the book was challenged for censorship in North Virginia, but officials unanimously voted to keep the title on library shelves. Martinez has 10 traditionally published novels, as well as numerous short stories known for their comedic and traditional pulp adventure elements.

See also: Apocalypse; Comedy; Young Adult Fiction

Alicia Ahlvers

"GILGAMESH"

"Gilgamesh" is an epic poem from Mesopotamia which follows the mythical exploits of Gilgamesh, historically the fifth king of the Dynasty of Kingship of Uruk (modern-day Iraq), believed to have reigned circa 2800 BC. In the epic, Gilgamesh is revered as a demigod, a great king, and a mighty warrior, but he is also a tyrant. In response to the complaints of the people, the goddess Aruru creates Enkidu, who lives in the wilderness as a confidant to the animals there, causing grief for the farmers and trappers. Enkidu is to become Gilgamesh's friend and equal, thus ending his tyranny. When Enkidu makes love to Shamhat, a woman that Gilgamesh has sent to seduce him, Enkidu's animal friends forsake him. Shamhat takes Enkidu to Uruk, where he prevents Gilgamesh from lying with a bride on her wedding night. Gilgamesh and Enkidu afterward fight, then become friends and go on an expedition into the Forest of Cedar. With the aid of the sun god Shamash, they kill Humbaba, the guardian the gods placed in the forest. Once back in Uruk, Gilgamesh insults the goddess Ishtar by refusing her advances, citing how poorly she has treated past lovers.

The trope of the undead appears when Ishtar asks her father, Anu, to let her send the Bull of Heaven to kill Gilgamesh, threatening to raise the dead to devour and outnumber the living if her father does not allow her to so use the Bull. Ishtar sends the Bull of Heaven, which Gilgamesh and Enkidu kill. Enkidu then dies after a 12-day sickness; his demise is an act of retribution by the gods for the deaths of Humbaba and the Bull. After Enkidu's funeral, Gilgamesh sets out to meet the immortal Uta-napishti to learn his secret. He follows the path of the sun and crosses the Waters of Death. Uta-napishti challenges him to go a week without sleep, but Gilgamesh fails and realizes that death is inevitable. However, Uta-napishti tells Gilgamesh to dive under the sea for a plant that has the power of rejuvenation. Gilgamesh does so, but the plant is stolen by a serpent. Gilgamesh returns home, defeated, and shows the ferryman the walls around the city of Uruk, the one thing for which he will be remembered.

In the epic, it is clear that power over life and death belongs to the gods. Ishtar threatens, apparently convincingly, to single-handedly release all of the dead from the netherworld to eat the flesh of the living. This threat is nearly identical to the threat of zombie apocalypse that Ishtar (or Inanna in the Sumerian) makes in the tale of her descent into the underworld found in other myths of the goddess. Ishtar's threat also bears a striking resemblance to the threat of the dead returning from hell to walk on the earth in George Romero's *Dawn of the Dead* (1978). This indicates that the concept of resurrected human corpses as flesh-eating monsters has existed in nearly the same form for thousands of years.

See also: Cannibalism; Ishtar; *Night of the Living Dead* Series

Derek Manuel

GOLEM

The golem is an animated, anthropomorphic creature in Jewish folklore created entirely from inanimate matter, usually earth or clay. In their strictest iteration, they are created only by holy men who are close to God and therefore understood the power of creation of life. Like zombies, golem are mute and lack free will; however, the golem is comparable to the mummy and the Voodoo zombie in that it normally must follow the bidding of one person, and in some accounts, the golem can be made to perform manual labor.

The creation of the golem is comparable to the making of the *jiang shi,* or Asian hopping vampire, a zombie-like creature that can be controlled by notes posted onto its forehead. Similarly, the power of language is used to create the golem: animation of the golem can be achieved by a shem, or a piece of paper, that contains various letters of the Hebrew alphabet, which is either inserted into the golem's mouth or affixed to its forehead to bring to life the humanoid mass of clay. In some myths, the golem can be controlled or deactivated by changing the spell on its shem. The golem is the most popular artificial creature created by magic in Jewish mysticism. The word golem appears once in the Bible and appears in the Talmud as well. One legend has it that the prophet Jeremiah animated a golem.

"The Golem of Prague" is the most famous golem narrative. In it, Rabbi Judah Loew ben Bezalel (1520–1609) created a golem named Josef (aka Yossele) out of clay from the banks of the Vltava River to defend the Prague ghetto from anti-Semitic attacks; he used a mystical incantation and a shem to give it life. In literature, Gustav Meyrink's (born Gustave Meyer, 1868–1932) 1914 novel *Der Golem* is loosely inspired by golem folktales, and it in turn led to the filming of Paul Wegener's (1874–1948) Golem series, including *The Golem* (1920) and Julien Duvivier's (1896–1967) *Le Golem* (1936), a French and Czechoslovakian sequel to the Wegener film. Related to the golem and zombie is Mary Shelley's (born Mary Wollstonecraft Godwin, 1797–1851) classic novel *Frankenstein, or The Modern Prometheus* (1818), which features Victor Frankenstein's creature, a reanimated corpse made of parts of various bodies. In the early 20th century, several plays, novels, movies, musicals, and a ballet have their basis on the story of the golem, including Karel Capek's (1890–1938) play *R.U.R.* (1920), Isaac Bashevis Singer's (1902–1991) *The Golem* (1969), and Marge Piercy's novel *He, She and It* (1991). A golem museum can be found in the Jewish Quarter of Prague.

See also: Asian Cinema; *Jiang Shi*; Mummies

Anthony J. Fonseca

GOON, THE

The Goon is a comic book character created by Eric Powell (1975–). The character, a seemingly indestructible bruiser, visually resembles a blend of the Marvel comic book character The Thing, created by Stan Lee (born Stanley Martin Lieber, 1922–) and Jack Kirby (born Jacob Kurtzberg, 1917–1994), and Popeye, the creation of E. C. Segar (born Elzie Crisler Segar, 1894–1938). The Goon's partially scarred face also recalls the lead character of *Phantom of the Opera,* by Gaston Leroux (born Gaston Louis Alfred Leroux, 1868–1927). Assisted by his loyal sidekick, the diminutive and feisty Franky, The Goon is a force to be reckoned with in his strange world, the secret power behind a far-reaching and prosperous criminal organization. Although it bears similarities to our own world, The Goon's reality is inhabited by more than a few supernatural and preternatural creatures, including undead mobsters, wicker men, ghosts, ghouls, goblins, bog monsters, vampires, cannibals (aka "hobos"), aliens, robots (aka Brunos), mad scientists, mages, necromancers, and zombies.

The Goon debuted in a four-page preview in the March 1998 issue of *Dreamwalker* (#0), published by Avatar Press. The character starred in his own book (also from Avatar), but the run ended after three issues and was collected by Dark Horse Books in graphic novel format in 2004 under the title *Rough Stuff*. Powell self-published the character's second series, with four issues collected in *Nothin' but Misery*. The third (and ongoing) series has been published by Dark Horse Comics since 2003. Powell has written and drawn each series. He is a five-time Eisner Award winner, picking up his first in 2004 and his latest in 2008.

One of The Goon's major adversaries is the man known as The Zombie Priest, a necromancer and the creator and commander of a large army of zombies. Like Haitian Voodoo zombies, The Zombie Priest's zombies are for the most part brainless: The Goon and Franky disparagingly refer to them as slack jaws. They are capable only of carrying out the orders of their maker. Unsuccessful in his personal struggles with The Goon, The Zombie Priest has had to ally himself with other denizens of the text's odd world. One such ally is The Communist Airborne Mollusk Militia, a squadron of giant octopi who traveled by personal zeppelins. The Goon has also faced off with the Hags, whose benign appearance conceals their true, bloodthirsty nature. These despicable creatures nurture the strange beings known as Chug-Heads, the malformed progeny of their leader, Mother Corpse. The dwarf-like, potato-headed Chug-Heads are capable of merging into one another to form a larger, more deadly version of their race. Ultimately, The Zombie Priest comes to rely on Chug-Heads over the less-effective zombies. In 2008, an animated version was commissioned by the award-winning Blur Studio, to be directed by David Fincher and written by Eric Powell. As of 2014, the film is still in the early production stage.

See also: Graphic Novels and Comics; Haiti; Voodoo

Hank Wagner

GORDON, STUART

Stuart Gordon (1947–) is an American director, writer, and producer of horror and science fiction films who has adapted H. P. Lovecraft stories to the screen. One of his films, *Re-Animator* (1985), is based on Lovecraft's collection of stories, "Herbert West—Reanimator." These six stories, and Gordon's film, are about a scientist who attempts to reanimate dead bodies, with various levels of success and horrifying side effects. Gordon had an early stint in television, and at one point attempted unsuccessfully to interest networks in a series the Herbert West tales. Producer

American director Stuart Gordon is known for his film adaptations of the works of H. P. Love-craft, including *Reanimator* (1985), a comic and gory rendition of "Herbert West—Reanimator." (Associated Press)

Brian Yuzna (1949–) convinced him to make a film instead. Gordon used his commercial art background and special effects (with makeup) experience to create the film's gory effects.

Re-Animator is a cult horror comedy known for its extreme gore. It begins at the University of Zurich Institute of Medicine, where West gets into trouble for reanimating his mentor, a professor at the school. He is forced to leave, and comes to the United States, where he attends Lovecraft's fictional Miskatonic University. He rents a room with a basement, which he turns into a laboratory, but he soon finds himself in trouble again, running afoul of a professor and his roommate's fiancée, after he reanimates his roommate's cat. This all leads to another reanimation in the local morgue, the death and reanimation of the school's dean, a decapitation and reanimation of the headless body (and the head), more zombies, an eventual showdown among zombies and a headless corpse, and a face-off between West and a mutated zombie. The film ends with a nod to the Rom Zom Com, as West's roommate is forced to reanimate his fiancée, who has been killed by one of the undead corpses. The film did rather well, grossing over $543,000 in its opening weekend and ultimately earning more than twice what it cost for production. *Re-Animator* became an international hit, earning acclaim at Cannes and the distinction of first horror film to be included in the London Film Festival.

Gordon also directed three other films based on Lovecraft: *From Beyond* (1986), *Castle Freak* (1995), and *Dagon* (2001). In 2009, he directed a one-man theatrical show called *Nevermore: An Evening with Edgar Allan Poe*. In 2011, he produced, directed, and partially scripted the highly successful *Re-Animator: The Musical*. In 2005 and 2007, he directed two segments for the *Masters of Horror* Showtime series. One was based on Lovecraft's "Dreams in the Witch-House" and the other on Edgar Allan Poe's "The Black Cat."

See also: Comedy; Cult Film; "Herbert West—Reanimator"; Lovecraft, H. P.; *Re-Animator* Series; Television

Anthony J. Fonseca

GRANT, MIRA

Mira Grant (born Seanan McGuire, 1978–) was raised in northern California and studied folklore and herpetology at the University of California, Berkeley. She is known for *Newsflash*, a trilogy of political zombie novels with the titles *Feed* (2010), *Deadline* (2011), and *Blackout* (2012). *Blackout* won the 2013 Hugo Award for Best Novel, and Grant received a record five Hugo nominations that year.

Newsflash merges Grant's love of zombies with the online world. The series is set in 2039. The world has seen the rise of the zombie, and the human population has adapted, in large part thanks to the blogging community which was instrumental in exposing the zombie infection and providing the general population with survival strategies. Bloggers have, in fact, become the investigative journalists of this new age. The *Newsflash* series features a brother-sister blogger duo, Georgia and Shaun Mason. Georgia and Shaun's blogging team, including their friend Buffy, has become famous for documenting life after zombies because of their journalistic integrity. It also has been selected as the official bloggers for presidential candidate Peter Ryman. As they tour with the candidate, Georgia becomes increasingly aware of government secrets about the zombie infection and determines to expose the truth.

Before the release of the third book in the trilogy, *Blackout,* Grant released a free e-book alternate ending for *Feed* entitled *Fed*. The book can be found on her Facebook page or on Orbit's, her publisher's, website. Grant's *Newsflash* series is known for its characters' awareness of the zombie mythology. Grant explores not only the reality of living with a deadly contagion threat in everyday life but also the psychological damage that can be done because of fear and paranoia.

Grant's first novel was published in 2009, and since that time, she has accumulated a number of science fiction awards, including five Pegasus awards, one Hugo award, the John W. Campbell Award for Best New Writer (in 2010 for her urban fantasy/detective story "Rosemary and Rue"), and one Fancast Award, not to mention a truly impressive number of nominations in every category. Grant was an inductee into the 2012 Darrell Awards Hall of Fame. In addition, a 2010 National Public Radio fan poll ranked *Feed* as one of the top thriller novels of all time. Grant released a new series, *Parasitology*, in 2013. Grant is also a musician with three albums, whose music is categorized as filk, which is folk music with a science fiction or fantasy theme. Grant has written *October Daye* and *In Cryptid*, two successful series, under the name Seanan McGuire, as well as many short stories and works of nonfiction. Grant's short fiction often appears in *Apex, Fantasy Magazine,* and *Lightspeed.*

See also: Apocalypse; Science Fiction

Alicia Ahlvers

GRAPHIC NOVELS AND COMICS

Graphic novels and comics differ only in the preservation concerns of their format. In short, the graphic novel is intended to be less ephemeral than the comic book. Comic books are printed on cheap newsprint, while graphic novels are printed as either softcover or hardcover, on high-quality paper. As a result, graphic novels tend to cost more than comic books do. However, both comic books and graphic novels can introduce epic zombie series, with recurring characters and literary themes, as well as high-quality art work.

The most popular graphic novel zombie series, as of 2013, is Robert Kirkman's epic *The Walking Dead* (2003–), which contained 126 issues in 2014. *The Walking Dead* follows the adventures of Sheriff Rick Grimes and his friends and family as they try to survive in a post-apocalyptic world where the dead have begun returning to life. The series is notable because of its length, not just in the number of books, but in how long it follows its characters through a hellish world where it might seem that character growth and plot variation are not possible. Kirkman's characters, however, continue to evolve. Each day brings new challenges since all of the stabilizing institutions of civilization have broken down, and the survivors are running out of bare necessities that they could have easily depended on in the pre-zombie world, such as a food, even the simplest of modern medicines, and clothing. Moreover, Rick and his friends have had to learn to do things that would have been morally repugnant to them, such as kill other humans who would harm them, and even ignore the pleas of those in distress as every new person in the group is at the very least someone with a claim on their diminishing resources. The series is drawn in black and white, a decision the self-published author made in the beginning due to cost considerations (it is cheaper to produce a black-and-white graphic novel than it is one in full color.) The black-and-white drawings, however, are also reminiscent of George Romero's groundbreaking zombie film *Night of the Living Dead* (1968), which was also filmed in black and white since the young filmmaker could not afford at the time to produce his movie in color, which was still very expensive. As a result, Kirkman persisted in drawing the series in black and white, even after securing a publisher and achieving sufficient popularity with fans to publish in color. Kirkman's *The Walking Dead* has become enormously popular, particularly after the American Movie Classics network made a television series of the same name based on it of the same name, which first aired in 2010. There are now several novelizations based on the graphic novel and television series, as well as video games and even action figures.

Other notable, though less-well-known, zombie graphic novels include *Crossed,* another post-apocalyptic series. While Kirkman is clearly influenced by Romero, the *Crossed* series channels Danny Boyle's *28 Days later,* as its zombies are the living who become infected with a virus that causes them to both become impervious to their own suffering and have their wills effaced by the drive to harm others. However, the infected zombies are different from Boyle's in that they retain enough sentience to enjoy the suffering of their victims, and in fact are able to make plan elaborate tortures for them. The crossed, as they are called, as the infection causes a group of boils to erupt on the face in a cruciform shape, having an appearance that is more of a diseased animal than human. The infection causes the crossed to turn on loved ones, even going so far as to hunt them down in order to rape, torture, and kill them with the ferocity of a werewolf. In this fictional universe, the infection has spread rapidly throughout the world, toppling governments and leaving the uninfected to survive as best as they can in the ensuing chaos. The graphic novel series features scenes of horrific violence perpetrated by the crossed, such as the crucifixion of a priest, another scene of the uninfected being gleefully flung to their deaths in a moving plane, and crossed children bludgeoning to death by a mall Santa with their toys. The first 10 issues of *Crossed* were written by Garth Ennis (1970–). However, other breakaway issues were written by David Lapham (no date available). Ennis also wrote a spin-off series, *Crossed: Badlands,* as well as produced a web comic of *Crossed.*

Other comics and graphic novel series offer different degrees of playfulness with the zombie theme. The *Raise the Dead* series is another narrative set in a post-apocalyptic zombie world. But what makes this series unique is the artwork, which re-creates American popular culture icons as zombies, including a zombie Andy Warhol portrait of Marilyn Monroe, a zombie photo of a soldier kissing a girl in Times Square on V-J Day, and the Coppertone tan girl having her bikini bottoms tugged down by a zombie rather than a puppy. The *Raise the Dead* series is by the husband and wife team John Reppion and Leah Moore. Moore is the daughter of graphic novelist Alan Moore. The *Revival* series posits yet another apocalyptic scenario, though on a smaller scale, when the dead return to life on one day in rural Wisconsin. The resulting situation causes religious and political conflicts between the living and the revived dead. Other graphic novel series are based more clearly on films or literary works, such as the *Night of the Living Dead* graphic novels, created by various artists, or the graphic novel version of *Pride and Prejudice and Zombies.*

Sometimes it can be difficult to tell the difference between a graphic novel and a comic. This is compounded by the fact that some graphic novel series begin as comics, and once several issues achieve popularity, they are rebound by the publisher into a graphic novel format. Comics have featured zombies ever since 1944. It was then that the DC comics character Solomon Grundy was introduced to the American public. Grundy was introduced as a zombie super villain in the October 1944 edition of *All-American Comics* #61, pitted against the original Green Lantern. The next appearance of a zombie in comics came in an unexpected venue, Disney's *Donald Duck* comics. Bombie the Zombie first appeared in the story in *Donald*

Duck Four Color #238. A zombie sent by a witch doctor named Foola Zoola to get revenge on Scrooge McDuck for using imperialist tactics to destroy his village, Bombie stalks Scrooge for decades, pursuing Scrooge to the North Pole, an iceberg near the RMS *Titanic*, and finally to the isle of Ripan Taro.

Zombies more or less fell out of fashion in cartoons and comics, due to the Comics Code Authority (CCA), a self-policing organization formed by the Comics Magazine Association of America in the 1950s, which became the main censor for the U.S. comic book industry in the 20th century. Despite this, in 1973, Marvel Comics reintroduced the zombie character Simon William Garth in the black-and-white series *Tales of the Zombie* (1973–1975). Garth, a Voodoo and undead zombie rolled into one, had originally been introduced in 1953, just before the CCA gained power. Marvel Comics abandoned the CCA by 2001. Since 2005, Marvel Comics has published *Marvel Zombies*, an apocalyptic series in which Marvel superheroes have been zombified. Meanwhile, DC Comics, which had introduced the Black Lantern Corps (the animated corpses of DC metahumans), continued producing zombie comics through the imprint Zuda Comics.

In the last decade, zombies have made their way into many comedy horror cartoons and comics. *Tales from the Crypt's Diary of a Stinky Dead Kid,* published in 2009, stars the series' trademark characters, the Vault-Keeper, the Old Witch, and The Crypt-Keeper, as they tell parody stories, including a zombie version of *Diary of a Wimpy Kid* (2007), one of which includes his battle against an evil presence in *Guitar Hero. The Hardy Boys* series offered its own zombie fare in 2010 with the issue *Crawling with Zombies,* where an alien plague turns teenagers into the mindless, shambling undead. As of 2013, some of the top zombie-oriented comics titles included the aforementioned series, as well as the following: *The Victorian Undead*; *iZombie*; *Star Trek: Infestation*; *Jesus Hates Zombies* (featuring *Lincoln Hates Werewolves*); *Zombies vs Cheerleaders*; *A Very . . . Zombie Christmas*; *Zombies vs Robots*; and *Black Rio.* The zombie metaphor has even made its way into the comic-strip industry, where a zombie strip is one whose creator has died (or retired), and yet continues to exist in publication, drawn and scripted by others.

See also: Apocalypse; Bombie the Zombie; Comedy; *Marvel Zombies*; *Night of the Living Dead* Series; *Tales from the Crypt* (Comic); Television; *28 Days Later* Series; *Walking Dead, The* (Comic)

June Michele Pulliam and Anthony J. Fonseca

GREATSHELL, WALTER

Walter Greatshell (1962–) is an artist, painter, and young adult author known for his *Xombies* trilogy, a series of darkly comic novels that includes *Xombies* (2004), which was later retitled *Apocalypse Blues* (2009), *Apocalypticon* (2010), and *Apocalypso* (2011). The novels concentrate more on the stories of the survivors of a zombie apocalypse than on the zombies themselves.

According to Greatshell, *Apocalypse Blues* was originally to be titled Dead Sea, a title the author himself preferred because of the setting of the novel (a submarine during a zombie apocalypse), as well as the references to George Romero, the Dead Sea Scrolls, and the menstrual cycle (the X in Xombies refers to the female chromosome). *Apocalypticon* continues the story told in the first novel, the saga of the USS *No-Name*, an Ohio-Class submarine which becomes the vehicle for survivors during the apocalypse. Like the previous novel, it is more concerned with those survivors, namely the doctor whose research helped spawn the plague, a navy submarine commander, a BMX champion, and the series heroine, and teenager Lulu Pangloss, who is immune to the mutation. *Apocalypso* finishes the tale of human mutation, as Pangloss and submarine crew wander the world looking for survivors who they can convert into a new race of humans that can fight the xombie infestation. Greatshell's xombies are virtually impossible to kill; have bright blue skin; are fast, quick, strong, and bestial; and they can continue to attack when body parts are chopped off. Their body parts retain sentience and can continue to attack. Generally speaking, they are sentient beings, often even intelligent beings.

Greatshell currently lives in Providence, Rhode Island, where he continues to write (sometimes under the name W. G. Marshall) what he considers satirical horror, while dabbling in freelance illustration (children's books, comics, and graphic novels). His other novels include *Mad Skills* (2010), *Terminal Island* (2012), *Enormity* (2012), and *The Leaf Blower* (2013), and he has contributed to two anthologies, *The Undead, Volume 3: Flesh Feast* (2007) and *The Living Dead 2* (2010).

See also: Children's Books; Sentience; *Xombies* Trilogy; Young Adult Fiction

Anthony J. Fonseca

GRINDHOUSE

Grindhouse (2007) is the theatrical double feature release of the films *Planet Terror,* directed by Robert Rodriguez and *Death Proof,* directed by Quentin Tarantino (born Quentin Jerome Tarantino, 1963–). *Planet Terror* specifically is concerned with the living dead. It is a zombie film rife with references to the zombie canon, especially the first two *Return of the Living Dead* films (1985, 1988).

Rodriguez's zombies are created by chemicals contained in barrels that release infectious gas, and the film involves suspicious military personnel squaring off against innocent (and colorful) townsfolk. Sick verbal jokes, such as the line "this one's a no-brainer," stomach-churning special effects, and absurd action exploitation scenes, such as when the character Cherry Darling, played by Rose McGowan (born Rose Arianna McGowan, 1973–), gets her leg amputated and replaced with a machine gun, play up the dark, over-the-top humor in the film. The script is known for its slick writing, which invites serious scholarly study and academic interest in pastiche, or in the genre's penchant for post-9/11 critique of military extremism. The film simulates the feeling of attending what were called the grindhouse theaters and drive-ins of the 1970s—which specialized in exploitation films, especially pornography, martial arts films, and slasher horror. It uses cheap production values, resulting in scratched film and missing reels, especially those scenes containing sex, in this case complemented by apology inserts from the management. It

Cherry Darling (Rose McGowan), whose leg has been amputated and replaced with a machine gun, squares off against vicious military personnel and zombies in the film *Grindhouse* (2007). (Dimension Films/Photofest)

also contains false trailers for nonexistent exploitation films, as does its *Grindhouse* double features. These trailers showcase fake films by well-known filmmakers.

In 2007, *Planet Terror* and *Death Proof* were released separately on home video, delaying the theatrical cut in the United States until 2010. Whether the double feature was actually a single artistic product is a question for debate, but clues such as cross-casting and allusions that link the storylines together, combined with the double feature release strategy, make it seem that both films were meant to be viewed together. This is fitting for two films that rely heavily on packaging. *Death Proof*'s title refers not to the undead but to how antagonist Stuntman Mike, played by Kurt Russell (born Kurt Vogel Russell, 1951–), feels when he is driving one of his specially rigged stunt cars. These cars are designed to keep him alive at the wheel, while the women he lures into their passenger seats literally get torn limb from limb during high-speed collisions. Unluckily for Mike, a group of tough women share his interest in muscle cars, and after a slow build, they chase him down. The conclusion implies that exploitation films no longer need aging tough men as long as young, tough women have an appreciation for action exploitation. Grindhouse cinema, like the zombie, is death proof.

See also: Existentialism; Gender; *Return of the Living Dead* Series

L. Andrew Cooper

HAITI

Haiti, despite being the birthplace of many celebrated artists, writers, and intellectuals of progressive ideals, is still defined by its history as a savage nation: it is highly militaristic and hostile to the liberalizing effects of representative government. To a large extent, its citizens are enslaved by what most Western cultures would view as a superstitious worship of strange gods. Once declared as a fourth world by Mother Teresa, Haiti is a country trapped in a recurring nightmare of its own tragic history, one that has been perpetually shaped by its legendary revolution and subsequent exploitation by foreign and domestic powers. Haiti is also, with its long history of slavery and economic exploitation by outside forces, is the birthplace of the zombie, a creature whose single most defining characteristic is its lack of free will.

Upon discovering the island of Hispaniola in 1492, of which the present-day Haiti occupies the western third, Christopher Columbus remarked in his diary that the Taino Indians that he found there were ideally suited for enslavement. Before the island was taken over by the Spanish crown, the indigenous population of Hispaniola may have been in the millions. By the time Spain surrendered the colony of Saint-Domingue to France in 1697, only 30,000 Indians remained. The Spanish began importing African slaves as early as 1517, a practice that the French colonial administration pursued in earnest. By the eve of the Haitian Revolution (1791–1804), the population of African slaves would be over 450,000, compared to a free population of 55,000. With slave labor, the colony of Saint-Domingue quickly became the prime producer of sugar in the New World, exporting as much as 192 million pounds by 1791. The mechanized nature of sugar production, with its rigid production timetable and the inherent dangers of the refining process, made Saint-Domingue one of the most barbarous and cruel slave regimes in history. Slaves were abducted from the Kingdom of Dahomey and other communities adjacent to the Gulf of Benin, including the Adja, Ewe, and Fon. After a harrowing Atlantic passage—where one in seven would perish from dysentery—most slaves were put to work in the northern province of Saint-Domingue, where savannah was plowed and rivers diverted to cultivate sugar cane on a massive scale. Those who did not succumb to tropical disease and could endure the torture of captivity faced the prospect of being flogged for disobedience, maimed by the iron blades of the sugar mill, or worked to death in the field.

Depending on their origin, the African slaves spoke many different languages. They bridged their respective language barriers by creating Kréyol, a language consisting of French, Breton, and African tribal languages. They also integrated their native tribal religions with their masters' Catholicism to form Voodoo, which provided a cultural narrative grounded in the identity of Haitians as survivors of slavery and ultimately as victors over colonial oppression. The Vatican decreed that all slaves had to be properly catechized, but the masters seldom demanded anything beyond the customary baptism of infants. This unintentional neglect gave the Voodoo faithful an opportunity to fully articulate a belief system that would inspire trust and loyalty among large networks of slaves throughout the colony.

In 1789, the Parisian demand for "Liberté! Égalité! Fraternité!" was heard by Haitian ears as well as European. A growing upper class of free mixed-race Haitians fought for equal rights by appealing to the French crown but to no avail. In 1791, they joined forces with African slaves in planning a complex insurrection that would synchronize the murders of planters, overseers, and their families, with an immense scorched earth campaign. Armed with cannons provided by the mulatto landowners, the insurrection proved a ghastly success. The revolutionary leader Toussaint L'Ouverture (born François-Dominique Toussaint L'Ouverture, 1743–1803), a former African slave, united his countrymen in a military and political movement to banish the colonial powers from the island. After defeating the Spanish and British occupational armies by 1798, L'Ouverture was captured by the French who invaded Haiti with a 50,000 man army. The defeat of Napoleon's army (1804) by yellow fever and L'Ouverture's lieutenants marked the end of the revolution. By then, almost all white landowners were either dead or in exile. With the master class extirpated, the immense military apparatus created by the revolution quickly established itself as the ultimate authority. Officers in the Haitian army and their political allies were given substantial landholdings. A minority of mulatto freedmen and African military leaders gained enormous power, as Haiti's economy depended on the productivity of the sugar and coffee plantations. The African peasantry was forced into labor and most of them returned to work on the plantations where they had once been enslaved. In addition to these internal conflicts, in 1825, Charles X of France (born Charles Philippe, 1757–1836) extorted an indemnity of 150 million francs. Payment on this loan and many others exhausted the national treasury, extended the feudalist labor scheme, and destabilized the country. In 1843, a second revolution rocked Haiti, which experienced persistent political chaos and military coup d'états throughout the 19th century, as one military strongman after another rose and fell in lugubrious succession.

Haiti's immense international trade debt and strategic location attracted the interest of the United States. Using the recent assassination of the Haitian president as a pretext for invasion, the Woodrow Wilson administration dispatched the marines in 1915, and setup a sham government that organized all able-bodied men into forced labor battalions. The ultimate goal was the destruction of a guerilla army and the conversion of Haiti into an economic client state, which was best accomplished by installing a dictator that would exercise power for its own sake rather than for civil governance. By the time the marines left in 1934, Haiti's government was much more efficient in the pursuit and prosecution of anti-establishment forces. President Francois Duvalier (1907–1971) and his successors used surveillance networks and death squads to squelch dissent, while a small group of political insiders functioned as an ersatz bureaucracy that was actually a front for filching financial spoils. These practices have now become a time-honored political tradition, most recently evidenced by the chronic disappearance of international aid packages during the earthquake crisis of 2010, which resulted in over 230,000 deaths.

Against this historical and political backdrop, Haitian folk culture is informed by the figure of the zombie. The zombie is, among other things, a symbolic or metaphoric personification of the colonial slave culture. During the American occupation of Haiti in the 20th century, tales of zombies proliferated in the United States. *The Magic Island* (1929), by W. B. Seabrook; the film *White Zombie* (1932), directed by Victor Halperin (born Victor Hugo Halperin, 1895–1983); and the memoir *Tell My Horse* (1936), by Zora Neale Hurston all reinforce the popular image of Haiti as a place where one can witness zombies trundling along dusty rural roads, in thrall to their master, the Voodoo

Felicia Felix-Mentor is the alleged zombie photographed by Zora Neale Hurston during her visits to Haiti in 1936, while she was doing research for her book *Tell My Horse*. (Courtesy of June Michele Pulliam)

sorcerer. Ever since the revolution, Haitians have attempted to overcome powers that would hold the country captive. The figure of the zombie is intertwined with Haiti's history as a slave colony. Indeed, to be a zombie is in essence to be a slave for eternity, and Haitian folk culture resounds with references to the drudgery of those doomed to repeat the routines of their hellish lives.

See also: Africa; Class; "Country of Comers-Back, The"; Hurston, Zora Neale; Race; Seabrook, W. B.; Voodoo; *White Zombie*

Michael E. Matthews

HAMMER FILM PRODUCTIONS

Hammer Films is a production company formed in 1934 by London jeweler and comedian William Hinds (1887–1957), who performed under the stage name Will Hammer. Appropriately, Hammer's first feature was a comedy, *The Public Life of Henry the Ninth*. Owing to constant problems, bankruptcy, and total liquidation in 1937, Hammer Studios ceased production during World War II. The company's foray into horror occurred in 1955 with the television serial *The Quatermass*

Xperiment. In 1957, it released its first horror film, *The Curse of Frankenstein,* and followed that success with *Dracula* (1958).

Hammer Studios' most notable films relating to the zombie are *The Mummy* (1959) and *The Plague of the Zombies* (1966). Hammer Studios produced *The Mummy* after it acquired the rights to Universal Studios monsters in the 1950s. Hammer Studios' *The Mummy* is loosely based on Universal Studios' *The Mummy* (1932), as well as Universal's sequels *The Mummy's Hand* (1940), *The Mummy's Tomb* (1942), and *The Mummy's Ghost* (1944). However, Hammer Studios' mummy Kharis is more like a zombie than is Universal Studios' mummy in that he is not only a reanimated corpse, but he is also completely under the control of the man who has possession of The Scroll of Life through which he is commanded.

Hammer Studios' *The Plague of the Zombies,* however, was more directly related to the creature. Set in a Cornish village in the 1800s, the film chronicles a mysterious plague that approaches epidemic. A local physician, Peter Thompson, sends for outside help in the form of his former professor and mentor, Sir James Forbes, who arrives with his daughter. Empty coffins of the recently buried lead the doctors to zombies of the Haitian variety. Clive Hamilton, the local squire who has just returned from Haiti, uses these zombies to labor in his family's tin mine, which had fallen into disuse after living locals refused to work in this dangerous industry. After a fire is set by the doctors, the plague is ended. In this small-budget production, the eeriest scene may be Peter Thompson's recently dead wife's rising from her coffin, not with the typical confused shamble and mindless eyes of the zombie but with a sensuality, power, sexual hunger, and the subtlest flicker of a smile, apparently a recognition of the living, which includes her husband, before she is decapitated by a spade. The scene also alludes to one in the 1897 classic *Dracula,* by Bram Stoker (born Abraham Stoker, 1847–1912), where the undead Lucy rises from her grave with a seductive smile on her lips, inviting her horrified fiancé to kiss her.

Hammer dominated 1960s and early 1970s horror with vampire, science fiction, and monster movies, and its highest grossing (when adjusted for inflation) film was from 1966, *One Million Years B.C.* The studio halted production a second time from the mid-1980s until 2000 after Hammer's once-novel approaches had become dated; they were accused of tawdry cheapness in sets and of attiring actresses in near-pornographic costumes, and contracts were not reissued with prominent and profit-assuring female stars such as Ursula Andress (1936–) and Raquel Welch (born Jo Raquel Tejada, 1940–). The studio flickered back to life recently, with major horror films including *Let Me In* (a 2010 English remake of the Swedish film *Let the Right One In*), *The Resident* (2011), and *The Woman in Black* (2012). In 2013, Hammer Studios is slated to produce an adaptation of Cherie Priest's (1975–) 2010 Hugo Best Novel Award nominee *Boneshaker,* a steampunk zombie novel.

See also: Haiti; *Mummy, The; Plague of the Zombies, The;* Universal Studios; Voodoo

Danel Olson

HANDLING THE UNDEAD

Handling the Undead is a 2005 horror novel by Swedish author John Ajvide Lindqvist (1968–). It is his fictional reaction against contemporary American representations of the zombie as an abject Other, or a raving cannibal who must be terminated with extreme prejudice. To Lindqvist, this representation denies the creature's humanity, as the zombie was formerly a human being who was someone's loved one when alive. In *Handling the Undead,* after a freakish 24-hour surge of electrical power, the dead mysteriously return to life, with the phenomenon limited to parts of Sweden. After some recently dead reanimate in a hospital, the government quickly realizes that other dead might also be reawakening and sends the military to open graves to free the occupants.

Lindqvist's zombies are not cannibals, and so pose no danger to the living. In contrast to how Americans have been depicted in fiction responding to zombies, the Swedish government moves to ensure that the newly awakened dead are treated gently, and also with sensitivity. A special complex is found to house the newly reanimated to protect them, and the living are enjoined to use respectful language to describe the undead. After an official refers to the awakened dead as zombies during a press conference, his superiors declare that the animated dead must be referred to as the reliving in order to preserve their dignity. Still, the reliving unsettle the living because they can hear their thoughts and become menacing when the living feel revulsion for them, which happens when the reanimated bodies are visibly traumatized and/or decaying. The living become telepathic in the presence of the reliving, leading to many fights after people are able to hear the thoughts of others.

Lindqvist's story follows three protagonists, each with reliving family members who challenge beliefs that there is a clear distinction between life and death. David's wife Eva dies in a horrific traffic accident, yet the suddenness of her death makes her passing feel less final. Elvy's reliving husband had died after a lengthy battle with Alzheimer's, which has made him as good as dead to her for nearly a decade while she nursed him. And Gustav's six-year-old grandson Elias, who had died a month prior to the action, is kept alive in memory through Gustav's grief for the child. Gustav keeps Elias's toys in his apartment as if the boy will soon play with them again. As a result, these characters experience their reliving loved ones with a disturbing mixture of elation and revulsion. Lindqvist's ending suggests that the dead have been awakened through divine intervention, as several of the living whose loved ones have reanimated have visions of the Virgin Mary or other mythical beings like the Fisher King, a character from a popular series of Swedish children's books who brings the living to the next world that is located under the water.

A month after they have been reanimated, the reliving collapse, their spirits leaving their bodies in the form of a caterpillar that burrows into the ground and disappears. Lindqvist posits that the dead have been reawakened in the first place because of how we are no longer able to accept the presence of death in our lives. *Handling the Undead* was first published in Sweden in 2005 as *Hanteringen av odöda.* It was translated into English in 2009, and the first American edition, by

St. Martin's, appeared in 2010. As of 2013, Lindqvist's novel is scheduled to be made into a feature film.

See also: In the Flesh; Reanimation

June Michele Pulliam

"HERBERT WEST—REANIMATOR"

"Herbert West—Reanimator" is an episodic short story by H. P. Lovecraft, published serially between October 1921 and February 1922. It was first published in six installments in *Home Brew* in 1922. Considered to be a Lovecraft classic, it has since been collected in *Beyond the Wall of Sleep* (1943) and *Dagon and Other Macabre Tales* (1943). Regarded generally as a *jeu d'esprit* which Lovecraft wrote for a friend, according to *H. P. Lovecraft: A Life* (1996) by S. T. Joshi (born Sunand Tryambak Joshi, 1958–), Lovecraft received a mere one-fourth cent a word. It is a story involving medically reanimated corpses and Lovecraft's most conscious excursion into zombie fiction.

The six episodes of "Herbert West—Reanimator" are told in the first person by a nameless narrator, and the stories he recounts occur before, during, and after World War I. West is a quintessential mad scientist who, like Victor Frankenstein, refuses to concede that some sorts of knowledge should not be pursued. In the first episode, "From the Dark," the narrator describes himself as the closest companion of Herbert West, a fellow medical student at Miskatonic University in Arkham, Massachusetts. West, an effete little man described as having a slightness of form, yellow hair, spectacled blue eyes, and a soft voice is said to possess a diabolical, cold-natured disposition; he is obsessed with the possibility of overcoming death. To this end, he has developed a variety of sera and has experimented with reanimation using rabbits, guinea-pigs, cats, dogs, and monkeys as test subjects. The narrator assists West in opening a recent grave and transporting its occupant to a makeshift laboratory in an old farmhouse, where they attempt to revive it. When they believe that they have failed, they bury the corpse, but later hear screams that force them to leave the farmhouse in a panic. They learn afterward that the newly dug grave was disturbed a second time, and that the farmhouse was burned to the ground.

In succeeding episodes, the narrator describes West's attempts at procuring ever fresher bodies and the results of his experiments on them. "The Plague-Demon" details West's feud with Dr. Allan Halsey, dean of Miskatonic University, a tale that terminates in Halsey's unpleasant fate. After Halsey dies unexpectedly, West experiments on him, reanimating him into a raving madman who beats West and the narrator into unconsciousness and kills over 20 people before being captured and put into an asylum. In the next episode, "Six Shots by Moonlight," the narrator and West move to Bolton, a factory town near Arkham, and obtain the body of boxer Buck Robinson, nicknamed The Harlem Smoke. The story involves local Italians who are missing a child, perhaps the only crime for which West is not directly responsible, though the conclusion involves seeing Robinson's reanimated form with a small arm between its teeth, indicating one of the subjects of West's experiments killed the little boy. In "The Scream of the Dead," West has perfected a fluid that when injected into a fresh corpse preserves it from decay and leaves it ready for resurrection. He briefly revives a traveling salesman who died during West's examination of him after he fell ill. The salesman's final words reveal both that West killed him and that the victim is horrified at being reanimated.

In "The Horror from the Shadows," the penultimate episode in the career of Herbert West, the action is transposed to Flanders in 1915, during World War I. The narrator is now a physician with the rank of first lieutenant in a Canadian regiment, while West is a celebrated Boston surgical specialist. West has joined the military so he can more easily obtain fresh bodies on which to test his theories. His attempts at reanimating the headless body of the regiment's surgeon, Major Sir Eric Moreland Clapham-Lee, and he succeeds, revealing that the body has a memory of the terrible events that led to its death. The final episode, "The Tomb-Legions," occurring six years after the events in Flanders, reveals a depth to the relationship that has hitherto been neglected: the narrator now fears for his own safety but still assists West in his charnel experiments. West has moved to a house overlooking one of the oldest cemeteries in Boston, where he is sought by what are obviously animated corpses, led by Dr. Clapham-Lee, who is wearing a wax head on the stump of his neck. Clapham-Lee and West's other victims liberate Halsey from the asylum and then call upon West. Unable to escape, West is torn to pieces by his reanimated victims, who leave no trace of the doctor. Afterward, the unreliable narrator is suspected of the murder or madness by the detectives who question him, but who cannot locate a body.

The stories in "Herbert West—Reanimator" are generally considered by literary critics to be among Lovecraft's weakest, amounting to formulaic fiction with unpleasantly racist elements, written out of friendship and for low pay. The series is, nevertheless, not without interest. It is the first story to make use of Miskatonic University, the fictional institute of higher learning that is based in the imaginary town of Arkham. Lovecraft obviously realized that Miskatonic University was well worth revisiting, for it and Arkham figure in a number of his more notable stories, including "The Dunwich Horror."

The series is also notable as an early example of scientific zombie fiction. Though it is difficult to say where such a subgenre begins, one can certainly argue that "Herbert West—Reanimator" was inspired by Mary Shelley's *Frankenstein* (1818), as well as by Jack London's (born John Griffith Chaney, 1876–1916) more contemporary *A Thousand Deaths* (1899). Nevertheless, Lovecraft's treatment of his themes is more modern than both his predecessors, including his recognition that, in the 20th century, the university and its scholars would provide the source for scientific developments. Furthermore, in making use of the events of World War I and bending the horrors of that war to serve his fictional purposes, Lovecraft was among the first, if not the first, to recognize that the horrors emergent from this war were uniquely suitable for fictionalization. Finally, the series is not without a sly sense of humor that is all the more amusing for its manifestation in inappropriate moments. This is perhaps most evident in "The Tomb Legions," when the undead close in on West and ring the doorbell of the house in which he and the narrator are waiting. The suspense level is high when the narrator opens the door, and instead of attacking, one of the assembled undead gives the narrator a large square box and grunts, in a highly unnatural voice, "Express–prepaid." All the undead thereupon leave. The narrative implies that inside the box is Dr. Clapham-Lee's severed head. For scholars interested in the history of zombie fiction, "Herbert West—Reanimator" is a benchmark text.

See also: Lovecraft, H. P.; *Re-Animator* Series; Race; Science Fiction; Sentience

Richard Bleiler

"HISTORY OF GHERIB AND HIS BROTHER AGIB, THE"

"The History of Gherib and His Brother Agib" is included in *One Thousand and One Nights,* also known in English as *Arabian Nights,* a collection of stories from various sources, authors, and time periods from across the Middle East and South Asia. These stories were compiled during the Islamic Golden Age. The tale of Gherib and Agib takes place in and around Iraq and Persia and contains one of the oldest known references to ghouls.

One Thousand and One Nights was first translated into English in 1706. The frame story revolves around a Persian king who marries a series of virgins and then has them executed in the morning before they can have a chance to dishonor him with infidelity. Eventually, the kingdom begins to run out of virgins and the king's vizier, whose job it is to provide his sovereign with new wives, offers his daughter, Scheherazade, as the next bride. But Scheherazade, aware of the king's treatment of his wives, begins a story for the king each night, postponing the ending until the next night and thereby forcing the king to delay her execution to hear the end of the story, at which point she starts a new story that must be finished the next night. These stories continue for one thousand and one nights.

In the story, Agib, who ascended to the throne by murdering his father, has a dream that prophesizes that a brother will cause him conflict, so he orders his father's pregnant concubine drowned to prevent the problem. Instead, the concubine escapes into the forest and has her child, Gherib. Afterward, Prince Merdas discovers the concubine while hunting and is captured by her beauty, so he invites her and her son Gherib to live with him. Among Prince Merdas's tribe, Gherib is raised along with his half-brother Sehim and taught princely conduct and the art of combat. Gherib is tasked by Merdas to defeat Saadan, the ghoul of the mountain, to win the hand of Merdas's daughter. Along the way, Gherib embraces Islam and converts his men. The ghoul of the mountain eats only the flesh of men and is also called a beast, a giant, and the-ghoul-who-eats-men-we-pray-God-for-safety. The ghoul has five flesh-eating sons, who are much stronger than normal warriors. Nevertheless, they are eventually defeated by Gherib and converted to Islam.

The ghouls in the story bear a marked resemblance to modern ghouls. They live in the mountains in a remote castle littered with corpses. While the ghouls are not specifically described as undead, the ancient and decayed castle where they reside and their old age points to the possibility. These ghouls differ from modern portrayals of the creature in that they have the power of speech and intelligence and are capable of serving a holy cause after their conversion to Islam. In the ghoul's remote mountain castle, Gherib finds a beautiful Persian princess, whom he returns to her father and marries. Later, Gherib is joined with the ghoul to battle his brother and Merdas's armies. The ghoul proves a loyal and useful soldier: he roasts and then eats many infidel champions, and then rescues Gherib after he is captured by Agib. For good reason then, the enemy is terrified of the ghoul. After the battle, Gherib has a son by his Persian wife and rules Iraq, ousting his brother Agib, and his son rules Persia in his name.

See also: Ghoul; Sentience

Braden Dauzat

HOMECOMING

Homecoming (2005) is the sixth episode of the first season of the *Masters of Horror* television series, and its zombies are notable because while they are undead, they are not mindless. Instead, they are the reanimated bodies of soldiers sent to die in the United States' war on terror after 9/11 when President George W. Bush falsely claimed that Iraq had weapons of mass destruction.

The dead soldiers begin reanimating after the president's speech writer, David Murch, responds on a political talk show to Janet Hoffsteader, a grieving mother who is reminiscent of Cindy Sheehan in her attempts to ask the president in person why her soldier son had to die in the war. Hoffsteader, like Sheehan, is detained by the Secret Service for her persistent pubic questioning. After Murch tells Hoffsteader that he wishes that he could revive her son Gary so that the boy could tell his mother that he died for a good cause, dead soldiers arriving at Reagan Airport in Washington D.C. rise from their flag-draped coffins. Unlike zombies who operate by Romero's Rules, these reanimated soldiers do not wantonly eat human flesh. In fact, when one of the undead servicemen rises from his coffin, he walks up to the frightened soldier who is shooting at him, puts a hand on his shoulder, and tells him "at ease." The zombies only kill those responsible for sending them to war, such as the president's advisor. After the undead vote, their purpose for reviving has expired and they die anew.

Murch, who narrates the story after his own death, tells us that the fallen servicemen only wanted the people responsible to look them in the face and know what they had done by sending them to war. Alarmed by the spectacle of undead soldiers voting a president out of power and the act's potential to cause living voters to stop supporting the war, the administration uses conservative pundits to muddy the message. When an undead soldier announces during a press conference that he was killed for a lie, Jane Cleaver, an Ann Coulter-like television celebrity, denounces him and his fellow reanimated soldiers as traitors who should not be allowed to vote because they are dead, and therefore no longer citizens.

While these zombies are characterized by gruesome wounds and decomposing flesh, they are also relatively humanized. In one scene, a zombie soldier on his way to vote is treated with deferential respect rather than loathing when he is brought in from the rain by a couple who ask his name and thank him for his service to the nation. When it seems as if the undead soldiers have cost the president the election, his people attempt to steal the race, changing the polling results in Ohio. As a result, the dead in Arlington National Cemetery rise from their graves in outrage to make sure that their fellow soldiers' votes are counted. The tombstones of the dead in Arlington bear the names of famous directors of zombie films. The episode concludes with the now-dead narrator informing viewers that if the government ever again sends soldiers to die for a lie, then we will see the true face of hell.

Homecoming is loosely based on Dale Bailey's (no date available) short story "Death and Suffrage," published in 2002, in which the dead return to life to vote for a presidential campaign manager's leftist candidate after the manager debates a pro-Second Amendment pundit on a talk show. Robert, the campaign manager, tells the pundit that if there is any justice in this world, then Dana Maguire, a little girl recently murdered by gun violence, will rise up from her grave to haunt him. The next day, several of the dead do leave their graves to vote for Robert's candidate, who wins the election. Bailey's reanimated dead are more typical zombies in their inability to speak. At the end of the story, when the dead begin rising worldwide amid political injustice, the president quips that they are our conscience because by reanimating, they remind the living what they died for.

See also: Free Will; Television; Sentience

June Michele Pulliam

HOUSE OF THE DEAD SERIES

House of the Dead is a film series based on the action-horror light gun video game series by Sega, *The House of the Dead*. It consists of two films, *House of the Dead* (2003) and the television movie *House of the Dead 2* (2005), alternately titled as *House of the Dead II: Dead Aim*.

The first film, directed by Uwe Boll (1965–), is a prequel to the video game series. It involves a group of young adults who travel to a secluded island for a rave party. They show up late and miss the first boat. While chatting with a boat captain, they learn the island has a sinister reputation and is named La Isla del Muerte, or the Island of Death. They arrive on La Isla del Muerte to discover that it is deserted, except for the flesh-eating zombies that have risen from the graveyard and devoured the rest of the partygoers. The members of the new group of partygoers split up and begin wandering around until night; at that point, the zombies appear and attack. The group finds a small number of survivors who inform them

House of the Dead (2003) is based on an action-horror video game series of the same name. (Artisan/Photofest)

that the zombies attacked the rave party, and those who tangled with the undead have reanimated as zombies themselves.

Most of the zombies appear as rotting corpses or the freshly dead, but some look as though they have been stitched back together, resembling a swamp creature, or are in mummy-like wrappings. All are portrayed as quick and deadly, with an infectious bite and a hunger for human flesh. The remaining gang of partygoers must fight off the zombie horde with a cache of machine guns and other weapons that they discover as they attempt to escape the island. In the process, they find the man responsible for creating the zombies. Hundreds of years previously, he created an immortality serum and injected himself with it in order to become the first zombie, who subsequently infected the island. The group defeats the original zombie but loses one of their own in the process. This member is revived with an injection of the serum. The film is sporadically interspersed with brief scenes from the video game that have no connection to the plot, showing flashes of video game zombies attacking and being blasted by the light gun.

House of the Dead opened to an overwhelmingly negative reception, yet still made a small profit on its $12 million budget through box office and DVD sales. The director later released a director's cut so-called funny edition that incorporated bloopers. The director's cut was also universally panned by critics. Shot mostly in British Columbia, Canada, *House of the Dead 2* premiered on the SciFi Channel, and is a sequel to *House of the Dead,* where the female infected survivor from the first film is treated in a hospital in California. A doctor attempts to create an immortality serum from her blood and inadvertently creates a zombie infestation at the fictional

Cuesta Verde University. Soldiers must battle the zombie hordes before the government bombs the campus, but they are too late to stop the infection from spreading throughout the city.

See also: Cannibalism; Romero's Rules; Science Fiction; Television; Video Games

Braden Dauzat

HOW TO BE A ZOMBIE

How to Be a Zombie is a 2010 tongue-in-cheek self-help volume by Serena Valentino (1973–), author of *How to Be a Werewolf* (2011) and *Nightmares and Fairy Tales* (2007), as well as the GloomCookie children's series. As of 2013, it is by far her most popular book. It purports to assist those who have recently been made into the living dead who are attempting to adapt to their new lifestyle. A work of young adult fiction written for an 12- to 18-year-old audience, the text is careful to include helpful cautionary statements reminding teens to ask parents before moving on to more mature zombie media. The volume informs users that the newly undead must make many decisions, including but not limited to deciding whether to roam alone or in a pack, whether or not to eat brains, and if it is wise to befriend the living. The volume includes helpful tips for readers on how to inform their families about their new lifestyle, and gives advice on dressing stylishly for a hunt and dealing with decaying and missing body parts. The volume also identifies various types of zombie personalities for those attempting to understand the undead.

The guide is divided into three sections: "How to Join the Hideous Legions of the Undead," "Fearsome Fashion and Frightful Fun," and "Adventures in Advanced Zombiedom." Of particular relevance are the thoughtful, well-researched short lists of zombie topics such as books, movies, games, and music, making this an excellent resource for living readers who wish to explore the world of zombies in a humorous way. Additionally, how-to sections include instructions on throwing the perfect zombie bash with decorating and refreshment ideas, as well as lists of zombie-friendly bands and playlists designed to make the shyest undead feel comfortable. The section on applying realistic zombie makeup and fashioning believable zombie dress are useful to the living who are planning on attending a Zombie Walk. Tips on dating the undead and a zombie love story attempt to inspire those already involved in relationships that cross the living/undead lines. The artwork in this guide includes eye-popping and colorful graphic illustrations. *How to Be a Zombie* includes humorous and inviting subtext that teen readers will relate to as they struggle with their search for identity, work on developing worthwhile friendships, and talk to their family about serious issues. This zombie self-help title also does a particularly effective job of giving positive messages to teen readers about embracing differences in themselves and others, making this a more serious work than it first appears.

Valentino is a comic book and young adult author based in San Francisco, as of 2013. In 2012, she published a sequel, *Undead: Everything the Modern Zombie Needs to Know,* which purports to contain all the current information on zombies that zombie-loving teens (or the aspiring young adult zombie-killer) could possibly desire. Like its predecessor, *Undead* contains tips on fashion, zombie makeup, and dating the undead. Valentino's two zombie books are known for being quirky and visually compelling.

See also: Young Adult Fiction

Alicia Ahlvers

HUMANS VS. ZOMBIES

Humans vs. Zombies is a multiplayer, live-action role-playing game. It began on college campuses in the United States, where it is still predominantly played. Most players are cast as humans at the game's onset, but they can be turned into zombies as play continues, and the game ends either when all humans are turned into zombies, or when a goal is reached by the humans, such as surviving for a previously established amount of time or completing a mission like defending a specified building on campus, or safely moving a pre-arranged character (e.g., a scientist who has invented a cure) into a safe zone. The zombies in the game operate loosely by Romero's Rules in that they are cannibalistic (a zombie must eat a human every 48 hours in order to stay alive) and a zombie's bite can turn a human into one of the undead. Various organizations and even departments, such as biology or chemistry, usually host the games. Some universities, such as Bowling Green State, even create elaborate websites where gameplay and characters are tracked on a virtual map.

Generally, play, which is controlled by administrators who create and modify the narrative as play progresses, begins with a narrative where a zombie infestation begins. Typically, zombies are identified by bandanas worn around the head or neck. Humans, who are typically identified by wearing bandanas around one of their arms, can defend themselves using any approved weapon. These are designated with safety in mind, and normally include balled up socks, marshmallows, and Nerf style guns; weapons can be thrown or shot to momentarily kill a zombie. Zombie players are unarmed; they must catch or tag humans to kill and/or infect them. Many campuses add other safety rules such as an off-limits rule for players traveling on wheels or for players who have left campus. In some iterations of the game, zombies have to make a kill in a specified amount of time, after which they collect the human player's I.D. card to prove the kill, or the zombies starve and are then ejected from gameplay. Safe zones, such as dorms, student unions, cafeterias, classroom buildings, and the library, are often established so that human players can eat, sleep, attend class, do research, and complete assignments.

The earliest version of the game is recorded as having been played at Goucher College in 2005. Since then, as its official website notes, the game has developed an international fan base. Prominent news outlets such as *The New York Times, The Washington Post, National Public Radio,* and *The Associated Press* have covered the games, which are currently played on six continents, at reportedly over 1,000 locations. The game is free and available under a Creative Commons license. At campuses that are more technologically advanced, zombies are required to input identification numbers of all humans they kill or turn these numbers into a database. Though innocent and playful, the game has not been without controversy and detractors. Some campuses banned it after the Virginia Tech shootings in 2007 because of its use of toy guns (Nerf launchers) and the propensity of ex-military players to wear fatigues. While predominantly played on college campuses where it is officially sanctioned, the game has branched out to residential neighborhoods, camps, and military bases.

See also: Cannibalism; Epidemics; Romero's Rules

Anthony J. Fonseca

HURSTON, ZORA NEALE

Zora Neale Hurston (1891–1960) was an American writer, anthropologist, and drama teacher who served briefly as a story consultant for Paramount Studios in Hollywood in the 1940s. The daughter of a clergyman/politician and a teacher, she attended Howard University, Barnard College, and Columbia University, and was a member of the American Folklore Society, the American Anthropological Society, and the American Ethnological Society. At one point she was the most published black female author and collector of African American folklore.

In 1921 Hurston published her first story, and in 1925 she won second place in a prestigious National Urban League contest, bringing her to the attention of the Harlem Renaissance writers, including Langston Hughes (born James Mercer Langston Hughes, 1902–1967). Already known as an expert storyteller, she studied at Columbia under anthropologist Franz Uri Boas (1858–1942), and continued publishing in literary magazines—with newfound interest in anthropology. Her early failed folklore collecting trip to the South led to an interest in Voodoo, and ultimately she visited Jamaica and Haiti to gather information, purportedly photographing a zombie. Because of her respect for Jamaican and Haitian cultural traditions and belief in Voodoo, she was allowed to participate in rites that would have been off limits otherwise. *Tell My Horse* examines Jamaican and Haitian Voodoo in a series of stories depicting unexplained spiritual phenomena in a land where spirits are assumed to abide in all humans, living and dead, and can influence the living to create unusual occurrences. *Tell My Horse* also discusses the importance of chants and songs of worshipful respectfulness, along with rituals.

Hurston describes the emergence of Haiti's people from slavery, French colonization and influence, and American occupation, noting that the largely poor and uneducated Haitian population in the 20th century was deeply religious and finds in Voodoo some solace from the widespread poverty and uninspiring government. Hurston's stories about Voodoo in Haiti descriptively chronicle actual occurrences during ceremonies that Hurston participated. Hurston's writing in *Tell My Horse* is clear and engaging and affords easy mental images of the events that include the use of symbols, artifacts, celebratory songs, and laudatory chants. Also included throughout the book are more than two dozen photographs and an appendix that contains the actual music of the songs. In Chapter 10, Hurston establishes early on that "Voodoo is a religion of creation and life," noting that symbolism and ceremony play significant roles. She further offers a summary of its significance: the rituals offer appeasement and worshipful respect to the gods who, it is believed, influence life through spirits. Through Voodoo, believers expect that bad fortunes can be reversed, ill health can be over-

Tell My Horse, an ethnography by American author and anthropologist Zora Neale Hurston, examines Jamaican and Haitian Voodoo in a series of stories depicting unexplained spiritual phenomena in a land where spirits are assumed to abide in all humans, living and dead, and can influence the living to create unusual occurrences. (Library of Congress)

come, and even difficulty in love can be positively resolved. In Haiti, ceremonies occur frequently, and anyone needing relief from an affliction need attend only one (and bring along an offering for the gods). Subtitled *Voodoo and Life in Haiti and Jamaica,* the book was published in the United States in 1938. Hurston professes to have encountered an actual Voodoo zombie in the yard of a hospital in Haiti. This woman, according to Hurston, had died in 1907, and no one had seen her until 1936, when she was found naked by the side of the road. The woman had little memory of her past, but did recall her father's plantation where she lived, which had since passed into the possession of her brother. The woman was eventually identified by her brother and ex-husband. Hurston photographed the woman in 1936, and the photograph was first published in *Life* magazine before appearing in *Tell My Horse*. Hurston reiterated her claim about the existence of zombies when she was interviewed on *The Mary Margaret McBride Show* on January 25, 1943. Hurston's other books include *Jonah's Gourd Vine* (1934), *Mules and Men* (1935), *Their Eyes Were Watching God* (1937), *Moses, Man of the Mountain* (1939), and *Dust Tracks on a Road* (1942). She also authored one play, *Mule Bone: A Comedy of Negro Life* (1991).

See also: Davis, Wade; Haiti; *Tell My Horse*; Voodoo

Anthony J. Fonseca

I AM LEGEND (FILMS)

I Am Legend has had three film adaptations as of 2012: *The Last Man on Earth* (1964), starring Vincent Price (born Vincent Leonard Price Jr., 1911–1993); *The Omega Man* (1971), starring Charlton Heston (born John Charles Carter, 1923–2008); and *I Am Legend* (2007), starring Will Smith (born Willard Christopher Smith Jr., 1968–). All are based on Richard Matheson's contemporary classic novel *I Am Legend* (1954), with its viable combination of massing zombies/vampires against a solitary survivor (Robert Neville) holed up in a fortified home in Los Angeles suburbia. Just three years after the release of Matheson's novel, Hammer Films engaged Matheson to pen a film treatment, which he titled *The Night Creatures,* but Hammer scrapped the venture after the British Board of Film Censors threatened an outright ban in England. Nevertheless, Matheson's narrative framing and the horror conventions he envisioned in his screen treatment led to an early, faithful adaptation on film, *The Last Man on Earth,* a cult classic that subsequently formed the basis of a secondary strain of screen incarnations.

The Last Man on Earth (*L'ultimo uomo della terra* in Italian), is an Italian production directed by Ubaldo Ragona (1916–1987) and written for the screen. It was penned in part by Matheson himself, credited as Logan Swanson. The film's grainy, black-and-white quality and bleak atmosphere, in combination with Price's sympathetic portrayal of Los Angeles suburbanite Robert Morgan (Robert Neville renamed), have secured its cult following for 50 years. *The Omega Man*, directed by Boris Sagal (1923–1981), boasts a larger budget and action star, as Heston portrays Los Angeles urbanite Robert Neville. Finally, *I Am Legend*, directed by Francis Lawrence (1971–), boasts an even bigger budget, extensive computer generated images, and top box-office draw Smith as Manhattan urbanite Robert Neville.

Within just a few years of *The Last Man on Earth*'s release, Matheson's novel had already set the stage for a vastly larger second strain of filmic offshoots, inaugurated in 1968 by George Romero and John A. Russo's (1939–) black-and-white contemporary classic *Night of the Living Dead*. Indeed, *Night of the Living Dead* does preserve two essential elements of Matheson's original novel, namely the apocalyptic vision and the idea of a survival space, or enclosure, in which human survivors have no other alternative but to fortify and defend. Perhaps, the element introduced by Romero and Russo that has produced a far more prolific strain of films is their decision to replace Matheson's sole survivor with multiple survivors, a small yet vital change to Matheson's formula that engendered a socially and politically volatile space that has survived ever since in countless sequels, versions, and remakes. The

Vincent Price stars as Robert Morgan (Robert Neville, renamed) in *The Last Man on Earth* (1964), the first of three film adaptations of Richard Matheson's novel *I Am Legend* (1954). (AIP/Photofest)

idea of a group of survivors, or a multi-occupancy, creates a much more porous space that seems not only to transcend time but also to organically cater to dialogic negotiation.

See also: Apocalypse; Epidemics; *I Am Legend* (Novel); Matheson, Richard; *Night of the Living Dead* Series; Romero, George; Vampires and Werewolves

John Edgar Browning

I AM LEGEND (NOVEL)

I Am Legend is a 1954 post-apocalyptic zombie/vampire novel by Richard Matheson. Considered a contemporary horror classic, it has seen at least four editions in its first couple of years alone, as well as international editions: *Je suis une legende* (1955), the U.K. version of *I Am Legend* (1956), and *Soy leyenda* (1960). The story's protagonist, Robert Neville, is the only survivor of a pandemic whose sufferers have returned from the dead, hiding out by day, venturing about by night in search of human blood. The pandemic is the result of germ warfare and a nuclear exchange abroad, which readers gather through Neville's flashbacks as he performs his monotonous daily routine of fortifying his home against nightly assaults by the blood-thirsty walking dead, gathering supplies in now-deserted Los Angeles, sharpening wooden stakes, and destroying any infected he finds along the way. Neville, whose daily routine includes researching a cure, is immune to the disease, a result, he thinks, from being bitten previously by a vampire bat. Although *I Am Legend* is revered for its vampires, equally of note is its creation of an entirely new breed of zombie.

The living dead of Matheson's text break radically from the traditional literary archetype of the Romantic and Victorian Periods. Instead, Matheson's vampires resemble the older, preliterary vampire of the folklore of European peasantry, the revenant. This creature is typically a villager who resurrects, in state of decay, and feeds upon the blood or life force of family and neighbors. Matheson's zombie/vampires, however, are like neither their European kindred nor their screen cousins in previous zombie films, both of which posed a geographically isolated and relatively surmountable threat. Rather, Matheson reimagines the zombie en masse, and reorients conventional Gothic space and geography by setting the story in "white" suburbia, around a Gothicized, domestic enclosure rather than inside it. Neither victory nor triumph over evil, but mere survival is all that one can hope for.

Matheson's infected undead are zombies in that they are mindless due to the brain damage incurred before reanimation. They wish to drink blood, not from any need but due to a faulty understanding of their condition: the infected undead believe they are vampires because they are allergic to sunlight and garlic. Matheson's infected undead are eventually contrasted with his infected living, who are similarly allergic to sunlight and garlic but who are not zombies, as they have retained the full use of their faculties and are working to rid the world of the diseased undead. *I Am Legend*'s iconic status is marked by at least 64 print editions in at least 14 different languages, three straight filmic adaptations, and a host of other offshoots. To mark the centenary of Bram Stoker's death, the Horror Writers Association honored Matheson's novel with the "Bram Stoker Vampire Novel of the Century Award" at its annual Bram Stoker Awards banquet in 2012, the first award of its kind.

See also: Apocalypse; Epidemics; Matheson, Richard; Vampires and Werewolves

John Edgar Browning

I WALKED WITH A ZOMBIE

I Walked with a Zombie is a 1943 zombie retelling of *Jane Eyre,* directed by Jacques Tourneur (1904–1977), produced by RKO Pictures to cash in on the popularity of Universal Studios' horror films in the 1930s and 1940s. RKO executives came up with the title, lifted from an *American Weekly* article of the same name, even before a script was created. Producer Val Lewton (born Vladimir Ivanovich Leventon, 1904–1951), however, disliked Wallace's formulaic story, so he used a script that was a reworking of *Jane Eyre.*

The plot opens with nurse Betsy Connell taking a job in the West Indies to care for Jessica, the comatose wife of Paul Holland, a wealthy planter whose family controls life on the island. Jessica's malady has rendered her mute and trance-like, devoid of all will but still desirable. Dr. Maxwell, the island's one physician, diagnoses Jessica's condition as caused by a tropical fever that has destroyed her higher brain functions. Jessica can walk when directed to do so, and at night sleepwalks through the house. The island's black inhabitants believe she is the victim of sorcery and can be cured only by Voodoo, and the desperate nurse clandestinely takes her patient to a ceremony. But Jessica is not cured; instead the participants fear that she is the walking dead and demand that island law enforcement investigate what they believe Holland has done to his wife to prevent her from running away with Wesley, his half-brother with whom she had an adulterous relationship. Like many other of Tourneur's films, *I Walked with a Zombie* ends ambiguously: Paul's mother confesses to using Voodoo to zombify her daughter-in-law before she could tear the family apart; Dr. Maxwell patronizingly contradicts Paul's mother, convincing her that she is merely an "imaginative, fanciful" woman. While it is unclear whether Jessica is the victim of dark magic or of a brain fever, she is a zombie, nevertheless, due to her lack of free will.

The 1943 film *I Walked with a Zombie* dealt with white anxieties about blacks. In this shot, the shadow of the black zombie Carrefour towers over Betsy Connell, awakening her from her slumbers. Carrefour's presence in this intimate space hints as miscegenation. (John Springer Collection/Corbis)

The film elucidates American anxieties about race and gender in the 1940s. The island's black inhabitants, who wish to learn definitively if Jessica is a zombie, send one of their own who has been zombified to retrieve her from her bedroom in the middle of the night. At the time this film was made, white audiences would have read this scene as one implying the threat of miscegenation. Horror scholar Peter Dendle (1968–) argues that Depression-era and wartime zombie films raised awareness of gender issues and female empowerment by depicting zombified women as subservient men but not conquered. In her zombified state, Jessica is stronger than the other men around her, which makes her a threat to patriarchal order. Paul and Wesley still fight over possession of the comatose Jessica. Patriarchal order can be restored only after Jessica is dead, euthanized by Wesley, who commits suicide afterward, freeing Paul to marry the more appropriately subordinate Nurse Betsy.

See also: Gender; Race; Voodoo

June Michele Pulliam

IN THE FLESH

In the Flesh is a 2013 television miniseries produced by the BBC. It is told through the perspective of the zombie Kiernan Walker, who suffers from partially deceased syndrome (PDS) which reanimates the dead and turns them into zombies who roughly follow Romero's Rules. However, these zombies do not usher in the apocalypse, since soon after the Rising, as the initial outbreak of PDS is referred to, a cure is discovered, and the British government puts its afflicted citizens through a reconditioning therapy so that they can be reincorporated into society.

Still, everyone is not enthusiastic about the returning home to their families of the so-called rotters. In order for PDS victims to better deal with the guilt they feel after remembering killing people while in the throes of the disease, the doctors, nurses, and psychiatrists who treat them encourage their patients to think of themselves as akin to those suffering a serious mental illness were not fully responsible for their actions as they were not receiving the relatively new treatment for their condition. Unfortunately, members of the Human Volunteer Force (HVF), the armed militia who had to kill the rotters during the early days of the outbreak in order to protect the living, are not so forgiving. Four years after the Rising, members of the HVF continue to patrol the rural areas, including the fictional rural town of Roarton in the United Kingdom where *In the Flesh* is set, looking for rotters to execute. They also express anger over the rotters' being sent back to live among them, as after the Rising, the government was initially slow in sending troops to the rural areas to help residents deal with the zombies, who were tearing apart the living. People are, therefore, understandably skeptical, as well, when the government tells them they have effectively treated those who suffer from PDS so that they are no longer a threat to the living.

Those suffering from PDS must be given drugs on a regular basis in order to remain stable, but even doctors seem to have their doubts about the efficacy of the treatment: when Kiernan is returned to live with his parents, they are given a taser in case he gets out of hand. Meanwhile, Kiernan is tormented when his memories return to him and he recalls those he killed while in the throes of the disease. At home, Kiernan must stay hidden in his parents' house lest members of the local HVF learn that he is there and kill him.

In the Flesh was created by the BBC after the phenomenal success of American Movie Classics's television series *The Walking Dead* (2010–). However, the series is only similar to *The Walking Dead* in that both are about zombies. Instead, *In the Flesh* is another example of how differently other cultures envision the creature as someone who retains some of its humanity in spite of its condition, rather than an abject Other that can be terminated with extreme prejudice. While the HVF are resentful of the rotters, it is notable that the British government has provided for their care, viewing them as not that much different from people suffering from any other illness that causes the body and/or mind to deteriorate. In this way, *In the Flesh* is similar to Swedish writer John Ajvide Lindqvist's novel *Handling the Undead* (2005), in which the government immediately sets up a care program for its deceased citizens after they begin to reanimate. The BBC has renewed *In the Flesh* for a second season to air in 2014.

See also: Cannibalism; Dementia; Epidemics; *Handling the Undead*; Romero's Rules; Television; *Walking Dead, The* (Television Series)

June Michele Pulliam

INFERI AND THE IMPERIUSED

The Inferi and the Imperiused are two types of zombie-like beings that exist in the Harry Potter universe created by J. K. Rowling. The Inferi are actual reanimated corpses, and the Imperiused are living characters who have been deprived of their will via the Imperius Curse.

The Inferi appear in *Harry Potter and the Half-Blood Prince* (2005), the sixth book in the series, though they are mentioned in passing in earlier books. In *The Half-Blood Prince,* Harry encounters them when he travels with his mentor Albus Dumbledore, the headmaster of Hogwarts School of Witchcraft and Wizardry. In order to stop Voldemort, the series' antagonist, Harry and Dumbledore must destroy his horcruxes, which are objects containing part of his soul in order to render him invulnerable; Voldemort cannot be killed while part of his soul is secured outside of his body. Voldemort has protected one horcrux with an army of Inferi, who more closely resemble earlier versions of the Voodoo zombie: they do not hunger for human flesh and they follow the command of a master. However, Inferi can be directed to kill, and Voldemort has programmed his undead to rise from the underground lake where this horcrux lies. When Harry and Dumbledore attempt to leave with the horcrux, the Inferi try to drag them beneath the water. But because Inferi fear light, Dumbledore drives them away by surrounding them with a ring of fire. The 2009 film version, *Harry Potter and the Half-Blood Prince,* directed by David Yates (1963–), envisions the Inferi as even more menacing than they are in

Rowling's novel. Yates's Inferi are a CGI generated army of gaunt, naked, hollow-eyed undead who actually succeed in pulling Harry underwater before Dumbledore can subdue them.

Since the zombie is also defined as a humanoid creature lacking in free will, *Harry Potter* characters victimized by the Imperius Curse also fit this category. The Imperius Curse, one of the three unforgivable curses in the series, places victims under the control of the wizard who has used dark magic against them. Characters who have been imperiused are zombies comparable to those described in some Haitian accounts, as they remain under control until the enchantment is lifted. However, the Imperiused are different from other types of zombies in that it is not immediately obvious to others that they have been deprived of their free will. Rather, the Imperiused appear to behave normally, and their compromised conditions are not detected until the wizard controlling them directs them to do something that may be out of character. Examples of the Imperiused include Minister of Magic Pius Thicknesse, introduced in the seventh book of the series, *Harry Potter and the Deathly Hallows* (2007), who is cursed by Voldemort and established as a puppet ruler. In *Half-Blood Prince,* keeper of the Three Broomsticks (Madam Rosmerta) and Hogwarts student Katie Bell become members of the Imperiused when Draco Malfoy uses them to deliver a cursed necklace to Dumbledore. The vulnerability to the Imperius Curse is not universal: some characters, such as Harry, are able to resist by using extraordinary skill.

See also: Free Will; Haiti; Voodoo; Young Adult Fiction

June Michele Pulliam

ISHTAR

Ishtar, also known as Ashtart, Ashtoreth, Astarte, Inanna, and Isis, is generally represented as the daughter of Anu, the sky god, and Sin/Nigal, the moon god, and has the lion as her cult animal. A Babylonian and Assyrian goddess of battle, fertility, and sexual love, whose name literally means "Star of Heaven" (or "The Evening Star"), Ishtar's worship is thought to reach back as far as the third millennium in the Middle East, and survived until the rise of Christianity. Ishtar's connection to zombies comes from her frequent threats to raise the dead and command them to feast on the living if she does not get her way.

In Sumeria, Ishtar became associated with the fourth millennium goddess Inanna, and may have been contemporary with the appearance of the wheel in Mesopotamia (c. 3000 BCE). The highest goddess in the Babylonian pantheon, sometimes revered as "Opener of the Womb" and "She Who Begets All," Ishtar married her brother, Tammuz, god of agriculture and regeneration. Following Tammuz's death, Ishtar traveled the underworld to retrieve him, challenging the personification of darkness Ereshkigal ("Queen of the Damned" or "Queen of Death"), who is also in some accounts her sister: Ishtar threatens to release the dead from the underworld to devour the living if she is not allowed to bring back her husband. Ereshkigal permits conditional entry in that Ishtar must remove a piece of clothing as she moves through each gate. By the seventh gate, and half-mad with the strip-tease, Ishtar attacks Ereshkigal, only to be subdued and given 60 infections. As Ishtar nears death, all earthly regeneration ceases, and King of the Gods Ea sends a eunuch to revive her with the waters of life.

Another Ishtar-related zombie infestation is promised in the *Epic of Gilgamesh*. In this case, the gods send Ishtar to seduce and kill both Gilgamesh, one-third mortal, two-thirds divine King of Uruk (Iraq), and his half-brother Enkidu. But when Gilgamesh scorns her, Ishtar demands her father Anu send the Bull of Heaven to smash the gates of Hell and menace Gilgamesh's lands. She once again threatens to raise the dead to devour the living, this time if her father does not give her the Bull of Heaven. Modernized versions of Ishtar have appeared in films such as *Blood Feast* (1963), *Blood Diner* (1987), and *Blood Feast 2: All U Can Eat* (2002), as well as in literature. In 2012, Gilgamesh Press published *Ishtar,* a collection of novellas. Ishtar's role in "Gilgamesh" was also rewritten in 1993 as a juvenile text, *The Revenge of Ishtar,* by artist/author Ludmila Zeman (1947–). Ishtar's ancient power resurfaces in some of the best zombie fiction of recent years, such as *Monster Island* trilogy, by David Wellington (1971–), in the form of a godlike presence from an ancient civilization, able to summon and direct otherwise incoherent and lost zombies that threaten all humanity.

See also: "Gilgamesh"; *Monster Island* Trilogy; Wellington, David

Danel Olson

ITALIAN CINEMA

Italian cinema ranges from art house favorites such as Vittorio De Sica's (1901–1974) *Bicycle Thieves* (1948) and Federico Fellini's (1920–1993) classic *8½* (1963), which consistently make *Sight and Sound's* top-ten lists, to B movies in virtually every genre. Italian filmmakers played key parts in the explosion of zombies in global cinema during the late 1970s and 1980s, beginning with the success of *Zombi 2.*

Italian cinema made an early impact in film, with extravagant historical epics, such as Giovanni Pastrone's (aka Piero Fosco, 1883–1959) *Cabiria* (1914), the commercial success of which profoundly shaped the silent era, particularly films by D. W. Griffith (born David Llewelyn Wark Griffith, 1875–1948) and other masters of the Hollywood style that would define many long-lasting conventions of cinematic narrative. After World War II, Italian film distinguished itself with new styles, often grouped together under the term Neo-Realism, that challenged Hollywood filmmaking through audacious visions of the financial and spiritual ruin that pervaded Europe. This movement gave rise to some of the world's most revered auteur directors, such as De Sica, Fellini, and Roberto Rossellini (born Roberto Gastone Zeffiro Rossellini, 1906–1977). Although noted for using pseudo-documentary cinematographic style and nonprofessional actors, which contributed to a raw view of reality (particularly life in impoverished urban areas), these filmmakers did not limit themselves to depicting concrete, external experience. Fellini, in particular, turned increasingly toward exaggerated, fantastic events in order to give form to psychological states, all the more realistic for appearing physically unreal on the screen.

While helping to establish the postwar international art cinema, the Italian film industry also made major contributions to more commercial genre traditions, including horror. Italy's horror cinema was well established before Dario Argento brought it to new heights with his directorial debut *The Bird with the Crystal Plumage* (1970). His most significant predecessor is Mario Bava, whose *Black Sunday* (aka *The Mask of Satan,* 1960) is a classic of supernatural terror and whose *Blood and Black Lace* (1964), along with Alfred Hitchcock's classic *Psycho* (1960), is the clearest forebear for the subgenre of slasher or body count horror. Bava's science fiction/horror film *Planet of the Vampires* (1965) features reanimated corpses that anticipate *Night of the Living Dead* (1968). Although Italian horror is often derided for being exploitative and derivative, Bava's and Argento's films innovated the genre by fusing many elements from the Italian art house with more commercial storylines about ghosts and killers. For example, *Blood and Black Lace* uses dream-like, exaggerated set-pieces as well as intensely saturated colors that have clear kinship with Fellini's *Satyricon* (1969), which Fellini directed the year after he contributed to the anthology horror film *Spirits of the Dead.* Argento perfected Bava's stylistic innovations with his uber-violent masterpieces *Suspiria* (1977) and *Inferno* (1980), the latter of which features a sequence that is Bava's final (uncredited) directorial effort.

Argento also brought his artful, uber-violent sensibilities to the American cinema by collaborating with George Romero on *Dawn of the Dead* (1978), which was released the same year in Italy under the title *Zombi.* Although the film credits Argento only as a script consultant and a contributor to the band Goblin's musical score (Goblin had already scored *Suspiria* and other Argento films), he took responsibility for reediting the Italian release. His brother Claudio Argento (1943–) is also credited as associate producer. Dario Argento and Romero have long enjoyed a strong creative connection; they went on to codirect the film *Two Evil Eyes* (1990), which adapts stories by Edgar Allan Poe and adds extremes of style, not to mention a few zombies. Together, all of these factors suggest that Argento was a major creative force behind the cinematic zombie renaissance that *Dawn of the Dead* inaugurated.

Other Italian filmmakers were influential in the new explosion of zombies in global cinema during the late 1970s and 1980s. The success of *Zombi* inspired Lucio Fulci, who had been making exploitative and artful B films for a decade. He created *Zombi 2* (1979, aka *Zombie*). Connected to *Dawn of the Dead* only by name, and thus often dismissed as a rip-off, *Zombi 2* combines wild and unlikely events with gore that arguably exceeds even Romero's extremes. The island setting and racist depiction of natives connects Fulci's film to another famous trend in Italian horror, the cannibal cycle. Although cannibalism is already one of the zombie's many traits in *Night of the Living Dead*, the gruesome expansion of cannibalism's role in *Zombi* and *Zombi 2* likely owe something to Italian films such as Sergio Martino's (1938–) *The Mountain of the Cannibal God* (1978) and Ruggero Deodato's (1939–) *Last Cannibal World* (1977), a forerunner of Deodato's gory classic *Cannibal Holocaust* (1980). Questions of origin aside, the phenomenal success of *Zombi 2*, which did better at Italy's box office than *Zombi*, ensured a host of other Italian zombie films. Fulci also directed the *Gates of Hell* trilogy. In addition to other films by Fulci, Bruno Mattei's (1931–2007) *Hell of the Living Dead* (1980) and Umberto Lenzi's (1931–) *Nightmare City* (1980) are among the best known from this cycle, which also has a strong connection to *Demons* (1985), a film about fast-moving zombie-like creatures directed by Mario Bava's son, Lamberto Bava (1944–), and produced by Dario Argento. While Romero purists often question the shaky storylines and bad acting that characterize films by Fulci, Mattei, and others, these films' stylistic excesses, especially their extremes of violence, have achieved cult status on their own merits and bear many of the features that place Italy's among the world's most influential and beloved cinematic traditions.

See also: Cannibalism; Cult Film; Fulci, Lucio; *Gates of Hell* Trilogy; Mattei, Bruno; *Night of the Living Dead* Series; Romero, George; *Zombi* Series

L. Andrew Cooper

JACKSON, PETER

Peter Robert Jackson (1961–) is a New Zealand director best known for his adaptation of J. R. R. Tolkien's (born John Ronald Reuel Tolkien, 1892–1973) *The Lord of the Rings,* as well as his 2005 remake of the classic *King Kong.* His main contribution to the zombie genre is *Dead Alive* (1992), released by WingNut Films in New Zealand as *Braindead.* In it, Jackson takes carnage to comic extremes. His only foray into the zombie film genre, the film has endured as a cult classic, widely regarded as perhaps the goriest film in the history of cinema. The infection-borne New Zealand zombies of *Dead Alive* are nearly invincible and continue to be animated even after being chopped into multiple pieces.

Jackson is a self-taught director who began shooting short films on his family's eight millimeter camera after seeing the original *King Kong* (1933) at age eight. Filmmaking became his primary interest after dropping out of school at 16. He applied for an entry-level position at the New Zealand production company The Film Unit but was not hired. Jackson spent the next several years working in the photography department of a local newspaper, living with his parents and spending his wages on film equipment that he used to shoot short subjects in his spare time. In 1983, Jackson purchased a 16-mm camera and started work on the sci-fi horror comedy with WingNut films, 1987's *Bad Taste.* What began as an amateur production starring Jackson and his friends was released as a feature film in after late-stage funding from the New Zealand Film Commission. *Bad Taste* features gory special effects that were influenced by Tom Savini in *Dawn of the Dead* (1978). *Bad Taste* was followed by the grotesque puppet satire *Meet the Feebles* (1989), inspired by Jackson's experiences visiting screenwriter, producer, and musician Fran Walsh (born Frances Rosemary Walsh, 1959–) on the set of a New Zealand children's show. Walsh and Jackson married and have since collaborated on all major projects.

Jackson's next film, *Heavenly Creatures* (1994), earned an Academy Award for Best Original Screenplay nomination for him and Walsh. The mainstream attention landed Jackson his first Hollywood movie, *The Frighteners* (1996). The horror-comedy was not successful but helped promote the digital talents of Jackson's effect studio Weta Workshop. Weta later returned to the horror genre on multiple occasions, including the 2006 zombie comedy *Black Sheep.* Weta creations were key to Jackson's vision of *The Lord of the Rings* trilogy, which grossed nearly $6 billion globally as of 2012. It won multiple Oscars, including Best Picture and Best Director (2004). Realizing a childhood dream in 2005, Jackson remade his favorite film, *King Kong,* for Universal Studios. He also directed the film adaptation of the novel *The Lovely Bones* for DreamWorks (2009), before returning to Tolkien for a three-part version of *The Hobbit* in 2012–2013 (*An Unexpected Journey, The Desolation of Smaug,* and *There and Back Again*). Jackson was knighted by the New Zealand Order of Merit in 2010. He has also won Australian Film Institute Awards, British Academy Film Awards, Critics' Choice Awards, Golden Globes, and Saturns.

See also: Comedy; *Dawn of the Dead*; *Dead Alive*; Savini, Tom

Kevin Dole

JIANG SHI

The *jiang shi* is a zombie-like monster in Asian folklore dating from the Qing dynasty. The term *jiang shi* is generally translated as "stiff corpse." These creatures are also known as "hopping vampires" because rigor mortis stiffens their limbs, resulting in outstretched arms and limiting its movements to hopping. One possible source of the legend comes from the folk tradition of transporting a corpse over a thousand *li*. Poor families would hire a Taoist priest to reanimate the corpse of a dead loved one and command it to hop to its ancestral burial site. In other tales, a *jiang shi* can return from the dead and suck the life force from human victims, a deadly process that results in the creation of a new *jiang shi*.

This Chinese monster has been portrayed as a hungry ghost and as a reanimated corpse that appears in various stages of decomposition. These early zombies—either raised from the dead by an evil necromancer or returning from the grave due to improper burial, a sinful life, or suicide—have pale skin, claw-like fingernails, and long prehensile tongues. A *jiang shi* can be defeated in a variety of ways, including showing it its own reflection, stabbing it with a peach-wood branch, and burning it. In some films, *jiang shi* are put to sleep when yellow slips of paper containing spells are affixed to their foreheads and their evil spirits can be drawn out with sticky rice.

In recent years, the *jiang shi* has been featured across Asian and Western popular culture. The monster appears in a number of horror films from Hong Kong and China, including Sammo Hung Kam-bo's (1952–) *Encounters of the Spooky Kind*, originally titled *Gui da gui* (1980). The creatures also appear in Ricky Lau's (1949–) comedy *Mr. Vampire*, originally titled *Geung si sin sang* (1985) and its numerous sequels, as well as Wei Tung's (born Stephen Tung Wei, 1954) *Magic Cop*, originally titled *Qu mo jing cha* (1990). Versions of the *jiang shi* appear in the television series *My Date with a Vampire*, originally titled *Ngo wo geun see yau gor yue wui* (1998), and a *jiang shi* is the primary villain in the "Chi of the Vampire" episode of the animated *Jackie Chan Adventures* television series (2002). *Jiang shi* foes and bosses also appear in a variety of video games, including the *Darkstalkers* series (Capcom, 1994), *Castlevania: Order of Ecclesia* (Koji Igarashi, 2008), and *Sleeping Dogs* (United Front Games, 2012).

See also: Asian Cinema; Comedy; Cult Film; Ghosts; Television

Kyle William Bishop

JUAN OF THE DEAD

Juan of the Dead, also known as *Juan de los Muertos,* is a 2011 comedy zombie film written and directed by Argentinian Alejandro Brugués. Juan, the title character, is a 40-year-old slacker, and he and his libertine friend Lázaro are both estranged from their children. When the two friends find themselves in the middle of a zombie infestation, Juan uses it as an opportunity to get the money to reconnect with his daughter Camila. He sells his services as a zombie assassin, with his slogan being "Juan of the Dead. We kill your beloved ones." Lázaro, his son Vladi, and Camila become Juan's army of zombie killers. Soon, the group finds itself overwhelmed, and they are faced with the possibility that they, like many of the citizens of Havana, will have no choice but to take a boat off the island.

While some of zombies in the film are realistically gory, with twisted appendages that have bones sticking out of them, others look quite amateurish in their special effects. Brugués's zombies follow Romero's Rules and are easy to defeat; only their sheer numbers make them a challenge. The movie is also known for its unlikeable protagonists, as well as its political subtext, as it uses the zombie trope to criticize Cuba's leaders. The government not only writes off the infestation as nothing more than dissidents in the employ of the United States, but it also makes matters worse by keeping public transportation running during the outbreak. Brugués scripted the film so that it commented on both the zombie-like quality of the citizens of Cuba and the 50 years of confrontational posing against the United

Zombie bride (Senia Veigas) and groom (Jazz Vila) on the set of *Juan of the Dead* (2011), billed as Cuba's first horror film. (Desmond Boylan/Reuters/Corbis)

States characteristic of the Cuban government. Juan and Lázaro are aimless, much like the protagonists in *Shaun of the Dead* (2004), the film's inspiration. *Juan of the Dead* also satirizes what Brugués states on the film's website are the three methods that Cubans deal with problems: turning them into business opportunities, ignoring them, and running away from them completely by taking to the sea in order to leave the island. Juan deals with the problem of the dead returning to life in the first two ways before he eventually chooses to stand and fight to defend his country.

Despite its audience accolades, the film had moderate success in a limited release at the box office. In its opening weekend, it made $12,000 on only one screen in the United States; its gross as of 2012 was $18,000. The film, first shown at the 2011 Toronto International Film Festival, is in Spanish, and is billed as Cuba's first horror film. It won the 2012 silver medal for the Best European/North-South American Feature Audience Award at the Fantasia Film Festival in Montreal, as well as the 2012 Audience Award at the Toronto after Dark Film Festival Summer Screening Series.

See also: Apocalypse; Class; Comedy; Romero's Rules

Anthony J. Fonseca

KEENE, BRIAN

Brian Keene (1967–) is a horror novelist who gained widespread attention and eventually made a name for himself after winning the 2003 Bram Stoker Award for Best First Novel, for *The Rising*. Keene's zombies differ from more traditional representations of the creature in that they are not the result of science gone wrong, of an infection, or of a Voodoo curse; rather, they are the result of demonic possession. Keene's zombies can sprint, shoot weapons, and even operate motorized vehicles. Animals present an added danger in Keene's zombie world.

In *The Rising*, Jim Thurmond has survived the sudden zombie apocalypse by hiding out in the West Virginia shelter he had built to survive Y2K. From this shelter he watches as the bodies of his friends, neighbors, and even his beloved pregnant wife are taken over by demons. Almost without hope, he receives a desperate call from his young son, living in California with his first wife. The two are trapped in a rapidly deteriorating situation, with little hope of holding out against the zombie horde. Thurmond gets out of his shelter, where he meets a minister, Martin, and a prostitute, Frankie. They join forces and travel across the country. While Thurmond searches, one of the scientists who caused the dimensional rift that let in the demons communicates with a zombie-demon named Ob, offering the reader clues to the cause of the apocalypse. Eventually, these characters converge for a climactic and gory ending. In the sequel, *City of the Dead* (2005), Jim finally locates his son but must work quickly to rescue him before the zombies invade. In the mêlée, Frankie is grievously wounded by the zombies, and a next-door neighbor named Don helps them to escape and joins the group. As they flee, a vengeful Ob becomes obsessed with Jim. Ob steps up the hunt for the group, which, of course, leads to another suspense-filled and violent climax.

Keene has since shifted the mythology of his zombie novels from supernatural causes to viral infection. His next set of connected full-length works include *Dead Sea* (2007), which features survivors who isolate themselves at sea, to try to protect themselves against the zombie threat started by diseased rats, and a graphic novel, *Entombed* (2011), set in the same world. In 2012, he also released the short story "Couch Potato," featured in *21st Century Dead: A Zombie Anthology*. Keene also has a stand-alone chapbook with Camelot Press featuring zombies, *Fast Zombies Suck* (2011), and a graphic novel series, *The Last Zombie*.

See also: Apocalypse; Epidemics

Alicia Ahlvers

KING, STEPHEN

Stephen King's (born Stephen Edwin King, 1947–) name is synonymous with American horror fiction. Although he rarely uses the zombie trope in his stories or novels, he has produced two works that have been influential in the subgenre: *Pet Sematary* (1983), which was made into a film in 1989, and *Cell* (2006), which is rumored to be made into a film, listed as in production as of 2014. The former introduces the possibility of undead animals returning from the grave and ties the zombie to Native American mythology. The latter features a world in which technology, in the form of a cell phone burst, interferes with brain waves and causes human beings to become mindless killers who usher in the apocalypse, like the creatures in Danny Boyle's *28 Days Later* (2002) and the ensuing series.

King's interest in horror can be traced to various influences, many of which are known for their treatment of the terror of the undead, in one form or another. King was a young fan of EC's horror comics, including *Tales from the Crypt*. In fact, he later exhibited this influence in his scripting for the film *Creepshow* (1982), in which his scripts were an homage to *Tales from the Crypt*, which often features stories of the walking undead (often as humans who did not realize they were dead, a theme which made its way into feature film with the cult classic *Carnival of Souls* [1962] and the blockbuster *The Sixth Sense* [1999]). King has cited as his influences many authors who have dabbled in the returning undead trope, namely Richard Matheson, whom he calls his greatest influence; Ray Bradbury; H. P. Lovecraft; and Bram Stoker. King has also worked with and noted the influence of George Romero, and has, in fact, partially dedicated *Cell* to Romero and written an essay for the Elite DVD version of *Night of the Living Dead* (1968). King, who also writes under the pseudonym Richard Bachman, has sold over 350 million copies of 50 novels and collections and five nonfiction books. He has received Bram Stoker Awards, World Fantasy Awards, British Fantasy Society Awards, and the O. Henry Award.

See also: Bradbury, Ray; *Cell*; *Creepshow*; Matheson, Richard; *Pet Sematary* (Novel); Romero, George; *Tales from the Crypt* (Film); *28 Days Later* Series

Anthony J. Fonseca

LABRUCE, BRUCE

Bruce LaBruce (born Justin Stewart, 1964–) is a Canadian writer, director, and photographer known for queer media. LaBruce studied film at York University in Toronto, and began his career writing for publications such as *Cineactio* and his editing career with e-zines such as *J.D.'s*. He later made two gay pornographic zombie films, *Otto, or, Up with Dead People* (2008) and *L.A. Zombie* (2010).

Otto premiered at the Sundance Film Festival, while *L.A. Zombie* premiered in competition at the Locarno Film Festival. *Otto* is a metatextual film about a zombie named Otto who travels to Berlin, where he is discovered by an underground filmmaker, Medea Yarn, who decides to make a documentary about him. To this point in the narrative, she has been attempting to finish a political zombie film, *Up with Dead People,* and she convinces its star to allow Otto to stay in his guest room, where Otto finds his wallet containing information about his pre-zombie life. This prompts memories of Rudolf, his ex-boyfriend. Otto subsequently decides to reunite with the boyfriend in the school playground where they first met, a meeting that proves disastrous. In *L.A. Zombie,* whose tagline is "It came from beneath the sea . . . to fuck the dead back to life," a zombie emerges from the ocean and wanders the streets of Los Angeles, finding dead men and bringing them back to life via penetration of their wounds with his penis. *L.A. Zombie* is more abstract than *Otto,* even while the structure reflects that of a traditional sex-driven pornographic film, albeit with unconventional, gory sex scenes punctuating the meandering narrative. The film's

Canadian director, writer, and photographer Bruce LaBruce's contributions to the zombie genre include the gay pornographic films *Otto; or, up with Dead People* (2008) and *L.A. Zombie* (2010). (WireImage)

poster artwork pays homage to the iconic poster design for George A. Romero's *Dawn of the Dead*.

Both *Otto* and *L.A. Zombie* were released in soft (simulated sex with no graphic shots of penetration or ejaculation) and hard (unsimulated sex, including shots of penetration and ejaculation) cuts to allow for maximum distribution. Both films toured the festival circuit and were critical successes, noted for their hybridization of porn and indie film. According to Jamie Duncan, the home of Melbourne Underground Film Festival director Richard Wolstencroft (1969–), also known as Richard Masters, was raided by police after word spread that *L.A. Zombie* was featured at the summer film festival. The Australian Classification Board banned the soft cut of the film immediately prior to its premiere at the festival. Because it was labeled as an unclassified film, detectives questioned Wolstencroft, who claimed that all copies of the film had been destroyed.

See also: Cult Film; Pornography

Laura Helen Marks

LANSDALE, JOE R.

Joe R. Lansdale (born Joe Richard Lansdale, 1951–) in Gladewater, Texas, is a writer known for his genre-bending fantasy, mystery, detective, and horror fiction, which often utilize zombies. Though set in different historical eras, his horror tales contain zombies that owe much to the concepts first postulated by George Romero in *Night of the Living Dead* (1968). Lansdale's zombies are animated corpses who are infected with some type of disease that spreads through a bite. In Lansdale's earlier stories, zombies are explained scientifically, created by a man-made laboratory virus that is accidentally unleashed. In Lansdale's later works, zombies are caused by mysterious colored lights which kill and reanimate.

Lansdale's 1984 novella *Dead in the West* (first serially published in *Eldritch Tales*, 1984–1987, and reissued as a novella in 1986) features the sharpshooting Reverend Jebediah Mercer, who roams the American Southwest after the Civil War. It was inspired by comic books, B movies, and by the lethal Puritan swordsman Solomon Kane, created by Robert E. Howard. Arriving in Mud Creek, Texas, later the setting of Lansdale's mummy/zombie tale *Bubba Ho-Tep* (2003), Mercer learns the town had been visited by a Native-American shaman and his African American mistress, who healed many of the townspeople but were tortured and executed after they were mistakenly accused of causing the death of a child. His last breath a curse, the shaman returns and begins to transform the townspeople into zombies in order to destroy Mud Creek. Mercer and a small group must then defend Mud Creek against the zombies. In a later adventure, Lansdale's 2007 story "Deadman's Road," the solitary Mercer learns of Gil Gimet, an evil beekeeper whose reanimated corpse preys upon passersby.

Lansdale's 1989 story "On the Far Side of the Cadillac Desert with Dead Folks" and his 2010 story "Christmas with the Dead" are modern explorations of the zombie prototypes postulated by Romero. In the former, set in the American Southwest, a bounty hunter named Wayne takes on a murderer and the never-seen Meat Boys, who operate a club that permits humans to exploit zombies. Wayne is victorious and prepares to jail the murderer, but before he reaches Law Town, he is waylaid by one of the scientists who created the zombie virus, Brother Lazarus and his followers, who have enslaved zombies, forcing them to sing hymns upon command. The tongue-in-cheek "Christmas with the Dead" follows Calvin, a man who lost his wife and daughter to the zombie lights, as he fights to install Christmas decorations and celebrate the holiday, learning that Christmas can bring out the best in the dead. Lansdale has won the Bram Stoker, British Fantasy, and American Mystery Awards, and has served as vice president of the Horror Writers of America. He has also published under the name Ray Slater.

See also: Bubba Ho-Tep (Film); "Bubba Ho-Tep" (Short Story); Cult Film; *Night of the Living Dead* Series; Romero, George

Richard Bleiler

LAST MAN ON EARTH, THE
See I Am Legend (Films)

LAZARUS

Lazarus of Bethany is a biblical figure who has become representative of the idea of bodily resurrection. Although this is a central motif in zombie fiction, the tale of Lazarus differs greatly in that he retains his soul and his humanity. In the Gospel of John, Lazarus's sisters send word to Jesus that Lazarus is ill, and Jesus returns to Bethany after Lazarus has died. Mourning, the sisters tell Jesus that he could have prevented their brother's death. Four days after the body's interment, Jesus tells a group of men to remove the stone blocking the entrance to the tomb, and he commands Lazarus to come out, which he does, alive and well. The resurrection of Lazarus is the sixth miraculous sign of Jesus's divinity in the Gospel of John. It prompts the crucifixion of Jesus. The chief priests of the Jews also contemplate killing Lazarus because his resurrection has caused many to follow Jesus.

The name Lazarus is so strongly associated with the idea of bodily resurrection that it is used to describe medical phenomena that resemble it. The "Lazarus sign" is a reflex which sometimes occurs after brain stem failure, wherein the patient will raise both arms briefly before dropping them on the chest. Numerous references to Lazarus can be found in popular culture, many of which appear in works where characters return from the dead. Stephen King's novel *Pet Sematary* (1983), in which a child interred on an ancient burial ground returns from the dead, now evil and desiring to kill his living loved ones, opens with a paraphrase of a passage from the Gospel of John's referring to Lazarus. The video game *Darkwatch*, put out by MobyGames (2005), prominently features a villain named Lazarus who was reputedly an ancient Roman who still exists, undead, in the American West, as a vampire. The short story "Lazarus" (*The New Dead*, 2010), by John Connolly (1968–), actually casts the biblical Lazarus as a zombie. The story opens with Lazarus's waking from the dead, bound and numb, unaware of his name or his surroundings. He realizes that he was once called Lazarus, but he does not identify with his former name anymore. His sisters at first rejoice his return but eventually realize that he is no longer the brother they loved: his flesh is decaying, he has no hunger, he does not taste food, and he feels no joy. As a consequence, everyone is afraid of and disgusted by Lazarus. Eventually, the priests decide to destroy Lazarus, in part because his resurrection glorifies Jesus but more importantly because he is inhuman, an abomination.

While the biblical account of the resurrection of Lazarus was intended to demonstrate the power of Jesus, the name of Lazarus has become associated more generally with circumventing death, often in an imperfect manner. Many fictional works alluding to Lazarus involve the influence of evil forces or the dangers and downfalls of resurrecting the dead.

See also: King, Stephen; *Pet Sematary* (Novel); Video Games

Derek Manuel

LEFT 4 DEAD

Left 4 Dead (*L4D*), developed and published by Turtle Rock Studios/Valve in 2008 for the Xbox 360, PC and Mac OS X, is a cooperative first-person shooter game with survival horror elements. What differentiates *L4D* from the majority of zombie-themed video games is its emphasis on team play. The game centers on a group of four survivors who can be controlled by up to four players, with the game itself controlling any unselected characters. The three male characters (a Vietnam veteran, a biker, and an IT analyst) and one female character (a college student) begin the story in Pennsylvania after an apocalyptic outbreak of what is called the Green Flu. They spend the game battling their way to new locations in search of safety. The virus, which can spread via bites, engenders uncontrolled aggression and causes mutation. The resulting zombies share similarities with the infected in the film *28 Days Later,* and indeed are called the infected, as well as zombies. The most common infected are fast-moving and most dangerous in numbers. The number and speed of zombies (which aggressively charge and pursue players), limited inventory, and varying levels of darkness create a hectic and claustrophobic atmosphere. Special types of zombie enemies also appear, as for example those that explode or large and muscular variations (the classes of zombie in the later *Dead Island* games are very similar to those in *L4D*).

Combat is primarily firearm-based, and players can attach flashlights to most guns, allowing for better vision in the dark but attracting infected. Players can also attract and distract enemies with certain noises. Gameplay focuses on teamwork: players must help, heal, and revive other survivors and can also injure them on any setting above easy. The final level of each campaign requires players to hold off a horde of zombies until rescued. Players can take different routes through these levels, and in addition, the game alters in-game events (enemies, item placement, and music) based on factors such as player performance, health status, and stress level for a more dynamic and replayable experience. Online multiplayer allows players to inhabit either zombies or survivors, in two teams of up to four each.

Valve released *Left 4 Dead 2* for the Xbox 360, PC, and OS X in 2009. The game elicited some prerelease controversy over its violent content and cover art featuring a mangled hand, as well as over worry that the short time between the release of the two games would mean reduced or eliminated support for the first title. *L4D2* offered four new survivor characters, again three males (a high-school football coach, a gambler, and a mechanic) and one female (a television production assistant). It also offered new weapons and more realistic damage to the infected. Additional special enemies were also added, including new infected unique to different levels. The sequel additionally introduced what is called the realism mode, with less onscreen information displayed, altered effectiveness of enemy damage (such as more need for headshots), and more limited options for players who have been killed to return to gameplay. Finally, the dynamic artificial intelligence rewarded players for taking longer or more difficult paths through levels. A limited-run weekly digital comic titled *The Sacrifice* that served as a prequel debuted in 2010. A downloadable content package of the same name bridges the two *L4D* games, and a second, *The Passing,* takes place between the first and second levels of the sequel and makes reference to the game *Dead Rising*. A downloadable-content crossover with *Resident Evil 6* became available for PC users in 2013, and a third *L4D* is currently planned.

See also: Dead Island; *Dead Rising*; *Resident Evil* (Video Game); *28 Days Later* Series; Video Games

John R. Ziegler

LIFEFORCE

Lifeforce is a 1985 film directed by Tobe Hooper (born William Tobe Hooper, 1943–) for the film company Cannon. A mega-budget adaptation of *The Space Vampires,* a novel by Colin Wilson (born Colin Henry Wilson, 1931–2013), it was coscripted by Dan O'Bannon. The film details the discovery of an immense alien ship by an exploratory space team. The aliens are brought to earth, and there they feed on human energy, creating an epidemic of the walking dead; London is placed under military rule.

Found in the tail of Halley's comet, the ship is filled with the corpses of giant bat-like creatures, as well as three naked humanoids, including a beautiful young female, in three stasis containers. The three specimens are taken back to the *Churchill,* Tom Carlsen's ship, but the crew members are systematically killed off. Only Carlsen escapes, in a space capsule, when the ship is gutted by fire. He lands in Texas. Meanwhile, the burned-out *Churchill* is retrieved and taken back to London, where the three humanoids are placed under observation. One of the humanoids awakens and literally sucks the life out of a guard, leaving him a dried out husk. In turn, the guard, now a desiccated corpse, drains the life out of a scientist. Ultimately, the female humanoid escapes into London, and she sustains her existence by regular infusions of energy drained from human victims, creating walking zombies, desiccated corpses that have to in turn drain the energy from another human, lest they crumble to dust. What follows is an apocalyptic disaster as the numbers of the walking dead swell. Carlsen, with the help of a doctor and colonel of the Special Air Service, must destroy the female alien before the planet is threatened.

The creatures in the film straddle the fence between being zombies and vampires: they are literally walking corpses. They shuffle and crawl their way through the streets, and only their sheer numbers allow them to overtake faster humans. They use what amounts to a kiss, rather than a bite, to spread their contagion, but the infection is nonetheless spread via the mouth, as with zombies. Critics of the film panned it, citing its tortuous plot structure, with the story of what happened on Carlsen's ship presented in a disjointed manner, as well its convoluted attempts to include references to vampire mythology. Part of the problem was that the film was recut so much for theatrical release. However, it did receive positive reviews for its special effects, such as the animatronic shriveled corpses. Released almost contemporaneously with O'Bannon's own take on the zombie genre, *Return of the Living Dead* (1985), *Lifeforce* uses the traditional zombie motif of a plague spread by infected victims. The film failed to make much of an impression on its initial release, either critically or financially. It was made with a budget of $25 million, but its opening weekend take was only $4.2 million and its gross was $11.6 million. It has since become a cult film.

See also: Apocalypse; Epidemics; *Return of the Living Dead* Series; Science Fiction; Vampires and Werewolves

John Llewellyn Probert

LIVE AND LET DIE

Live and Let Die is the eighth James Bond film, released in 1973. Produced by Harry Saltzman (born Herschel Saltzman, 1915–1994) and Albert R. Broccoli (born Albert Romolo Broccoli, 1909–1996), and directed by Guy Hamilton, it marks the first performance by Roger Moore (born Roger George Moore, 1927–) in the title role. It is loosely adapted from the Ian Fleming (born Ian Lancaster Fleming, 1908–1964) novel of the same name, the second in the James Bond series, first published by Jonathan Cape in 1954. The film revolves around gold smuggling and Cold War tensions and is the only Bond film to incorporate supernatural elements into the plot by way of Haitian Voodoo and Voodoo zombies.

After three British operatives are killed in rapid succession, one at the United Nations headquarters in New York, one in New Orleans, and one as the sacrificial object in a Voodoo ceremony on the fictitious Caribbean island of San Monique, Bond must discover links between the killings. Dr. Kananga, played by Yaphet Kotto (born Yaphet Frederick Kotto, 1939–), based on the novel's underworld Voodoo leader Buonapart Ignace Gallia (or Mr. BIG), is San Monique's diplomat to the United Nations. In the film, he uses poppies grown on the island to make heroin in New Orleans, which he then sells in New York. Assisting Kananga is Solitaire, a Voodoo priestess who loses

Geoffrey Holder portraying Baron Samedi, the Voodoo god of the dead, in the James Bond film *Live and Let Die* **(1973). (United Artists/Photofest)**

her second sight after she is seduced by Bond, which makes her useless to Kananga. Kananga takes Solitaire to San Monique to kill her in a second Voodoo ceremony, but Bond destroys the poppy fields and rescues her from one of Kananga's henchmen, including the zombie Baron Samedi, described as the man who cannot die. The pair discover Kananga's underground hideout, and Bond kills Kananga.

Voodoo serves as a backdrop for the action in the film, and Bond continually runs into problems when seeking help among locals because of their belief in zombies created through Voodoo, as they are understood in Haiti. The film also offers a few scenes of snake dancing and Voodoo ritual. In the commentary on the 1999 DVD, it is revealed that Trinidad's Geoffrey Holder, who played Samedi, choreographed the San Monique Voodoo sequences and authenticated the different Voodoo elements in the film, including his makeup. Although both Voodoo and zombification play roles in the film, very little serious discussion occurs in the script as to their meaning. Critics saw the film as a by-the-numbers adventure that traded on the Blaxploitation movement of early 1970s cinema. Roger Moore was also criticized in comparison to Sean Connery, who had relinquished the role of Bond two years earlier.

See also: Baron Samedi; Davis, Wade; Haiti; *Serpent and the Rainbow, The* (Book); Voodoo

Titus Belgard

LOVECRAFT, H. P.

H. P. Lovecraft (born Howard Phillips Lovecraft, 1890–1937) was a novelist, poet, short-story writer, critic, and scholar. A resident of Providence, Rhode Island, he lived briefly in Brooklyn, and visited cities as separate as Toronto and New Orleans. Although the word zombie does not appear in Lovecraft's letters or fiction, the reanimated dead are featured, most notably in "Herbert West—Reanimator," although Lovecraft used the trope in a variety of other stories. "Herbert West" is an episodic short story first published in six installments in *Home Brew* in 1922 and features six tales of reanimation of the dead, discussed in a separate entry.

"In the Vault" (*Tryout,* 1925) describes the actions of the undertaker and coffin-maker George Birch when he is trapped in a cemetery vault in the winter; it concludes with the revelation that Birch suffered injuries that would have had to have been caused by bites from an angry corpse. "The Horror at Red Hook" (*Weird Tales,* 1927) describes the fate of elderly mystic and magician Robert Suydam and his new bride, who are murdered while aboard ship, their bodies clawed and exsanguinated. The Yezidees that Suydam has smuggled into New York revive his corpse and take it to be sacrificed, but Suydam resists sacrifice and manages to disrupt the ceremonies. "The Thing on the Doorstep" (*Weird Tales,* 1937) initially seems to describe a failed marriage between Edward Derby and Asenath Waite, the only female student of Miskatonic University, but it is gradually revealed that Asenath is, in fact, possessed by the mind of Ephraim, her wizard father. In an attempt at resisting the usurpation of his own will and the loss of his body, Derby kills Asenath in order to strike at Ephraim, but the wizard forces Derby's spirit into Asenath's corpse, allowing Ephraim the use of Derby's body. This story is recounted, on paper, by Derby in Asenath's decaying corpse. The reanimated corpse is not a zombie in the usual meaning of the term as it retains volition and memory.

"Cool Air" (*Tales of Magic and Mystery,* 1928) and "The Outsider" (*Weird Tales,* April 1926), on the other hand, are major stories and show most of Lovecraft's considerable strengths. "Cool Air" is about a narrator who befriends a fellow boarder, Dr. Muñoz, discovering him to be an erudite gentleman who favors cool climates and cold rooms. All is well until a power failure and a heat wave, and the narrator discovers that what remains of Dr. Muñoz is a dark, slimy trail that leads to a little pool of putrescence. A note from Dr. Muñoz explains that he died 18 years earlier and kept himself alive through refrigeration, and though this resolution is not a complete surprise, the unpleasant physicality of his demise is disturbing. "The Outsider" tells of a mysterious individual born in an old gothic castle. This individual is almost completely isolated, possessing only dim memories of being nursed by an aged person. After a lengthy, almost epic climb, the nameless individual discovers he has merely reached the solid ground, though the land he explores is hardly less nightmarish than the castle, being full of ruins. He enters a brightly lit castle filled with revelers, but all flee in horror, and he sees himself reflected: a ghoulish, decaying corpse. It is a powerful conclusion to an intriguing story.

Although Lovecraft's fiction frequently made use of the irrational, Lovecraft himself was a rationalist and a materialist, evolving a personal philosophy of cosmicism, a belief that humans are insignificant in the vast universe. Lovecraft thought consciously about what he was trying to achieve through his writing, and he explicated many of his ideas in his *Supernatural Horror in Literature* (1927; corrected edition, Hippocampus Press, 2000), beginning with the premises that the oldest and strongest emotion of mankind is fear, and the oldest and strongest kind of fear is fear of the unknown. To evoke fear of the unknown, particularly a cosmic fear, was then a noble tradition for Lovecraft, and to do so he created a pantheon of deities inimical to humanity. At the top were Yog-Sothoth and Azathoth, and beneath them he established a hierarchy of dangerous and merciless beings to whom humanity and its concerns are at best trivial.

See also: "Herbert West—Reanimator"; *Re-Animator* Series

Richard Bleiler

LUGOSI, BELA

Bela Lugosi (born Béla Ferenc Dezso Blaskó, 1882–1956) was a Hungarian actor who made the character Count Dracula iconographic in *Dracula* (1931), a classic directed by Tod Browning (born Charles Albert Browning Jr., 1880–1962). He is also known for his roles in various Haitian-based Voodoo and zombie films, often depicted as a master mesmerist capable of hypnotizing potential victims with a simple stare. Lugosi's acting career began modestly, with minor roles in Hungarian stage plays, but it took wing in 1927 when he was selected to play Count Dracula on Broadway, in the Hamilton Deane (1880–1958) and John L. Balderston (1889–1954) version. This led to his being cast in *Dracula*, as well as his becoming synonymous with the 1930s horror film scene, often paired with Boris Karloff. Lugosi was typecast as a horror villain in various Universal films, and was then picked up to star in the independent *White Zombie* (1932), *Voodoo Man* (1944), and *Zombies on Broadway* (1945), all of which cast him as a bokur, commanding a legion of zombies.

In *White Zombie,* Lugosi stars as Murder Legendre, a Voodoo master who turns people into zombified slaves to run his sugar mill. Legendre is approached by a plantation owner who wishes to possess the body and soul of a young, beautiful woman, so he pays to have her placed under a zombie spell. The two fake her death using poison, and Legendre performs a fake resurrection, after she is turned over to the plantation owner. When the plantation owner has a change of heart, the villain Legendre zombifies him and attempts to make the female zombie murder her fiancé. In the film's finale, Legendre loses control of his zombies who attack and kill him. In *Voodoo Man,* Lugosi is a mad scientist, Dr. Richard Marlowe, who captures young women to use Voodoo and hypnosis to transfer their life force to his zombified, dead wife. Placing the women in a state of suspended animation, he finally resurrects his wife, but she dies again after Marlowe is shot by police. Lugosi played the role more for pathos or sympathy, emphasizing the love the character possesses for his wife, especially in scenes where she briefly comes to life but then reverts back to an unresponsive, zombie state. In *Zombies on Broadway,* Lugosi plays zombie expert Professor Paul Renault. Where *White Zombie* and *Voodoo Man* are more traditional horror films that treat Voodoo-related zombies in a serious light, *Zombies on Broadway* gives the zombie a comic touch, much like the later Bud Abbott (born William Alexander Abbot, 1895–1974) and Lou Costello (born Louis Francis Cristillo, 1906–1959) comic horror films. Like *White Zombie*, the film ends with a broken spell and Lugosi being attacked by one of his own zombies. In all three films, zombies are represented as recently resurrected or hypnotized humans who are forced to do the bidding of a Voodoo master, that is, until some outside force breaks the control of the bokur.

See also: Bokur/Caplata; Comedy; Universal Studios; *Voodoo Man*; *White Zombie*; *Zombies on Broadway*

Anthony J. Fonseca

MABERRY, JONATHAN

Jonathan Maberry (1958–) is a *New York Times* best-selling and multiple Bram Stoker Award-winning author, magazine feature writer, playwright, and writing teacher/lecturer. His fiction includes *The Pine Deep* trilogy, *Ghost Road Blues* (2006), *Dead Man's Song* (2007), and *Bad Moon Rising* (2008); the Joe Ledger series of action thrillers; *The Wolfman* (2010), which is based on the 2010 Universal Pictures film; *Dead of Night* (2011); and the Benny Imura series of Young Adult zombie thrillers *Rot and Ruin* (2010), *Dust and Decay* (2011), and *Flesh and Bone* (2012).

Maberry has an affinity for zombies. His 2009 sci-fi horror thriller, *Patient Zero*, opens as Baltimore cop Joe Ledger encounters a zombie who turns out to be a bio-engineered weapon. Ledger uncovers various problems, namely international terrorism and espionage. *Rot and Ruin* tells the tale of an apocalyptic future filled with zombies. Lead character Benny Imura was born into California's zombie apocalypse, and his parents were killed. At age 15, he joins his older half-brother Tom to become a zombie killer. *In Dead of Night,* a death row prisoner named Homer Gibbons is infected with Lucifer 113, a zombification drug, so that he might suffer through consciousness while in his grave. A relative requests that his body be transferred to a local funeral home, where the killer resurrects, with an insatiable hunger for humans; in addition, his bite infects survivors, who then become zombies. A significant portion of Maberry's work for Marvel Comics features zombies: *Marvel Zombies Return* and both *Marvel Universe vs. The Punisher* and *Marvel Universe vs. Wolverine* use a zombie apocalypse as their raison d'etre. Mayberry conducted dozens of interviews with experts in several disciplines to publish *Zombie CSU: The Forensics of the Living Dead* (2008), wherein he posits the zombie apocalypse as a result of both supernatural and scientific origins, such as a plague or pandemic. The text contains various digressions: a discussion of slow versus fast zombies, a consideration of military reaction to zombies, and a hypothetical chronology of zombie art.

His nonfiction works include *The Vampire Slayer's Field Guide to the Undead* (2001), *Vampire Universe* (2006), *The Cryptopedia: A Dictionary of the Weird, Strange, and Downright Bizarre* (2007), the aforementioned *Zombie CSU*, *They Bite!* (2009), and *Wanted: Undead or Alive* (2010). In 2004, Maberry, an eighth degree black belt in Jiu-Jitsu, was inducted into the International Martial Arts Hall of Fame mostly because of his extensive number of martial arts guides.

See also: Apocalypse; Epidemics; Vampires and Werewolves; Young Adult Fiction

Hank Wagner

MAGIC ISLAND, THE

The Magic Island (1929) is a travelogue written by journalist W. B. Seabrook in which he recounts his experiences as a white man in Haiti being initiated into mysteries of Voodoo. The book is credited with introducing the American public to the trope of the zombie, though this is not the primary focus of the work.

The Magic Island blends fact with fiction, eroticizing Haiti and its black inhabitants with lurid accounts of their beliefs and religious practices, indicating that this is a special place where anything can happen. In keeping with this style of writing, "Dead Men Working in the Cane Fields," the chapter in which the author mentions zombies directly, is formatted as a frame tale, where the author's Haitian friend Polyniece tells him folklore about the creature, which he represents to Seabrook as fact. In the first story, when the Haitian American Sugar Company factory offered bonuses for new workers in 1918, Ti Joseph, an overseer from the country, brought a string of ragged men to the plant and collected their wages himself every Saturday. The men had vacant stares and were in a daze, and shuffled behind Ti Joseph, who explained their lethargy as due to their being from the country and so overwhelmed by life in the city. But if zombies are permitted to taste meat or salt, the magic reanimating them would be undone. This happens when Ti Joseph's kindhearted wife Croyance takes pity on the creatures and gives them pralines with pistachios during a holiday when her husband is away. Croyance, however, does not realize that the pistachios in the candies are salted. Once the zombies taste the salt, they wail in pain because they suddenly realize that they are dead. Immediately, the zombies run to their graves, clawing at the earth until they can lie down in their original resting places and be dead once more. A second story at the end of the chapter tells of a young bride married to a wealthy older planter. She discovers that her husband's laborers are all zombies and is so horrified that she goes mad.

In addition to telling Seabrook supposedly true stories about zombies, Polyniece showed to the author people he swore were the dead who had been raised from their graves through Voodoo. The alleged zombies were laboring under the hot sun in the cane fields: their faces were devoid of expression, and they stared vacantly into space, even when they were introduced to the author. Still, Seabrook has doubts about Polyniece's story, and indicates that the people his friend believes are zombies are in fact profoundly retarded adults who had been forced to toil in the fields. Polyniece attempts to persuade his incredulous white friend that zombies are real by citing a section of the Haitian penal code that defines as murder the act of administering a substance to someone that puts the person in the coma and causes his or her family to bury the victim, believing that he or she is dead, regardless of the final results. The implication is that this law would not exist if the island did not have a problem with bokurs' turning people into zombies. Polyniece also reminds Seabrook that even the poorest Haitian peasants bury their dead beneath masonry to make it more difficult for the bodies to be removed from the grave and made into zombies.

See also: Bokur/Caplata; "Country of Comers-Back, The"; Haiti; Race; Seabrook, W. B.; *Tell My Horse*; Voodoo

June Michele Pulliam

"MALTHUSIAN'S ZOMBIE"

"Malthusian's Zombie" is a short story by Jeffrey Ford (1955–) which appears in the 2008 anthology *The Living Dead* and offers an original take on the creature. The story pays homage to "The Facts in the Case of M. Valdemar" (*Broadway Journal* and *American Review*, 1845), by Edgar Allan Poe, a proto-zombie short story in which a terminally ill man is hypnotized moments before his death, so that the mesmerist can remain in contact with him as his soul makes its journey from this world to the next one. Although the tale borrows from Poe, it diverges significantly in that it allows the mesmerist to absolutely control the undead subject.

Ford's story is similar to Poe's in a number of ways. First, the plight of the zombie is related by an observer, but in this case, the narrator is a professor of literature rather than a medical doctor. Malthusian, a retired psychologist, is the narrator's new neighbor who fascinates him with his knowledge of literature and stories about how he worked for the U.S. government on a clandestine and questionable project, as he agreed to engage in some super-secret work for the government during World War II in exchange for the safe passage of his mother, father, and sister to the United States. Before long, the elderly Malthusian is dying, and wrests a promise from the narrator that he take care of his zombie, a man who was kidnapped away from his family nearly 40 years earlier and whose will and memories of his former life were overridden by Malthusian, for the purpose of creating an assassin devoid of volition and willing to do anything he was told to do by those who controlled him.

Malthusian's zombie, however, is capable of more than killing others. He can be commanded to do things that would seem impossible, such as play a Chopin nocturne on the piano after hearing it only once, or growing fatter or thinner or halting the aging process entirely. After the project had been cancelled, Malthusian was ordered by his superiors to set fire to his lab and thus eliminate the zombie. Malthusian, however, has pangs of conscience, and takes his zombie home to live with him, thus voiding his contract and keeping him apart from his family. Now that Malthusian is dying, he can no longer care for the zombie, and so he requests that the narrator take him until what Malthusian describes as his transformation is complete. Malthusian dies shortly thereafter, and the zombie comes to live with the narrator and his family. After a few months, the narrator notices that the zombie begins to age suddenly, since his former master is no longer present to command him to stop getting old. Then the zombie, seeming to remember his past life, draws what the narrator believes is a picture of his previous residence. When the narrator brings the zombie to this place, ostensibly to reunite him with his long-lost family, the creature begins to morph into Malthusian's likeness. At this point, it becomes clear to the narrator that Malthusian's final order to his zombie was that he assume his master's form, and even retain his memories, so that he could be reunited as Malthusian with his master's family.

See also: Existentialism; "Facts in the Case of M. Valdemar, The"; Free Will; Poe, Edgar Allan

June Michele Pulliam

MARVEL ZOMBIES

Marvel Zombies was originally a five-issue series (2005–2006) published by Marvel Comics, following their Fantastic Four characters into a parallel universe where the world's superheroes have been infected with a virus that turns them into zombies. The series is written by Robert Kirkman, who is best known to zombie enthusiasts for his self-published epic *The Walking Dead* series of graphic novels. The popularity of the limited-run series encouraged Marvel to collaborate with Dynamite Entertainment and produce several sequels. *Marvel Zombies vs. the Army of Darkness* and *Army of Darkness* explain the origins of the infection, whereas *Marvel Zombies 4* included characters from Marvel's horror comics. Additionally, the *Marvel Zombies* have inspired a set of action figures.

See also: Epidemics; Graphic Novels and Comics; *Walking Dead, The* (Comic)

June Michele Pulliam

MASH-UPS, LITERARY

A literary mash-up is a work that combines two or more sources into a new work that sheds new light on the original, while modernizing it with references to current popular culture.

This is the case with Seth Grahame-Smith's novel *Pride and Prejudice and Zombies* (2009), which combines Jane Austen's (1775–1817) *Pride and Prejudice* (1813) with the trope of the zombie that operates by Romero's Rules in that it is undead, violent, mono-focused, and cannibalistic. In Grahame-Smith's version of the novel, the Regency England of Elizabeth Bennett and Fitzwilliam Darcy is beset by zombies, or dreadfuls, as they are called, and Elizabeth wins Darcy's heart through her zombie-fighting prowess as well as her sharp intellect. While Grahame-Smith's novel is the first literary work to be described by this term, the mash-up predates his work, and the term was originally used to apply to a song that is created by blending two or more existing musical compositions.

The popularity of *Pride and Prejudice and Zombies* prompted Grahame-Smith's publisher, Quirk Books, to commission more works along this model, including Grahame-Smith's *Abraham Lincoln: Vampire Hunter* (2011) as well as *Sense and Sensibility and Sea Monsters* (2009), by Ben H. Winters (no date available) and *Jane Slayre* (2010), a mash-up of Charlotte Bronte's (1816–1855) *Jane Eyre* (1847) and the trope of the vampire, by Sherri Browning Erwin (no date available). Moreover, the popularity of *Pride and Prejudice and Zombies* caused other publishers to follow suit, releasing titles such as *The Adventures of Huckleberry Finn and Zombie Jim: Mark Twain's Classic with Crazy Zombie Goodness* (2011), by Gallery Books; *Alice in Zombieland* (2011), by Sourcebooks; and *The Undead World of Oz: L. Frank Baum's The Wonderful Wizard of Oz Complete with Zombies and Monsters* (2009), by Coscom Entertainment.

Well-known children's works that are in the public domain have also been made into zombie mash-ups. These titles include *Pat the Zombie* (2011), a parody of the children's picture book *Pat the Bunny*, but meant for adults; *Jack and Jill Went Up to Kill: A Book of Zombie Nursery Rhymes* (2011); and *The Zombie Night before Christmas* (2010).

See also: Children's Books; *Pride and Prejudice and Zombies*; Romero's Rules

June Michele Pulliam

MATHESON, RICHARD

A prolific author of fantasy, science fiction, and horror, Richard Matheson's (born Richard Burton Matheson, 1926–2013) biggest contribution to zombie fiction is his 1954 novella *I Am Legend*, positing a post-apocalyptic world in distant 1976. The resulting radiation after a nuclear exchange between the United States and the Soviet Union has radically transformed the natural world, causing, among other things, an epidemic of flies and dust storms. The altered environment produces bacteria that infect nearly 100 percent of the human race, reviving the newly dead and making the living allergic to sunlight and garlic. Civilization quickly topples after many of the living succumb to the virus, while the living infected are severely limited in their ability to conduct their daily activities because they must take shelter during the daylight hours. Robert Neville, who believes himself to be the last man on earth, barricades himself in his home every night against the reanimated dead, who gather outside and howl for his blood. The reanimated dead are mindless and cannot fully understand their condition; they seek human blood because they believe that they are vampires rather than out of any need for sustenance. During the day, Robert kills as many of the infected as he can, not realizing that some are dead and mindless, and therefore, beyond redemption, while others are the living infected. The living infected, who are in the process of re-establishing civilization, view Robert as a legendary serial killer who must be caught and executed.

I Am Legend prefigures the modern zombie narrative with its post-apocalyptic setting and mindless undead who lack a leader. While zombies created by Voodoo are equally mindless, they are always under the control of a master. Matheson's undead, on the other hand, prefigure the zombie as represented in George Romero's film *Night of the Living Dead* (1968) in that they are controlled by a drive instead of a master. In fact, George Romero names Matheson's *I Am Legend* as one of the texts that influenced the making of his groundbreaking zombie film. Also, in Matheson's novella, when the dead begin to rise, civilization shortly thereafter comes to halt. Romero's take on the zombie similarly topples civilization.

Matheson is best known for *I Am Legend*, which has been made into a film three times. Matheson is also the author of such well-known works including the novels *The Shrinking Man* (1956), *A Stir of Echoes* (1958), *Hell House* (1971), and *What Dreams May Come* (1978), which were also made into films. Matheson is also known for his work as writer for *The Twilight Zone* as well as penning the screen plays for "The Enemy Within" (1966), an episode of *Star Trek* and the teleplay "The Night Stalker," a television movie that preceded the series *Kolchak: The Night Stalker*.

Matheson received many awards for his work during his career, including The World Fantasy Award for Life Achievement (1984) and from The Horror Writer's Association, The Bram Stoker Award for Lifetime Achievement (1991). He was inducted into the Science Fiction Hall of fame in 2010, and died days before he was to receive the Visionary Award in 2013 during the annual Saturn Awards ceremony.

See also: I Am Legend (Film); *I Am Legend* (Novel); *Night of the Living Dead* Series

June Michele Pulliam

MATTEI, BRUNO

Bruno Mattei (1931–2007) was an Italian filmmaker who directed more than 50 films and worked on dozens more. Although he is remembered mainly for his zombie movie *Hell of the Living Dead* (1980), his work spanned five decades and many genres, emphasizing low-budget exploitation that falls into categories like nazisploitation and nunsploitation. He is also known for his longtime collaboration with Claudio Fragasso (1951–), the director behind *Troll 2* (1990). When director Lucio Fulci became too ill to finish *Zombi 3* (1988), Fragasso and Mattei completed the film.

Mattei shared with Fragasso both directing and writing responsibilities on *Hell of the Living Dead,* along with José María Cunillés (1943–), who is credited with the story and screenplay. The film is also known for its use of original music by the band Goblin. This music is similar to that used by George Romero in *Dawn of the Dead* (1978), as is Fragasso's and Mattei's graphic depiction of the zombie as cannibalistic. However, the film offers originality in that it veers away from the typical vague explanation for the cause of the zombie apocalypse. Here the story accounts for the apocalypse by blaming scientists who created a zombie virus to reduce human overpopulation by causing humans to eat one another. The overpopulation of a tribe in New Guinea is handled thusly by white scientists and soldiers. Such political subtext would later come to inform films such as Romero's *Day of the Dead* (1985) and *28 Days Later* (2002) by Danny Boyle. The film's ending, in particular, is important in this respect: it shows the spread of the contagion from New Guinea into first-world commercial centers, suggesting the threat of reverse colonization. More memorable than *Hell of the Living Dead*'s politics are its gruesome scenes, which reach heights of taboo and disgust, particularly when a young boy eats his father.

Gore and visceral horror also characterize Mattei's *Rats* (1984), a post-apocalyptic tale inspired by the success of *Mad Max* (1979). Near the end of his life, Mattei returned to zombies with *Island of the Living Dead* (2006) and its sequel, *Zombies: The Beginning* (2007). Here, zombies infect the world after one of them is accidentally raised from the sea. Overall, his films are likely better known than his actual name, perhaps owing to the fact that he used more than 10 pseudonyms. These include Jimmy Matheus, Vincent Dawn, Stefan Oblowsky, and Pierre Le Blanc.

See also: Dawn of the Dead; Fulci, Lucio; Italian Cinema; Nazi Zombies; Romero, George

L. Andrew Cooper

MOCKUMENTARIES

Mockumentaries, or mock documentaries, featuring zombies typically either follow a film crew during a zombie apocalypse or attempt to illustrate the truth of the zombie status as secondary citizens. Despite being similar in many ways to the so-called found footage format of vérité horror films such as Michael Bartlett's (1976–) and Kevin Gates's (1976–) *The Zombie Diaries* (2006), Jaume Balagueró's (1968–) *[REC]* (2007), or George Romero's *Diary of the Dead* (2008), mockumentaries are generally more invested in comedy than these films, relying on the contrast between the simulated earnestness of the people interviewed (both zombie and human) and the traditional horror tropes of unthinking zombies who attack humans to eat their flesh.

In Laura Moss's short mockumentary *Rising Up: The Story of the Zombie Rights Movement* (2009), a female professor in an office says that laws dictate where, how, and what zombies can eat, as the images on the screen flip from a zombie eating the intestines of a dead dog to a zombie chewing on a disembodied arm, to a zombie straining to reach a young child who is smiling and waving at the camera—a disparity designed to provoke laughter. Perhaps the most famous professionally produced zombie mockumentary is *American Zombie* (2007), directed by Grace Lee, who also co-wrote the screenplay. The film follows Lee as she creates a documentary about the zombie population of Los Angeles. The crew interviews three zombies in particular: Ivan, a convenience-store clerk; Judy, a representative for a health-food producer; Lisa, a florist, who specializes in funeral arrangements. They also interview Joel, the director of ZAG, the Zombie Advocacy Group. Like other zombie mockumentaries, *American Zombie* relies upon the contrast between horrific images, such as Lisa's maggot-infested stomach wound or Ivan's blood-encrusted head wound, and the more mundane comments of the zombies themselves, as when Judy says she is just like everyone else, or Joel's proclamation that ZAG's tagline is a parody of a past gay rights' movement tagline. The film takes a darker turn when the crew goes to Live Dead, a Burning Man–inspired festival of the undead, where they uncover the flesh-eating monsters John has been hoping to find.

More common than full-length films, however, are short zombie mockumentaries, often produced by amateur filmmakers and posted to video-sharing sites. Like the professional versions, these shorts often draw on the ideas of zombies as misunderstood social outcasts and generally end in crew members being attacked by the zombies whose image they hope to rehabilitate. Despite their often derivative content, these amateur mockumentaries, by far the most common form of short zombie videos, highlight the continuing popularity of the genre.

See also: Comedy; *[REC]* Series; Romero, George; Sentience

Margo Collins

MONSTER ISLAND TRILOGY

The *Monster Island* Trilogy was originally published serially in 2003 on David Wellington's website. The actual published trilogy of novels was to ultimately include *Monster Island* (2006), *Monster Nation* (2006), and *Monster Planet* (2007), all with Thunder's Mouth Press. Covering 12 years, in locales including New York City, Colorado, Egypt, and Somalia, Wellington's novels chronicle an infestation of the unliving, as the word zombie is seldom used. These creatures threaten to eradicate the human race.

Wellington's cannibalistic undead are controlled by an ancient spirit, Mael Mag Och, who in life was a willing sacrifice, strangled in an Orkney Island bog so that his culture could have a better harvest season. The series is distinguished by its articulate descriptions of survivor loneliness, its accurate detail of military hardware and biological and/or chemical war agents, its depiction of military strategy, and its constant plot twists and uses of dramatic irony. Moreover, readers are given a glimpse into the minds of the undead, conveying a sense of what the undead think and feel before killing. The series also makes some overt political statements as, for example, when it argues that no girl should ever again be infibulated and then sold into marriage as a child.

The series is also defined by Wellington's practice of having his living heroes converted to the undead as the story progresses. Dekalb, a U.N. weapons inspector who is captured in Somalia by an English-speaking commander of the Somaliland Girl Army, is the series' primary character. Dekalb leaves his daughter Sarah in Somalia to become a soldier in the Girl Army, the best fate he can hope for his child in this post-apocalyptic world, while he helps the commander and her sister soldiers boat all the way to the U.N. Secretariat building in New York City to obtain AIDS treatments for the leader of the newly formed Free Women's Republic of Somaliland. Gary Fleck, an undead doctor, menaces the living until the end of the series, scheming to keep enough humans alive to serve as livestock that he can feed off. *Monster Nation,* a prequel, is set five years before *Monster Island.* In this novel, readers discover how the disease leading to reanimation began, when undead cells began to divide or reproduce, thanks to the investigations of the American Captain Clark, who tries to track one of the earliest victims, Nilla, also known as Julia. *Monster Planet,* the final novel of the trilogy, returns the action to Africa, with Dekalb's daughter Sarah and an eventual showdown with Mael Mag Och and Dr. Fleck.

See also: Africa; Apocalypse; Cannibalism; Epidemics; Romero's Rules; Sentience; Wellington, David

Danel Olson

"MR. GARRITY AND THE GRAVES"

"Mr. Garrity and the Graves" is a 1964 episode (Season 5) of *The Twilight Zone* featuring the reanimated dead rising from their graves. In it, Jared Garrity, a travelling peddler, arrives in the small Western town of Happiness, Arizona. Garrity is informed that previously, the newly renamed town was known for its gunfights and violent deaths, as well as its number of corpses buried at Boot Hill Cemetery. Garrity, a con artist, offers to restore complete happiness by reanimating the town's loved ones, offering this service for free. In front of a dozen or so townspeople, he then resurrects a dog which had just been run over by a delivery wagon. That night Garrity goes out to the cemetery and performs his ritual, which he claims is based on a scientific principle he learned while in the Himalayas. By the end of the episode, he has created an undead army.

After going out to resurrect the dead at night, Garrity returns to the saloon, and a body can be seen in the mist which looks eerily like the deceased brother of Mr. Jensen, one of the town's residents, as the body walks with the sibling's distinctive limp. Jensen, who killed his brother in a business disagreement, almost immediately offers Garrity money to send his brother back to the grave. The other townspeople, having seen the resurrected brother, also become antsy about their own loved dead returning, and all offer Garrity cash to send them back to their graves. As Garrity is leaving town in his wagon that night, the dog comes running from the wilderness to join him, followed by his assistant and wagon driver, an ex-stage actor, who pretended to be the resurrected brother. Garrity and his confederates ride away with the money, joking about the smoke and mirrors trick. As they drive off, the dead begin rising from their graves. While they shamble toward Happiness, one of the reanimated dead comments that the peddler did not do himself justice, that he "sure can do a job of resurrectin.'" A few of the resurrected dead mention the harm they intend to their loved ones when they find them.

Although the word zombie is never used in the episode, and the resurrected dead are not decomposed and do speak, the image of the graves moving slowly as dirt is pushed off of them, followed by bodies emerging from the ground, are both early versions of the motifs used in resurrected zombie films, as is the distinctive emotionless shambling gait of the undead, walking with their arms held lifeless by the side, and their blank stares while walking. This is especially evident in the extras comprising the resurrected crowd in the background of the main action. Three possible sources have been identified for "Mr. Garrity and the Graves," which is credited as a teleplay by Rod Serling (1924–1975), based on a story by Mike Korologos (likely a pseudonym used by Serling). Another theory is that a short story by Philip José Farmer (1918–2009) titled "Uproar in Acheron" (*The Saint Mystery Magazine,* 1962) is the source for the charlatan ruse. A third possible source is a tale titled "Mister Lazarus," found in *Historic Haunted America* (1995). All scholars agree that the twist ending was original to *The Twilight Zone* episode.

See also: Reanimation

Anthony J. Fonseca

MUMMIES

Mummies in fiction and folklore are normally not considered zombies, but there are some notable exceptions. In most fictional representations of the mummy, the creature does not even reanimate; instead, it frightens the living by inspiring terrifying dreams or perhaps exacting revenge through a curse laid on anyone who destroy or enter its tomb. However, if zombies are to be understood as creatures who generally lack free will and who are often the walking dead, then a few notable cinematic and literary mummies can be categorized as zombies. These mummies are similar to earlier representations of the zombie as the reanimated dead who have been deprived of their will through magical means, usually through Voodoo or Haitian mysticism. In the case of some mummies, a curse prevents their souls from departing for the afterlife. Some more famous mummies who fit this description would include Kharis in the Hammer Studios film *The Mummy* (1959) and Bubba Ho-Tep in both the titular short story (published in *The King Is Dead: Tales of Elvis Post-Mortem,* 1994), by Joe R. Lansdale, and the 2002 film version of it, directed by Don Coscarelli.

In the Hammer Studios film *The Mummy,* Princess Anarka's high priest, named Kharis, is caught trying to reanimate her after her death. Kharis is then buried alive for committing sacrilege and sentenced to eternally guard Anarka while suspended between life and death. Four thousand years later, when a British archeological team unearths Anarka's tomb, the leader accidentally reanimates Kharis by reading the *Scroll of Life* that was buried with him. Mehmet Bey, an Egyptian who is faithful to the old gods, is incensed by the British archeological expedition that despoils his country's sacred treasures and uses dark magic to turn the reanimated Kharis into an instrument of revenge. Bubba Ho-Tep is mummified alive as punishment for a sexual transgression, sleeping with one of the Pharoah's women. Like Kharis, Bubba Ho-Tep is similarly suspended between life and death. Unearthed in the 20th century, the creature is eventually sold to a small-time travelling carnival to become a roadside attraction, but he disappears after the tour bus carrying him skids off a bridge, releasing him into the creek below. Now Bubba Ho-Tep wanders the halls of the Mud Creek Shady Grove Convalescent Home, driven by the insatiable need to suck souls from the living to compensate for the soul that was taken from him when he was first mummified.

Despite these examples, most fictional mummies are not zombies. For example, the mummy Ramses in *The Mummy or Ramses the Damned,* by Anne Rice (born Howard Allen Frances O'Brien, 1941–) is a reanimated corpse, but he is not driven by a consuming desire, such as the need to take revenge on those who have disturbed his tomb or to find a lost love. Rather, Ramses awakens in the Victorian era with his free will intact, and is as capable of carrying out his wishes in the 19th century as he was during the time of the pharaohs. The mummy Imhotep in the 1932 Universal Studios film *The Mummy* is also not a zombie; the 1959 film *The Mummy* follows much the same plot as this version. Imhotep as envisioned in 1932 by Karl Freund (born Karl W. Freund, 1890–1969) is similar to Kharis in that both are buried alive for sacrilege and accidentally reanimated after an archeologist reads aloud their burial scrolls. However, Imhotep has more agency than does Kharis, or than any typical zombie, for that matter. Once Imhotep is reanimated, he walks out of the tomb that has been his prison for nearly 4,000 years, removes his bandages, dresses in modern clothes, and searches for his lost love, Princess Anck-es-en-Amon, who has been reincarnated in the 20th century as Helen Grovesner. While Imhotep is certainly undead, he is as articulate as Rice's Ramses and not subject to anyone else's will. In fact, Imhotep can mesmerize others to make them subject to his will.

Moreover, Ramses and Imhotep do not look like corpses. Ramses's form is still pleasing. And while Imhotep does not have a youthful appearance (his desiccated skin makes him look like someone with a bad case of sun damage), he does not look like a walking corpse. Thus, both Ramses and Imhotep can pass among the living without alarming them. Kharis and Bubba Ho-Tep, on the other hand, do resemble walking corpses. Bubba Ho-Tep is a dried out husk whose bandages are so brown and rotted that they have dissolved into his withered, preserved flesh. Like most contemporary zombies, Bubba Ho-Tep's appearance is fearful because he is so obviously a walking corpse. The flesh on his lips has rotted away, freezing his face in a rictus of pain, but his eyes are very much alive and animated with a malevolent fire, suggesting that he is imprisoned within his decaying flesh. Kharis presents a similar picture of decay. His cerements are gray with age and rot, and his eyes are similarly animated. However, whereas Bubba Ho-Tep's face is set in a perpetual snarl, Kharis's mouth has been sealed shut with bandages. We learn that before Kharis was mummified alive, his tongue was cut out to prevent his cries from offending the gods. In fiction, the voice is symbolic of agency, so Kharis's inability to speak and his lack of a functioning mouth or tongue shows us to what degree he has been deprived of his will. Finally, both Kharis and Bubba Ho-Tep have the shambling gait of the zombie, which further suggests that they are reanimated corpses, although both can move quickly when it is necessary. So while the mummy is a variety of the undead, the creature can only rarely be classified as a zombie unless certain other conditions are met.

See also: Bubba Ho-Tep (Film); "Bubba Ho-Tep" (Short Story); Haiti; *Mummy, The*; Voodoo

June Michele Pulliam

MUMMY, THE

The Mummy (aka *Terror of the Mummy*) is a 1959 Hammer Studios film directed by Terence Fisher (1904–1980). It follows the same plot as the 1932 Universal Studios film of the same name: The mummy Kharis, played here by Christopher Lee (born Christopher Frank Carandini Lee, 1922–), was Princess Ananka's high priest and lover. He is caught trying to reanimate the princess after her death and punished for his sacrilege by having his tongue cut out before he is buried alive, then sentenced to eternally guard Ananka while suspended between life and death.

Four thousand years later, John Banning, played by Peter Cushing (born Peter Wilton Cushing, 1913–1994), leads an archeological team that unearths Ananka's tomb, and Banning accidentally reanimates Kharis when he reads the *Scroll of Life* that was buried with him. Mehmet Bey, an Egyptian who is faithful to the old gods,

In Hammer Studios' film *The Mummy* (1959), the mummy Kharis (Christopher Lee) attempts to throttle John Banning (Peter Cushing), whose archeological team has unearthed the tomb of his 4,000-year-old lover, Princess Ananka. (Universal International Pictures/Photofest)

is incensed by the archeological expedition for despoiling his country's sacred treasures, and so uses dark magic to turn the reanimated Kharis into an instrument of revenge against the team's members, whom he considers infidels. Bey's plans are thwarted after Kharis sees Banning's wife Isobel, who is the spitting image of Ananka. Kharis is distracted by Isobel long enough for Banning and his party to definitively kill him. The film was a result of Hammer Studios' acquiring the rights to Universal Studios' monsters in the 1950s. Hammer Studios soon after put out its own version of Universal Studios' 1932 film *The Mummy*, which was loosely based on the original, as well as Universal's sequels *The Mummy's Hand* (1940), *The Mummy's Tomb* (1942), and *The Mummy's Ghost* (1944).

While most mummies are not zombies, the mummy Kharis is a notable exception in that he looks and behaves like many iterations of this creature. First, he is undead, something underscored by his gray bandages and decaying face. These features give him the appearance of a moldering corpse. Kharis is deprived of free will, another trait shared with the Voodoo zombie. Kharis's will is subordinated to whoever controls the *Scroll of Life*. At first, Bey commands Kharis through this document, but Bey's commands are not Kharis's prime directive because Kharis was sentenced to eternally protect Ananka. So when the mummy mistakes Isobel for the princess, he is subordinate to her, which allows Isobel to command him to stop throttling her husband John. Kharis's lack of agency is emphasized by his missing tongue. The voice is a long-standing metaphor for agency in fiction, so Kharis's inability to speak signifies his loss of his will. Kharis's missing tongue is indicated in his mummified face, in which his mouth has been bandaged shut, while his piercing eyes are left uncovered.

See also: Hammer Film Productions; Mummies; Universal Studios

June Michele Pulliam

MY BOYFRIEND'S BACK

My Boyfriend's Back is a 1993 comedy horror film directed by Bob Balaban, a well-known character actor who had two years previously directed an episode of the television series *Eerie, Indiana* (1991–1992) titled "Zombies in PJs." *My Boyfriend's Back* was only Balaban's second film, following the cultish 1989 dark comedy *Parents,* which likened meat-eating to cannibalism. The 1992 *Eerie, Indiana* episode spoofing consumerism featured zombies more related to the Voodoo zombie in that they were living beings who had been turned into mindless slaves forced to do their master's bidding. Balaban's 1993 film, on the other hand, concentrated on the undead, cannibalistic version of the zombie.

The film, whose title is based on the 1963 rock hit by The Angels, tells the story of Johnny Dingle, who returns from the dead as a zombie to fulfill his dream of dating Missy McCloud, the girl he has loved since he was six years old. Johnny is killed while trying to stop a robbery at the shop where Missy works. Just before the shy and lovelorn teen dies, he elicits from Missy a promise to go to the prom with him. This promise is enough to cause him to rise from his grave, reanimated by his single-minded desire. But as Johnny prepares for his big night, his body parts fall off and decay. An old woman, played by Cloris Leachman (1926–) who knows about Johnny's condition, reveals to him the terrible truth about what he must do to stave off decay—consume human flesh, as each bite will give him about 20 minutes before his body decays once again. But Johnny must fight more than his revulsion at eating human flesh in order to remain intact long enough to take Missy to the prom. He must also battle Missy's insanely jealous boyfriend Buck and his friends, who are disgusted by the presence of a dead boy among them. Meanwhile, the local doctor who first examined Johnny after he returned from the dead has discovered that his flesh has the ability to rejuvenate the bodies of the living, and he schemes to kill Johnny and use the boy's body to become wealthy, marketing cosmetic surgery without the surgery.

Johnny's zombiism is a combination of the zombie created through magical means and ones following Romero's Rules. Love is the magical force that brings Johnny back from the dead, but he also needs to consume human flesh if he wishes to forestall returning to the grave. It is a fairly typical teen sex comedy in which the shy and un-athletic boy eventually wins the girl of his dreams from the popular jock. The story is told through the frame of a comic book narrative: each chapter opens with the scene illustrated as a comic book before transitioning into film. The film is also an early example of the Rom Zom Com, or romantic zombie comedy, a term popularized in 2004 with the film *Shaun of the Dead*. The film did not do well at the box office, grossing only $3.3 million, despite a $1.5 million opening weekend on 1,165 screens. *My Boyfriend's Back* was originally slated to be titled *Johnny Zombie,* and received uniformly negative reviews.

See also: Cannibalism; Comedy; Rom Zom Com; Romero's Rules; *Shaun of the Dead*

Anthony J. Fonseca

NARCISSE, CLAIRVIUS

Clairvius Narcisse (1922–) is a Haitian man who was reported to have been turned into a zombie (a Voodoo zombie returned from the dead). This prompted Canadian ethnobotanist and Harvard-educated scholar Wade Davis to travel to Haiti, at the behest of a pharmaceutical company, to discover what drugs may have been used to zombify Narcisse. Davis, who had done some research on drugs and hypothesized that tetrodotoxin (TTX), a potent neurotoxin, was used, chronicled his studies in *The Serpent and the Rainbow* (1985) and later in *Passage of Darkness: The Ethnobiology of the Haitian Zombie* (1988).

Narcisse was rumored to have been turned into a living zombie, but researchers (Davis and those who followed him) theorized that he had received a dose of zombie powder, a mixture of various chemicals, including TTX, which had been extracted from the liver of the puffer fish, or perhaps bufotoxin, which had been extracted from toad. This zombie powder would bring the victim close enough to death to induce a coma; in a third-world country like Haiti, it was easy to pass this coma off as death, at which time the victim could be buried, to be later exhumed since his or her breathing had been slowed to the point of almost ceasing. Narcisse, who was exposed to the powder through skin contact while he was out, returned home and fell into a death-like coma and was buried by his grieving family. After a requisite number of days, the zombie master (bokur) who poisoned him retrieved his ostensibly dead body and then gave him doses of the hallucinogenic zombie cucumber (*Datura stramonium* or nightshade) to put him into a trance state where he could be commanded to do anything, thereby making him into a zombie—someone that the people of his village viewed as undead. The zombified Narcisse was sent to work on a plantation as slave labor for two years until the property owner died and there was no one to give his slaves regular doses of zombie cucumber in order to maintain their zombification. Once he was no longer being drugged, Narcisse recovered his memory and left the plantation. Narcisse returned home after 18 years and convinced his sister that he was indeed the man they had buried. Because Narcisse's death had been verified by two American doctors, he became famous and caught Davis's attention.

Further investigations revealed that Narcisse fought with his brother over land, thereby making him a violator of the village code. His zombification was considered a type of imprisonment, as it were, hard labor alongside other offenders on a sugar plantation. Moreover, Narcisse's recovery from the effects of the drug was remarkable, which brought his case to the attention of American scientists. Narcisse's alleged undead existence as a slave made him famous among Haitians, who at the time possessed an unshakable belief in the reality of zombies and bokurs.

See also: Bokur/Caplata; Davis, Wade; Haiti; *Serpent and the Rainbow, The* (Book); Tetrodotoxin; Voodoo; Zombie Cucumber

Anthony J. Fonseca

NAZI ZOMBIES

Nazi zombies are a curious subspecies of the walking dead known for being violent, malevolent, and militaristic. They reanimate with a spectrum of zombie characteristics but often retain their ability to think on their own, organize under a commander, and use weapons rather than just their teeth. Only in a few cases do they infect their victims with their condition. These Nazi revenants vary from immortal super soldiers, to supernatural monsters, to traditional infectious zombies.

Reanimated Nazis first appear in Ken Wiederhorn's (no date available) film *Shock Waves* (1977), in which the zombie-like monsters are immortal and aquatic SS super soldiers, developed through occult Nazi experiments on convicted murders and psychopaths. A German hermit, played by Peter Cushing, explains to a group of shipwrecked survivors that he commanded a group of immortal Nazis during World War II. These so-called Death Corps could serve indefinitely on submarines because they are undead. Disturbed from their rest by the outsiders, the soldiers rise from their sunken ship to kill, and they no longer obey the commander's orders. Like zombies, the impassive creatures do not breathe, never speak, and lumber relentlessly, but they kill their victims by drowning and strangling (not biting). The only way to incapacitate them is to remove their goggles in the sunlight. Their defining feature is their ability to rise straight up out of the water.

Nazi zombies next appear as vampire hybrids in *Zombie Lake* (originally *Le lac des morts vivants*, 1981), a French-Spanish movie directed by Jean Rollin (born Jean Michel Rollin Roth Le Gentil, 1938–2010). After a young woman takes a swim in a quarantined lake, a French village is attacked by a platoon of undead Nazi monsters, which kill people by biting them on the neck and drinking their blood. The mayor reveals that the locals had killed a number of Nazi soldiers during World War II and hidden their bodies in the lake, which had once been used for pagan rituals and human sacrifice. He explicitly calls the creatures zombies. The monsters act for the most part like typical zombies, except for one, who recognizes the daughter he had with a local French girl. Motivated by the mayor's suggestion that they will free her father's damned soul, the girl lures the zombies into a trap. The townsfolk burn the monsters to ash.

The Treasure of the Living Dead (originally *La tumba de los muertos vivientes*, 1982), known as *Oasis of the Zombies* in the United States, is another French-Spanish collaboration, written and directed by Jess Franco. The protagonist, Robert Blabert, acting upon his father's tales of Nazi gold lost in northern Africa, takes his friends into the desert on the trail of a German treasure hunter. The locals they encounter explain how the walking dead have awakened, and that their victims must be burned before they rise as zombies as well. Undeterred, the treasure hunters go to the oasis, where they are soon attacked by a host of weathered and rotting Nazi monsters, understandably desiccated and slow moving, but Robert fights back successfully with fire. Unlike the previous Nazi zombies, these desert foes do not reside in water; however, they rise slowly up out of the sand in a visually similar manner.

Since the zombie renaissance of the 21st century, a handful of new Nazi zombie films have appeared. The first of these films, *Horrors of War* (2006), directed by Peter John Ross (1972–) and John Whitney (no date available), is a B-level film that recasts World War II as a battleground for supernatural creatures. Unlike the previous films, *Horrors of War* is a period piece and war movie. The Nazis have engaged in Project Osiris, developing a formula to create unstoppable super soldiers, monsters that resist bullets and attack their victims like zombies but that transform physically like Dr. Jekyll and Mr. Hyde. Lieutenant John Schmidt is part of a special-ops detail, including a French werewolf who works with the Allied forces. They are ordered to seek out the secret Nazi bunker to destroy the monstrous soldiers and capture the super soldier formula. Along the way, they battle different beasts and mutated humans, all incredibly strong and fast, and they ultimately succeed at their mission when Captain Joe Russo sacrifices himself for his fellow soldiers. *Outpost* (2007), directed by Steve Barker (1971–), is a similar film, featuring less traditional zombie monsters. *Outpost* is a contemporary tale of mercenaries hired to find an abandoned Nazi research bunker in Eastern Europe. Hunt, the protagonist, seeks a legendary machine designed by German scientists to create invulnerable super soldiers. When Hunt finds the lab, his team disturbs a host of undead Nazi monsters, powerful revenants with supernatural abilities (e.g., ghost-like teleportation) that torture and murder their human victims, usually with bayonets. *Outpost*'s zombie-like super soldiers show no evidence of cannibalism and do not lack but attack with organized and brutal purpose, and they cannot be destroyed, not even by a point-blank shot to the head; furthermore, their condition is not contagious. As the monsters succeed in killing all the human protagonists, Barker followed *Outpost* with the sequel *Outpost: Black Sun* (2012), where the Nazi zombies menace a new group of people. A third *Outpost* film, *Rise of the Spetsnaz,* was in production in 2013. *War of the Dead* (2011), directed by Marko Mäkilaakso (1978–), claims to be inspired by actual Nazi so-called anti-death experiments performed on Russian soldiers during World War II. In the film, a coalition of Allied and Finnish soldiers, led by Captain Martin Stone, are sent to locate and destroy the hidden lab. In much the same way as the two previous movies, the protagonists of Mäkilaakso's film are repeatedly attacked by voracious super soldiers—often the same ones—and it becomes clear they are reanimated, undead monsters; however, these zombies can and do infect their victims with their condition. These Nazi-created monsters (they are technically former Russian soldiers) are also indicative of the recent fast-moving, super-strong, and ultraviolent zombies.

Arguably the most successful film to feature Nazi zombies—or zombie-like, undead monsters—is the 2009 Norwegian movie *Dead Snow* (originally *Død snø*), directed by Tommy Wirkola. The film opens with a group of college students' retreating to a

In Tommy Wirkola's film *Dead Snow*, a group of college students on holiday in the mountains of Finland discover a hoard of gold beneath the floorboards of the cabin where they are staying. The group is terrorized by the Nazi zombies, who stashed the treasure there over 60 years ago. (IFC /Photofest)

remote cabin for the weekend, in an open homage to American slasher movies. They are visited by a mysterious wanderer in the middle of the night, Turgåer, who explains the history of the nearby town that rebelled against Nazi occupation and chased a platoon of German soldiers into the woods to die. After the stranger's departure, one of the students, Erlend, finds a wooden chest filled with gold and jewelry stolen from the locals by the Nazis. By disturbing the treasure, the group raises the violent Nazi monsters, which act in most regards like zombies, or at least that is what Erlend tells his friends they are. In reality, because the decomposing soldiers attack and kill their victims with fists and bayonets, as well as their teeth, and because their bite does not communicate their condition to their prey, the foes are more like *draugar,* animated corpses that protect burial sites and treasure. The Nazi hordes are relentless and organized in their quest to reclaim all of the stolen gold, and largely because the students do not understand what they are up against, Oberst Herzog and his undead troops achieve a brutal and violent victory over the trespassing students.

In addition to the films, Nazi zombies feature in various video games and graphic novels. They first appeared in the video game *Wolfenstein 3D* (1992), followed by its prequel *Spear of Destiny* (1992) and the various sequels *Return to Castle Wolfenstein* (2001), *Wolfenstein RPG* (2008), and *Wolfenstein* (2009). Nazi zombies can also be found in mini-games in *Doom II* (1994), *Call of Duty: World at War* (2008), *Call of Duty: Black Ops* (2010), and *Call of Duty: Black Ops 2* (2012). The monsters are featured in the Japanese manga series *Hellsing* (1997–2009), written and illustrated by Kouta Hirano (1973–); *War of the Undead* (2007), written by Bryan Johnson (1967–) and illustrated by Walter Flanagan (1967–); and *Marvel Zombies Destroy!* (2012), written by Frank Marraffino (no date available) and Peter David (1956–).

See also: Africa; *Dead Snow*; Draugar; Franco, Jess; Sentience; Vampires and Werewolves; Video Games

Kyle William Bishop

NECROPOLIS

Necropolis is a 2004 comic noir zombie novel by Tim Waggoner (no date available). The main characters of the story are supernatural creatures who make up the citizenry of Necropolis, which they built to escape the encroachment of human beings. These include demons, vampires, and ghouls, as well as a hard-boiled, zombie private eye named Adrion.

Adrion's task is to discover why Necropolis seems to be headed into a downward spiral, as the Lords of Necropolis engage in a power struggle. His problem is that he himself is deteriorating as quickly as his surroundings, which include drug-addicted cyber-vampires, monstrous insects, golem, and werewolves. Waggoner fashioned the novel to be a parody of Raymond Chandler's (born Raymond Thornton Chandler, 1888–1959) Philip Marlowe books. *Necropolis* holds the distinction of being a zombie narrative that is told by a zombie who makes the requisite snide comments and engages in sick humor as he attempts to salvage body parts as they fall off. The plot involves one of the female dark lords' attempts to steal the brains of humans. It is during this investigation that Adrion, a police detective, is turned, via a spell, into a zombie, but one which retains its sentience and free will.

Fortunately, Adrion is revived as a sentient zombie, and as a supernatural monster, he is limited to existence in Necropolis, where a Voodoo practitioner warns him that his reanimation spell is failing. Out of desperation, Adrion, now a private investigator, agrees to help a dark lord named Galm, who has been robbed of a valuable and powerful magic stone that could end the eternal night that makes Necropolis thrive. He joins forces with a half-vampire, half-human woman. Aside from the noir detective genre, Waggoner also incorporates elements of cyberpunk, role-playing games, action adventure, and dark comedy.

See also: Comedy; Golem; Sentience; Vampires and Werewolves; Voodoo

Anthony J. Fonseca

NIGHT OF THE COMET

Night of the Comet is a 1984 film directed by Thom Eberhardt (born Thomas Everett Eberhardt, 1947–). It is a parody of 1950s and 1960s science fiction B-movies, with obvious homage being paid to *The Day of the Triffids* (1962) and *Plan 9 from Outer*

Space (1959). The film also contains allusions to the futuristic science fiction film *THX1138* (1971). Trading on the public's fascination with Halley's comet, which was scheduled to come close enough to Earth for viewing in 1986, the film begins with worldwide comet viewing parties; those who are unfortunate enough to view the comet's passing while outdoors are showered with a red powder that turns them into dust. Meanwhile, viewers in airtight rooms emerge to find the streets of Los Angeles empty, covered with a patina of red dust and littered with clumps of clothing. Those who are only mildly exposed to the dust, however, are turned into zombies.

The movie's heroines are Valley girls Regina and Samantha. They survive in part because their Green Beret father made sure that the sisters were well versed in the martial arts and in the use of automatic weaponry. Since both were locked in air tight rooms while the comet approached, they remain human. Regina confronts the first zombie early in the film, at first believing that he is a drug-crazed mugger. The film's zombies do not follow Romero's Rules. While they are cannibals, they are also intelligent and able to speak. One zombie uses a pipe wrench to brain his victim. Physically, they do not resemble corpses. They are very pale, with a hint of red coloring, ostensibly from the dust. Such sentient zombies present a challenge for Regina and Samantha, who use their firepower and fighting skills to survive. They go in search of other survivors and safety, wind up at a radio station still on the air, where they find Hector, a street-wise thug who partners with the two to survive. A group of evil scientists surface as co-survivors attempting to capture the remaining humans to drain their blood, in order to find a cure for themselves. Regina, Samantha, and Hector rescue two children from the scientists and leave to restart civilization. The film ends with Regina's and Hector's becoming a couple and parenting the children, while the younger Samantha leaves on a date with one of the last surviving boys her age. As of 2013, *Night of the Comet* grossed $14.3 million.

See also: Apocalypse; Cult Film; Gender; *Plan 9 from Outer Space*; Science Fiction; Sentience

David E. Cowen

NIGHT OF THE LIVING DEAD (1990)

Night of the Living Dead is a 1990 remake by Tom Savini of the iconic 1968 George Romero film. More than a simple colorization of Romero's black-and-white film, Savini's remake explores the sexual politics of the original. Savini remains faithful to Romero's story line: seven people are trapped in a farmhouse by the living dead.

Savini's remake also includes the same characters found in Romero's original, going so far as to cast similar-looking actors. Tony Todd (born Anthony T. Todd, 1954–) as Ben brings the same intensity as did Duane L. Jones (1936–1988), and Tom Towles (1950–) as Harry Cooper is as truculent as Karl Hardman (1927–2007). Even in a minor role, Savini's choice of actor, Bill Moseley (born William Moseley, 1951–) as Johnny does a masterful job of channeling Russell Streiner (1940–) in the graveyard scene, making disparaging remarks about the dead and frightening his sister Barbara. But Patricia J. Tallman (1957–) as Barbara is pivotal to Savini's remake. The red-haired and athletically built Tallman, an accomplished stuntwoman as well as an actress, does not resemble the willowy Judith O'Dea (1945–), who originally interpreted Barbara as a shell-shocked damsel in distress. Over two decades shaped by second-wave feminism span O'Dea's and Tallman's interpretation of this character, and Tallman plays her in a time when women in horror film no longer merely scream and fall on their high heels; instead, they rescue themselves and others too.

After Barbara makes her way to the farmhouse and meets Ben, she becomes a formidable fighter of the undead, better than her fellow survivors. In a defining moment of her character, after Barbara has come to grips with some of the situation, she changes clothing, trading her skirt and flats for a pair of overhauls and work boots that she finds in the house, signifying that she is ready to fight. But most importantly, Barbara is better equipped to analyze their situation in order to survive. While Ben and Cooper continue to fight about whether or not the basement or the upstairs part of the house is the safest place, Barbara has a third, and ultimately, better option: escaping the house entirely. As she shoots at the zombies through a boarded-up window, she observes that they are slow and stupid, and so it would be easy enough to leave the house with a gun and some ammunition and outrun them. But Ben and Mr. Cooper, the two adult males in the group, will not listen to her, and the other survivors are too willing to be led by male authority to consider her idea. Cooper is particularly hostile to her theory, in part because she is a woman. During the disastrous escape attempt by Ben, Judy Rose, and Tom, Cooper attempts to take control of the house, wrestling the shot gun from Barbara, and leaving her and Ben to fight off the zombies. Armed with a pistol, Barbara makes her way through the zombie-infested countryside, eventually finding safety with a band of redneck survivalists who accompany her to the farmhouse to rescue the others. But when the rescue party arrives, Ben has died in the night and reanimated, so he is appropriately shot, unlike in the original, when Ben, the only person to live through the night, is shot by a trigger-happy redneck. Cooper, however, has lived through the night by hiding in the attic. Cooper reaches out toward Barbara, telling her "you came back." Barbara promptly shoots Cooper between the eyes. It is unclear whether or not Cooper merely frightened Barbara and she defended herself or if she shot him out of anger toward his behavior the night before.

The zombies in this remake follow Romero's Rules but are far more gory and frightening than the undead in Romero's original. The first zombies that Barbara encounters in the cemetery provide an excellent example. In Romero's film, this zombie could be confused for a deranged and dangerous old man. In Savini's film, however, our first glimpse at the zombie establishes how this monster is horrifying because it straddles the boundaries between life and death. As Barbara's brother Johnny is attacked by the ghouls, Barbara screams for help from a well-dressed handsome man who is slowly making his way toward her, as if responding to her call of distress. But as the man comes closer, he begins to step on his trousers, which pull his burial suit down his body, as the garment is one piece that opens in the back. When the man's autopsy scar is revealed, there is no longer any doubt that he is one of the living dead rather than a potential source of assistance. Later zombies are covered in gore and are similarly disturbing. Finally, Savini's remake considers some of Romero's other *Dead* films in its tentative exploration of the coming post-apocalyptic world. Barbara has a glimpse into this world when she briefly visits the camp of heavily armed survivors. While she spent the night horrified that she must dispatch the formerly human, the survivors in the camp seem to have been waiting for this moment all of their lives. The camp is a carnival in the literal sense of the word, where the survivors pass the time baiting zombies kept in a corral and shooting at several of them who have been hung from a tree. Barbara quips about the zombies and survivors that "we're them and they're us," commenting on the carnivalesque nature of the encampment where the values of civilization have been abandoned, and the living are more monstrous than the undead that they torment.

The film was Savini's directorial debut, though he was previously well known in the horror industry as a creator of gory special effects. He had worked with Romero on two previous occasions: on the 1978 film *Dawn of the Dead* (in which he also played a small role) and on the 1985 film *Day of the Dead*. He was originally supposed to be a special effects makeup artist on the set of the original *Night of the Living Dead,* but he was drafted by the U.S. government for military service and subsequently shipped to Vietnam.

See also: Apocalypse; *Dawn of the Dead*; Gender; *Night of the Living Dead* Series; Race; Romero, George; Romero's Rules

June Michele Pulliam

NIGHT OF THE LIVING DEAD SERIES

The *Night of the Living Dead* series is synonymous with George Romero's representation of the zombie, beginning in his 1968 film *Night of the Living Dead*. That film was groundbreaking, crystallizing earlier representations of the creature as a mindless being while blending supernatural and scientific causes for the sudden reanimation of the dead. Romero particularly draws upon Richard Matheson's novella *I Am Legend* (1954), where the dead have been reanimated by a virus. Matheson's and Romero's zombies differ from earlier representations of the creature as a victim of sorcery who is subordinate to the will of their master. Romero's and Matheson's creatures have no master but are driven by the need to consume human flesh, in the case of Romero's zombies, or to drink blood, in the case of Matheson's zombies.

Romero's *Night of the Living Dead* series consists of six films, beginning with the black and white, low-budget *Night of the Living Dead,* where seven strangers take refuge in a farmhouse outside of Willard, Pennsylvania. When the house is soon surrounded by the recently dead who have suddenly begun returning to life and attacking the living, the group spends the night defending their stronghold. Because the phone network has crashed, survivors cannot call for help. Nor can they receive much information from the media about the crisis, as radio and television stations are for the most part off the air. As a consequence, the seven are

The recently dead have risen from their graves and swarm outside of a farm house in rural Pennsylvania in George A. Romero's iconic film *Night of the Living Dead* (1968). (Continental Distributing Inc./Photofest)

forced to hatch a desperate plan for escape in the absence of useful information. The plan for escape fails however, partly because the survivors cannot suppress their petty squabbles to work together. Each film in the series focuses on a different band of survivors at different times during the apocalypse; the inability of humans to collaborate in order to ensure their long-term survival is a constant theme. The film concludes with Ben, the only African American of the group, living through the night, only to be mistaken for a zombie and shot by a member of a militia that is patrolling the countryside looking for people in need of rescuing. The film was criticized upon its release for what at the time were considered graphic scenes of gore and violence. However, it was eventually selected by the Library of Congress's National Film Registry for preservation for its cultural significance.

The second film in the series, *Dawn of the Dead* (1978), opens the morning after the zombie apocalypse. It follows a television news crew who flees zombie-infested Pittsburgh in news chopper, eventually taking refuge in an abandoned shopping mall several hours outside of the city. Critics generally describe it as a film that connects the zombie metaphor with rampant consumerism, as the majority of its action takes place in the mall. The mall represents not only a refuge from the undead but also a return to pre-apocalypse normalcy for both the living and the zombies. The survivors spend several months setting up housekeeping and then binging on what the mall has to offer before their shelter is eventually overrun with zombies. The zombies who amass outside of the mall are attracted to it as somewhere they felt fulfilled during their lives. Once inside, the zombies are ideal shoppers, behaving much more respectfully in this space than do the humans, who have looted the stores and appropriated the living quarters for themselves.

Day of the Dead (1985) exemplifies another of Romero's innovations in reimagining the zombie, the blurring of the boundary between monster and human. This causes us to question the creature's essential difference from ourselves. This theme is continued throughout the rest of the series in unique ways. *Day of the Dead* is set many months after the zombie apocalypse. Before the U.S. government completely collapsed, it tasked a group of research scientists to discover a way to reprogram zombies into docility, as the creatures now so greatly outnumber humans that complete extermination of the undead is impossible. The scientists shelter in a nuclear silo, protected by a small cadre of soldiers, who are often as mindless as the zombies in their own pursuit of sex, alcohol, and marijuana, while their insatiable blood lust makes them far more brutal than the undead. Meanwhile, Dr. Logan, the head of the research team, manages to teach the zombie Bub to suppress his cannibalism and to take pleasure in reading (or at least, flipping through the pages of a book) and listening to classical music. Bub is Romero's first truly intelligent and sympathetic zombie—the earliest fully developed zombie character in the series. The characterization humanizes the creature, thereby blurring the lines between the monster and the victim. In life, Bub was in the military, something we learn when he recognizes the sadistic Captain Rhodes as a superior officer and salutes him. Rhodes, who is disgusted by zombies and scientists alike, scorns to return the salute, enraging Bub. Wondering how his charge would behave, Logan gives Bub his own unarmed sidearm, which the angry zombie points at Rhodes, who responds by pointing his own gun. The scene illustrates that there is not that much difference between human and zombie. Logan's attempts to domesticate zombies, however, are in vain. The compound is soon overrun by the undead when once again humans cannot put aside their differences to work together.

Land of the Dead, set many years after the initial zombie apocalypse, continues to humanize the zombie. Kaufman, played by Dennis Hopper (born Dennis Lee Hopper, 1936–2010), a wealthy capitalist from the old world, has set up a small community, protected from zombies by the military he finances. The community reproduces the same savage inequalities found in the old world: wealth is still in the hands of a few white males who live in Fiddler's Green, the luxury condominium towers that include a fully stocked mall and many restaurants. The remaining residents of the compound serve the wealthy and live in slums. The social order created by Kaufman is challenged when Cholo, his Latino henchman, realizes that this world is not a meritocracy. Although Cholo has finally made enough money to purchase a condominium in Fiddler's Green, Kaufman refuses to sell one to his employee because he is too brown and too working-class to be a desirable resident. An enraged Cholo steals Dead Reckoning, the million-dollar armored vehicle used to raid zombie towns for supplies, and threatens to shell the compound if Kaufman does not pay him ransom. While Kaufman scrambles to find Dead Reckoning before Cholo makes good his threat, the zombies of Uniontown collaborate to take over the compound, as they are angry after Kaufman's raiders looted their settlement and shot up many of them. Zombies in the film are capable of complex thought—they can learn, as we see when they pick up tools and use them in new ways and figure out how to cross the river to get into the city, and are driven by more than the insatiable drive for human flesh. Rather, what motivates these zombies is a feeling of solidarity for one another. This film too ends with the living being driven out of their compound after they cannot work for the common good. In the film's last scene, the zombies are establishing peaceful residency in the compound, while a few survivors leave in Dead Reckoning in search of a place where they can presumably be equal and safe, from the zombies and other humans.

Diary of the Dead (2007) goes back in time to the first night that the dead begin reanimating. It follows seven University of Pittsburg film school students and their professor, who are in the woods filming a horror movie when they first hear reports of rioting and mass murder. Afterward, they begin to shoot a documentary about the dead returning to life, *The Death of Death,* and upload it on the internet with the hope that this technology survives long enough so that others can learn from their experiences dealing with zombies. The film also goes forward in time with its foregrounding of 21st-century technology such as cell-phone videos, the internet and laptop computers, to tell the story in complex and metatextual ways. These technologies were unavailable to the band of survivors in *Night of the Living Dead,* a lack that can only partly be explained in *Diary of the Dead* by the 1968 film's rural location. *Diary of the Dead* is also unique in how it uses these technologies to blur the lines between the undead and the living. Romero's earlier works, with their standard narrative format that does not break the proscenium, make it easier for the viewers to think of the zombie as an abject Other that must be exterminated rather than as someone's loved one who used to be alive. But this film's self-referential story-telling, which constantly changes perspective as each character uses a different video camera or cell phone to record events, makes it difficult to objectify anyone, or to even clearly identify the monster in some cases.

The plot of *Survival of the Dead* (2009), the final work in Romero's *Dead* oeuvre, is chronologically closer to the 1968 classic in that the story begins six days after the dead have begun to reanimate. However, it is thematically more closely affiliated with *Land of the Dead* in how it humanizes the zombies. Set on Plum Island, a Delaware community that has housed only two families for the past century, the Muldoons and the O'Flynns, *Survival of the Dead* presents a world where no strangers exist. The O'Flynns insist on euthanizing the undead, while the Muldoons have held on to their revived dead, chaining them to their beds in an upstairs room in the family home, or tethering them outside where they can continue to perform work that was meaningful to them in life, such as farming or delivering the mail. The Muldoons see the undead as ill loved ones to be cared for rather than as abject Others with no right to human compassion. Mid-film, the Muldoon patriarch explains that he believes that he is doing the Lord's bidding by keeping the undead alive rather than killing them. However, Muldoon's daughter realizes that keeping undead family members close is dangerous after she is bitten by her zombified twin sister. The film ends with no clear position about how the undead should be treated by the living. Zombies are teachable, as Romero has already shown viewers, and so humans might be able to coexist with them, something demonstrated in *Survival* when one of Muldoon's undead children finally learns to eat animals rather than humans, a behavior that Muldoon had been attempting to encourage in the undead all along. Humans, however, continue to be unable to minimize their differences in order to survive, which is shown in Muldoon's and O'Flynn's lethal exchange of gunfire by way of settling their feud.

The trope of the zombie apocalypse and its consequences on the human race is reproduced in many epic works of 20th- and 21st-century film and fiction, and Romero's *Night of the Living Dead* series is the Ur text for all of these works.

See also: Apocalypse; Cannibalism; Class; *Dawn of the Dead*; *Day of the Dead*; *I Am Legend* (Novel); Matheson, Richard; *Night of the Living Dead* (1990); Race; Romero, George; Romero's Rules

June Michele Pulliam

OMEGA MAN, THE
See I Am Legend (Films)

P

PAFFENROTH, KIM

Kim Paffenroth (1966–) is the author of the *Dying to Live* trilogy: *Dying to Live: Valley of the Dead* (2010), *Dying to Live: Life Sentence* (2012), and *Dying to Live: Last Rites* (2012). He also is the editor of *History Is Dead: A Zombie Anthology* (2007) and has one projected title, *Pale Gods*, in the works, all published by Permuted Press. Paffenroth is a professor of religious studies whose scholarship examines the portrayal of zombies in popular culture. His book *Gospel of the Living Dead: George A. Romero's Visions of Hell on Earth* (2006) argues that zombie movies help human beings form ideas about humanity and God. He claims that much of the imagery of zombie movies is derived from *Dante's Inferno*, and examines the moral issues in George Romero's films to illustrate that zombie movies engage in social criticism and the examination of human nature.

In Paffenroth's self-consciously philosophical novel *Dying to Live* (2010), Jonah Caine, a former English professor-turned zombie killer, teams up with ex-military man Jack and half-zombie guru Milton in their fortified compound (formerly a museum) to ponder the issues of life, death, and undeath—and what it means to be human in a post-human world. The characters in his first novel engage in involved discussions of the theological implications of the zombie apocalypse; the second and third novels provide interesting examinations of those same topics without monologues. *Dying to Live: Life Sentence* is set 12 years later. It is alternately narrated by an adult named Zoey, looking back at her childhood, and the self-aware zombie Wade Truman. *Dying to Live: Last Rites* (2012) follows two couples, the humans Rachel and Will and two zombies, Lucy and Truman, as they travel in their exile from the world they knew. In these novels, the zombies stand in for all the dispossessed in our own society, highlighting issues of race, class, and gender. *Valley of the Dead*, subtitled *The Truth behind Dante's Inferno*, tells the story of a Dante Alighieri (1265–1321), who stumbles upon a zombie infestation and, rather than face being considered mad, weaves the experience into a story that becomes his famous *Inferno*. *Valley of the Dead* offers a mash-up of classic literature and typical zombie fare in a clever combination, though it is not in the style of *Pride and Prejudice and Zombies* (2009).

In *Pale Gods*, Paffenroth again uses his characters to prove the point that zombie narratives explicate human morality. In this novel, also set in a post-zombie-apocalypse world, Ridley ships out on the *Hyperion* with King, a religious man, and the atheist Captain Jacob, exploring not the ruins of civilization but the nature of religion itself. Thus, Paffenroth's fiction illustrates his claim that depictions of zombies save us from becoming the philosophical zombie, or humans who fall prey to the misguided urge to degrade and dehumanize themselves, becoming soulless machines.

See also: Apocalypse; Mash-Ups, Literary; Permuted Press; Romero, George; Zombie Studies

Margo Collins

PASSAGE OF DARKNESS

Passage of Darkness: The Ethnobiology of the Haitian Zombie (University of North Carolina Press, 1988) is Wade Davis's scholarly treatise that is a follow-up to his 1985 book, *The Serpent and the Rainbow*. In *Passage of Darkness,* Davis expresses awareness of criticism of his previous book, *The Serpent and the Rainbow,* by both the scientific and anthropological communities, so he presents much of the same information in a different manner: where *The Serpent and the Rainbow* had been an autobiographical account of Davis's journey to Haiti in order to determine whether or not there was a factual basis behind the legend of the zombie, *Passage of Darkness* allows Davis to eschew the first-person narrative style in favor of a more measured, clinical approach.

Davis lays out his arguments methodically, first presenting a cultural history of Haiti, followed by case studies cataloguing reports of zombie sightings and a brief history of premature burial, and concluding with an in-depth look at the ingredients and preparation of both the "zombie powder" and its antidote. The more careful, less anecdotal manner in which Davis relates information in *Passage of Darkness* helps to bolster his claim of verifying the existence of the zombie, a creature of folklore which had captured popular imagination through the years. *Passage of Darkness* also goes into more detail in regard to the principal case study featured in *The Serpent and the Rainbow,* that of Clairvius Narcisse. Here, Davis paints a more complete picture of Narcisse's former life, illustrating him as someone who had transgressed against the social mores of his community. This transgression made Narcisse a more likely candidate for a transformation into a zombie, since Davis categorizes the process of zombification as a culturally sanctioned act, carried out by a secret society (Bizango) against individuals who have violated a particular code of ethics.

Davis also addresses specific complaints in regard to his scientific methodology, particularly criticism of the efficacy of the samples of "Voodoo-powder" that he had obtained. With a two-pronged argument, Davis states that no two concoctions assembled by bokurs (magicians or witch-doctors who practice dark magic) will be of the same potency. In many cases, the poisons contained within the powder may kill the victim outright; in other cases, the powder may have little or no effect. In cases in which a zombie is not produced, a bokur will not question his own competence in preparation; rather, some supernatural agent will be blamed for the failure of the process. Davis does not give a great deal of credence to the fact that the powders he obtained did not pass muster in a laboratory environment, arguing that instances of the actual, successful creation of a zombie are fairly rare anyway. Further, Davis devotes a chapter of his book to illustrate the emic viewpoint that a belief in the magical properties of the process and the psychological implications of this belief are equally as important in the success of the process as the effectiveness of the actual poisons utilized. Davis states that in order for the process to work as it should, the victim must believe that the bokur is actually capturing his or her soul during the process of his or her faked death and subsequent zombie rebirth. Only then will the psychotropic substances and physiological aspects of zombification work (in tandem with the fear produced by the victim's own mind) to produce a true zombie.

See also: Bokur/Caplata; Davis, Wade; Haiti; *Serpent and the Rainbow, The* (Book); Tetrodotoxin; Voodoo; Zombie Cucumber

Robert Butterfield

PERMUTED PRESS

Permuted Press had inauspicious beginnings in 2004, but the American small press has grown to become the preeminent specialty publisher of zombie-oriented fiction. Founded with the intent of publishing a single anthology, Permuted quickly expanded its ambitions and became the first press to focus primarily on zombie fiction, although it prefers the broader description of post-apocalyptic and survival horror fiction. Other publishers with a zombie focus, such as Creeping Hemlock's Print is Dead imprint, Books of the Dead Press, and Living Dead Press, have subsequently appeared, but Permuted's position as the primary and most prolific zombie publisher remains unchallenged.

The launch of Permuted coincided with a growing surge in zombie popularity across popular culture. Several zombie-based video games were best sellers in the late 1990s and early 2000s. As well, films such as *Resident Evil* (2002), based on the video game, *28 Days Later* (2002), the remake of *Dawn of the Dead* (2004) and *Shaun of the Dead* (2004) achieved significant popularity, and notable novels such as *Blood Crazy* (2001) and *The Rising* (2003) and *City of the Dead* (2005) emerged. Permuted started relatively slowly, publishing three titles in 2005, including the anthology *The Undead,* and three more works in 2006. In 2007, output ramped up to 10 titles. Permuted's pace has continued with at least nine books published in every year since then, with a peak of 23 titles in 2011. Permuted has specialized more in publishing new and up-and-coming authors, with relatively few titles by well-established authors. As one might expect, with a backlist of more than 75 titles, the quality of Permuted's offerings has varied, with texts being later purchased by publishers such as St. Martin's, along with movie adaptations. Permuted has made a habit of publishing novel series, as reflected by their list of best-selling titles.

Evidence of Permuted's rise beyond its small press origins can be seen in the details of two ventures entered into with major corporations. First, Permuted inked a deal in 2009 with mass-market publisher Simon and Schuster, which called for the publication of co-branded editions of some of Permuted's most popular titles, as well as the launch of some of the press's original titles. The arrangement eventually included 12 titles. Second, Permuted entered into a relationship with Audible. com in 2010, resulting in the publication of audio book editions of 11 of Permuted's most popular titles. The press has employed a variety of artists for book covers and has managed to consistently produce striking and professional illustrations, often eschewing standard zombie imagery in favor of different subjects and unusual perspectives. Permuted's titles are published in trade paperback editions, produced using print-on-demand technology, and as e-books. More than half of the press's catalog is available in e-book format, which now comprises more than 60 percent of Permuted's total sales. Permuted promotes its titles primarily via internet marketing. As of 2012, Permuted has a website that averages 5,000 unique visitors per month.

See also: Blood Crazy; Dawn of the Dead; Paffenroth, Kim; *Resident Evil* (Video Game); *Shaun of the Dead; 28 Days Later* Series

Robert Morrish

PET SEMATARY (FILM)

Pet Sematary is a 1989 film by Mary Lambert (1951–). A relatively faithful interpretation of Stephen King's novel of the same name, published in 1983, it is particularly notable for how it visually connects various undead to the cinematic figure of the zombie. The reanimated dead are not identified per se as zombies, but they fit many broad definitions of the creature. Like the zombie created by Voodoo, the undead in *Pet Sematary* are reanimated through magical means. Moreover, they crave human flesh, similar to zombies created by George Romero. They also visually reference cinematic zombies in several ways: one has the burning stare characteristic of many zombies, and its mouth is smeared in gore similar to the blood-encrusted mouths of Romero's zombies; another is visibly decaying in a way that also references Romero. Even the character Victor Pascow, a ghost rather than one of the reanimated dead, resembles the zombie. He appears to the audience in the form he had at the moment of his death when he was hit by a car: with livid flesh and a visibly broken skull displaying part of his brain, along with his mismatched eyes, one of which is clouded over in a way reminiscent of the eyes of zombies in Romero's later films.

When Dr. Louis Creed moves his family to Ludlow, Maine, to take a job as the head of the infirmary at a small college, his five-year-old daughter Ellie is disturbed when she learns about the concept of death after their neighbor, Jud Crandall, shows the Creeds the nearby pet "sematary" where local children have been burying their beloved animal companions for nearly a century. The visit to the pet cemetery disturbs young Ellie, in part, because she suddenly realizes that her beloved cat Church will also die one day. When Ellie is visiting her grandparents with her mother and

When Gage Creed (Miko Hughes) is reanimated in the Micmac burying ground by his grieving father Louis, the boy is not the sweet child that his parents remembered, but a murderous demon in Gage's decomposing body. (Paramount Pictures / Photofest)

little brother during the Thanksgiving holidays, Church in fact does die after being hit on the road. Hoping to prevent Ellie from having to learn about life's ugly realities too soon, Jud has Louis bring Church's body to the Micmac burying ground, a piece of earth with the magical ability to reanimate the dead. Louis buries Church here, and the cat returns home, albeit not quite the same animal that he was when alive the first time. Church now smells of the grave and takes delight in killing animals and leaving them on the Creeds' doorstep. While Ellie too senses a difference in her pet when she returns, she does not know that her cat had died and has been resurrected.

When Louis's toddler son Gage is killed by a truck, the desperate father inters his child in Micmac burying ground against Jud's advice about the horrifying results of reanimating humans in this manner because the ground is haunted by a windigo, a demonic spirit from Algonquin folklore that can possess human or animal bodies, turning them into cannibals. While a cat with a taste for flesh is not terribly disturbing, a toddler is another matter. Gage reanimates, with horrific results. The boy returns home and tears out Jud's throat and then attacks his mother. When Louis sees that Gage has become an unspeakable thing in the body of his child, he destroys his reanimated son. Still, Louis does not learn from his mistakes. Grieving for his now-dead wife Rachel, he buries her in the Micmac burying ground, reasoning that his attempts to reanimate Church and Gage were failures only because their bodies had been dead too long before he made these attempts. The film ends with a hideous revived Rachel returning home to kiss her waiting husband. A sequel, *Pet Sematary II,* was made in 1992, also by Mary Lambert. As of 2013, rumors that Paramount Studios is planning to remake *Pet Sematary* have surfaced.

See also: Cannibalism; King, Stephen; *Pet Sematary* (Novel); Reanimation; Romero, George

June Michele Pulliam

PET SEMATARY (NOVEL)

Pet Sematary is a novel by Stephen King, published in 1983. It is notable for its unique interpretation of the zombie, a creature not identified per se as a zombie but which fits many broad definitions of the undead which operate by Romero's Rules. Like the zombie created by Voodoo, the undead in *Pet Sematary* are reanimated through magical means—the bereaved inter their dead pets and loved ones in the Micmac burying ground. There they are reanimated via magical means but with horrific results, as the land has been profaned by a windigo, a demonic spirit from Algonquin folklore that can possess human or animal bodies, turning them into cannibals.

The novel's protagonist, Louis Creed, discovers the Micmac burying ground shortly after moving his family to Ludlow, Maine, to take a job as the head of the infirmary at a small college. The family becomes intimately acquainted with death over the next few months. Five-year-old daughter Ellie becomes upset after the Creeds' neighbor Jud Crandall take her to visit nearby pet "sematary," where local children have been burying their beloved animal companions for nearly a century. She comes to realize that her beloved pet cat Church will also die one day, and soon after, Church is killed while crossing the road. Louis tries to prevent Ellie from learning about life's ugly realities too young by interring the cat in the Micmac burying ground. Church returns the next day, albeit not quite the same animal that he was when alive: the cat now stinks of the grave and takes delight in killing animals and leaving them on the Creeds' doorstep. Ellie senses a difference in her pet, but she does not know that he has died and has been revived. Then, toddler Gage is hit by a truck and is killed, and a grieving Louis inters his son in the Micmac ground against Jud's advice about the horrifying results of reanimating humans in this manner. Gage reanimates, tears out Jud's throat, and then murders his mother, Rachel, causing Louis to realize that he must destroy the thing that his child has become. Still, Louis does not learn from his mistakes. He euthanizes Gage but takes his wife's body to the profaned ground, reasoning that his attempts to reanimate Church and

Gage were failures only because their bodies had been dead too long. The novel ends with a hideous-looking revived Rachel returning home to kiss her waiting husband.

Pet Sematary is a unique contribution to the zombie genre in how the creature is one of many supernatural entities in a fictional world where the lines between death and life, the supernatural and the natural, are blurred. Louis, a physician and a man of science, is guided by the spirit of Victor Pascow, a student who is brought to the infirmary after being struck by a car on Louis's first day on the job. Victor is a rather corporeal ghost, always appearing to Louis in his hideously maimed form, brain pan exposed from the impact of the accident. Furthermore, the reanimated dead of the novel are not easily categorized into any zombie mythology. *Pet Sematary* was made into a film of the same name in 1989.

See also: Cannibalism; King, Stephen; *Pet Sematary* (Film); Reanimation; Romero, George

June Michele Pulliam

PHANTASM SERIES

The *Phantasm* films are a series consisting of, as of 2013, *Phantasm* (1979), *Phantasm II* (1988), *Phantasm III: Lord of the Dead* (1994), and *Phantasm IV: Oblivion* (1998). All four were written and directed by Don Coscarelli, who uses recurring

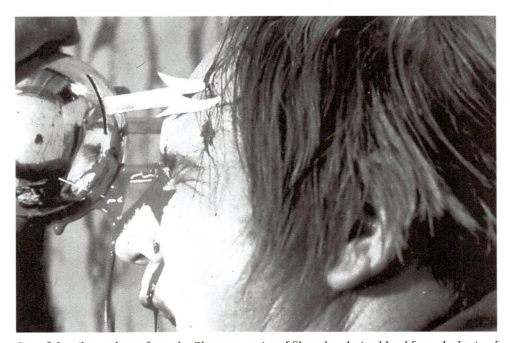

One of the silver spheres from the *Phantasm* series of films that drains blood from the brain of its victim prior to converting him into a zombie slave. (MGM/Photofest)

cast members, characters, and score music. The plot of *Phantasm* concerns the efforts of teenager Mike Pearson to discover the reasons behind a series of deaths in a rural American town. He realizes that the local mortician, known only as The Tall Man, is an alien who kills, steals corpses, shrinks them, and reanimates them as grotesque, dwarfish zombies. The zombies are then transported to another planet via a space gate and are used as slave labor.

Mike, with his brother Jody and their friend Reggie, defeat The Tall Man by trapping him in a mine shaft. An ambiguous ending, which is perhaps a nightmare, suggests that the alien may have escaped. The film relies more on juxtaposition, dream imagery, and illogic, all common in German expressionism. Despite the film's low budget, Coscarelli created an atmospheric masterpiece, with the iconographic image of the flying silver sphere containing drills, suction pumps, and other mechanical devices used to drain the blood from the brain.

In *Phantasm II,* two of the main actors, Reggie Bannister (1945–) and Angus Scrimm (1926–) return a decade later to reprise their roles as Reggie and The Tall Man, but other principals were replaced. The film has much the same plot as the first but expands the action. The Tall Man has been moving across small-town America, emptying graveyards to create dwarfish zombie slaves, destroying towns in the process. Mike and Reggie pursue him with the aid of two women, Liz and Alchemy. The sequel features a quick shot of the alien planet, seen briefly in the first film. There are several silver spheres as well, each possessing its own way of killing. This time The Tall Man meets his end by being embalmed with acid, although a coda suggests once again that he is not actually dead. *Phantasm III: Lord of the Dead* brings back Bill Thornbury (1952–) as Jody, despite this character's apparent death in *Phantasm*. A. Michael Baldwin (1963–) returns as Mike, and Bannister and Scrimm return as well. After being dissolved in acid, a new Tall Man emerges from the space gate. The third installment in the series spends more time developing the mythology of the silver spheres. Jody's spirit is now contained within one, and various characters are shown to have had their brains replaced with spheres, the most important revelation being that Mike has a sphere in his own head. This time The Tall Man is killed with liquid nitrogen, and the movie ends on a cliffhanger as Reggie is pinned to the wall by hundreds of spheres as a new Tall Man appears.

Phantasm IV: Oblivion suffered from the series' ever-dwindling budgets, the film going into production only after Coscarelli realized he had enough unused material from *Phantasm* to avoid shooting too much new footage. The combination of new and old footage resulted in the film's being the most dreamlike of all four. It begins where *Phantasm III* left off, with Mike's fleeing and Reggie's being released by The Tall Man from the grip of the spheres. Jody convinces Reggie to go after Mike, who is on a physical and mental journey, through both abandoned towns and his imagination. Mike finds himself being forced to remember incidents from his youth, and eventually he ends up in the desert, where he attempts suicide before passing through another space gate, to find himself in the 19th century. He meets Scrimm as character Jebediah Morningside, and the story line suggests that Morningside will become The Tall Man once the mechanical device in his mortuary has been put into action. Mike returns to the present with The Tall Man in pursuit, attempting to retrieve the sphere in Mike's head. An explosion destroys The Tall Man, but yet another appears through a space gate; this one takes the sphere from Mike before returning through the gate. As of 2013, the possibility of a fifth *Phantasm* movie has produced potential scripts by Coscarelli and others.

See also: Coscarelli, Don; Science Fiction

John Llewellyn Probert

PHILOSOPHICAL ZOMBIES
See Existentialism

PLAGUE OF THE ZOMBIES, THE

The Plague of the Zombies is a film released in 1966 by Hammer Studios as the B Feature of a double bill, the other half being the return of Christopher Lee in *Dracula, Prince of Darkness*. Producer Anthony Nelson Keys (1911–1985) got behind the film because distributors wanted Hammer to make movies more cheaply. He, there-

fore, shot two films back to back, so both *The Plague of the Zombies* and *The Reptile* (1966) share sets and actors. John Gilling (1912–1984) directed both. *The Plague of the Zombies* is a loose rewriting of Bram Stoker's novel *Dracula*. It transplants the traditional story of zombies used as slave labor from its original Caribbean setting to the tin mines of Cornwall, England.

Professor of medicine Sir James Forbes receives a letter from Peter Tompson, his brightest student, requesting that he come to Cornwall to help him diagnose a spate of sudden deaths. Sir James's daughter Sylvia travels with her father so that she can visit her best friend Alice. When Sir James and Sylvia arrive, Alice is unwell and has a cut on her hand that she will not let anyone look at. That evening, an entranced Alice

A dead man in a Cornish village is reanimated through Voodoo in *The Plague of the Zombies* (1966). (Hammer/Photofest)

walks over the moors to Squire Hamilton's estate, where she is seized by a zombified villager and hurled to her death in front of a horrified Sylvia, who was concerned about her friend and followed her. Sir James and Peter perform an autopsy on Alice but find nothing to explain her illness before her death. Van Helsing-like, Sir James is willing to entertain the possibility of the supernatural. Thus, he and Peter later visit Alice's grave to discover that she is not in her coffin but has reanimated as a zombie. The zombie Alice approaches in a seductive manner that is similar to the vampire Lucy's overtures in *Dracula*. Like Lucy, Alice too is beheaded. Meanwhile Squire Hamilton, who has spent some time in Haiti learning how to dispatch and resurrect villagers to serve his evil purpose, has his eye on Sylvia and begins the laborious process of bewitching her in order to turn her into a zombie. The film concludes when Sir James and Peter dispatch Squire Hamilton, breaking his control over Sylvia and his other zombies in a way that is similar to how Bram Stoker's vampire hunters rescue Mina.

The film's zombies are a metaphor for the British class system, with the reanimated villagers used as cheap mining labor. The film also explores xenophobia and nationalism, in the villagers' mistrust for outsiders, and in their need for a strong, learned authority figure to defeat the zombies: Forbes, as a professor of medicine and a maverick, is prepared to subvert the law and get his hands dirty (literally) by digging up corpses when superstitious villagers refuse to allow him to perform autopsies on their dead. The film is best remembered for the sequence in which a reanimated Alice is beheaded, followed by Peter's hallucinatory dream sequence where the dead claw their way out of their graves.

See also: Class; Gender; Hammer Film Productions; Vampires and Werewolves

John Llewellyn Probert

PLAN 9 FROM OUTER SPACE

Plan 9 from Outer Space is a 1956 cult science fiction horror film written and directed by Ed Wood. The film bills Bela Lugosi, but it was made posthumously. Prior to Lugosi's death, Wood had filmed the actor for other projects, and he used the footage plus a stand-in for Lugosi for action shots not yet filmed. Although it adds very little of significance to the zombie trope, the film is a pre-1968 (the year George Romero directed *Night of the Living Dead*) example of a storyline involving undead humans resurrected by aliens.

These extraterrestrials react to news of the human creation of a weapon of mass destruction by unleashing what they refer to as Plan 9. The plan calls for the reanimation of the human dead, in the form of zombies or ghouls. Set in California, the story begins when two gravediggers are killed by a reanimated corpse. Nearby, two pilots encounter a flying saucer. A police detective investigating the murders in the cemetery is likewise killed by two corpses. One of the pilots begins to suspect a connection between the murders and the UFO, especially once other sightings make the news. As the story progresses, a government conspiracy is revealed, and the zombies attack the alien leader. Ultimately, the pilot and some police officers are lured to the spaceship, where they are lectured on the foibles of developing more powerful weapons, including the inevitable discover of a substance that can detonate hydrogen, thus destroying the universe. After a fight with the aliens, their ship is set afire and explodes in their attempt to escape.

The film, originally titled *Grave Robbers from Outer Space*, is often criticized for the poor quality of its special effects, as well as the ridiculousness of Wood's having hired his wife's chiropractor as Lugosi's stand-in—he was almost a foot taller than Lugosi. The film was shot in 1956, and finished in 1957 but not released until 1959, although it did preview in Los Angeles. In 1992, the film was the subject of *Flying Saucers over Hollywood: The Plan 9 Companion* and, in 2006, was mentioned in segments of another documentary called *Vampira: The Movie*. It is widely considered the worst film in the history of cinema.

See also: Cult Film; Lugosi, Bela; Romero, George; Science Fiction

Anthony J. Fonseca

PLANTS VS. ZOMBIES

Plants vs. Zombies is a humorous video game originally published in 2009 by PopCap Games. In the game, players grow plants which have the ability to stave off a zombie attack, as the zombies attempt to capture and feast on the brains of player avatars.

The game involves players placing different plants around their avatars' houses. The plants have both attack and defense capabilities, which allow the player to fight a zombie invasion: for example, sunflowers enable players to harvest sunlight, which keeps plants viable; potatoes serve as landmines that kill zombies; peas shoot the zombies repeatedly to decapitate them; and walnuts serve as barriers to zombies. The game rules establish that zombies must move in horizontal lanes that are similar to furrows in a garden into which the screen is divided. Zombies move toward the house of the player along one of the prescribed lanes. In the early levels, only plants located in the travel lane of a zombie were capable of attacking or defending; as players move through levels, plants have more flexibility.

The first level takes place in the player's front yard during the day, when the plants are at their strongest. The second level takes place at night, where plants are weakened due to the lack of sunlight. Additionally, the screen becomes much darker as night falls. At this point, zombies can also attack via the back yard (which has a swimming pool through which zombies pass using lifesaver-shaped floaties). In the third level, fog makes visibility difficult so that it is harder to see the zombies. In the final level, the player must face a giant zombie-controlled robot. Players receive warnings from characters to help them prepare for the infestation, during which time they can defeat zombies by either using the plants or rolling large nuts at them. Each player starts with a prescribed number of seeds and growing spots, with the latter increasing with purchases made with virtual money. The player is warned about the impending attack, allowing him or her to quickly select plants to fight off the approaching zombies. Nocturnal plants, such as mushrooms, are included to help provide energy to the other plants, as the sunflowers do during daylight attacks. Each plant is most effective against specific zombie types, that have unique qualities such as speed, the ability to fly and/or jump, robustness against attack, and peripherals (such as helmets and armor). Comic interludes such as dancing zombies and cultural references in naming occur. For example, gravestone inscriptions reference the "Dead Parrot" Monty Python sketch and the openings of *The Simpsons* Halloween specials, which both popularized the idea of humorous engravings on gravestones. The game can be played by a single player or by multiple players. Like most games, it includes extra features that are unlocked as play progresses. Various versions of the game designed for different platforms have been released, including iOS, iPad, Android, Xbox Live Arcade, Blackberry, Nintendo DS, and PlayStation 3. Each iteration has unique features and modes, and both Windows and Mac versions have been updated. A sequel was released in 2013.

See also: Comedy; Video Games

Anthony J. Fonseca

POE, EDGAR ALLAN

Edgar Allan Poe (born Edgar Poe, 1809–1849) is best known as the American master of the macabre, authoring gothic horror tales steeped in realism, such as "The Tell-Tale Heart" (*Boston Pioneer,* January 1843) and "The Pit and the Pendulum" (1843). Poe also ushered in the modern detective story with "The Murders in the Rue Morgue" (*Graham's Magazine,* April, 1841) and composed horror poetry. A running theme in Poe's stories is the living dead or of being buried alive. Poe's theme of living death endures through the modern zombie trope, with his "The Facts in the Case of M. Valdemar," where he introduced the idea of the undead into American fiction.

In "Loss of Breath" (*Southern Literary Messenger,* September 1835), Mr. Lackobreath is erroneously pronounced dead but evades autopsy by jumping out a window, landing aboard a passing hangman's cart. Lackobreath then survives his own hanging, waking in a tomb where he discovers a prematurely interred gentleman. Roderick Usher, in "The Fall of the House of Usher" (*Burton's Gentleman's Magazine,* September, 1839), entombs his sister Madeline while she is alive but she rises. The narrator of "The Black Cat" (*United States Saturday Post,* August, 1843) walls up his murdered wife and, inadvertently, the family cat. The hideous feline calls from the tomb, indicting the killer while perched atop a corpse. In "Some Words with a Mummy" (*American Review,* April 1845), Count Allamistakeo is embalmed alive and, centuries later, reanimated. In "The Facts in the Case of M. Valdemar" (*American Review,* December, 1845), a hypnotist places the dying Valdemar under a trance, causing Valdemar to remain in an intermediate state as his body decomposes. In "The Cask of Amontillado" (*Godey's Magazine,* November, 1846),

Montresor murders his enemy by entombing him, alive, in a wine cellar. Rather than attribute Poe's fascination with living death to morbid curiosity, derangement, or an unwillingness to accept the finality of death, current scholarship emphasizes that Poe's subject matter reflects anxieties of his generation. Though rare, premature burials of coma patients, due to fallible medical science, led to coffins being outfitted with bells attached to the dead.

Born to traveling actors, Poe was orphaned at the age of three and remained at odds with his foster father, John Allan, a Richmond tobacco exporter who would leave Poe out of his will. Following stints at the University of Virginia and West Point Academy, Poe moved to Baltimore and published short stories while serving as editor for numerous periodicals.

American author Edgar Allan Poe wrote about themes commonly found in the zombie narrative, such as premature burial and reanimation. (National Archives)

Poe suffered from depression and alcoholism, struggled financially, gambled, and further damaged his reputation by lampooning New England literati for their pretentiousness. The death of Poe's wife, Virginia, devastated him, and he died within three years; the cause of death remains a subject of fascination, with theories ranging from alcohol poisoning to rabies.

See also: "Facts in the Case of M. Valdemar, The"

Matthew McEver

POETRY, HAITIAN CREOLE

Haitian Creole poetry utilizes images from Haitian folklore and religion to reflect societal, cultural, and political issues, particularly in its connection to the Haitian revolution. The Voodoo zombie slave is an important trope in this literary tradition.

Haitian Kreyòl (Creole) poetry stems from a conscious effort to express the uniqueness of Haitian culture and politics through the use of the Kreyòl language, one of the many Creole tongues that developed in the Caribbean from mixtures of French, English, Spanish, Portuguese, and African languages. Kreyòl is currently the vernacular language spoken by the majority of people in Haiti and is similar to the language used by slaves on the island during the Haitian revolution (1791–1804).

This use of Kreyòl by Haitian poets illustrates a solidification of a religious, racial, and national consciousness. The development of literature written in Kreyòl, especially poetry, reflects past and present political and cultural struggles that stem out of a history of colonialism and revolt. Religion, especially Haitian Vodoun, is a rich source for imagery in this poetry, expressing resistance to injustice. The zombie, an important supernatural figure in Haitian folklore and literature, commonly appears in Haitian Kreyòl poetry as it is a metaphor for the effects of slavery. The zombie as it is represented in Haitian folklore and literature is a creature lacking agency; it is forced to work for a cruel master and is unenlightened as to its subservient state. In Haitian Creole poetry, there are a moments of zombification and dezombification, instances where images of zombies represent allegories to political repression and strife. Such poems may be deceivingly straightforward in their treatment of the image of the zombie, but they imply that even zombies can die if exploited. The poetry also often captures folkloristic themes in and uses the vernacular Kreyòl as an appropriate and powerful authorial choice to deal with the trope.

Three literary movements are generally recognized in the history of Haitian Creole contemporary poetry: Pyonye (The Pioneers, 1950–1960), Sosyete Koukouy (The Society of Fireflies, 1960–present), and Lamadèl (The New Generation, 1990–present). Each generation of Haitian Creole poets have poems dedicated to the image of the zombie. The poets of the Sosyete Koukouy movement also utilize the figure of the zombie to make political and social commentaries, especially about the bloody Duvalier (born Jean-Claude Duvalier, 1951–) regime. Some of these poems mention "zonbi," the Kreyòl word for zombie and use the image to illustrate both the personal and the social struggle. The image of the zombie is a figurative device that brings various themes of these poems together in an allegorical sense. Writers from the Lamadèl movement also focus on Haiti's economic and political dilemmas through folklore, religion, and culture and have a greater number of women poets among their ranks. Historian Colin Dayan contrasts the image of the warrior female (the Voodoo loa or spirit lwa Ezrulie) against the passive image of the zombie to reconfigure Haitian history and culture from Caribbean women's perspective of empowerment. The idea of zombification is a powerful cultural referent in Haiti, and zombifying powder in Haitian Creole poetry can be used to make a political statement, in some poems being placed on a personified landscape by an outside power wishing to exploit Haiti.

Haitian Creole poetry offers a unique image of the zombie that grows directly out of the nation's folklore. As with other religious and supernatural elements that provide a fertile iconography for expressing the historical struggle and freedom in Haiti, the zombie provides a metaphor for expressing individual and collective numbness. Through the motif of the zombie, three generations of Creole Haitian poets offer a powerful tool for expressing salient social critiques.

See also: Africa; Class; Free Will; Haiti; Race; Voodoo

Solimar Otero

PONTYPOOL

Pontypool is a 2008 Canadian psychological thriller, with elements of dark comedy peppered throughout, directed by Bruce McDonald and adapted by novelist Tony Burgess, based on his novel *Pontypool Changes Everything* (1998). The film, like the novel, is set in the fictionalized version of the real-life town of Pontypool, a municipality in Ontario. But where the novel follows the adventures of drama coach Les Reardon as he tries to outrun the cannibalistic undead in the Canadian countryside during the dead of winter, the film is focused on a minor character from the novel, former shock-jock turned radio announcer Grant Mazzy, played by Stephen McHattie (born Stephen McHattie Smith, 1947–). With the exception of the first five minutes, the entirety of the film takes place within the confines of a radio station. As such, the film is an homage to the 1938 *War of the Worlds* radio broadcast. The overall plot device created by Burgess is that certain uses of endearing words the English language makes humans into crazed quasi-cannibalistic undead who try to eat other's mouths, thereby creating more undead. Filming was done in Pontypool itself, as well as in Toronto.

The film begins outside of the station, when Mazzy encounters a panicked woman on the side of the road during his drive in to work on Valentine's Day. She forces him to stop his car, speaks gibberish at him and then disappears. The scene then switches to inside of the radio station, where Mazzy, technical assistant Laurel-Ann Drummond, and station manager Sydney Briar begin a normal show, only to bunker down for the ensuing attack. During a report from their weather and traffic reporter, the trio hear about a riot at the office of a doctor in Pontypool. They attempt to confirm and finally manage to clarify the scene: Pontypool citizens are mysteriously walking around mumbling to themselves, becoming violent, and biting others. After a transmission in garbled French warns the trio to remain calm and speak no words in the English language, the radio crew learns that Pontypool has been quarantined. Laurel-Ann, who had earlier translated the French message into English, becomes transfixed on a word; infected, she attempts to attack the others, but since they are inside the sound booth, she can only slam her head against the glass partition that separates them until she eventually dies from lack of victims.

Meanwhile, the town's doctor, known only as Dr. Mendez, fights his way into the studio. Mendez explains that a virus transmitted via the English language causes the infected to succumb to the words on which they fixate. The film is notable for its lack of gore (with the exception of Laurel-Ann's death), as well as the rarity of the screen time for the monsters; other transfixed cannibalistic humans enter the station only within its final 15 minutes, and they are not seen until they press against the sound booth's glass. As they do, Mendez begins babbling, so Mazzy and Briar leave him. They become trapped upstairs; Mendez, who has only been babbling to stave off an infection, arrives and saves the two by running outside so that the transfixed fixate on his voice and follow him. The film ends with Mazzy and Briar back on the air, transmitting linguistic contradictions in an attempt to break the virus's spell. Unfortunately, just as they do so, the military bombs the radio station. As credits roll, various news reports and interviews are heard, all degenerating into gibberish; the virus has spread. An enigmatic epilogue ends the film surrealistically, with a stylized, black-and-white version of Mazzy and Briar bantering. Although the film employs the zombie trope, the word itself is never uttered. McDonald uses constant camera movements, blue lighting, and a ubiquitous low buzzing alternated with complete silence in the backing soundtrack, which accompanies Mazzy's constant talking on the microphone. These add an eerie quality to the film. Burgess, who has a cameo as part of a ridiculous singing troupe, wrote his own name into the script and cleverly interspersed subtle commentary on the novel's themes and motifs into the dialogue.

See also: Apocalypse; Cannibalism; Epidemics; *Pontypool Changes Everything*

Anthony J. Fonseca

PONTYPOOL CHANGES EVERYTHING

Pontypool Changes Everything (1995) is an experimental, metaphorical zombie novel by Canadian author Tony Burgess (no date available). The book inspired the 2009 film *Pontypool,* which had a screenplay by Burgess and was directed by Bruce McDonald (1959–). Burgess's zombies are a combination of the undead zombies made popular by George Romero in *Night of the Living Dead* (1968) and the mutated fast-moving zombies made popular by Danny Boyle in *28 Days Later* (2002). The zombies in the novel are caused by a language-based virus, which occurs when a person fixates on a particular English word; the infected human then repeats the word over and over until it drives him or her insane, at which point the individual attacks others and tries to eat through victims' mouths. The creatures are unstoppable: they continue to assault their victims until their necks are broken or they break their own necks in the attack.

Burgess's novel is set in an actual small Ontario town named Pontypool. While the film based on the novel is an homage to Orson Welles's (born George Orson Welles, 1915–1985) Mercury Theatre on the Air Halloween radio play *The War of the Worlds* (1938) and deals with the zombie attacks off-screen, the novel foregrounds the attacks and is much more graphic and visceral in its treatment of violence. The novel, which for the most part follows the character Les Reardon, a high school drama teacher, can best be described (as it has been by most scholars) as hallucinatory. Its characters are uncommon, in some cases weird and nightmarish, and the novel's editing cuts between characters and scenes are extremely jarring. Burgess also constantly introduces main characters and kills them off, even if chapters are told through their point of view. The virus which infects humans is nothing created by scientists or the military; instead, it has been mutating slowly over time along with the human race and has only now reached its present dangerous state.

Burgess's zombies are as vicious and frightening as any in the tradition of zombie fiction: they are fast, relentless, and cannibalistic. Comparable to much zombie fiction, the novel contains scenes of human atrocity, with very young brother and sister survivors/zombie killers who live as husband and wife. Burgess, a semiotics scholar, creates descriptions and dialogues that are simultaneously taboo and gruesome, yet elegantly written and pensive.

See also: Cannibalism; Epidemics; *Night of the Living Dead* Series; *Pontypool*; Romero, George; *28 Days Later* Series

Anthony J. Fonseca

PORNOGRAPHY

Pornography often stretches the boundaries of the socially and culturally acceptable. One of the oldest human taboos is necrophilia, or intimate contact with the deceased. While the use of zombies in pornographic film has not been as common or consistent as that of vampires, the other undead, the zombie trope has reoccurred throughout the history of adult film, spanning the golden age, the video age, and surviving the Internet gonzo age unscathed.

Zombie porn sites emerged recently, and since the mid-2000s zombie porn films have had a brief but notable resurgence, with movies such as *Re-Penetrator* (2004), *Porn of the Dead* (2006), *Zombie Nation* (2006), and *Dawna of the Dead* (2008). This resurgence is due predominantly to the growth in popularity of zombies in mainstream film and television shows such as *The Walking Dead* (2010–) but also due to a rapid rise in production of porn parodies in 21st century. Very recently, Joanna Angel and Tommy Pistol (1976–) have spearheaded zombie porn as part of the alt-porn movement with film company BurningAngel's *Evil Head* (2012) and *The Walking Dead XXX* (2013), directed by Pistol and Angel. Yet, hardcore pornographic zombie films have faced criticism from both horror and pornography genre purists who believe that the union of the two satisfies neither audience, an attitude which may account for the relative scarcity of zombie porn.

Hardcore pornography came on the scene in a commercial sense in the early 1970s, with an explosion of hardcore feature films, many of which utilized existing Hollywood genres, narratives, and structures on which to build hardcore sex scenes. Horror genres were predictably tapped, and horror porn proved very popular. Nonetheless, zombies were not as fruitful a pornographic source as vampires and Satanists—tropes that came with preexisting sexual connotations. It is worth noting, however, that some satanic ritual porn films, such as *Devil's Ecstasy* (1977) and *Hot Nasties* (1976), feature corpses re-animated via witchcraft and Satanism. By the early 1980s, however, films that appealed to those desiring to see the undead in flagrante delicto had emerged. Examples of pornographic riffing on mainstream zombie texts include *Driller* (1984), a bizarre and ambitious porn version of Michael Jackson's (born Michael Joseph Jackson, 1958–2009) video *Thriller* (1983). *Porno Holocaust* (1981) is regarded as the first hardcore zombie film, as the protagonist is a sexually active male zombie who wanders a Caribbean island killing off a group of vacationers, before ultimately raping the females. While there were hardcore films featuring zombie elements in the 1970s, namely *Hot Nasties* and *Naked Lovers,* also known as *The Porno Zombies* (1977), *Erotic Nights of the Living Dead* is the first full-fledged hardcore zombie film. It combined the popular zombie horror movie plot development (gore and zombie effects) with full frontal nudity and graphic depictions of a variety of sexual acts. This marriage of the elements of horror and pornography was done in a way that was previously disregarded as too risqué for even the hardest works of the genre, yet in this early example there is no sexual activity involving zombies. In this sense, *Mansion of the Living Dead* (1985) is regarded as the first hardcore zombie film. While it incorporates a loosely woven plot and minimal character development, the film centers on women's postmortem sexual relations. Allusions to mainstream and Hollywood texts continue to this day, as evidenced by titles such as *Night of the Giving Head* (2008). There are, however, examples of hardcore zombie films that move beyond paying lip service to famous nonpornographic examples. *Dark Angels 2: Bloodline* (2005) develops a plot in which zombies and vampires merge, creating a new race called slags, while *Succubus,* also known as *Raven Riley: Demonslayer* (2007), incorporates the resurrection of the dead, not zombies per se, into a pornographic retelling of the Lilith tale. While gay pornography is a smaller industry than its heterosexual counterpart, and as a result works with lower budgets, producing fewer feature films, there are two celebrated pornographic gay zombie films directed by Bruce LaBruce: *L.A. Zombie* (2009) and the hardcore *Otto: or Up with Dead People* (2010), both of which were released in hard and soft cuts.

Interest in hardcore zombies goes beyond film and video. In 2007, Image Comics distributed *XXXombies,* part of an anthology titled *Crawl Space.* The story's integral plot points center around a zombie outbreak near a pornographic movie set and the producer's attempts to corral undead celebrities to join in the filming. Within XXX fan fiction, there is a thriving interest in zombies of both the heterosexual and homosexual variety. Most recently, like film pornography, fan fiction has drawn on the popularity of *The Walking Dead* to create X-rated literary extensions of the comic book and television show. In addition to fan fiction, published anthologies of zombie erotica, such as *Fifty Shades of Decay: Zombie Erotica* (2013), have emerged in recent years.

See also: Angel, Joanna; LaBruce, Bruce; Romero's Rules; *Thriller;* Vampires and Werewolves; *Walking Dead, The* (Television Show)

Celise A. Reech-Harper and Laura Helen Marks

POST-HUMAN ZOMBIES

Post-human zombies adhere to the theory of the post-human, or super-human, which is a speculative being reflecting radical considerations of what it means to be human. Several recent iterations of the zombie characterize it as post-human, for in these narratives, the zombie is not an undesirable abject Other, but a being that has arrived at a desirable, albeit disturbing, stage in evolution. This is the case in

The zombie Big Daddy, in George A. Romero's *Land of the Dead* (2005) is post-human in that he and his fellow zombies have evolved to do what the living cannot, namely, forming the class-consciousness necessary to set aside differences to effectively come together for the common good. (Universal Studios/Photofest)

Daryl Gregory's novel *Raising Stony Mayhall*, published in 2010; George Romero's film *Land of the Dead* (2005); Andrew Currie's film *Fido* (2006); Kit Reed's (1938–) short story "The Zombie Prince" (2004), collected in *Zombies: The Recent Dead* (2010); and Jeffrey Ford's short story "Malthusian's Zombie" (2000), collected in the anthology *The Living Dead* (2008). Each represents the zombie as having desirable qualities that humans lack, and in some cases, can never possess.

Tommy the zombie in Ford's "Malthusian's Zombie" is a representation of the creature as a being uniquely capable of transcending the limitations of the human body. Malthusian, a military psychologist, made a zombie by kidnapping an ordinary citizen and subjecting him to a rigorous form of hypnotism that turns him into an assassin devoid of volition, who will do anything that his handlers require of him. Tommy, the resulting zombie, is a secret weapon who can be deployed against the United States' enemies during the Cold War. However, Tommy's hypnotism not only enables him to murder without the limitations of conscience but changes the physical make up of his body. Over the decades that Malthusian controls Tommy, he successfully orders the zombie to become fatter or thinner, taller or shorter, and to not age. Malthusian's ability to manipulate Tommy's body on this level calls into question the limitations on the human flesh: his body is not controlled by observable biological processes but by the force of the will, giving the zombie advantages over the human.

In Reed's "The Zombie Prince," zombies are superior to humans in that they are free of emotion. Reed's zombie does not hunger for human flesh but is a stealer of souls. Zombies also lack individuality in that they do not remember their former names, and in fact know nothing of their previous lives, which means that they can no longer feel pleasure or pain. For this reason, Dana Graver, reeling from a recent break up that is so painful that she would do anything to make the hurt go away, including commit suicide, finds the idea of being a zombie appealing. As a result, Dana willingly lets the zombie X (zombies are so lacking in individuality that they are known to one another as only X) take her soul and change her into a zombie. Yet, as X takes Dana's soul and transforms her into a zombie, he too is altered, as he has allowed himself to come too close to a human: X suddenly recalls that he is Remy L'Hereaux, who was turned into a zombie by his father-in-law, a powerful bokur who never approved of his daughter's marriage. Remy's grieving wife Sallie, believing him to be dead, put a silver bracelet on his cold wrist, binding him to the world of the living. As a result, once Remy remembers who he is, he is driven to see his wife and child once more and can only hope that his rapidly decomposing body falls apart before he locates them, and they see the horror of what he has become.

In *Land of the Dead,* the fourth film in Romero's *Night of the Living Dead* series, zombies are post-human in their ability to form class-consciousness, a way of thinking about each other that lets them look past differences created by race, class, and gender. Class-consciousness is a precondition for enabling humans or zombies to collaborate in order to seize the means of production from the ruling classes for the common good. Some unspecified time after the initial zombie apocalypse, the wealthy capitalist Kaufman has established a fortified enclave on the ruins of old Pittsburg. Here, the wealthy few live in the expensive and exclusive condominium development, Fiddler's Green, where they can still enjoy world-class shopping. Meanwhile, the majority of the survivors, whose labor runs the enclave, live in squalor in the slums outside of this development, unable to afford many of the basic necessities of life, such food or antibiotics. Moreover, the survivors in the slums are so brutalized by Kaufman's henchmen that they have too little hope to seize the means of production for the common good. Zombies, on the other hand, can form class-consciousness. Death has freed them of the prejudices that color human behavior, and in one of the film's first scenes, we see zombies of all races, sexes, and classes peacefully coexisting in the aptly named Uniontown. After Uniontown is raided by a group of Kaufman's men on a foraging mission where they delight in senselessly slaughtering many zombies as they pillage for supplies, the African American zombie Big Daddy leads his fellow undead to destroy the human compound, effectively seizing the means of production that is controlled by Kaufman. Once the compound is destroyed, the zombies return to peaceful coexistence. Romero's representation of the zombie as post-human has been evolving through his previous three films, where they begin as loathsome abject Others in *Night of the Living Dead* and *Dawn of the Dead,* and must be destroyed because there are in thrall to the need to consume human flesh, to creatures who are sympathetic because they can learn and have feelings, as we see with the teachable zombie Bub in *Day of the Dead.*

In Currie's *Fido,* zombies are post-human in their superior appreciation for the small pleasures in life and their refusal to be enslaved by limiting social roles. *Fido* is set in an alternative 1950s North America, where humans are experiencing unparalleled prosperity after the Allies had defeated the zombies (rather than the Nazis) only a decade earlier. Victory against the undead was possible, however, not due to the bravery of the soldiers but the triumph of capitalism. Dr. Hrothgar Geiger, founder of Zomcom, invents an electronic collar that can be fitted on a zombie to transform it from a ravening cannibal into a docile creature whose labor can be appropriated for menial tasks such as repetitive factory work or domestic service. So now, in an alternative version of an idyllic 1950s drawn-from-television situation comedy of the era, father still knows best, women and children are still subordinate to him, and the living dead are not thought of as human. People remain within these roles whether or not they are fulfilled by playing them. When the Robinsons get their own zombie servant, Timmy and his mother Helen become fond of the creature that Timmy nicknames Fido. Timmy interacts with the zombie in a way typical of a boy and his dog. Helen, meanwhile, starved for affection from her husband, discovers that Fido has a better appreciation of what is valuable than does Mr. Robinson. While Mr. Robinson rushes off to play golf with men he hates, Timmy, Helen, and Fido cavort while washing the car and enjoy cool drinks. By the end of the film, it is clear that zombies have a better ability to form bonds with those they love than do many of the living.

In Gregory's *Raising Stony Mayhall,* zombies defy all previous representations as soul-less undead who are either controlled by a zombie master or harmful to humans. Gregory's zombies are sentient and intelligent, rather than the mindless cannibals represented in Romero's *Night of the Living Dead.* Here, zombies are caused by a 48-hour brain fever that temporarily makes the sufferer into a ravening fiend whose intellect is subordinated to the drive to rip apart the living. Most of the living in the novel see the living dead (or LDs, as they prefer to be called) as a threat to their existence, and so attempt to exterminate them soon after they first begin to reanimate. As a result, approximately 50 years later, only a handful of LDs exist worldwide, struggling to survive in safe houses with the help of sympathetic humans, who attempt to keep their undead friends and family members from being killed or locked up in Dead Town, the special secret prison where the government performs experiments on a captive population of LDs. This is done despite the fact that LDs' homicidal condition is temporary, and the LD are human except that their bodies do not deteriorate, feel pain, or require food, water, or sleep. As a consequence, the LDs are a type of post-human whose bodies have transcended many of the limitations of mortality. However, the LD body is not impervious to injury: rather, as the body has stopped regenerating, these injuries can never be fully repaired. The LD can sometimes also be destroyed by a bullet to the head. Nevertheless, the LDs' static flesh gives them a type of supernatural invulnerability unavailable to the living: they can run without ceasing, and because they never need to sleep nor eat, they can be more productive than the living. But the most startling post-human quality of the LD is their ability to live through force of their wills and to expand the parameters of the body itself. If an LD loses a body part like a toe or finger, he or she can prevent it from decomposing by continuing to think about the severed part. Moreover, the LDs' consciousness can overflow their boundaries of their flesh, which the titular character Stony Mayhall discovers when he tries to escape some chains that he has been bound with, as he can open the locks by merely thinking about them as an extension of his own body. At the end of the novel, when Stony has supposedly been killed in a house fire that changed his body into ash and bone shards, his consciousness still exists and he can make the small atoms of his remains move if he wished. Instead, Stony opts to remain in this state to observe the interactions of the living and LD, as a sort of sprit who has passed into a superior plane of existence that is similar to Buddhahood, a state of enlightenment where all suffering due to attachment has passed.

See also: Apocalypse; Bokur/Caplata; Class; Existentialism; *Fido*; Free Will; "Malthusian's Zombie"; *Night of the Living Dead* Series; *Raising Stony Mayhall*; Romero, George; Sentience; "Zombie Prince, The"

June Michele Pulliam

POULTRYGEIST: NIGHT OF THE CHICKEN DEAD

Poultrygeist: Night of the Chicken Dead is a horror comedy directed by Lloyd Kaufman. It was shot on location in Buffalo, New York, and produced by Troma Entertainment, the infamous low-budget horror-gore production and distribution company founded in 1974 and known for such titles as *Toxic Avenger* (1985), *Redneck Zombies* (1987), *Surf Nazis Must Die* (1987), and *Cannibal! The Musical* (1993). *Poultrygeist* is a combination of genres, from horror to comedy to musical and includes scenes of gory special effects utilizing prosthetics and makeup. It features a notable cameo appearance by adult film actor Ron Jeremy and a soundtrack including punk, punkabilly, and ska bands, such as the Dwarves, Scatterbox, and Zombina and the Skeletones.

This satire of the fast food industry is set in a fictionalized, military-themed fried chicken franchise, the American Chicken Bunker (ACB). An ACB store unwittingly built atop a sacred Native American burial ground becomes overrun with zombie chickens that have been transformed by the evil spirits inhabiting the Tromahawk Indian site. A storyline involving the principal characters, Arbie and Wendy, connects them as a one-time couple who had (at the beginning of the film) made love in the same spot where the ACB store now stands. The pair has grown apart since: Wendy left for college and became a lesbian and political activist. She and her lover Micki protest the construction of this particular ACB franchise, which is owned by the racist General Lee, a parody of Colonel Sanders. Arbie becomes an employee of the restaurant in order to get close to Wendy and win her back. After several customers and coworkers are slaughtered by possessed raw chicken carcasses, the protesters are given free fried chicken, which makes them violently ill. Soon after, the General fights a zombie chicken and becomes infected, while the slaughtered victims are also reanimated as zombie chickens. As the scene escalates into a full-fledged massacre, Old Arbie (an older version sent back from the future, played by director Kaufman) shoots up the zombie mob until he is killed. Arbie, Wendy, and the remaining survivors attempt to fend off the attack but are vastly outnumbered; as new hatchlings emerge and the General chicken zombie threatens to finish off the protagonists, the remaining coworker Hummus (a burqa-clad Muslim woman) detonates herself, along with the zombies, allowing Arbie, Wendy, and a small girl to escape. The film ends when the girl lays an egg, and the ensuing horror leads to a car crash and explosion, presumably killing everyone inside. *Poultrygeist* enjoys the critical reception typical of a cult film, where critics from venues such as the *New York Post, The Calgary Herald,* and the Toronto after Dark Film Festival have generally acknowledged its salient satirical effectiveness, alongside the juvenile humor, use of stereotypes, and crude horror effects.

See also: Apocalypse; Comedy; Epidemics; Romero's Rules

Ben McCorkle

PRIDE AND PREJUDICE AND ZOMBIES

Pride and Prejudice and Zombies, subtitled *The Classic Regency Romance, Now with Ultraviolent Zombie Mayhem,* is a novel by Seth Grahame-Smith. Published by Quirk Books in 2009, it is often credited with being the first popular literary mash-up, or a hybrid of a work of classic literature interwoven with a second story that transforms the original, where the mash-up is narrated as the actual version of the events that were fictionalized in the original. In Grahame-Smith's retelling, the Regency England of Jane Austen is plagued with zombies.

Therefore, the Bennett sisters must worry about more than finding suitable spouses. Instead, in this world where the dead reanimate, if a young woman wishes to be considered accomplished, she must be mistress of the deadly martial arts, in addition to being able to play a spinet or paint china. Mr. Bennett has spent much of his meager family fortune educating his daughters in China so that they can defend themselves against the dreadfuls, as zombies are called in the novel. Moreover, the Bennett sisters' martial arts skills have a second practical benefit: they can make their living as body guards and hired assassins should they be unable to find suitable spouses who would marry them in spite of their paltry fortunes.

The presence of zombies in this mash-up does little to alter Austen's plot: Elizabeth and Jane still marry Mr. Darcy and Mr. Bingley, respectively; Lydia runs away with the villainous Mr. Wickham, who must be coerced into marrying the girl whose reputation he has ruined; and Charlotte Lucas weds the Bennetts' pedantic cousin, Mr. Collins. The zombies in the story also emphasize Elizabeth's proto-feminism: her martial arts prowess and zombie-killing abilities are in keeping with her lack of interest in conventional femininity in Austen's version, something demonstrated in both versions through her muddy petticoats, tanned skin, and ability to walk long distances without tiring, as well as her willingness to speak her mind. Zombies take the place of the very human revolutionary forces in Austen's *Pride and Prejudice,* which is set during the Napoleonic Wars, 16 years after the French Revolution. In Austen's version, the King's troops are stationed all over England in 1813, the publication date of Austen's novel, in part to quell any similar revolutionary fever that might topple the existing social order. In Grahame-Smith's novel, the King's army floats around the country to suppress zombie outbreaks, which have been plaguing the nation for at least a generation.

The popularity of Grahame-Smith's novel spawned a prequel and sequel not penned by the author, *Pride and Prejudice and Zombies: Dawn of the Dreadfuls* (2010) and *Pride and Prejudice and Zombies: Dreadfully Ever After* (2011), as well as a graphic novel by the same name. The success of *Pride and Prejudice and Zombies* encouraged Quirk books to create a line of mash-ups, including *Sense and Sensibility and Sea Monsters* (2009), based on Austen's novel *Sense and Sensibility* (1811), and *Jane Slayre* (2010), a rewriting of *Jane Eyre* (1847), by Charlotte Brontë. A film version of *Pride and Prejudice and Zombies* is rumored to be in production for 2014, but as of this writing, no director or stars had been named.

See also: Cannibalism; Comedy; Epidemics; Mash-Ups, Literary; Romero's Rules

June Michele Pulliam

QUARANTINE

Quarantine is a 2008 virtual shot–by-shot American remake of the 2007 Spanish horror film *[REC]*. Jennifer Carpenter (born Jennifer Leann Carpenter, 1979–), of the American Movie Classics series *Dexter* (2006–), leads a strong ensemble cast, directed by John Erick Dowdle (1973–). The film is a riveting tale of an outbreak of a rapidly spreading disease that causes the affected to become savage and violent. Like *28 Days Later* (2002), infected victims do not actually die and reanimate, so *Quarantine* is not a zombie film in the vein of *Night of the Living Dead* (1968). However, the behavior of the victims is consistent with that of zombies who follow Romero's Rules.

When reporter Angela Vidal (Jennifer Carpenter) shadows a local fire company as they answer a seemingly routine call about an emergency in an apartment building, she is trapped with the crew after all are suddenly quarantined along with the residents, who are infected with a mysterious ailment that makes them incoherent and blood-thirsty. (Screen Gems/Photofest)

The first section of the film introduces Carpenter's character, local television personality Angela Vidal, as she and her cameraman Scott go on location. The pair is assigned to follow members of a Los Angeles fire company as they proceed through the typical activities of their night shift. *Quarantine* is a "found footage" horror film, comparable to *Cloverfield* (2008) or *The Blair Witch Project* (1999), and the point of view is entirely composed of what is seen through the lens of Scott's camera. Vidal and Scott accompany the two firefighters assigned to escort them through the shift on an emergency run to an apartment building. The call quickly escalates into a disturbing and dangerous situation as the incoherent, elderly woman they are called to check on first attacks and bites a member of the Los Angeles Police Department and then attacks and throws one of the firefighters over a railing to the floor several stories below. More residents appear to fall prey to the mysterious condition as the Centers for Disease Control and Prevention (CDC) utilizes military force to quarantine the building. One building resident, a veterinarian, attempts to tend to the injured as the other residents and building manager collect in the lobby. Lawrence surmises that, impossible as it seems, the affected may be suffering from an accelerated form of rabies, with symptoms that should take months to occur presenting in minutes after the initial infection.

Power to the building is cut off as residents are held at gunpoint to prevent them from leaving. Things go from bad to worse—members of the CDC come in, and several (along with Lawrence) are attacked by a suddenly resilient and rage-filled firefighter as they attempt to take a brain sample; other residents appear rabid and begin to attack anyone in sight, and Scott is forced to kill one rampaging resident with his camera. The one surviving CDC member, who is pressured into revealing what he knows about the situation, states that a sick dog had been traced to the building by his registration tags. The previous day, the dog had become vicious while at a veterinarian's office and had attacked other animals, who rapidly displayed the same rabies-like symptoms and aggressive behavior. The situation quickly spirals out of hand. Vidal and Scott, eventually the only non-infected surviving members of the group, barricade themselves in the attic, in the supposedly vacated apartment of a tenant, originally from Boston, who has not been seen for several months. There, using the light of the camera to navigate the room, they find evidence of the manufacture and dissemination of the virus by the former resident, a member of a doomsday cult. The emaciated, ghoulish apartment resident eventually appears, killing Scott, and dragging Angela Vidal, screaming, into the darkness. The film's final segment is the only real variation from the plot of *[REC]*, which had utilized supernatural and religious themes to posit the cause of the outbreak as a virus that caused demonic possession.

See also: Apocalypse; Epidemics; *Night of the Living Dead* Series; *[REC]* Series; Romero's Rules; Television; *28 Days Later* Series

Robert Butterfield

R

RACE

Race is an inevitable part of day-to-day life, but it seems less obvious in zombie fiction. The contemporary zombie operating by Romero's Rules can be any race or sex. While the modern zombie is more obviously a metaphor for class, it is sometimes more subtly one for race or ethnicity.

Nonetheless, the earliest zombie, the Voodoo zombie, was a result of fears of Haitians in the 19th century that they would be re-enslaved by powerful corporations who had set up plantations on the island, changing its economy so that peasants had to leave their land and work for starvation wages in the fields and factories. The zombie in Haitian folklore is a creature who is brought back from the dead by a bokur, or a Voodoo priest who practices black magic. The bokur robs the zombie of its will and uses it as an undead slave who performs menial tasks, such as toil in the fields or the factories for no compensation. The zombie's reanimated (supposedly) dead body represents the horrors of slavery, as it deprives the victims of free will and reduces them to the status of an abject Other. In *Tell My Horse* (1938), folklorist Zora Neale Hurston claims to have seen actual zombies during her travels in Haiti, living beings who had been drugged by a bokur and enslaved either to pay off a debt or out of revenge. Haitian Creole poetry also connects the trope of the zombie to race in that it uses the creature as a metaphor to explore the horrors of slavery and colonialism.

Yet, when the zombie created by Voodoo first appeared in American popular culture, it reproduced racial prejudices of the time. So in W. B. Seabrook's enormously popular travelogue about Haiti, *The Magic Island* (1929), the author recounts some of the more sensationalist folk tales about zombies that were told to him by a black islander. The tone is one of incredulity, as if his informant were too ignorant to realize that what he is passing off as fact is actually a fantastic folk tale. The same informant later shows Seabrook men that he claims are zombies, but according to Seabrook, are merely mentally retarded adults who were forced to harvest cane in the broiling sun. The film *White Zombie* (1932), whose fictional depiction of the zombie is loosely based on Seabrook's accounts of the creature from *The Magic Island*, represents the zombie as less able to maintain its free will if it is not white. Of all of the bokur Murder Legendre's zombies that he has created through Voodoo and kept subordinated through a powerful combination of magic and the force of his will, only the white zombie Madeline can resist his efforts to control her. Legendre's black zombies somnambulate through their labors in his sugar mill; they are unspeaking, vacant-eyed human cogs in his machinery. Legendre's mixed-race zombies are slightly more intelligent in that they retain enough of their sentience to be effective henchmen for him. But the white Madeline retains enough of her will to resist Legendre's attempts to make her kill others. This hierarchy is in keeping with commonly held beliefs about race at the time in which nonwhites were viewed less intelligent and more submissive than whites.

H. P. Lovecraft reproduces this type of racial hierarchy in detail in his six-part short story "Herbert West—Reanimator," where the white and upper-class Major Clapham-Lee is the only one of Dr. West's experiments in reanimation that retains sentience after zombification. An angry Clapham-Lee leads the rest of the doctor's failed experiments to exact a grizzly revenge on their creator. The others, including an African American boxer and white farm boy, who is presumed to be unintelligent due to his class status, lack the intellect to be more than mere brutes when reanimated. A notable exception to this generalization is Dr. Halsey, the dean of Miskatonic Medical School, a man who puts West out of the program because he believed his experiments to be immoral: Lovecraft represents the character as unintelligent due to his rigid morality.

George Romero's film *Night of the Living Dead* (1968) examines race in an oblique but complex way. Ben, the only African American character trapped in the farmhouse with six other white survivors, touches upon some of the issues of race that were being openly debated due to the Civil Rights Movement. Ben butt heads with the older and white Mr. Cooper for dominance of the group, and their fight is as much about masculine and white privilege as it is about the best way to defend themselves from the zombies outside. Cooper is given the courtesy title Mister. Other members of the group address him thusly, whereas Ben, who is only slightly younger, is called by his first name. In a time when younger people demonstrated respect for their elders by addressing them by their last names and a courtesy title, nonwhite adults were not afforded this courtesy. Cooper does not even address Ben by his first name, a sign of his disrespect for someone that he clearly considers to be his social subordinate. The theme of race is once again addressed at the end of the film. After the zombies swarm the farmhouse, only Ben survives. However, in the morning when the sheriff and a local militia doing a search and rescue mission come across the house, they are understandably anxious and shoot Ben when they see movement, believing him to be a zombie. The audience can never be certain if racial bias was a factor in Ben's shooting. However, the images that run behind the film's credits hint at a subtle racism that might have influenced the group to shoot before coming any closer. In a montage of newspaper photographs of the aftermath of the first days of the zombie apocalypse, the militia uses hooks to drag the bodies of dead zombies onto a pyre to burn them. The images are reminiscent of photographs taken of lynching parties in the late 19th- and early 20th-century United States, featuring jovial parties of whites standing next to the mutilated corpses of African Americans.

As the figure of the zombie has evolved, it has become a potent metaphor for the intersection of race and class. Because the single most defining characteristic of the zombie is a lack of free will, the creature is generally associated with the working classes, who have little or no control over the means of production. The zombie's working class association can also be linked to race in the United States, since nearly three times as many blacks as whites live in poverty, according to the U.S. government's poverty rate statistics. Romero considers race and class in his 2005 film *Land of the Dead* through the character of Big Daddy, the zombie who leads his fellow undead to raid the nearby fortified human compound in retaliation for an earlier invasion that their residents conducted on the zombies' peaceful enclave of Uniontown. While the humans came to Uniontown to scavenge essential supplies like food and drugs, they also kill and mutilate many zombies just for sport. The African American Big Daddy is working class: in life, he ran a small gas station, something we know when he emerges from the building after a human accidentally runs over the cable outside connected to a bell indoors. Big Daddy is wearing a uniform shirt with his name embroidered on the pocket. This character cleverly combines the themes of race and class. The zombies' ability to overthrow the human enclave is possible only because they have formed class consciousness, a state of mind in which the subordinate classes see their common oppressed condition and understand that commonality is greater than any distinctions of race, class, or gender that might otherwise divide them. Karl Marx (born Karl Heinrich Marx, 1818–1883) viewed class consciousness as a precondition to revolution. The film's zombies' class consciousness is demonstrated both through their ability to work together and their diversity as a group, which includes blacks and whites, men and women, and people in a variety of professions, as is seen by their attire, since they wear the clothes they died in. Humans, however, are arguably unable to form class consciousness, which is demonstrated by the vast inequalities in the human enclave, where a small group of wealthy whites control the majority of the resources, leaving poor whites, Hispanics, and blacks to live in the slums outside.

Diana Rowland's *White Trash Zombie* series also considers the theme of race as it is connected to the zombie. Rowland's heroine Angel Crawford is poor and white, and before she is made into a zombie, she embodies nearly all of the negative stereotypes about people like her, including being a pain-pill-addicted high-school dropout who lives in a trailer with an alcoholic father. Only after Angel becomes a zombie who requires brains to continue her undead existence does she begin to expect better of herself and work to improve her life. As a member of the working class, Angel calls attention to how whiteness too is a racial category, though it is often not seen as such, since to be white means to have access to race and class privilege that is taken for granted and so is invisible. Because Angel is poor and white, however, she lacks access to much of this privilege, which exposes its existence to readers.

See also: Bokur/Caplata; Class; Gender; Haiti; Hurston, Zora Neale; *Night of the Living Dead* Series; Poetry, Haitian Creole; Romero's Rules; Seabrook, W. B.; *Tell My Horse*; Voodoo; *White Trash Zombie* Series

June Michele Pulliam

RAIMI, SAM

Sam Raimi (born Samuel Marshall Raimi, 1959–) is an American film director best known for his big budget *Spider-man* series of movies and his independently produced *Evil Dead* trilogy. Raimi is a self-taught director who began making short films at 13 with an eight-millimeter camera. In 1978, after a series of student productions, Raimi decided to attempt a feature film. Originally hoping to make a comedy, Raimi decided that a horror film would be more practical to produce on a small budget. He shot a prototype short *Within the Woods* starring his friend, longtime collaborator, and actor Bruce Campbell, who has appeared in many of Raimi's projects to date, under the production label Renaissance Pictures. After showing *Within the Woods* to potential financiers, he raised over $300,000 from investors in suburban Detroit. With the working title *The Book of the Dead*, Raimi began a grueling, intermittent production that would take nearly two years. The result, *The Evil Dead* (1981), was

American director Sam Raimi, whose most significant contribution to the zombie genre is his *Evil Dead* trilogy of films. (Getty Images)

a financial success upon theatrical release. *Evil Dead II* (1987), not a true sequel so much as remake, introduced the elements of slapstick humor that are the trilogy's hallmark and considered Raimi's most significant contribution to the horror genre. Raimi followed his first mainstream picture, *Darkman* (1990) with *Army of Darkness* (1992), the last and most popular of the *Evil Dead* films with the widest theatrical release.

The monsters in the first two *Evil Dead* films are humans possessed by evil spirits that have been released by their having read passages aloud from a copy of *The Necronomicon,* or *The Book of the Dead.* The resulting possessed people serve the same function as the ghouls in the archetypal modern zombie film *Night of the Living Dead* (1968): their wills are subordinated to a drive to kill all humans, including their former friends, who are now trapped with them inside of the cabin where all were vacationing. In *Army of Darkness,* bumbling use of *The Book of the Dead* resurrects legions of the deceased, animating them into deadites, creatures who can be easily recognized as zombies for the first time in Raimi's body of work. The titular army is colorfully dispatched with novel weaponry and wisecracking humor before the hero can finally go home. After *Army of Darkness,* Raimi returned to mainstream Hollywood, making a western, *The Quick and the Dead* (1995); a crime drama, *A Simple Plan* (1998); a sports drama, *For Love of the Game* (1999); and a supernatural drama, *The Gift* (2000), before striking it big with the superhero franchise *Spider-man,* with Columbia Pictures. He returned to the horror genre for *Drag Me to Hell* (2009). A remake of *The Evil Dead,* produced by Raimi and Campbell, was released in 2013.

See also: Campbell, Bruce; *Evil Dead, The* (Films); *Evil Dead: The Musical*; *Night of the Living Dead* Series

Kevin Dole

RAISING STONY MAYHALL

Raising Stony Mayhall is a 2011 novel by Daryl Gregory in which zombies defy all previous representations as soul-less undead who are either under the control of a zombie master or harmful to humans; rather, they are sentient and intelligent and are not cannibals. The novel references the film *Night of the Living Dead* (1968), by George Romero, as a backstory.

Raising Stony Mayhall begins with what the narrator calls Romero's documentary, a 1968 film which captured the dead's return to life in rural Pennsylvania on the first night of a mysterious outbreak. In Gregory's fictionalization, Romero's documentary inaccurately represents the living dead, or LDs, as they prefer to be called, as cannibals. The LDs are only dangerous to the living during the first 48 hours of their transition; when their fever abates, they regain sanity and can safely coexist with the living. Unlike the living, the LDs do not deteriorate or feel pain, and they do not require food, water, or sleep. Their bodies, however, can be damaged, and those injuries can never be fully repaired. Also, they can sometimes be destroyed by a bullet to the head.

Gregory's protagonist, John "Stony" Mayhall, is unique among the LD: he did not rise from the grave, nor was he one of the living who was turned by a zombie bite. Instead, he was created when his runaway teen mother was bitten during the last hours of her pregnancy, turning Stony into a fetal LD who clawed his way out of the womb, leaving his mother to bleed to death. The infant Stony is found by Wanda Mayhall, an Iowa nurse who raised him in stealth, lest the government destroy him as it does other LDs. As baby Stony matures into an adult, he remains hidden in the family farmhouse during his formative years while his three older sisters and mother homeschool him. When Stony's presence in the household is eventually discovered by the authorities, he narrowly escapes capture. Members of Stony's family, however, are punished for concealing him: his mother Wanda is jailed as a terrorist, and his older sister Alice, a physician, is barred from practicing medicine. Over the next 30 years, Stony learns about the world's quickly dwindling LD population as he first hides in safe houses set up by LD sympathizers, and then is later imprisoned in Deadtown, a facility established to contain and experiment on the LDs, before finally reuniting with his remaining relations.

Narrated as a third-person account, the novel is full of interruptions in the story that reflect on how Stony's life will come to be recreated in mythic ways once the planet is fully transformed after world governments can no longer contain the virus that causes the dead to reanimate. Stony's existence is a miracle itself, as he is the only zombie-born infant who matured. Gregory's unique iteration of the zombie trope represents the creature as post-human. The LDs' static flesh gives them a supernatural invulnerability. Comic scenes in the novel show Stony's best child-hood friend shooting arrows at him and getting him to jump from great heights in order to test this. The LD can run without ceasing, and because they never need to sleep nor eat, they can be more productive than the living. But the most startling post-human quality of the LD is their ability to live through force of their wills and to expand the parameters of the body itself. A part severed from an LD's body can be kept from deteriorating so long as the LD continues to think about it. Moreover, the LD's bodies can overflow their flesh, which Stony discovers when he tries to escape some chains that he has been bound with, as he can open the locks by merely thinking about them as an extension of his own body. Stony is also represented as a Christ figure meant to unify the living and the LD. The novel ends when some of the LDs decide to increase their numbers through the Big Bite, a day during which several LDs transform hundreds of humans into zombies to more rapidly spread the virus through the population. The Big Bite brings about an apocalyptic collapse of civilization, and Stony is purportedly killed attempting to save his family. Afterward, human-friendly LDs memorialize him as a religious leader. Here, the reader learns that Stony, the narrator, still lives. He can choose to make the small atoms of his remains move if he wished. Instead, he opts to observe the interactions of the living and LD as a sort of sprit who has passed into another plane of existence.

See also: Apocalypse; Epidemics; Free Will; *Night of the Living Dead* Series; Post-Human Zombies; Romero, George; Romero's Rules; Sentience

June Michele Pulliam

REANIMATION

Reanimation after death is virtually synonymous with zombie fiction. A preponderance of zombies are the reanimated dead who, in their revived state, lack reason and are either subordinate to the person who put them in this condition or in thrall to the single-minded drive to consume flesh or tear apart humans.

The earliest examples of the creature are reanimated through magical means by a bokur or Voodoo priest who uses black magic. This method of reanimation is seen in William Seabrook's "Dead Men Walking in the Cane Fields," which recounts two Haitian folktales about how Voodoo was used to revive the dead, who were then used as slave labor. The bokur named Murder Legendre enslaves the living (and perhaps reanimates the dead), using Voodoo in the film *White Zombie* (1932).

Madeline, the zombie of the title, is put into a death-like trance by a magical powder that Murder arranges to have her come into contact with. Madeline's loved ones believe that she has died, so they bury her. Murder then retrieves Madeline's body on the night that she is interred and revives her through magical means, transforming her into a beautiful puppet, who is devoid of free will and has little memory of her former life. It is unclear whether Murder's other zombies are the reanimated dead or had never really died, as we are not privy to how he made them. John Gilling's *The Plague of the Zombies* (1966) similarly represents the dead being reanimated through Voodoo, though the story is set in Victorian England rather than Haiti. In 1983, ethnobotanist Wade Davis concluded that zombies do exist in Haiti. These are people who are slipped tetrodotoxin (TTX), a toxic substance found mainly in the liver and ovaries of certain fish, by a bokur. The TTX puts victims into a coma resembling death. After victims are buried, the bokur retrieves their bodies and then administers *Datura stramonium,* more commonly known as zombie cucumber, a substance that produces amnesia, delirium, and suggestibility in victims. The victims are then regularly dosed with *Datura stramonium* and are manipulated by a bokur as part of a Voodoo ritual to create the illusion that they are zombies.

Magical or supernatural means of reanimation persist in contemporary zombie fiction, though this magic is not always related to Voodoo. For example, in "Homecoming," an episode of the *Masters of Horror* television series, soldiers are revived by their sense of moral outrage after being sent to die in the Middle East due to the erroneous claim that Iraq had weapons of mass destruction. When the bodies of the fallen soldiers are returned to the United States, they rise from their coffins and make their way to the polls to vote the current administration out of office. In David Wellington's *Monster Island* trilogy (2006–2007), the zombie apocalypse is precipitated when Mael Mag Och, who was preserved for millennium after he was sacrificed in an Orkney Island bog so that his people could have a better harvest season and, is sent by the Old Ones to "turn out the lights" on the human race and bring about the end of the world. The dead are also revived by magical means in Stephen King's *Pet Sematary* (1983) and the *Evil Dead* series (1981–2013): in the former, grieving family members who inter their deceased humans and pets in a plot of land cursed by a windigo can have their dead revived, while an accidental reading of the *Necronomicon* revives the dead in the later. A cogent explanation of why the dead begin returning to life is never given in George Romero's films, in the graphic novel epic *The Walking Dead* (2003–) and the television series based on it (2010–), or John Ajvide Lindqvist's novel *Handling the Undead* (2005), so supernatural agency is about as likely a cause as any. The film *Shaun of the Dead* (2004) also never gives views and explanation as to why the dead begin returning to life but plays with the various explanations offered for this phenomenon in other zombie texts.

However, many works of zombie fiction show the dead return to life via scientific means. Notable among these are Richard Matheson's novella *I Am Legend* (1954), where the dead begin reanimating due to a bacteriological mutation that occurred after a global nuclear exchange permanently changed the environment. In *Night of the Living Dead* (1968), in the first days when the dead begin returning to life, pundits speculate that their reanimation might have been caused by radiation emitted by a satellite that recently returned to Earth's orbit. This reference is a nod to *I Am Legend,* which greatly influenced director George Romero when he was writing the script for *Night.* In Max Brooks's *The Zombie Survival Guide* (2003) and *World War Z* (2006), the solanum virus is responsible for reanimating the dead. The virus has been reviving the dead into ravening cannibals for centuries, but humans have been unaware of its presence until the 21st century, since the outbreaks were put down before they caused a pandemic; the resulting violence was attributed to genocidal warfare or mass hysteria. While zombies are also created by a virus in the *28 Days Later* films (2002–), the virus does not reanimate the dead but transforms the living, who eventually starve since their cerebral cortex becomes so compromised that they no longer even attempt to find sustenance.

The dead can also be revived with cosmic dust, technology whose harmful effects we do not fully appreciate, or scientific experimentation gone wrong. In *Night of the Comet* (1984), the dead are brought back to life after coming into contact with dust released after Halley's comet enters the planet's atmosphere. Cell phones inadvertently turn people into zombies in King's novel *Cell* (2006). Chemical agents reanimate the dead, deliberately in H. P. Lovecraft's serialized short story "Herbert West—Reanimator" (1921–1922) and Stuart Gordon's comic version of it made in 1985, *Re-Animator,* and accidentally in the *Return of the Living Dead* films, where corpses stored in the basement of a Veterans Administration hospital are revived by 2-4-5 Trioxin, an herbicide originally created by the U.S. military in order to destroy marijuana plants.

See also: Bokur/Caplata; Brooks, Max; Davis, Wade; Haiti; *Handling the Undead;* "Herbert West—Reanimator"; *Homecoming; I Am Legend* (Novel); King, Stephen; *Monster Island* Trilogy; *Pet Sematary* (Novel); *Plague of the Zombies, The; Re-Animator* Series; *Return of the Living Dead* Series; Romero, George; Seabrook, W. B.; Television; Tetrodotoxin; *28 Days Later* Series; Voodoo; Wellington, David; *White Zombie;* Zombie Cucumber

June Michele Pulliam

RE-ANIMATOR SERIES

The *Re-Animator* series is a group of films including *Re-Animator* (1985), *Bride of Re-Animator* (1990), *Beyond Re-Animator* (2003), *An Imperfect Solution: A Tale of the Re-Animator* (2003), and *Re-Animator: 1942* (2008). Although some critics characterize the *Re-Animator* series as heterogeneous and thoroughly repetitive, others point out that the series does hold true to the overall premise: when a human (notably not Victor Frankenstein) dabbles in reanimating the dead, results will be predictably and generally disastrous. Also, true to their source in the tales of H. P. Lovecraft, all *Re-Animator* movies must have as their protagonist a character named Herbert West, a scientist who wants to bridge the boundaries between life and death. West must have an assistant who occasionally offers advice or espouses different ethical stances. Each film also makes reference to Miskatonic University's Medical School, where West has access to cadavers (corpses) and various laboratories where he can concoct the requisite reanimating serum, usually characterized by its green glow.

Dr. Herbert West (Jeffrey Combs) and one of those he brings back from the dead (Kathleen Kinmont) in *Bride of Re-Animator* (1990). (50th Street Films/Photofest)

The films differ from Lovecraft's stories in that they also feature various good-looking young women who comprise the university's student body (Lovecraft's Miskatonic University was not co-ed, and the author only mentions one female student in his oeuvre). The zombies, reanimated corpses in this case, must behave carnivorously, albeit mindlessly, necessitating their immediate termination, although dispatching the reanimated corpses is difficult, as the first film in the series made clear. Zombies in the series are also characterized by their ability to move rapidly; and their individual body parts can reanimate separately and act independently. Another of the *Re-Animator* series' recurring motifs is devising inventive ways to stop zombie attacks.

True to its source material, the film series does not address questions that were left unanswered by Lovecraft himself. Chief among these is the question of why a medical school, presumably while training physicians and surgeons in the technology of saving lives, would not be interested in West's theories of resurrection, which could save lives by restoring the recent dead to life. Surely a successful experiment (and West's were successful) would take the medical profession by storm and make Miskatonic University's Medical School the envy of the nation, if not the world. In the world of Lovecraft's "Herbert West—Reanimator," Miskatonic Medical School's professors and residents choose to not pursue West's experiments, perhaps because they might probe too deeply into the mysteries of life and death. Although this reluctance is never specifically addressed, such lack of interest among West's colleagues may stem from religious issues or the politics of academia: other professors and administrators are portrayed as interested mainly in petty office politics, in maintaining the status quo that has empowered them. In their world, Herbert West is not so much a colleague as a distraction. He is definitely not seen as a brilliant scientist, and in both the stories and the films, this makes for a curious, unresolved, and untenable tension.

Unlike the world inhabited by Lovecraft's characters, which is well rounded, recognizing different ethnicities and ancestries, the world inhabited by the principals in the films of the *Re-Animator* series is hermetic. Viewers have little backstory; whether the characters had lives prior to the advent of the films themselves is never addressed. Viewers are left to wonder where West hails from, where West's parents are, and what they must have done to encourage their son's peculiar interest. Similarly, while there is little of the overt racism that critics have noted occasionally mars Lovecraft's tale, the world of the *Re-Animator* series is a white patriarchy: all of the positions of authority are occupied by white males. Where the series and Lovecraft's tales intersect is in their use of humor. Lovecraft's Herbert West stories possess a tongue-in-cheek quality, overt tinges of humor that show that the author does not always take his material seriously. This is also the case with the majority of the film series: there are odd moments in which it seems actors were told either to improvise or to have fun for a scene. In the first film, for example, West battles an unhappily reanimated cat, and it is obvious that he is fighting a stuffed animal. In the second, there are risible images that involve a flying head.

The general consensus is that the films of the series excel in three areas. The first is their representation of violence and visceral horror. The episodes that comprise Lovecraft's serially produced tales that make up "Herbert West—Reanimator" are hardly free of explicitly detailed horrors, as the conclusion of "Six Shots by Moonlight" demonstrates. In it, West and his assistant resurrect the bestial and recently deceased boxer, the so-called Harlem Smoke. Following this, an Italian child disappears, and though they are innocent, suspicion settles on the two scientists. Expecting the worst from the Italians, the two men receive instead a nocturnal visitor, "a glassy-eyed, ink-black apparition nearly on all fours." The creature is covered with mold, leaves, and blood, and carries in its mouth a pale object terminating in a tiny hand. The *Re-Animator* series is full of similar horrific episodes, though children are, as is usual in film, generally off-limits.

Where Lovecraft purists may have issues with the series is in its acceptance of sexuality, namely in its casual presentation of nude or scantily clad women. From the very first film, the series introduces attractive women, and the series' directors find excuses to objectify them. Finally, in the series, as in "Herbert West—Reanimator," the methods for reanimating and dealing with the dead are rational. There are no pentacles and invocations, no blasphemies, no calling upon various deities to restore life to the dead and then to deal with the problematic reanimated corpses. Instead, in both, the scientific method is followed: a questing intelligence develops a method for reanimating corpses and conducts experiments to find the best way to do this.

See also: Comedy; "Herbert West—Reanimator"; Lovecraft, H. P.; Science Fiction

Richard Bleiler

[REC] SERIES

The *[REC]* series is a trilogy of Spanish horror films named after the abbreviation for the recording button on a video camera. *[REC]* is a 2007 film written by Juame Balagueró (1968–), Luis Berdejo (born Luis Berdejo Arribas, 1975–), and Paco Plaza (1973–),and directed by Balagueró and Plaza. *[REC]*², the 2009 sequel, is also directed by Balagueró and Plaza. *[REC]*³: *Genesis* (2012) is written by Plaza and Berdejo, and directed by Plaza. Two of the three films purport to be found footage taped by the doomed users of video cameras, who record the outbreak of a virus and the ensuing carnage. Like *The Crazies* (1973) by George Romero and *28 Days Later* (2002) by Danny Boyle, each of the *[REC]* films is a zombie movie in spirit if not in fact. The infected are not the living dead, but as explained in *[REC]*², victims of a virus that leads to demonic possession and the overwhelming to eat human flesh; one bite from any of the infected will create a new zombie. In this way, the infected in the *[REC]* series are similar to zombies who follow Romero's Rules.

Filmed using shaky handheld cameras and marketed as a found footage film, *[REC]* was remade in the United States as the 2008 film *Quarantine*. *[REC]* is presented entirely as the footage of a fluffy Spanish reality TV show *While You're Asleep,* produced by a local station in Barcelona which purports to present the nightly work life of the city. When firefighters answer a call from an apartment complex where a woman is supposedly trapped, *While You're Asleep*'s television crew follows them, capturing footage of the ensuing outbreak. The government, which has learned about the virus after one of the residents sent her infected dog to the vet, prevents everyone from exiting the building, trapping the firefighters and the television crew with the infected tenants. As more tenants and all of the firefighters become infected, the film crew makes its way to the penthouse at the top of the building to discover the link between the virus and the Catholic Church.

*[REC]*² begins moments after *[REC]* ends, as the government sends in its Special Forces with a doctor from the ministry of health, who is also revealed to be an emissary from the Vatican. Both they and a group of thrill-seeking teenagers have cameras. While viewers saw *[REC]* entirely from one cameraman's point of view, *[REC]*² jumps back and forth from the perspective of these two cameras. *[REC]*³ is so different in form and tone that it often feels like an unrelated zombie movie. The events of *[REC]*³ are roughly similar, and the first character to be infected mentions suffering from a dog bite. Unlike the first two films, only the very beginning of *[REC]*³ is presented as found footage. *[REC]*³ begins as the recording of a wedding and its reception. But once the majority of the guests are infected, the groom destroys the camera, leading the rest of the movie to be presented as filmed through the fourth wall. *[REC]* grossed $32.5 million, *[REC]*²$18.5 million, and *[REC]*³: *Genesis* $10.1 million. *[REC]*⁴: *Apocalypse* is scheduled to be released in October 2014.

See also: Crazies, The; *Quarantine*; Romero, George; Romero's Rules; Television; *28 Days Later* Series

Jason Dupuy

REFERENCE BOOKS

Reference books on zombies and zombie-related material have become more popular in recent years, with various encyclopedias, dictionaries, and guides to fictional representations of the creature. Bob Curran's (no date available) *Encyclopedia of the Undead: A Field Guide to Creatures that Cannot Rest in Peace* is a comprehensive study of zombies, along with other types of supernatural creatures that are similar, including vampires and golem. Curran, a broadcaster, writer, and researcher born in Northern Ireland, is best known for his guides to Celtic mythology and mythological creatures, such as the leprechaun, the werewolf, and the vampire. His 2006 reference book on the undead is organized as a list of essays/entries on various classes of undead monsters, with individual entries on each creature.

The text tracks diverse undead literary and folklore characters from what Curran terms the earliest times to modern day Europe and America. Chapters in his text include "A Carnival of Terrors," "Vampires," "Werewolves," "Zombies and Voodoo," "Ghouls and the Golem," and "The Terrors of H. P. Lovecraft," the last chapter offering a biographical overview of H. P. Lovecraft. In his introduction, Curran points out that the intent of his study is to examine the scientific and sociological possibilities of monsters, as well as their beginnings in lore and their evolutions through literature and film, such as through Hammer Studios films. In essence, he looks at both the history and mystery. In some cases, Curran writes of historical accounts of people reputed to be undead, or medically afflicted with symptoms that make them seem so. Curran's discussion of zombies is limited to those associated with Voodoo spells and black magic. He focuses on Africa, the Caribbean, and New Orleans, with concentration on Voodoo priests such as Marie Laveau.

In *Icons of Horror and the Supernatural: An Encyclopedia of Our Worst Nightmares* (2007), edited by Lovecraft scholar S. T. Joshi (born Sunand Tryambak Joshi, 1958–) writes perhaps the most comprehensive chronicle of the modern zombie as trope in her chapter on the historical and metaphorical meanings of the zombie motif, including examples from both literature and film. Other reference works, such as Dan Oliver's (no date available) *Zombies A-Z* (2011) are written more with fans in mind than researchers.

Zombie movies have inspired more works of reference than has zombie literature. Peter Dendle's *The Zombie Movie Encyclopedia* (2001) is a comprehensive alphabetical listing, including international zombie films as well, which have their own index for easier access. Dendle's introduction also serves as an interesting history and criticism of zombie mythology and fictions. Jamie Russell's *Book of the Dead: The Complete History of Zombie Cinema* (2005) is the most ambitious of these reference works, written for both scholars and fans. It includes lengthy discussions of the zombie trope in individual films as well as full color stills and fandom information. R. G. Young's (no date available) *The Encyclopedia of Fantastic Film: Ali Baba to Zombies* (New York: Applause Books, 2000) offers some discussion on the zombie motif in film. Glenn Kay's (no date available) *Zombie Movies: The Ultimate Guide* (2008) is an admirable collection of entries, including minor and lesser known films from the 1930s until the turn of the century, ordered chronologically. Kay also includes movie stills, informative interludes, and interviews.

See also: Africa; Ghoul; Golem; Hammer Film Productions; Lovecraft, H. P.; Vampires and Werewolves; Voodoo; Zombie Studies

Anthony J. Fonseca

RESIDENT EVIL (VIDEO GAME)

Resident Evil (*RE*) is a video game that was developed and published by Capcom (also responsible for the *Dead Rising* series) on the Sony PlayStation in 1996 and was later ported to the Sega Saturn and PC. The series is called *Bio Hazard* in Japan, but the name was changed in the United States for trademark reasons. *RE* is universally regarded as significant for initiating and popularizing the survival horror genre of video games. Survival horror, a phrase first used in *RE*, requires players to conserve supplies and ammunition, which means that combat is not always the best option, and extensive puzzle solving skills are essential. Games in this genre also attempt to be genuinely atmospheric and frightening. Thus, the *RE* series began to garner criticism beginning with *RE 4* for moving toward action gaming. Perhaps, in response, Capcom called the most recent game, *RE 6*, dramatic horror.

A *Director's Cut* of *RE* debuted in 1997, followed by the *Director's Cut: Dual Shock Version,* which added support for the PlayStation controller's analog sticks and vibration function. The title was remade again in 2002 for the Nintendo GameCube, with new graphics, gameplay elements, and storyline changes, and that version was ported to the Nintendo Wii in 2008. *RE* drew on the 1989 Japanese Capcom title *Sweet Home,* a horror role-playing game set in a haunted mansion, as well as the 1992 game *Alone in the Dark,* which allowed players to choose from a male or female character trapped in a mansion with enemies, including zombies. *RE,* set in fictional Raccoon City, similarly allows players to select Chris Redfield or Jill Valentine; it begins in a mansion overrun with zombies and other mutated creatures. The infestation is a result of illegal experiments by the Umbrella Corporation that exposed people and animals to the fictional T-Virus.

Zombies in *RE* can be either of the slow-moving or of faster, tougher varieties called Crimson Heads. Slower zombies, easy to kill from a distance but dangerous up close, can become Crimson Heads if their heads are not destroyed or they are not burned. Zombies will pursue the player even if they lose limbs, and some play dead before attacking. They are occasionally seen in this and other *RE* titles eating other zombies. The game also features zombie dogs. Hyper Zombies, capable of speed bursts, debuted in the *Director's Cut*. The third-person gameplay featured 3D player and enemy characters on pre-rendered backgrounds with a fixed camera. It limited both space in the player inventory and the ability to save. The game is the only one in the series to have multiple endings (four), and there was some censorship of the full-motion video cut scenes (replaced by CGI in the GameCube update) to bring the Japanese version to North America and Europe, but enough violence remained to earn it one of the first Mature ratings, applied to games recommended by the Entertainment Software Rating Board for those 17 and older.

In addition to the seven games comprising the main series (*RE 0* through *6*), there have been 12 further titles under the *RE* umbrella. These installments have been released for handhelds, consoles, and Windows, and include action, first-person, third-person, rail-shooter, and light-gun games. The series has developed a complicated mythology, with a number of recurring characters. *RE 6* was released in 2012 for the PlayStation 3, Xbox 360, and PC, is the most recent iteration, featuring Chris Redfield is one of the protagonists who must deal with the Neo-Umbrella organization and its use of the new C-Virus for bioterrorism. Beyond games, *RE* has spawned an array of merchandise, including toys, comics, novels, and a series of big-budget *RE* films.

See also: Apocalypse; Cannibalism; Video Games

John R. Ziegler

RETURN OF THE LIVING DEAD, THE

The Return of the Living Dead is a 1979 novel by John Russo that was meant to be the sequel to George Romero's film *Night of the Living Dead* (1968), for which Russo cowrote the screenplay and played a zombie. Though Russo meant the novel to be a treatment for a screenplay for a sequel, the film *Return of the Living Dead* (1985) bears no resemblance to his story.

The Return of the Living Dead takes place in rural Willard, Pennsylvania, the setting of *Night of the Living Dead,* 10 years after the dead first began returning to life. While the government has convinced most citizens that it has contained the threat of the living dead, the humble people of Willard know better, so they always put a stake or a bullet through the heads of their deceased to make sure that they do not reanimate. On the night that the action in the novel takes place, a bus crashes over a ravine, killing all 34 passengers on board, and Bert Miller takes his three daughters to the accident scene so all can help the locals neutralize the victims in this way before they become a threat. However, this method of dealing with the dead is not officially sanctioned by the authorities, so when law enforcement and emergency response personnel arrive after the small group has managed to disable 13 of the victims, the members of the assembly scatter lest they be arrested. Unfortunately, the remaining 21 victims reanimate after they are taken to a local funeral home, and escape into the night, only to turn others into flesh-eating zombies, referred to as ghouls just as they are in Romero's *Night of the Living Dead.* Soon the undead overrun the countryside and only a handful of people survive the night. The ensuing mayhem makes a degree of lawlessness possible that would not have been tolerated earlier, and the Miller sisters are kidnapped, one of them raped.

While *Return of the Living Dead* is not considered a well-written novel, some of its themes show up in later zombie fiction and film. One of the Miller daughters is pregnant and dies giving birth, and the last chapter of the novel indicates that her baby is a zombie as a result. Both Zack Snyder's remake of *Dawn of the Dead* (2004) and Daryl Gregory's novel *Raising Stony Mayhall* (2011) treat this theme. And the idea that a zombie apocalypse would enable humans to behave much more savagely than the undead is commonplace in zombie fiction. On the other hand, Russo's representation of his female characters is similar to those found in Romero's *Night of the Living Dead* but would become outdated by the 1980s. The Miller sisters are more adept at being victimized, first by their brutal father, and later by their captors, than they are at standing up for themselves or displaying any competence fighting the undead. They offer little resistance when they are beaten or insulted, and one of them trembles when she must pick up a firearm to protect herself against the undead. Women in later zombie fiction are more assertive and are much more competent at defending themselves and their loved ones against the undead. In 2010, Kensington Books reissued Russo's *Return of the Living Dead*, along with his screenplay for *Night of the Living Dead* in a volume titled *Undead*.

See also: Cannibalism; *Dawn of the Dead*; Gender; Ghoul; *Night of the Living Dead* Series; *Raising Stony Mayhall*; *Return of the Living Dead* Series; Romero, George; Romero's Rules

June Michele Pulliam

The dead, who have been revived by 2-4-5 trioxin, an herbicide originally developed by the military to destroy marijuana plants, in the film *Return of the Living Dead* (1985). *Return of the Living Dead* purportedly tells the "real" story behind George A. Romero's 1968 film *Night of the Living Dead*. (MGM/Photofest)

RETURN OF THE LIVING DEAD SERIES

The *Return of the Living Dead* series is a group of five American comedy-horror films produced between 1985 and 2005: *The Return of the Living Dead* (1981), *Return of the Living Dead Part II* (1988), *Return of the Living Dead 3* (1993), *Return of the Living Dead: Necropolis* (2005), and *Return of the Living Dead: Rave to the Grave* (2005).

The first installment of *Return of the Living Dead* centers around a character named Freddy's during his first night working at Unida Medical Supply, a company whose stock includes medical cadavers. While he is being shown around his workplace by Frank, his friends and girlfriend drive around, partying in the graveyard, waiting for his shift to end. During this time, Frank confides in Freddy that three canisters were accidentally delivered to Unida by the government many years prior. The canisters each contain a human body and a gas called trioxin that reanimates the dead. When Frank takes Freddy to see the canisters, he accidentally breaks one, releasing the gas into their faces and rendering them unconscious. Freddy and Frank proceed through the stages of death and eventually reanimate into zombies, as do the various cadavers in the supply company and in the nearby morgue and cemetery. Freddy and Frank return for the sequel, *Return of the Living Dead Part II*, in which a group of kids who discover one of the canisters must fight the reanimated dead.

The series' significance lies in its conception of zombies as rationally thinking, fast-moving creatures that are indestructible and have a desire for brains rather than just human flesh (the zombie cry of "brains!" originates from the first film). Destruction of the brain does not kill these zombies, and incineration of their bodies merely spreads the infectious gas through the airborne ashes; however, these features were dropped from the plot of the most recent two films in the series. In addition, the zombies of the first three films, generally considered by fans to be the only genuine installments of the series, are given a specific and empathetic reason for brain-consumption: their undead bodies are racked with constant excruciating pain that is only alleviated through the consumption of human brains.

The series also introduces the idea that zombies are created by secret government experiments: from an herbicide, 2-4-5 trioxin, developed by the military initially to destroy marijuana plants but later used to create super soldiers once the military realizes its unexpected effects. All of these details were established in the first film, written and directed Dan O'Bannon, writer of classic horror/sci-fi films such as *Alien* (1979) and *Total Recall* (1990), as well as the zombie film *Dead and Buried* (1981). The first film in the series establishes a punk aesthetic in look, characters, and soundtrack, featuring songs by The Cramps and The Damned, among others. It also plays out as a dark comedy in which the characters are aware of the zombie genre, citing George Romero's *Night of the Living Dead* (1968), while they are trying to figure out what is going on.

The Return of the Living Dead is not a sequel to *Night of the Living Dead,* however, and the inclusion of references to Romero's film demonstrates O'Bannon's desire to deviate substantially from that revered series. Rather, it has its roots in John A. Russo's novel, *Return of the Living Dead* (1979). Russo worked with Romero on the 1968 classic as a coproducer, and Romero developed his own franchise, while Russo retained the rights to his novel and sought a filmmaker to adapt it. O'Bannon assisted with the script, initially to be directed by Tobe Hooper. When Hooper backed out, O'Bannon was offered the director job. The film was critically successful and has become a beloved cult movie that has had substantial impact on popular culture, especially the zombie legend.

Return of the Living Dead 3, directed by horror legend Brian Yuzna of *Society*, *Bride of Reanimator,* and *The Dentist* fame, changes the tone of the series from black comedy to angst-filled teen romance. The film centers around Curt, whose father is a colonel involved in the continued military experiments using trioxin to reanimate the dead. When Curt and his girlfriend Julie have a motorcycle accident, Julie is killed. Grief-stricken, Curt brings her back to life using trioxin, and he attempts to continue their relationship in spite of her hunger for brains. Following the pair's efforts to evade capture, the film ends with Curt's and Julie's suicides. Although the film failed miserably at the box office, it has since become a cult legend thanks in part to the infamous video box cover depicting Julie in her zombie makeup, with shards of glass protruding out of her face and body like spikes, creating a striking, punk rock look. The film's censorship history has also contributed to its subsequent cult status, as the U.S. VHS/DVD R-rated release trims several seconds from the runtime.

After substantial gap in time, the low budget films *Necropolis* and *Rave to the Grave* were filmed back to back in 2005, both directed by Ellory Elkayem (1970), who directed *Eight Legged Freaks*. In *Necropolis*, a group of teens attempt to rescue their missing friend from a suspicious corporation, Hybra-Tech, which has purchased gallons of gas from Chernobyl. Once inside the facility, the friends accidentally release a horde of zombies. In *Rave to the Grave*, the trioxin gas has been processed into a new drug, akin to Ecstasy, and is handed around at a rave. Those who ingest the new drug experience unprecedented highs before ultimately dying and becoming reanimated as zombies. The entire rave becomes infected, via both drug ingestion and bites from zombified ravers. These attempts to capitalize on and reenergize the franchise were received with derision by many fans and critics alike.

See also: Apocalypse; Comedy; *Night of the Living Dead* Series; Romero, George; Romero's Rules; Science Fiction

Laura Helen Marks

ROAD, THE (FILM)

The Road is a 2009 film adaptation of the 2006 Pulitzer Prize-winning novel of the same name by Cormac McCarthy. Directed by John Hillcoat (1961–), it was released in the United States in November 2009 and stars Viggo Mortensen (born Viggo Peter Mortensen Jr., 1958–), Charlize Theron (1975–), and Robert Duvall (born Robert Selden Duvall, 1931–). Rather faithful to McCarthy's novel, the film renders the story of an unnamed man and son as they struggle to survive in the aftermath of an unspecified, ecologically devastating cataclysm. The father–son team migrates toward the coast, scrounging for food and shelter while constantly eluding bloodthirsty cannibal road gangs. Even to the casual viewer, it is apparent that zombie motifs are more pronounced in the movie than in the novel.

In multiple scenes, father and son dodge flesh-eating aggressors by taking refuge in houses, evoking 1968's classic *Night of the Living Dead*. Moreover, the post-apocalyptic world represented in the film is derivative of zombie fiction following Romero's Rules, where civilization is quickly toppled after the dead begin returning to life. The survivors of the nameless catastrophe that has turned the planet into a wasteland often seem like little more than zombies themselves. Not only have some of the survivors been reduced to cannibalism in order to live, but the destruction of the world as they knew it has simplified how they relate to their surroundings. The complex social interactions of the old world are now a luxury as all human desire has been reduced to foraging for food. The survivors even look like zombies with their often shell-shocked expressions. To replicate the scorched-earth setting of the novel, crews filmed the bulk of the movie in western Pennsylvania strip-mine territory and along an abandoned Pennsylvania freeway. Post-production teams then digitally decolorized the scenery, resulting in a landscape that appears drab and grungy. Upon the film's release, discussion ensued over Hillcoat's decision to omit a scene where Mortensen's character discovers the charred remains of a newborn infant, consumed by its own parents. In another deviation from the novel, filmmakers expanded the role of the wife via multiple flashback scenes, which are related in brighter colors than the rest of the film, emphasizing how the man is haunted by memories of a happier world that no longer exists. *The Road* drew both negative and positive critical responses.

See also: Apocalypse; Cannibalism; *Night of the Living Dead* Series; *Road, The* (Novel); Romero, George; Science Fiction

Matthew McEver

ROAD, THE (NOVEL)

The Road is Cormac McCarthy's (2006) novel recounting the story of an unnamed man and his pre-adolescent son as they struggle to survive in the aftermath of an unspecified catastrophe that has left the world awash in gray, drenched in ashes, and bereft of vegetation and wildlife. As the pair pushes a shopping cart of possessions toward the coast in hopes of finding a warmer climate, the reader learns that the earth is also saturated in human wickedness. Among the sparse population, religion and morality are as dead as the landscape, abandoned because such ideals seem irrelevant in a post-cataclysmic world. Most survivors, now fixated on biological necessities, devolve into barbarous cannibals, forming militias or cults, roaming the wasteland in search of living, human flesh to devour.

Much of the conflict in *The Road* involves the father's efforts to protect his son from the marauders, mostly by hiding in abandoned houses and bunkers. Should the flesh-eaters prevail, he intends to proactively euthanize his child. He carries a revolver with two bullets, the second intended for himself, no doubt influenced by his wife's preemptive suicide, revealed via flashback. Matters are further complicated, however, when the man must use one bullet to kill a raider. Language normally associated with the horror genre supplies McCarthy with appropriate metaphors to convey that people have abandoned all moral sense. Here, flesh-eating savages symbolize ultimate depravity. In one scene, a woman gives birth. Then her seemingly normal family roasts and consumes the infant. Usually, the cults murder on a whim. Sometimes, they harvest victims in an underground slaughterhouse. Always, these monsters field-dress their prey and leave skulls in their wake. Witnessing such evils, the man struggles to retain whatever humanity he has intact. He is not ready to start eating people, but he is lured into other forms of savagery.

Embittered and inclined to abandon all sense of compassion, he resists aiding others in need. Yet, such heartlessness is beyond the boy's comprehension, and the child continuously calls attention to his father's temptation to inhumanity, acting as a foil to all other characters. As father and son reach the coast, their lot does not improve. The man, now coughing blood, is shot by an archer. Dying, he charges his son to carry on, and following a three-day vigil, another man approaches, offering to adopt the boy, insisting that he is one of the good guys and that his family does not eat people. While *The Road* does not contain any creatures that could be easily considered zombies, it makes extensive use of the tropes common to the post-apocalyptic zombie narrative perpetuated by Richard Matheson's novella *I Am Legend* (1954) and George Romero's *Night of the Living Dead* series of films. *The Road* is set in a similarly bleak post-apocalyptic landscape. The collapse of civilization causes surviving humans to behave in ways that are similar to zombies, including resorting to cannibalism in some instances. Critics praised *The Road* for its emotional realism and lyrical prose. Ultimately, McCarthy was awarded the 2007 Pulitzer Prize for fiction for *The Road*.

See also: Apocalypse; Cannibalism; *Night of the Living Dead* Series; *Road, The* (Film); Romero, George; Science Fiction

Matthew McEver

ROM ZOM COM

The term Rom Zom Com is a contraction of Romantic Zombie Comedy and was coined by Simon Pegg and Edgar Wright to describe their 2004 film *Shaun of the Dead.* As a concept, the Rom Zom Com actually predates *Shaun of the Dead* by over a decade, beginning with the 1993 film *My Boyfriend's Back.* Similar to the romantic comedy genre on which it is based, in the Rom Zom Com, an amorous couple is parted, only to be reunited in the end but due to the presence of zombies.

This is certainly the case in *Shaun of the Dead,* when Shaun, the protagonist, is able to rekindle his girlfriend Liz's love after the two survive a night of fighting the undead. *Shaun of the Dead* is particularly comic in its narrative resolution. In the first 20 minutes of the film, Liz dumps Shaun because their relationship has stagnated due to his unwillingness to behave like a responsible adult: he spends his spare time playing video games in his unkempt flat with his slacker roommate Ed, or downing pints with him at their favorite pub, The Winchester. Yet, when Shaun and Liz reunite at the end of the film, little has changed. Liz now lives with Shaun in his flat, which is cleaner, yet Shaun is still an aging boy who plays video games with Ed, who is now a zombie pet, chained in the tool shed. Shaun's relationship with Liz is not the only romantic relationship in the film.

Although he did not coin the term, Bob Balaban directed the first Rom Zom Com, *My Boyfriend's Back.* The film tells the story of Johnny Dingle, who returns from the dead as a zombie to fulfill his dream of taking Missy McCloud, the girl he has loved since he was six, to the prom. Unfortunately, Missy is unaware of Johnny's love and does not see him as a potential romantic partner—until after he dies protecting her during a robbery of the convenience store where she works and then returns from the dead. One standard convention of the romantic comedy is the contrived meeting of lovers, which is reproduced in *My Boyfriend's Back*: Johnny arranges it so that his best friend dons a mask and pretends to rob her place of employment so that he can heroically save her and better present himself to her as a potential suitor. But Johnny's plans are thwarted when a real criminal robs the store and shoots Johnny for interfering. Another standard convention of the romantic comedy is the idea of a true love that can overcome all obstacles. True love is the force that reanimates Johnny, allowing him to return from the dead to take Missy to the prom, in spite of some inconveniences, such as his having to periodically eat human flesh to prevent the embarrassment of having parts of his body fall off in public.

The literary mash-up, a work of fiction that combines two or more established narratives, *Pride and Prejudice and Zombies* (2009), by Seth Grahame-Smith and the film *Zombieland* (2009) are further examples of the Rom Zom Com. Grahame-Smith's novel combines *Pride and Prejudice* (1813), the classic by Jane Austen with the typical zombie narrative. These zombies operate by Romero's Rules. In Grahame-Smith's text, Elizabeth Bennett and Fitzwilliam Darcy are lovers, similarly parted by their pride and prejudice, but they are reunited after Darcy comes to appreciate Elizabeth's superior zombie-slaying abilities. The addition of zombies to Austen's Regency England modernizes the author's romantic conventions so that they are more in keeping with those found in the romantic comedy genre of film. Here, Elizabeth and Darcy are thrown together by means that are more contrived than they are in Austen's novel: instead of the lovers first meeting when Darcy refuses to dance with her at a ball, they interact in a more protracted and contrived way when the dance is disrupted by a horde of zombies, and the five Bennett sisters in attendance display their zombie-killing prowess in order to save many of the guests.

Zombieland (2009), directed by Ruben Samuel Fleischer is another example of the Rom Zom Com, where the lovers are parted, repeatedly, only to be reunited in the end through the interference of zombies. Soon after the zombie apocalypse commences, the film's narrator, named Columbus, sets out to check on his parents. During his journey, Columbus meets another male survivor, Tallahassee, and later, two females, Wichita and Little Rock. The women lure the two men into a storage room by pretending to be in distress, only to rob them of their weapons and motor vehicle. Columbus and Tallahassee, however, meet Wichita and Little Rock again, only to be car-jacked by the duo. Still, Columbus is clearly attracted to Wichita, a woman who in the pre-apocalypse world would not be interested in him because he is not wealthy, powerful, or handsome. Wichita, on the other hand, is an attractive woman who is able to use her looks to manipulate men. The contrived conditions created by the zombie apocalypse make Columbus's romance with Wichita possible. He seems to be quite literally the last man on earth near her age. Their romantic relationship finally flourishes after Wichita takes Little Rock to Pacific

Playland, the last place where the girl remembers being happy before the collapse of civilization. The two women end up trapped by the zombies at the amusement park and must be rescued by Columbus and Tallahassee. In a pattern typical to the romantic comedy film, *Zombieland's* ending suggests that Columbus and Wichita begin a romantic relationship soon afterward.

The 2013 film *Warm Bodies,* directed by Jonathan A. Levine, is based on the novel of the same name by Isaac Marion. Both are examples of the Rom Zom Com. Marion's novel, a loose retelling of *Romeo and Juliet,* explores existential themes through the trope of the zombie, whereas Levine's film transforms the story so that it incorporates the conventions of the romantic comedy. The film is the story of the zombie R and his love for the human Julie, in a world where the dead reanimate as zombies who operate loosely under Romero's Rules. R deviates from these rules in that he is a sentient zombie who narrates the story. Still, his cognitive abilities are impaired: he can no longer remember his full name, his former occupation, or even his old friends and family. R and Julie fall in love, and they must pursue their relationship over the objections of their families, in this case, the zombies and the humans, rather than the Montagues and Capulets. Their relationship eventually revitalizes R, causing his heart to beat and making him lose his craving for human flesh, so that he becomes human again. His transformation affects the other zombies as well when their hearts also start to beat, and they no longer desire human flesh. Meanwhile, the remaining humans are changed when they start to see the undead as afflicted humans who are worthy of their care rather than as zombies who are to be terminated with extreme prejudice.

See also: Comedy; Mash-Ups, Literary; *My Boyfriend's Back*; *Pride and Prejudice and Zombies*; *Shaun of the Dead*; *Warm Bodies* (Film); *Zombieland*

June Michele Pulliam

ROMERO, GEORGE

George Romero (born George Andrew Romero, 1940–) is the director widely considered the father of the modern zombie film. His ground-breaking movie *Night of the Living Dead* (1968) crystallizes earlier images of the zombie, creating the iconic shuffling, glassy-eyed undead with an insatiable desire for human flesh. *Night of the Living Dead* achieved such wide-spread popularity that Romero's zombies influenced all other subsequent representations of the creature. All writers and directors must now either abide by the rules for zombies what were established in his film (Romero's Rules) or explain why these rules are wrong. To date, Romero has directed 19 films, mostly in the horror genre, and 7 of these titles are zombie films, including *The Crazies* (1973), and the 6 films in his iconic *Night of the Living Dead* series.

Though Romero was born in New York City, he made Pittsburgh, Pennsylvania, his home after moving there to attend Carnegie Melon University, where he studied the arts. In fact, all of the films in his *Night of the Living Dead* series are set in or near Pittsburgh. In his early career behind the camera, Romero shot commercials

and short films. His first paying job was making short films for the children's television show *Mr. Rogers Neighborhood,* which was also originally aired from Pittsburgh. According to author Peter Hartlaub (no date available), when Romero began casting for *Night of the Living Dead,* he originally wanted to use Betty Aberlin (born Betty Kay Ageloff, 1942–), who played Lady Aberlin on *Mister Rogers' Neighborhood,* in the role of Judy. However, Fred Rogers (born Fred McFeely Rogers, 1928–2003), a Presbyterian minister, vetoed the idea.

Romero's name has become so synonymous with the zombie that Hip Interactive asked him to help produce the video game *City of the Dead.* However, Hip Interactive never completed production of the game due to financial difficulties. Romero is, however, a zombie character in the video game *Call of Duty,* which has a secret zombie game embedded in it. One of Romero's character's nicknames in the game is The Father of All Zombies.

Described by Peter Dendle in his *Zombie Movie Encyclopedia* as the "Shakespeare of zombie cinema," American director George A. Romero, whose iconic 1968 film *Night of the Living Dead* transformed the figure of the zombie from a pitiful but not always dangerous victim of black magic into a ravenous undead cannibal whose existence ushers in the apocalypse. (Associated Press)

See also: Crazies, The; *Night of the Living Dead* Series; Romero's Rules; Television; Video Games

June Michele Pulliam

ROMERO'S RULES

Romero's Rules are the unspoken rules for zombies established by the films of George Romero. The term Romero's Rules describes the conventions by which zombies have been fictionalized since the 1968 classic *Night of the Living Dead.* The film serves as a prototype for almost all zombie fiction written and filmed since 1968, much in the same way that the 1897 publication of *Dracula,* by Bram Stoker, serves as the prototype for all vampire fiction of the 20th and 21st centuries.

Prior to 1968, representations of the zombie were primarily derived from Haitian folklore, in which zombies were recently deceased humans supposedly raised from the dead by a bokur, or Voodoo priest who practices black magic. These zombies were purportedly humans who were slipped a serum by the bokur, inducing a death-like trance. Then, after they were buried by their grieving families, the bokur disinterred them and administered a second serum that revived them, while suppressing all but their most basic motor functions, rendering them docile so they can be used as slave labor. These zombies are frightening because they are in a liminal state of existence between life and death and are at the mercy of the bokur who has deprived them of free will and is now their master. However, zombies created by Voodoo are never a danger to the living.

Romero effectively transformed the creature in *Night of the Living Dead,* which crystallized representations of the zombie as a mindless ghoul, as is the case in the 1954 novella *I Am Legend,* by Richard Matheson, while adding his own innovations. Romero created zombies that are the glassy-eyed undead who shuffle aimlessly and who possess an inexplicable but insatiable desire to consume human flesh, a compulsion that would come to be associated with virtually all subsequent zombies. A popular misconception about zombies that operate by Romero's Rules is that they have an overwhelming desire to consume brains, and that their general cannibalism is merely part of their clumsy attempts to trepan their victims. However, the compunction of the zombie to consume brains specifically would not be articulated until the 1985 comic zombie film *Return of the Living Dead,* which purports to tell the real story about what was fictionalized in Romero's classic.

Romero's zombies are not created by Voodoo but through an outbreak of epidemic proportions whose cause is unknown. After the initial outbreak, people become zombies either reanimating moments after their deaths or becoming infected after being bitten by another undead. Zombies operating by Romero's Rules also differ from those created by Voodoo in how they can be killed—their brains must be destroyed. Zombies created by Voodoo can be destroyed in a number of ways, including feeding them salt, which reminds them that they are not truly alive and causes them to run for their graves. Zombies created by Voodoo can also be destroyed by the death of their master. Although Romero is credited with transforming the zombie into the creature we are familiar with today, the undead in *Night of the Living Dead,* his first film in his series, are never referred to as zombies. Instead, they are described as ghouls. Nevertheless, Romero's films have so influenced the genre of zombie fiction that all zombie texts after *Night of the Living Dead* either have zombies who loosely operate according to the rules established in 1968 or must explain why those rules are erroneous.

See also: Apocalypse; Bokur/Caplata; Cannibalism; Epidemics; Haiti; *Night of the Living Dead* Series; Romero, George; Voodoo

June Michele Pulliam

ROSE, TIMO

Timo Rose (1977–) is a director of German horror and science fiction. The Sword of Independence Filmworks, which became Rosecalypse Films and Records, is his creation. As a filmmaker, he is best known for the *Mutation* trilogy, beginning with *Mutation* (1999). These three films chronicle a zombie infestation created when Nazi-based toxic chemicals are rediscovered in the 21st century. The second and third films, *Generation Dead* (2001) and *Century of the Dead* (2002) were combined and edited with additional footage in 2007 into *Mutation: Annihilation.*

The series is more about the organized crime syndicates who discover and fight over the chemicals that will allow them to create undead *übermenschen* than it is about the zombies themselves. The zombies generally appear in very few scenes, and when they do, they simply shamble into harm's way and are usually easily dispatched individually. The films incorporate more violence than gore, with lots of scenes of beatings and torture. Both *Generation Dead* and *Century of the Dead* end with apocalyptic visions (which resemble video game scenarios). The series is heavily influenced by music videos, action movies, and video games. In many respects, the movies are more similar to James Bond films than they are to horror films. One character in the *Mutation* series, Goldman, is directly lifted from Sega's *House of the Dead* game, and when some characters are killed, the phrase "Game Over" appears. Rose purposefully films parts of his movies in English, and as of 2013, some his most recent films, namely *Barricade* (2007), *Fearmakers* (2008), and *Beast* (2009), have been in the English language, with some German. Rose works under his Rosecalypse trademark and doubles as a rap musician; he has released several music CDs as King Hannibal and is currently working on a new project group, King and Prinzessa.

See also: Live and Let Die; Video Games

Anthony J. Fonseca

SAVINI, TOM

Tom Savini (born Thomas Vincent Savini, 1946–) is an American award-winning special effects director of more than two dozen movies since 1972. He has also been involved with horror and mainstream film as an actor, stuntman, and director. Savini cites both his time in Vietnam as a war photographer and his love of Lon Chaney as the forces that made him interested in introducing realism into horror film special effects. He became famous for his special effects work associated with director George Romero, as the two are natives of Pittsburgh. As well, he has worked on cult classics like *Friday the 13th* (1980) and *Day of the Dead* (1985), winning a Saturn Award for the latter. As a director, Savini remade *Night of the Living Dead* in 1990. As an actor and stuntman, he has appeared in *Dawn of the Dead* (1978), *From Dusk Till Dawn* (1996), *Zombiegeddon* (2003), and the "Planet Terror"

Tom Savini is an award-winning special effects director and actor, whose work is primarily in the horror genre. His time in Vietnam as a war photographer and love of the actor Lon Chaney interested him in introducing realistic special effects into horror. (Getty Images)

segment of *Grindhouse* (2007), in which he fights to save his home from an invasion of zombies.

Savini's early effects display a preoccupation with gore and realism, as in the opening scene of Romero's vampire film *Martin* (1976), where Savini creates a realistic wrist slashing. *Dawn of the Dead* showcased two of his signature effects, severed limbs and bite marks, while *Friday the 13th* exemplified his use of over-the-top blood and gore, on a shoestring budget of $17,500. He eventually worked toward his signature effect, the exploding head. Savini used his effects in the zombie genre with Romero's *Day of the Dead*. Savini's innovative work in prosthetics and latex allowed for the evolution of horror film into the splatter subgenre; he is best known for not working with computer-generated images, preferring to do hours of makeup to create his effects. His zombies can best be characterized as walking corpses, in that they are known for their skeletal features, obvious missing body parts and bloody injuries, and the bluish gray coloring of their skin. Savini is also revered for the graphic special effects he produces in dispatching monsters, including decapitations and explosions. He has also worked on films by well-known horror directors Dario Argento and John A. Russo, who played a zombie in *Night of the Living Dead* (1968). Additionally, Savini acts in many of the films for which he creates effects. Considered to have achieved iconic status in the genre, Savini as a character has appeared in television series like *The Simpsons* and in novels such as *Bad Moon Rising* (2008) by Jonathan Maberry. He is the subject of the documentary *Smoke and Mirrors: The Story of Tom Savini* (2013), directed by Jason Baker (1982–). Savini is the author of several books on special effects.

See also: Dawn of the Dead; *Day of the Dead*; Maberry, Jonathan; *Night of the Living Dead* (1990); Romero, George

Anthony J. Fonseca

SCIENCE FICTION

Because science fiction is related to horror genre, both contain similar tropes. The zombie is one of these shared elements. The zombie is most commonly associated with the horror, a genre that is defined by the presences of monsters who operate by supernatural rules. Yet science fiction is a genre that rationally explores alternative reality, present and future, rather than dabble in supernatural speculation.

Max Brooks's *The Zombie Survival Guide* and the film *28 Days Later* can both be classified as works of science fiction, as they use science to hypothesize about a world transformed by zombies that have rational explanations for their existence. In *28 Days Later,* the rage virus, a science experiment gone wrong and transmitted by blood, turns the living into zombies by effacing their higher brain functions; they become nothing more than raging lunatics bent on tearing apart the uninfected. Because the infected lose even the most basic drive for nourishment, they starve to death within a month. In *The Zombie Survival Guide,* when the living become infected with the solanum virus, they die, only to revive into zombies who operate according to Romero's Rules: they have an insatiable desire for human flesh and their bodies are impervious to pain. They no longer need rest or even oxygen.

Works of zombie fiction that use scientific explanations are rooted in reality. The rage virus of *28 Days Later,* for example, is a metaphor for the zeitgeist of life in the 21st century, where the planet's population seems to be seething with anger and compromise is no longer desirable. The virus was first synthesized in lab by forcing chimpanzees to watch footage of the violence that humans perpetrate the world over. The virus is eventually released by two well-meaning animal rights activists bent on relieving the chimps of their suffering, and its rapid spread and the apocalyptic results are familiar to viewers who have seen pandemics sweep nations, and natural disasters and terrorist attacks forcing people in the first world to live under martial law without electricity and running water.

Two zombie Ur-texts can be logically categorized as science fiction crossovers. Richard Matheson's novella *I Am Legend* speculates about the future: written in 1954, it is set in 1976, after a global nuclear exchange has enabled the development of bacteria that infects the human race. The bacteria reanimate the dead into mindless ghouls who seek human blood because they believe they are vampires. Meanwhile, the living infected cannot tolerate sunlight, so much activity essential to human survival momentarily ceases while they figure out how to restart civilization. The first film in George Romero's *Night of the Living Dead* series, *Night of the Living Dead* (1968), tentatively offers a scientific explanation for zombies—radiation leaking from a satellite that has re-entered earth's orbit.

These stand in contrast to other works of zombie fiction that depend on a scientific explanation for the creature but are based on weird science or technology that is so loosely rooted in rationality that it is nearly supernatural. Examples of this type of fiction include H. P. Lovecraft's story "Herbert West—Reanimator" and the series of comic *Return of the Living Dead* films. Dr. Herbert West of Lovecraft's story is a mad scientist who revives the dead with a serum that he has been perfecting for 20 years. The story chronicles his use of the scientific method with disastrous results. West learns from his experiments how variables such as the freshness of the corpse, as well as its race and intelligence, determine whether he creates a mindless ghoul or a sentient being. The later proves to be more dangerous for West, as being brought back from the dead is painful, particularly if the subject's body was mutilated before death, and so Major Chapman-Lee, the most intelligent of the dead that he revives, organizes the remainder of his zombies into a group who take him away, presumably to kill him. *Re-Animator* (1985), the comic film version of "Herbert West—Reanimator," emphasizes the mad science of Lovecraft's story with its depiction of the reagent as a glowing, acid-green fluid that has nearly magical powers in its ability to revive dead flesh. The dead are revived in *The Return of the Living Dead* films by 2-4-5 trioxin, an herbicide created by the U.S. military to destroy marijuana plants. In this fictional world, the substance first brought the dead to life in 1968 when some of it stored in a Veterans Administration hospital seeped into the morgue below, reviving the corpses into the zombies who first operated according to Romero's Rules.

The zombie is a monster that lends itself to scientific explanations, as the border between life and death is not as absolute as most people think. When someone dies, all of the bodily functions do not immediately cease but turn off one by one: the speed of this process is determined by the cause of death. Also, the protracted legal battles about when life begins and ends, as well as the existence of terms such as *clinical death* and *legally dead,* indicate that the difference between life and death can be tenuous even for our authorities. Moreover, diseases such as bovine spongiform encephalopathy, otherwise known as mad cow disease, wipe away higher brain functions. This makes the concept of the zombie not so far-fetched.

Even the concept of the Voodoo zombie has some scientific explanation for its existence: Wade Davis, a Canadian, Harvard-educated photographer and anthropologist with a doctorate in ethnobotany, studied Haitian zombies created by ritual. With the 1985 and 1988 publications of *The Serpent and the Rainbow* and *Passage of Darkness: The Ethnobiology of the Haitian Zombie,* Davis became synonymous with scientific zombification theory. Davis focused on the traditional uses of psychotropic plants and chemicals and hypothesized that tetrodotoxin, known commonly as TTX, might explain zombification, causing paralysis through interference with neuromuscular conduction. This produces numbness, slurred speech, and paralysis. Victims could be buried and later resurrected and given regular doses of *Datura stramonium,* commonly known as Jimson weed, producing amnesia, delirium, and suggestibility. The victims could then be manipulated to create the illusion that they are zombies.

See also: Brooks, Max; Davis, Wade; "Herbert West—Reanimator"; *I Am Legend* (Novel); Lovecraft, H. P.; Matheson, Richard; *Night of the Living Dead* Series; Tetrodotoxin; *28 Days Later* Series; Voodoo; *Zombie Survival Guide, The*

June Michele Pulliam

SEABROOK, W. B.

W. B. Seabrook (born William Buehler Seabrook, 1887–1945) was an American explorer and journalist known for his studies of occultism and his experimentation with cannibalism. He served in World War I but was injured at Verdun in 1916. His was a journalist/editor for *The Augusta Chronicle* (Augusta, Georgia), *The Atlanta Journal,* and *The New York Times.* He cofounded the Lewis-Seabrook Advertising Agency and eventually worked as a farmer in Georgia. Seabrook published many books, as well as articles in *Cosmopolitan, Reader's Digest,* and *Vanity Fair.* By the 1930s, he had produced enough successful literature to earn a trip to Haiti, where he developed an interest in Haitian Voodoo. He described the folklore associated with Haitian Voodoo in *The Magic Island* (1929), the travelogue that is credited with popularizing the trope of the zombie with the American public. Seabrook became interested in witchcraft and sorcery in Africa as well and followed up his 1929 text with *Jungle Ways* (1931). By the time he published *Witchcraft: Its Power in the World Today* (1940), he argued that everything he had witnessed and described was rational and had a scientific explanation.

On one of his trips to the French Ivory Coast of West Africa in the 1930s, he was the guest of the Guere tribe, which practiced cannibalism. Reportedly, he later obtained from a hospital body parts from someone killed in an accident, which he claims he cooked and dined on and described as being indistinguishable from fully developed veal. He described minutely in *Jungle Ways* the experience of cannibalism in a matter-of-fact tone using the terminology of a gourmand. His reputation was cemented in 1919, when Aleister Crowley (born Edward Alexander Crowley, 1875–1947) spent a week at Seabrook's farm; Seabrook published a story on the experience, and revisited it in *Witchcraft*. His *Adventures in Arabia: Among the Bedouins, Druses, Whirling Dervishes and Yezidee Devil Worshipers* (1927) was based on his travels and visits with various Bedouin and the Kurdish Yazidi tribes.

A haunted individual, Seabrook's alcoholism and sadism cost him his first marriage and led to his ex-wife's (Marjorie Muir Worthington, 1900–1976) publication of *The Strange World of Willie Seabrook* (1966). Seabrook committed himself in 1933 to Bloomingdale, a mental institution near New York City, in order to get treatment for his alcoholism. After his release, he published an account of his experience in his book *Asylum* (1935), which became a best seller. His autobiography is titled *No Hiding Place: An Autobiography* (1942). In 1945, Seabrook committed suicide by drug overdose.

See also: Africa; Cannibalism; "Country of Comers-Back, The"; Haiti; Voodoo

Anthony J. Fonseca

SENTIENCE

Until recently, sentience was not often associated with zombies. Given that the most defining characteristic of the zombie is its lack of free will, the phrase "sentient zombie" might seem oxymoronic. However, recent zombies are sentient in spite of their condition. Zombies created through Voodoo or other quasi-magical means by a master or bokur are sometimes represented as able to assert their will in order to resist their maker's control, which means that they have retained some sentience. For most zombies who follow Romero's Rules, however, sentience is often not represented in fiction, perhaps because doing so would interfere with the living characters' (and readers') ability to view the creature as abject Other, with no claim to human sympathy. In cases where zombies are portrayed as being sentient, this is one of many signs that the creature may have enviable qualities unavailable to humans or may be post-human.

Race, class, and sex determine the ability of zombies created by magic to retain sentience and resist control. In the earliest narratives from the 1920s and 1930s, zombies are created by a bokur, or Voodoo priest who uses dark magic. Predictably, these narratives reproduce the prejudices of their eras about nonwhites and the working classes. Thus, white zombies are represented as better capable of resisting their makers than are nonwhite zombies, since dominant scientific discourses at the time viewed whites as intellectually and morally superior to nonwhites. Moreover, in these same narratives, working-class whites are represented as intellectually inferior to middle- and upper-class whites. This sort of hierarchy is reproduced in H. P. Lovecraft's serialized story "Herbert West—Reanimator" (1921–1922), where the titular character, a mad scientist, reanimates the dead with results that vary according to the subject's race and class. The reanimated dead, no longer restrained by their consciences, are in thrall to their basest instincts. West's early human experiments are conducted on members of the working classes of different ethnicities, such as an uneducated white farm boy and an African American prize fighter. While the resurrected farm boy cries out in pain and searches for his grave, the revived prize fighter, who is likened to a gorilla by Lovecraft, is found wandering on all fours after having consumed a missing child. Some upper-class whites, however, also lack sentience due to their feeble intellectual abilities. For example, Dr. Halsey, West's former teacher and the Dean of Miskatonic Medical School, goes on a murderous rampage once revived, confirming West suspicions that the man who threw him out of the program because he thought his experiments with reanimation were immoral was in fact an unintelligent Puritan with a feeble scientific mind. The white and upper-class Major Chapman-Lee is the only one of West's zombies who develops sentience. Chapman-Lee fully comprehends the horror of his undead condition after West has reanimated his decapitated body and exerts his will to exact a terrible revenge on the doctor by leading other zombies to bear him away to his unnamed punishment.

Yet, while race and class are represented in these narratives in ways that reproduce stereotypes that reinforce white male hegemony, women threaten this hegemony when they are turned into zombies. In the first ever zombie film, *White Zombie* (1932), Madeline Short, the "white zombie" of the title, shows signs of sentience in that she resists her maker, Murder Legendre, the powerful Creole bokur. In this way, Madeline is unlike Legendre's other zombies—all male and either black or of mixed race. In short, Madeline is not fully conquered; her sentience allows her to resist Legendre long enough to be rescued by her husband and others, who also destroy the bokur's power over his other zombies. Although Madeline's sentience eventually enables white males to reassert power over women and nonwhites in Haiti, the setting of *White Zombie,* her sentience still threatens the social order because it suggests that she and perhaps all other white women have the potential to resist other forms of control.

Sentient zombies who operate by Romero's Rules, on the other hand, call into question divisive hierarchies of race, class, gender, and nationality, by making it difficult to classify the zombie as abject Other. The creature is humanized by its sentience, while it possesses qualities that make it superior to humans. For example, in George Romero's *Land of the Dead* (2005), zombies are both humanized and represented as superior to the humans who hunt them. *Land* opens with a scene in which zombies run a peaceful small town, complete with a little white chapel and a bandstand on the public square. While the zombies are clearly not human, as shown by their inability to speak and their varying states of decomposition, they are similar to humans because they are individuals, demonstrated by varied clothing and facial expressions, rather than the stereotypical vacant stare of the zombie in *Night of the Living Dead*. Viewers realize that these zombies are sentient after one of them, Big Daddy, becomes enraged after several of his fellow undead are slaughtered or maimed by humans for sport during their raid on the zombie enclave to scavenge supplies. Big Daddy responds by organizing his fellow zombies into their own raiding party, leading the group to overrun the nearby fortified compound of survivors. The zombies' ability to overthrow the human enclave is possible only because they are capable of forming class consciousness, a state of mind in which the subordinate classes see their common oppressed condition, and understand that commonality is greater than any distinctions of race, class, or gender that might otherwise divide them. Karl Marx viewed class consciousness as a precondition to revolution. Humans, however, are arguably unable to form class consciousness, something not true of zombies, who through death are free of the conditioning in life that made them blind to what they had in common with their fellow humans. The zombie's ability to form class consciousness is proof of both its sentience and its superiority to the living.

Andrew Currie's film *Fido* (2006) directly questions the widely held belief that zombies are not sentient. *Fido* is set in an alternative universe where The Zombie Wars occurred, rather than World War II. This conflict was won with a device invented by Dr. Hrothgar Geiger, an electric collar that is fitted around a zombie's neck, rendering it sufficiently docile to appropriate its labor. Now during peacetime, Zomcon, the corporation that makes the collar, fortifies towns against remaining zombies while offering the residents within "peace through containment." Collared zombies mow lawns, deliver milk and newspapers, and even babysit the children. Young Timmy Robinson disturbs this world when he questions Zomcon executive Mr. Bottoms about whether the undead can feel pain. Timmy's inquiry threatens the status quo because it questions the rationale on which this society is based, namely, that zombies are subhuman because they cannot feel pain or even think, which makes their enslavement acceptable. Timmy's relationship with his family's zombie that he has nicknamed Fido reveals that the creatures can feel pain: they retain memories of their human lives and so they are sentient. Fido saves Timmy, and later his mother, from danger on several different occasions, but his sentience threatens the tightly structured social order, and if zombies are sentient, then enslaving them is inhumane. If the white males who control this world are wrong about whether zombies feel pain, they may also be wrong about the intellectual abilities of women and children, who they view as subservient.

William Sleator's young adult novel *The Boy Who Couldn't Die* depicts sentient zombies that also invite readers to question whether or not their own free will is an illusion. The astral zombie, a living human whose soul has been taken via a Voodoo ceremony, is sentient because the bewitched human is on some level aware of what his or her doppelgänger is being forced to do. The astral zombie appears to outsiders as normal human being, but a bokur can use the bewitched human's captured soul to do his or her bidding without the conscious knowledge of the human, though the human is aware on a subconscious level of what the soul is doing. After his best friend Rodger is killed in a plane crash, Ken is obsessed with fears about his own mortality, so he solicits Cheri Buttercup's services to protect him from death, not fully understanding what this bargain entails. Cheri's magic turns Ken into "the boy who couldn't die," rendering him invulnerable to death and even to pain. Ken loses control of his own body, something that he realizes after a series of disturbingly realistic dreams where he hurts or even kills someone. During one dream, Ken awakens clutching a butcher knife from which phantom blood disappears. When Ken later learns that a man was stabbed to death in the area near Cheri's apartment, he realizes that she has appropriated his soul to do her bidding while he sleeps. Ken's subsequent battle to regain his soul reveals how humans may be controlled by forces that they are not fully aware of, leaving them with the illusion that they have free will. Ken's sentience, however, or knowledge of what his astral zombie is enslaved to do, implies that even the astral zombie retains some awareness.

In both Isaac Marion's novel *Warm Bodies* and Jonathan Levine's film version, erotic love humanizes the zombie by making it sentient. In this zombie rewriting of William Shakespeare's *Romeo and Juliet,* the zombie R remembers his former life and can articulate his condition after falling in love with the human Julie. Eating brains makes him uniquely sentient in that it gives him direct access to the memories of another human. R's relationship with Julie eventually causes all zombies to become sentient and to lose their desire for human flesh, as well as leads to the human acceptance and embracing of the undead, rather than continued attempts to eradicate them. Daryl Gregory's novel *Raising Stony Mayhall* deconstructs previous representations of the zombie. Gregory's zombies are not mindless undead cannibals who are eternally enthralled to a desire for human flesh. Rather, the zombie's initial cannibalistic desires subside 48 hours after an infection-induced fever abates. Afterward, zombies are as capable as the living of complex thought and forming strong bonds of attachment to others. Zombies, in fact, have the potential to be more powerful than humans because they are not limited by the need for food or sleep. Zombies are so feared, however, that the humans have been attempting to eradicate them ever since the first outbreak of the virus in Pennsylvania in 1968. In fact, zombies' sentience endows them with posthuman qualities that humans lack. If a zombie's body part is severed, all he or she must do is think about the part to keep it alive. Conversely, there is no distinct boundary between the zombie's body and its surroundings, something that Stony, the titular character, demonstrates when he is chained to a chair and escapes by experiencing himself as one with the locks and so is able to open them. He eventually conquers death through this power.

While the sentient zombie is not typical of the genre, it appears with sufficient regularity to be notable in how it highlights the fears about how cultural forces that control women and nonwhites are not always terribly effective in subordinating them. Later iterations of the sentient zombie reveal how humans are all effectively zombies in that they lack free will because they are controlled by invisible, ubiquitous social forces.

See also: Bokur/Caplata; *Boy Who Couldn't Die, The*; Class; *Fido*; Gender; "Herbert West—Reanimator"; Lovecraft, H. P.; *Night of the Living Dead* Series; Race; Romero's Rules; Voodoo; *Warm Bodies* (Film); *Warm Bodies* (Novel); *White Zombie*

June Michele Pulliam

SERPENT AND THE RAINBOW, THE (BOOK)

The Serpent and the Rainbow, published in 1985 by Simon and Schuster, is a controversial account of the journey to Haiti taken by Harvard ethnobotanist Wade Davis. It also chronicles his subsequent investigation into the legend of the Voodoo zombie and the purported process of zombification. A fictionalization of Davis's Haitian expedition was later the basis of a Hollywood movie of the same name. Davis's book depicts his search for the truth behind the story of the apparent zombification and subsequent recovery of Clairvius Narcisse, a Haitian citizen who was pronounced dead at Albert Schweitzer Hospital in Deschapelles, Haiti, in 1962, only to reappear, very much alive in 1980 in his home village. Narcisse claimed that his brother had contracted to have him turned into a zombie as a result of a land dispute. The book, which reads like a 19th-century adventure novel, is also concerned with the history of Haiti, particularly in regard to the country's modern-day association with the religion of Voodoo.

In *The Serpent and the Rainbow,* Davis recounts his search for ingredients of a reported powder which will render victims catatonic, inducing apparent death, followed by a zombie-like state. Davis's quest took him into the realm of Haiti's secret societies. Davis met with bokurs (Voodoo priests who practice black magic) who purportedly can induce such a state of zombification and gained access to a list of potential ingredients used in the zombie-powder. Davis then investigated the efficacy of botanically derived poisons such as datura, albizia, and mucuna in the production of the powder, along with other animal-derived toxins such as bufotoxin, before deciding that the principal ingredient in the powder must be tetrodotoxin (TTX), a poison derived from several species of puffer fish. Davis surmised that the TTX was the main catalyst in regard to the zombification process. Davis also stated that the victim's belief in Voodoo and the possibility of a living death instilled the malleability necessary to perpetuate a zombie-like state in the individual; when the victim, presumed dead, is taken from his or her grave, the chemical processes of the zombie-powder interact with victim's own fear and oxygen deprivation to create a trance-like state. In combination with postburial applications of *Datura* in a paste form, Davis surmised that this state of mind led to the suggestibility which makes the zombie useful as a sort of slave.

Subsequent to the release of *The Serpent and the Rainbow,* Davis was criticized in regard to both his scientific methodology and his storytelling; it was implied that he cast himself in a swashbuckling, heroic light at the expense of factual analysis of his findings. The criticism of Davis's hypothesis in the scientific community following the release of the book was based upon the known effects of TTX. Some of the criticism ignores the fact that Davis does not postulate that the poison, in and of itself, can produce a sustained trance-like state in which the victim can still physically function on some level. Rather, Davis speculated that a specific dose may, combined with other chemicals, initiate a temporary, death-like trance. Davis attempted to address some of his critics' issues in his 1988 book, *Passage of Darkness: The Ethnobiology of the Haitian Zombie.*

See also: Bokur/Calpata; Davis, Wade; Haiti; Narcisse, Clairvius; *Serpent and the Rainbow, The* (Film); Tetrodotoxin; Voodoo; Zombie Cucumber

Robert Butterfield

SERPENT AND THE RAINBOW, THE (FILM)

The Serpent and the Rainbow is a 1988 film directed by Wes Craven, inspired by (but not based on or adapted from) the 1985 work of nonfiction of the same name by ethnobiologist Wade Davis. Both the book and film examine the possibility of that bokurs or Voodoo priests who practice dark magic are using a powerful combination of psychotropic drugs to turn the living into zombie slaves in Haiti.

The plot is as follows: in 1978 Haiti, Christophe Juran, a school teacher and political agitator, is pronounced dead, but a tear can be seen rolling down his cheek after he is lowered into the ground in his coffin. Seven years later in the Amazon basin, Harvard anthropologist and field researcher Dr. Dennis Alan, played by Bill Pullman (born William James Pullman, 1953–), undergoes a drug-induced vision in which he encounters his animal spirit guide, a jaguar, and sees a man he will come to know as Peytraud, the chief of the Tonton Macoute secret police in Port-au-Prince. Back at Harvard, Alan, a spiritual skeptic, is recruited by a pharmaceutical company to investigate any drugs that may have reanimated Juran, who is now believed alive and living in a zombified state. Alan's initial contact in Port-au-Prince is Dr. Marielle DuChamps, a psychologist who works at an over-strained and underfunded health clinic. Through DuChamps, he meets Lucien Celine, played by Paul Winfield (born Paul Edward Winfield, 1939–2004), a Voodoo priest who walks the thin line between the spirit world and the government of Haitian dictator "Baby Doc" Duvalier.

A zombie bride rises from her grave in the film *The Serpent and the Rainbow* (1988), which is very loosely based on ethnobotanist Wade Davis's account of the existence of zombies in Haiti. (Universal Pictures/Photofest)

While meeting Lucien, Alan encounters and is followed by Peytraud. Juran is found and tells Alan that a powder is used to control his mind and make him do evil things. Celine identifies the powder's manufacturer as Voodoo practitioner Louis Mozart. After an initial contact with Mozart, DuChamps and Alan join a religious pilgrimage to a healing waterway. The next day, Alan is interrogated by Peytraud and is advised to leave Haiti. Mozart agrees, for $1,000, to show Alan how the zombie powder is made, a slow, methodical process taking three days and nights. During that time, Alan is again held by Peytraud and is briefly tortured. Released, Alan helps Mozart finish making the powder but is captured by Peytraud a third time and framed for a murder. Peytraud shows Alan his collection of souls and tells him that he is powerful enough to reach Alan anywhere. Alan is forced from Haiti, but Mozart slips him a jar of the zombie powder, known as tetrodotoxin. Back at Harvard, research reveals that the paralyzing effects of the drug wear off after 12 hours, long enough to render political agitators in Port-au-Prince, such as Juran, powerless. Alan experiences hallucinations in Boston and decides to return to Haiti. The Duvalier regime is collapsing, and the streets of Port-au-Prince are rapidly descending into chaos. Alan is warned that his final conflict with Peytraud will take place within his mind. Peytraud's men decapitate Mozart, and Peytraud drinks Mozart's blood, embodying his soul. Celine dies in Alan's presence, and a man blows the zombie powder into Alan's face. Under Peytraud's influence for 12 hours, Alan is buried alive but is dug up during the night by Juran. The film's climax is a lengthy fight between Alan and Peytraud in which Alan's jaguar spirit finally defeats Peytraud. Alan and DuChamps emerge from Port-au-Prince amid a new day for Haiti, spiritually as well as politically.

Craven's film, like Davis's book, is respectful of Haitian Voodoo, presented as a multifaceted system of belief. In addition to the pilgrimage that Alan and DuChamps join, Celine can be seen at one point presiding over a marriage ceremony. No explanation is provided, but Celine can be seen moving a dove around a bride and groom, who each release a dove from a balcony after the wedding. DuChamps also shows Alan another ceremony, which is a blending of Voodoo and Roman Catholicism and features a likeness of the Virgin Mary. At all times, until the climax, Alan remains a skeptical Western intruder, despite the overall respectful tone of the film. During the filming of *The Serpent and the Rainbow*, Craven and some of the production staff were awakened one night and brought to a field where a crowd was drinking and dancing in a Voodoo ceremony and a pig was slaughtered, its blood passed around for participants to drink. One of the crew met with a Haitian magician and experienced such profound hallucinations that he locked himself in his hotel room, then flew back to the United States, where he stayed in a secured room for four more days, emerging with no memory of the event.

The film is faithful to Davis's book in several respects. In the first chapter, Davis recounts how he was led to safety from the Amazon by a jaguar in 1974. Chapter two discusses the pharmaceutical recruitment in Boston and how a Haitian man, Clairvius Narcisse supposedly died in 1962, yet was seen alive again in Haiti, believed to be a zombie, several years later. Chapter three does introduce the reader to the

Voodoo expert who was the model for Celine in the film. There are, however, some noteworthy differences between the book and the film. The female protagonist in Davis's book is the daughter of the Voodoo priest, whereas DuChamps and Celine are not related at all in the film. In the book, Marcel Pierre is a member of the Ton-ton Macoute, and Peytraud does not exist. Rather, secret societies maintain order in Haiti. Nonetheless, for serious students of the zombie, this film should be considered required viewing. Produced by David Ladd (1947–) and Doug Claybourne (1947–), the film was a follow-up effort by Craven to the 1984 film *A Nightmare on Elm Street*. It was his biggest budget project up to that time, costing between $9 and $10 million. The film grossed approximately $19.5 million.

See also: Bokur/Caplata; Craven, Wes; Davis, Wade; Haiti; *Serpent and the Rainbow, The* (Book); Tetrodotoxin; Voodoo; Zombie Cucumber

Titus Belgard

SHAUN OF THE DEAD

Shaun of the Dead is a 2004 British comedy directed by Edgar Wright, who coauthored the script with lead actor Simon Pegg. The two had worked together previously on the Britcom *Spaced* (1999–2001). In the film, Shaun is a directionless young manager of an appliance store who has a tenuous relationship with his girlfriend Liz due to his unwillingness to take their romance past the casual dating phase, and he still lives at odds with his stepfather, with whom he does not get along. *Shaun of the Dead* is arguably the first example of a growing subgenre of zombie literature known as the Rom Zom Com, or Romantic Zombie Comedy, in that the film is as much about Shaun's attempts to mend his relationship with Liz as it is about his efforts to survive the zombie apocalypse. A British Academy of Film and Television Arts nominee, the film showcases the ennui of an entire generation of directionless youth.

In the opening credits and early scenes, young men and women are shown in dead-end jobs where they seldom look up or disengage their iPods; rather, they go about their daily business in a zombie-like stupor. Shaun's job as a manager of a big box store is equally dead end: his teenaged colleagues realize this when they openly mock him and disrespect his authority. Shaun and his friend Ed, played by Nick Frost, are part of this slacker lifestyle, spending every night getting drunk in the local pub. Shaun and Ed are so disengaged from the rest of the world that they are actually clueless when they see the first zombie attacks, thinking that they are simply watching a couple making out. The two return to Shaun's house to be confronted by Shaun's housemate Pete, who is irritated by Shaun's late night drunken antics. Pete, who has been filling in for absent employees who have come down with a mysterious flu, was bitten on his way home by someone he believes to be a crack addict. In fact, Pete was bitten by a zombie and will turn into one on the following day.

The next morning Shaun and Ed, after a hilarious encounter with a female zombie, learn via the news that zombies are attacking London. They grab weapons

Shaun (Simon Pegg) and his friends formulate a plan to get to their favorite pub, The Winchester, so that they can have a cold pint and "wait for this all to blow over," while the living dead wander through the streets of London in *Shaun of the Dead* (2004). (Rogue Pictures/Photofest)

from the tool shed, a cricket bat and a spade, and decide to travel across town to rescue Shaun's mother and Liz, who had broken up with Shaun the night before. Shaun and Ed lead everyone to their favorite local pub, The Winchester, which to the amazement of all has a, working antique rifle hanging over the bar. There are many comic moments while Shaun and his friends demonstrate how they are very unlike protagonists in an American zombie film in that they are not terribly adept at shooting a gun and blasting away at the zombies who soon make it into the pub. During the ensuing battle with the undead, Shaun is forced to shoot his mother, who has been bitten by a zombie, and members of the group are dragged out to be dismembered and eaten. Ed too is bitten during the ensuing melee, and Shaun and Liz are the only two of the group to survive the night, to be saved at the last second by the British army. The film then fast-forwards six months, where surviving humans have returned to their old lives and have enslaved the undead, turning them into zombified versions of the cheap labor which they were as young adults in the film's early scenes. Liz, meanwhile, has moved in with Shaun, and his flat is now cleaner but little else has changed in his life. Shaun still spends his free time playing video games with zombie Ed, who is now chained up in the shed instead of perpetually sleeping on Shaun's couch.

The film's special effects are realistic, with emphasis on gore and dismemberment, and the zombies are the typical flesh-eating cannibals who follow Romero's Rules. A critical and financial success, the film, produced by Universal Pictures in conjunction with Working Title Films, cost an estimated £4 million to make but made over

£1.6 million in the United Kingdom in its opening week in April. It grossed almost $13.5 million in the United States in September, despite a limited release.

See also: Apocalypse; Comedy; Existentialism; Rom Zom Com; Romero's Rules

Anthony J. Fonseca

SOLOMON GRUNDY

Solomon Grundy, a DC comics super villain named after the nursery rhyme, was introduced a zombie nemesis of the Green Lantern. He also became an enemy of Superman and Batman. Grundy first appeared in *All-American Comics* #61, in October 1944, with cover art by Paul Reinman (born Paul J. Reinman, 1910–1988). The character is one of first zombies in the comics.

Grundy's alter ego was a 19th-century merchant named Cyrus Gold. Gold had been murdered and left in a swamp near Gotham City. After 50 years, his corpse reanimates, composed partly of swamp mud. His resurrection comes about because a high council of Plant Elementals (The Parliament of Trees) turns him into an elemental; but since he did not die in fire, he cannot be fully created, so he becomes a half-functional Plant Elemental. Since he cannot die, when he is supposedly dispatched, he reanimates once again from the swamp, and some versions are mindless zombies. Grundy has very little memory of his life. He gets his new name in a hobo camp because all he can remember is that he was born on a Monday. He degenerates into a criminal and attracts the attention of the Green Lantern, but Grundy cannot be killed because he is already dead and because part of his body is composed of wood from the swamp. At one point, Grundy masters the emerald energy he has absorbed over years from battling the Green Lantern, and develops mastery over all wooden objects. He also later develops telekinetic ability through various travels in alternate universes. He is also sometimes reborn with intelligence. His last appearance was in *Faces of Evil: Solomon Grundy* (2009). Grundymen, zombies raised by various means in some comics, are named after Solomon Grundy.

See also: Graphic Novels and Comics; Reanimation

Anthony J. Fonseca

STAKE LAND

Stake Land is a 2010 coming-of-age film directed by Jim Mickle (1979–), in which Martin, the teen protagonist, must learn how to be a man in a post-apocalyptic United States, after a virus turns many of the living into vampires, who must be staked so that survivors can re-create civilization. However, the vampires in *Stake Land* are more similar to the infected in *I Am Legend,* by Richard Matheson, some of whom believe themselves to be vampires but behave more like zombies in that they are so in thrall to the drive to drink human blood that they lack free will and reason.

Orphaned by the virus, Martin travels with a character named Mister, an older man who teaches him how to stake the infected without mercy and how to grow into a man. Martin and Mister travel through a ruined landscape in search of New Eden, the rumored place where humans are said to have made a new beginning. In the Deep South, Martin and Mister run afoul of The Brotherhood, a Christian militia with white supremacist leanings, who capture the duo for killing two of their members who are rapists who attempted to sexually assault a nun known only as Sister. Martin and Mister escape, and afterward pick up Belle, a pregnant young woman hitchhiking to safety, and then rescue Willie, an African American ex-marine who was tied up and left to die in a portable toilet after a run-in with The Brotherhood. After meeting Willie, the group decides to go after The Brotherhood's leader, Jebediah Loven—whom they eventually capture and leave him tied to a tree so that he will be killed by the vampires. But Jebediah survives his encounter with the vampires, and the virus mutates in his body, making him into a stronger vampire, one unlike a zombie in that he can reason. In a showdown between the group and Jebediah, Belle and Willie are killed and only Martin and Mister escape. Soon afterward, Martin meets Peggy, a girl his age in a truck stop, and so Mister decides that his work of raising the boy is now done. He leaves Martin on his own, and the film ends with Martin and Peggy driving off together, eventually finding New Eden.

Even though *Stake Land*'s creatures are described as vampires, the film is noteworthy as a zombie text in how it references so many other works of post-apocalyptic fiction that have either influenced the contemporary zombie narrative or are derivative of it. The most obvious comparisons are the 1954 classic novella *I Am Legend,* as well as all three films based on it. Notably, George Romero lists Matheson's novella as heavily influencing his groundbreaking zombies in his *Night of the Living Dead* (1968). *Stake Land* is also evocative of the 2009 John Hillcoat's film adaptation of *The Road,* a novel by Cormac McCarthy, for both its narrative technique and themes. Mickel's infected also physically resemble zombies: their skin is pale and cracked, their mouths and clothing are usually stained with the blood of their latest kills, and their bodies are broken. In addition, Jebediah Loven has much in common with the zombie-killing Reverend Jebediah Mercer, a character created by Joe R. Lansdale. In fact, the film is an impressive bricolage of so many 20th-century texts, ranging from the infamous novel *The Turner Diaries* (1978), by white supremacist William Luther Pierce III (1933–2002), to 1984's *Children of the Corn,* directed by Fritz Kiersch (born George Keith Kiersch (1951–).

Stake Land is not terribly well known. It was shown on only one screen for its opening week in 2011, after premiering at the 2010 Toronto International Film Festival, making little more than $7,000. The film's widest release was on five screens, and eventually grossed a little over $33,000. Nevertheless, it is important in the subgenre because it illustrates the ubiquitous influence of the post-apocalyptic zombie narrative.

See also: Apocalypse; Epidemics; *I Am Legend* (Novel); Lansdale, Joe R.; Matheson, Richard; *Night of the Living Dead* Series; *Road, The* (Film); Vampires and Were-wolves; Young Adult Fiction

June Michele Pulliam

STUPIDEST ANGEL, THE

The Stupidest Angel, subtitled *A Heartwarming Tale of Christmas Terror,* is a 2004 comic horror novel by Christopher Moore (1957–). In it, Moore revisits characters he created in *Lamb: The Gospel According to Biff, Christ's Childhood Pal* (2002) and *The Lust Lizard of Melancholy Cove* (1999), as well as his fictional coastal California paradise, Pine Cove. The novel's monster, Dale Pearson, is a well-to-do socialite who mistreats his ex-wife, Lena Marquez, whom he has left impoverished. Through a misunderstanding, he is turned into one of the undead, and the zombie Pearson, still bitter about his death, decides to go after his ex, encouraging the other undead to follow him so all can even scores with the living, and in stereotypical zombie fashion, eat their brains.

While Lena is stealing a Christmas tree because she cannot afford to buy one, Pearson, dressed in a Santa costume, accosts her, and she accidentally kills him with a shovel, severing the artery in his neck. Unfortunately, the death is witnessed by seven-year-old Josh Barker, who believes that the actual Santa has been slain. Barker is later approached by Moore's dimwitted angel Raziel, who is on a mission to find a child for whom he can grant one Christmas wish. Barker wishes to have Santa alive again, and so Raziel brings Pearson as Santa back from the dead. Unfortunately, the bumbling Raziel has also reanimated many of the town's dead as well. The final showdown, which involves martial arts, weaponry, and the realization that the newly stoned on marijuana is unhealthy for a zombie diet, occurs at the Christmas party in the nearby chapel.

Despite their insistence on eating the brains of their victims, Moore's zombies are played more for comedy than horror, and as such, break with stereotype. Moore's zombies are articulate. In fact, as soon as they rise from their graves, they bicker over minor issues, such as whether they should wait in the cemetery until the last zombie breaks ground or feast on the locals first. When they corner the locals at the chapel, they taunt their would-be victims by telling them that they are going to feast on their brains, and follow up by embarrassing the living by divulging their would-be victims' innermost secrets. The zombie infestation, which accounts for only the last third of the novel, is resolved: Moore's undead are easily dispatched via a samurai sword and are finally defeated when Raziel turns back time. Despite its iconoclastic nature and irreverence, Moore's novel has been widely praised by sources as varied as *The New York Times* and *Library Journal.* As of 2013, *The Stupidest Angel* is slated to be made into a film by Swim Pictures, LLC.

See also: Comedy; Romero's Rules; Sentience

Anthony J. Fonseca

TALES FROM THE CRYPT (COMIC)

Tales from the Crypt was a bimonthly horror comic anthology series. Each issue was hosted by The Crypt Keeper, who was originally a dark, sinister presence that later became more benign in appearance and manner, ultimately leaning on tortured puns and black humor to entertain readers, and supported by two co-hosts: The Vault Keeper and The Old Witch. Although many stories were original, the editors and writers were not above seeking inspiration in the works of horror masters, such as Arthur Machen (born Arthur Llewellyn Jones, 1863–1947), H. P. Lovecraft, and Ray Bradbury. Despite the presence of numerous undead entities, only one story in the *Gemstone* series deals with zombies per se. Appropriately titled "Zombie!" the tale, illustrated by Johnny Craig (born John Thomas Alexis Craig, 1926–2001),opens as journalist Daniel King arrives in Haiti, visiting at the plantation of a man identified as Mr. Richards. Richards informs King that he has arrived on Voodoo Night. Against the advice of his host, King rushes into the jungle and films a strange ritual in which the corpse of a white woman is reanimated to dance with the black inhabitants of the island. Richards tells King the corpse is that of the plantation's previous owner's wife, who was murdered by her brute of a husband (in true Entertaining Comics [EC] tradition), only to be revived as a zombie and sent to wreak vengeance on her spouse for his sins. Believing that he has a sensational story, King develops his photographs, only to find that the white zombie does not register in a single frame, leaving him with no evidence of his fantastic tale.

Along with *The Haunt of Fear* and *The Vault of Horror,* this infamous EC title began with Crime Patrol 15. *Tales from the Crypt* subsequently changed its name twice: first to *The Crypt of Terror* in Issue 17, and again to the more familiar *Tales from the Crypt* in Issue 20. The comic's legacy has been maintained in print, film, and television. A series of paperbacks featuring selected stories was issued by Ballantine in the mid-1960s. Most memorable was the full reprinting of the magazine in a five-volume set of oversized hardcovers as part of *The Complete EC Library* (edited by William M. Gaines in 1981 and 1982 in two sets of three and two volumes, respectively, West Plains, MO: Russ Cochran, 1981 and 1982), later to be issued as single issue reprints of the entire series. A film of the same name, adapting stories from several EC anthologies, was released in 1972. Four years later, *Tales* became Saturday morning cartoon fare with the animated series, *Tales from the Cryptkeeper.* In the mid-1990s, two films, *Demon Knight* (1995) and *Bordello of Blood* (1996), appeared under the *Tales from the Crypt* rubric. In 2007, the comic book series was resurrected by the publisher Papercutz for nine issues.

Despite its short run of 27 issues, it has had a profound influence on horror authors and illustrators. Over the years, a veritable who's who of comic book artists and writers contributed. Known for shock and gore, the comic caught the attention of parents, teachers, clergy members, psychiatrists, and, most importantly, Congress. Concern over the impact the comic had on the psyches of America's youth led to the eventual demise of the EC line and the creation of the Comics Code Authority, a set of industry guidelines that banned graphic representations of gore, violence, and sex in horror and crime comics.

See also: Bradbury, Ray; Comedy; Graphic Novels and Comics; Lovecraft, H. P.; Television

Hank Wagner

TALES FROM THE CRYPT (FILM)

Tales from the Crypt is a 1972 film directed by Freddie Francis (born Frederick William Francis, 1917–2007). The film features five stories from the Entertaining Comics canon. In the movie, five strangers touring some ancient catacombs are cut off from a larger group, and subsequently encounter the mysterious Crypt Keeper, played by Ralph Richardson (born Ralph David Richardson, 1902–1983), looking much more human than the mysteriously robed character from the comics, or the animated corpse of latter television series (1989–1996). The Crypt Keeper tells each character a story about his or her impending doom. The five tales are "And All through the House" (*The Vault of Horror* #35), "Reflection of Death" (*Tales from the Crypt* #23), "Poetic Justice" (*The Haunt of Fear* #12), "Wish You Were Here" (*The Haunt of Fear* #22), and "Blind Alleys" (*Tales from the Crypt* #46). Three of the five tales in the film utilize the trope of the walking dead, although the characterization lends itself more to the idea of the revenging revenant, rather than the ghoulish zombie popularized by *Night of the Living Dead*.

"And All through the House" features Joan Collins (born Joan Henrietta Collins, 1933–) as a character who kills her husband and has an encounter with a serial killer dressed as Santa on Christmas Eve. "Reflection of Death" is a tale of a man who believes he has survived a car accident but is actually the walking dead. "Poetic Justice" is a story about a man and his son who both torment a neighbor, who then commits suicide. One year later, however, the neighbor returns from the dead for vengeance. "Wish You Were Here" is a variation of the classic tale "The Monkey's Paw," by W. W. Jacobs. It ends with the protagonist's husband being transformed into a living corpse, condemned to experience terrible pain for every second of his eternal existence. "Blind Alleys" concerns the revenge that a group of blind people in a nursing home enact against their tormentor. After he tells these tales, the Crypt Keeper reveals to his five listeners that he was not speaking about what might happen but rather about things that had already occurred. The five then realize that they are about to be cast into hell, a fate which they accept with a sense of resignation.

The undead creatures in the vignettes do not shamble, nor do they randomly seek to do violence to humans. "Reflection of Death" changes the story from the comic book slightly, making the walking corpse a man involved in an affair, rather than one who was simply in a car with a friend, but keeps to the plot of the dead person's being unaware that he is a walking, rotting corpse—until he sees his reflection at the end. "Poetic Justice" also introduces a sentient walking corpse, though this time one that commits murder out of revenge. In both cases, the zombies are signified by blue or gray skin, skeletal facial features, and oozing pores. "Wish You Were Here" ups the gore factor. Here, the dead human continues to feel pain even as he slowly turns into a zombie-like creature with extremely pale skin and sunken eyes. By story's end, his wife, in attempts to end his liminal state of existence, has chopped his body into bits, yet his suffering does not end, as he continues to scream while in the coffin.

See also: Comedy; Ghosts; Graphic Novels and Comics

Hank Wagner

TALES FROM THE HOOD

Tales from the Hood is a 1995 Spike Lee–produced (born Shelton Jackson Lee, 1957–) comic horror film directed by Rusty Cundieff (born George Arthur Cundieff, 1960–), who cowrote the script. An anthology film, it consists of four short vignettes, each dealing with a black urban youth issue. These are framed by the story of three gangbangers who show up at a mysterious South Central Los Angeles funeral home where they have heard they can purchase drugs. Although all of the stories deal with death and hauntings, one deals specifically with the return of the undead.

The zombie motif is prominent in the first segment, "Rogue Cop Revelation." It tells of Clarence, an African American rookie officer who does not intervene when three of his white colleagues beat a local black activist to death and is then haunted by the man's spirit for one year and later his corpse. On the anniversary of the death of the activist Martin Moorehouse, the now alcoholic ex-policeman Clarence draws the three white officers to their victim's gravesite. Moorehouse reaches up from the grave to drag one of the officers underground then pushes up the coffin up from the ground to reveal the officer's body inside. Moorehouse kills the other two officers in equally horrific ways. Even though Moorehouse has the decaying body and shambling gait of a stereotypical zombie, he also possesses characteristics of the ghost, as well as abilities such as telekinesis, which he uses against one of the officers. The segment ends with Clarence in a mental hospital, accused of murdering the three white officers. The film was made for $6 million but grossed $11.8 million in sales in United States, making it rather successful for an indie horror film. It was made under Lee's 40 Acres and A Mule Filmworks label.

The film's main characters are the gangsters Stack, Ball, and Bulldog, as well as Mr. Simms, the mortuary's eccentric owner, played by veteran actor Clarence

Williams III (1939–). Simms leads the youth through the mortuary, ostensibly to help him retrieve the drugs, and en route shows them various corpses, each accompanied by a story. In the second tale, "Boys Do Get Bruised," a young boy named Walter is abused by his mother's live-in boyfriend. Walter stops his abuser after he discovers that he can injure his tormentors by drawing them, then mutilating the image. "KKK Comeuppance," the third segment, is loosely based on David Duke (born David Ernest Duke, 1950–), a well-known Louisiana politician with Ku Klux Klan connections. The main character, Duke Metger, is eventually eaten by African American Voodoo dolls originally created by an elderly slave woman to hold the souls of her fellow slaves who had been killed by their master. The fourth story, "Hard-Core Convert," is occasioned when the gangbangers are shown the corpse of a young man from their neighborhood, Krazy K. In this vignette, K is given a special hallucinogenic therapy by a doctor that allows him to interact with the deceased victims of his violence. When K refuses to take responsibility for murdering fellow African Americans, he too is cut down by a gang, the three young gangbangers who are now in Mr. Simm's Mortuary. The film ends when Simms leads into a basement of the funeral home, revealing that they have been killed by the police: their bodies lie in three of Simm's coffins, and their souls are in hell.

See also: Comedy; Ghosts; Race; Science Fiction

Anthony J. Fonseca

TALKING DEAD, THE

The Talking Dead is a live talk show hosted by Chris Hardwick (born Christopher Ryan Hardwick, 1971–) about the American Movie Classics (AMC) network television show *The Walking Dead* (2010–), which has set records for television viewership. *The Talking Dead* premiered on October 16, 2011, after the encore presentation of season two premier of *The Walking Dead.*

The Talking Dead proved so popular that AMC expanded it from a 30-minute into an hour-long format and moved its airing to 10:00 p.m. Eastern time after new episodes of *The Walking Dead* were shown. Hardwick's guests on *The Talking Dead* include cast and crew members from the show, as well as Robert Kirkman, creator of the graphic novel series that spawned *The Walking Dead,* and celebrity fans, including Joe Manganiello (born Joseph Michael Manganiello, 1976–), Wil Wheaton (born Richard William Wheaton III, 1972–), and Sarah Silverman (born Sarah Kate Silverman, 1970–). Other elements of the show include an In Memoriam segment that examines deaths of characters in the previous episode, as well as polls and trivia.

The Talking Dead is accompanied by an interactive website that allows for watching video clips of both *The Walking Dead* and *The Talking Dead,* downloading photos, blogging, joining discussion boards, and downloading a *Dead Yourself* app. It also hosts videos of interviews with producers about upcoming episodes, as well as clips of the filming crew and actors on the set. Polls include questions such as

"Did the character Carl go too far when he shot the surrendering boy soldier in the final episode of Season 3?" Such polls go to the heart of the television program, which offers storylines that challenge viewers to rethink ethics, especially in the context of an apocalyptic world where it is impossible to trust anyone and survive. The existence of a show such as *The Talking Dead* is testament to the popularity of AMC's *The Walking Dead*.

See also: Television; *Walking Dead, The* (Television Series)

June Michele Pulliam

TELEVISION

Television is a medium from which the zombie has been notably absent, until recently, despite the fact that the zombie has been a staple of horror cinema and comics since the 1930s. Perhaps this is because television as a medium relies heavily on advertisers, and pre-cable broadcasters have traditionally been reluctant to air programs that might be considered excessively violent. After all, the contemporary representation of the zombie is one that follows Romero's Rules, which typically translates into gore and violence.

Another possibility is that the zombie tends to be a flat character, and it is difficult to sustain a multi-episode narrative based on a creature that does not substantially evolve. It is just as difficult to create one that follows survivors, whose bleak, post-apocalyptic world only gets worse with each passing day. Perhaps this is the reason that the American Movie Classics (AMC), a cable rather than a broadcast channel, was the first network to bring the zombie to wide popularity. Like the graphic novel on which it is based, AMC's *The Walking Dead* (2010–) follows Sheriff Rick Grimes and his family and friends as they struggle to survive the zombie apocalypse. *The Walking Dead* is similar to George Romero's *Night of the Living Dead* series: its zombies follow Romero's Rules and their presence quickly topples civilization, leaving the survivors to re-create as best they can the security and order of their old lives. The show is filled with gore and violence of the type that could be depicted only on a cable television station, where producers do not have to be as concerned about offending public sensibilities as would producers of shows that air on broadcast television. *The Walking Dead* has enjoyed a record-setting viewership, with 12.4 million people watching the Season 3 finale in April of 2013. In fact, *The Walking Dead*'s immense popularity with viewers spurred AMC to make a talk show based on the series. *The Talking Dead*, a talk show where host Chris Hardwick discusses episodes with cast, crew members, and even celebrity fans, premiered on October 16, 2011, after the encore presentation of the second season of *The Walking Dead*.

The popularity of *The Walking Dead* encouraged BBC to make its own zombie miniseries, *In the Flesh*, which aired in three episodes in June of 2013. *In the Flesh* is notable in that it deviates from the standard trajectory of the zombie narrative following Romero's Rules where only the living are sympathetic characters capable of development. *In the Flesh* is told from the perspective of the zombie Kiernan Walker. The zombies in *In the Flesh* suffer from a condition known as partially deceased syndrome, or PDS, which can be cured, so the presence of the undead has not brought about an apocalypse the way it has in *The Walking Dead*. Those infected with PDS are given therapy to stop the cannibalism that is part of the condition, and afterward, returned to their homes and families. Nevertheless, many people are uncomfortable being around people who have been cured of their PDS, and they react violently when those who have gone through treatment for their PDS are returned to their communities. Walker faces this challenge when he is confronted by members of the Human Volunteer Force in his community, an armed militia group that dealt with zombies before there was a cure. These people want Kiernan to be held accountable for killings he did before he was treated for his PDS. Because the series focuses on zombies who are in the process of being cured, there is less blood and gore than what is characteristic in other zombie narratives.

Zombies have also appeared on television before *The Walking Dead*. The reanimated dead were featured in a 1964 episode of *The Twilight Zone* (season 5, episode 152) titled "Mr. Garrity and the Graves." In it, Jared Garrity, a con artist, comes to the small Western town of Happiness, Arizona, and offers at no charge to restore complete happiness to residents by reanimating their loved ones, many of whom have recently died untimely deaths due to the brutal nature of life in the 19th-century American West, in which the episode is set. Garrity intends to swindle the people of Happiness by getting them to pay him to return their dead to the grave once they are convinced that their deceased loved ones have returned to life, and so fear that their past secrets and misdeeds that were known only by the dead might be revealed. And this happens soon after—when the townspeople believe that their dead family members have been resurrected, they offer Garrity cash to return them to the grave. Garrity takes their money and assures the townspeople that the dead, which he never believed that he revived, have now safely been returned to their graves. Garrity, however, has powers that he did not know he possessed. As Garrity is leaving town, the dead can be seen rising from their graves, shambling toward Happiness and mentioning that they intend to harm their loved ones when they find them. Although the word zombie is never used in the episode, and the resurrected dead are not decomposed and can speak, the image of the graves moving slowly as dirt is pushed off of them, followed by bodies emerging from the ground, are early versions of the motifs occurring in zombie films, as is the distinctive shambling gait of the undead, who walk with their arms held lifeless by the side as they stare ahead blankly. *The Twilight Zone* originally aired on the broadcast television station CBS in a time before most homes subscribed to cable television.

Other notable representations of the zombie on television before AMC's blockbuster series include *Homecoming*, the sixth episode of the first season of the *Masters of Horror* television series. *Homecoming*, which aired in 2005, uses the trope of the zombie to comment on the United States' war on terror after 9/11. The episode follows what occurs after George W. Bush falsely claims that Iraq had weapons of mass destruction, giving him the justification to start a war. In the episode, the reanimated dead are not cannibalistic fiends but the bodies of soldiers who died in the war and who have returned from the grave to take action against the regime that sent them to die on false pretenses. When one of the undead servicemen rises from his coffin, he walks up to the frightened soldier who is shooting at him, puts a hand on his shoulder, and tells him "at ease." The zombies' violence is saved for those directly responsible for their deaths and who would prevent them from their goal, which is to make it to the polls on election day in order to vote the current regime out of office. After the undead vote, their purpose for reviving has expired and they die anew. The *Masters of Horror* series was free to represent violence and treat controversial subject matter because it ran on the cable television network Showtime, rather than on broadcast television.

In 2008, the British television station E4 aired *Dead Set,* a British Television and Film Award–nominated miniseries in which cast and crew from the show *Big Brother* become stranded on the set at the beginning of the zombie apocalypse. *Dead Set* was produced and distributed by the same company that produces and airs *Big Brother*. The zombies in *Dead Set* are similar to the fast-moving ones popularized in the *28 Days Later* series. Nonetheless, the series is more concerned with lives of the survivors than the undead, who are flat characters.

See also: Dead Set; *Homecoming*; *In the Flesh*; "Mr. Garrity and the Graves"; *Night of the Living Dead* Series; Romero's Rules; *Talking Dead, The*; Television; *Walking Dead, The* (Television Series)

June Michele Pulliam

TELL MY HORSE

Tell My Horse subtitled *Voodoo and Life in Haiti and Jamaica,* also known also as *Voodoo Gods: An Inquiry into Native Myths and Magic in Jamaica and Haiti,* was published in the United States in 1938. It is a seriously sincere and thoroughly enthralling account of Zora Neale Hurston's personal experiences during a visit to Jamaica and Haiti during 1936 and 1937. Historically, it is a significant work, and Hurston's anthropological training and superb storytelling technique provide unparalleled access to Jamaican and Haitian culture that is immediately illuminating and informative. In the text, Hurston professes to have encountered an actual zombie, defined as a human body that has lost its soul, in the yard of a hospital in Haiti; a photograph is included in the book as incontrovertible evidence that zombies exist.

The existence of zombies is sometimes dismissed as folklore or attributed to myth. However, the belief among Haitians is that there is a practical aspect to zombies: the dead can be summoned from the grave to labor, either as revenge or to pay an owed debt. A bokur (a Voodoo priest who practices black rather than white magic) can cause a person to die if he or she could not or would not perform a certain task while alive. As a zombie, the soulless body could be controlled and made to perform whatever work desired. Also, since the zombie is already dead, it does not have to be cared for or reimbursed. A special secretive Voodoo ceremony accompanies the making of a zombie, as suitable zombie candidates must be specially selected. Not every deceased person can become a zombie. For example, zombification of the deceased can be prevented by poisoning the body upon death. Furthermore, zombification can be reversed by feeding the zombie salt. This cultural belief that the dead can be brought back to life as zombies to serve some nefarious purpose has caused fear of the creature to run rampant among lower-class Haitians. Some upper class and educated Haitians also fear zombies.

Hurston attended Howard University and later studied anthropology at Barnard College, before publishing her first novel in 1934. Traveling on a Guggenheim Fellowship to study Obeah folklore in West Indian culture, Hurston immersed herself in the life and customs of the people in the countries she visited. *Tell My Horse* is presented in three parts: the culture of Jamaica; the culture of Haiti, with a description of the national development and politics of the country; and the ritualistic and ceremonial practices of Voodoo in Haiti. Recently rediscovered long after her death, *Tell My Horse* is a series of stories depicting the interplay of life and death in day-to-day experiences and as substantiation for unexplained spiritual phenomena in a culture where spirits are assumed to abide in the living as well as emanate from the dead; they can influence life and may also account for unusual or strange occurrences. Chants and songs of worshipful respectfulness, along with rituals, play important roles in understanding and managing the spirit world.

Moving on to Haiti, Hurston sets a transitional stage with a description of the emergence of the country and its people from slavery, French colonization and influence, and American occupation. She notes that the largely poor and uneducated Haitian population is deeply religious and finds in Voodoo some solace and refuge from the widespread poverty and uninspiring government. The stories about Voodoo in Haiti descriptively chronicle actual occurrences from ceremonies in which Hurston participated. Hurston's writing is clear and engaging and affords easy mental images of the events that include the use of symbols, artifacts, celebratory songs, and laudatory chants. Also included throughout the book are more than two dozen photographs and an appendix that contains the actual music of the songs. In Chapter 10, Hurston establishes early on that "Voodoo is a religion of creation and life," noting that symbolism and ceremony play significant roles. She further offers a summary of its significance: the rituals offer appeasement and worshipful respect to the gods who, it is believed, influence life through spirits. Through Voodoo, believers expect that bad fortunes can be reversed, ill health can be overcome, and even difficulty in love can be positively resolved. In Haiti, ceremonies occur frequently, and anyone needing to be absolved of any affliction needs to attend only one (and bring along an offering for the gods).

Ritual performers consist of houngans and mambos (Voodoo priests and priestesses) and their attendants (hounsi) who have specific training and, it is assumed, divine inspiration directly from the gods. The ceremonies begin slowly with specialized movements that repeat at an increasingly frenzied pace, until a spiritual presence is manifested or becomes internalized in one of the individual participants. The rituals may also involve animal mutilation and/or sacrifice, the collection and drinking of animal blood, and burning with fire. Some ceremonies take place over several days and involve eating special foods or nothing at all, anointing and the pouring of libations, and the laying on of hands. Houngans and mambos are knowledgeable and respectful of ritual in the ceremony, becoming that way through experience and lengthy practice. Such knowledge is passed on orally through guided tutelage from masters to selected apprentices. Powers and prowess among priests are achieved through daring performances and enhanced through exciting feats that appear to be magic, especially in high-profile ceremonies. Secret societies exist in Haiti specifically to perpetuate and protect secrets related to Voodoo. The phrase "tell my horse," or *parlay cheval ou* in French, refers to the "mounting" of a person by a spirit. Otherwise invisible, the spirits are called upon to do the work of the gods and can speak through the possessed "mounts" who relinquish, momentarily, their conscious selves to the gods.

See also: Bokur/Caplata; Class; Haiti; *Magic Island, The*; Voodoo

Will Hires

TENNEY, DEL

Del Tenney (born Delbert Tenney, 1930–2013) was an American B-movie director, screenwriter, and producer known for his low-budget horror films of the 1960s. His penchant for sexploitation in horror culminated in his most famous work, *The Horror of Party Beach* (1964), which originally had the working title *Invasion of the Zombies*. In 1964, Tenney made three zombie films, two of which were released in that year, and the third six years later. *The Horror of Party Beach* was an attempt to tie the horror genre with the then-popular beach party film. It was released as a double feature with Tenney's *The Curse of the Living Corpse*, about a well-to-do man who dies, is interred, and returns from the grave to exact revenge on his family. *I Eat Your Skin* was shot under the working title *Caribbean Adventure* so that no one would know it was a zombie film.

Made for $120,000, *The Horror of Party Beach* was originally going to be subtitled *The First Monster Musical*. The story begins in a small beach town. Mutated creatures are created by the combination of water plants, dead human tissue, skeletal remains, and radioactive waste. The creatures begin stalking and murdering bikini-clad women. Despite the killings, beach and slumber parties continue to attract young men and women. A scientist, his teen daughter Elaine, her boyfriend, and the housekeeper battle against the monsters. The film serves as a cautionary tale for young adults, as the first young woman killed is a result of alcohol consumption, flirting, fighting, and going off for a dangerous swim alone. Interestingly, some of the locals originally blame the killing on Voodoo, so that the film consciously incorporates two zombie tropes into its sea monster creatures: the dead returning to life and Haitian Voodoo. The creatures are only tangentially zombies, as they are sentient and possess emotional intelligence. The film is also well known for its music, which features The Del-Aires, and for the fact that it is set on the Atlantic coast.

The Curse of the Living Corpse was written, directed, and produced by Tenney. A wealthy, abusive father, whose will dictates that his family ensure he is not buried alive, is found dead and is buried by family members, each eager to get his or her inheritance. As family members gather at the estate for the will reading, they are killed off, one by one, by the resurrected father. The movie is best known as the debut film of Roy Scheider (born Roy Richard Scheider, 1932–2008). *I Eat Your Skin,* originally titled *Zombie Bloodbath* or *Voodoo Bloodbath,* is about a novelist in search of material on Voodoo. On a remote island, he discovers the laboratory where a scientist experimenting on reversing the aging process has created monsters. The film was released as a double feature with *I Drink Your Blood,* directed by David E. Durston (1921–2010), at which time it was renamed.

See also: Comedy; Cult Film; Ghoul; Science Fiction; Sentience; Voodoo

Anthony J. Fonseca

TETRODOTOXIN

Tetrodotoxin (TTX) is a potent neurotoxin whose name derives from the word Tetraodontiformes, an order that includes puffer fish, porcupinefish, ocean sunfish, and triggerfish. These fish carry poison in their organs, produced by bacteria, that serves as a defensive biotoxin. When administered to humans, it prevents nerve cells from firing by blocking their channels through selective blocking of sodium. While this effect has potential to treat some cardiac arrhythmias and has proven useful in the treatment of pain, if incorrectly administered it can cause death. It is also rumored to be the active ingredient in zombie powder, which is used to make a human fall into a death-like coma so that he or she can later be revived and drugged for further use as a zombie in Haitian folklore.

TTX can enter the body by ingestion, injection, inhalation, or abraded skin. Reports have it that Clairvius Narcisse, a Haitian man who supposedly turned into a zombie and used as slave labor for years as punishment for a land dispute with his brother, was given the poison by a bokur through abrasions in the skin. The TTX caused paralysis of his voluntary muscles, stopping his breathing and slowing his heart rate to approximate his death. Scientists have found that near-lethal doses of TTX can cause a state of near-death for several days, supposedly while the brain is conscious. Ethnobotanist Wade Davis theorized in a 1983 paper and a 1985 book, *The Serpent and the Rainbow,* that this is how the Haitian Voodoo zombie was created, an idea originally dismissed by the scientific community.

The first recorded cases of TTX poisoning were in 1774, and the toxin was first isolated and named in 1909. Poisonings from TTX are generally due to consumption of puffer fish, with reported poisonings in the United States ranging from the Atlantic Ocean to the Gulf of Mexico, and to the Gulf of California, although only a few cases have been reported.

See also: Bokur/Caplata; Davis, Wade; Haiti; Narcisse, Clairvius; *Serpent and the Rainbow, The* (Book); Voodoo

Anthony J. Fonseca

THRILLER

Thriller is a 1983 music video by Optimum Productions, starring Michael Jackson and Ola Ray (1960–), featuring narration by Vincent Price. It was directed by John Landis (born John David Landis, 1950–), known for *Animal House* (1978), *The Blues Brothers* (1980), *An American Werewolf in London* (1981), and *Twilight Zone: The Movie* (1983). Following a classic, three-act film structure, *Thriller* begins with a brief homage to the 1950s teenage creature feature *I Was a Teenage Werewolf* (1957): Jackson transforms into a werewolf and attacks Ray, his date. In a meta-film twist, the audience discovers Jackson and Ray watching said attack in a movie theater. Frightened, Ray insists on leaving. On their way out, the couple encounters a gang of zombies in various stages of decomposition and Jackson makes another transformation, this time into a zombie.

Comprising a zombie dance sequence, partially choreographed by Jackson, and a zombie chase scene, the second act of *Thriller* is a homage to the zombie cult classic *Night of the Living Dead* (1968). In this second act, Jackson and his crew of living dead chase down Ray and attack her in a farmhouse. In the third act, as Jackson and crew move in for the kill, the next twist of the film occurs when Ray discovers that she has been dreaming. Or has she?

Recognized for its famous zombie dance sequence and excellent special effects makeup designed and created by Rick Baker (born Richard A. Baker, 1950–), Jackson's *Thriller* ushered in a new era of music video production, raising the expectations for higher-quality filmmaking and storytelling, thus transforming the music

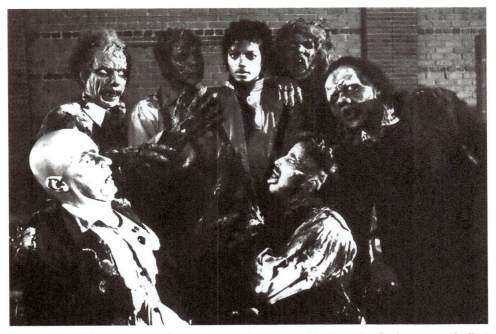

Pop star Michael Jackson transforms into one of the undead in the video for his song "Thriller" (1983). (MCA/Universal Home VideoPhotofest)

video from a mere commercial to sell albums to a true cinematic art form. *Thriller* was groundbreaking. It combined music and cinematic storytelling in 13:43 minutes, costing between $500,000 and $1.2 million to produce (depending on the source), at least 10 times more than the average music video at the time. To finance production, Landis approached the then-fledgling cable station Showtime, which agreed to front $250,000, with the stipulation that a 60-minute behind-the-scenes documentary accompany it. Titled *The Making of Thriller,* the documentary became the biggest selling music video of all time. When MTV learned of the deal with Showtime, the station offered to front the remaining $250,000, the first time that MTV ever paid to produce a video. *Thriller* won several awards, including the 1984 Grammy for Best Video; the 1984 American Video Award for Best Long Form Video; and the 1984 MTV Video Music Award for Best Overall Performance Video, as well as for Best Choreography, and the Viewer's Choice Award. Lauded by music critics as one of the greatest music videos of all time, in 2009, it gained recognition from the Library of Congress, becoming the first music video to be inducted into the National Film Registry.

See also: Comedy; *Night of the Living Dead* Series

Antoinette F. Winstead

28 DAYS LATER SERIES

28 Days Later is a 2002 horror film that revised the cinematic zombie almost beyond recognition. Directed by English auteur Danny Boyle, winner of the 2008 Academy Award for Best Director (*Slumdog Millionaire*), the post-apocalyptic zombie film imagines England 28 days after some well-meaning animal activists accidentally unleash the highly contagious rage virus which is being synthesized in a laboratory. Written by Alex Garland (born Alex Madawar Garland, 1970–) and produced by Andrew Macdonald (1966–), the film's story follows four major characters as they try to survive among hordes of relentless, rage-infected humans who are driven to savagely kill anyone who is not contaminated with the virus.

The plot focuses on Jim, who wakes from a coma in an abandoned hospital and makes his way outside to discover the entire city of London deserted. After wandering the streets, he seeks refuge in a church and meets his first zombie, a growling priest who moves in fits and starts and lunges for him. Jim escapes the priest but not without alerting a few amazingly fast infected zombies of his presence. As the infected chase Jim out of the church, survivors Selena and Mark rescue him and explain the events that have led up to the epidemic. The next day, they journey to Jim's childhood home, where he finds his parents have committed suicide rather than face the virus or its victims. As they sleep in the house that night, two of the infected see a candle burning through the window, smash into the house, and attack. In the fight, Mark is wounded and is covered in the highly contagious blood. Within seconds of realizing this, Selena violently kills Mark and explains to a shocked Jim the speed at which the infection progresses. Selena informs Jim that

Jim (Cillian Murphy) runs from one of the infected. (Fox Searchlight Pictures/Photofest)

if he were to become infected, she would kill him without a second thought. The next day, Jim and Selena meet two more survivors, Frank and his daughter Hannah, who invite them to stay in their apartment.

Low on supplies, especially water, and looking for answers, Frank shares a radio broadcast that promises the answer to infection for those who journey to a military blockade past Manchester. The four set out in Frank's car to find the people who made the broadcast. Upon their arrival at the blockade, calm, lovable Frank is infected and is promptly killed by soldiers, who take Jim, Selena, and Hannah to their fortress, which is led by the sadistic Major West. As is the case in many post-apocalyptic zombie films, the people inside the place of safety become more frightening than those outside, as multiple power struggles ensue. Major West confides to Jim that the answer to infection is giving his men access to women, who will give his soldiers hope that they can perpetuate the human race. When Jim objects to West's plan, his soldiers seize Hannah and Selena and prepare them to be raped while others take Jim outside to execute him in order to prevent his interference. Jim escapes and returns to the fortress, beating to death one of the soldiers who is about to rape Selena. Jim, Selena, and Hannah escape. After another 28 days, the three catch the attention of a military jet that is surveying the island for signs of life, and presumably, the trio is rescued.

While no dead return to life, viewers often place *28 Days Later* in the zombie subgenre because it possesses many of the characteristics that audiences have come to expect from zombie films. Set in a post-apocalyptic world filled with threatening transformed humans and where every social institution—religion, media, science, government, and the military—has failed to support and protect the people, the film introduces characters struggling with the desire to look out for themselves while still finding strength and hope in numbers. While not typical zombies, the infected share many similarities with the creature that operates by Romero's Rules: they do not communicate effectively and their wills are subordinated to the drive to tear apart any uninfected humans that they come into contact with. The infected also deviate significantly from Romero's Rules. The infected are alive, not undead; they eventually starve to death as the rage virus prevents them from even feeding themselves. But the infected zombie's speed is the most notable difference between themselves and prior representations of the creature. George Romero often gets credited for exploiting the metaphoric potential of the zombie to comment on human failures such as mindless consumption, consumerism, selfishness, and thoughtlessness. In its creative revision, *28 Days Later* adds savagery and vicious-ness to the list, characteristics that are communicated by the creature's speed and the name of the virus that animates it.

28 Days Later was a financial and critical success. With a budget of approxi-mately $8 million, the film has made almost $83 million worldwide. It won numer-ous awards, including the Saturn Award (The Academy of Science Fiction, Fantasy and Horror Films), the Empire Award for Best British Film, and the Narcisse Award for Best International Film. Boyle won the Grand Prize of European Fantasy Film in Silver and the International Fantasy Film Award for Best Director. The film also won awards for writing, cinematography, and acting, and was nominated for sev-eral others. Its success inspired a sequel, *28 Weeks Later* (2007), produced by Boyle, and directed by Juan Carlos Fresnadillo (1967–). The story picks up seven months after the initial outbreak, when the infected have starved to death; all seems to be under control. The U.S. Army is assisting in the United Kingdom's reconstruction. However, one of the returning refugees possesses a hereditary trait that makes her immune to symptoms of the virus, while still allowing her to be a carrier, and the pandemic begins anew, this time presumably to leave the British Isles and infect the world. *28 Weeks Later* enjoyed its own success at the box office, garnering approximately $64 million in profits. With the same style and tone as *28 Days Later,* the film was well received by critics and fans, winning the Empire Award for Best Horror and nominated for others. As of 2012, production has yet to start on the rumored third film, *28 Months Later.*

See also: Apocalypse; Epidemics; Existentialism; Gender; Romero's Rules

Tracy Stephenson Shaffer

UNDEAD EVIL

Undead Evil is a comic book series that tells the story of Alfred Carter, set in post–Hurricane Katrina New Orleans. After his mother dies, Alfred ventures into the attic of the family home that has been a forbidden place for decades. In the attic he finds an old travel chest owned by an ancestor, Maximillian Carter, a ruthless plantation owner at the turn of the 19th century. Carter also uncovers a family curse that involves deformed progeny and vengeful Voodoo-based zombies.

When Alfred opens the chest, he discovers an old album, a goblet, a top hat, and a book written in a strange text. As Alfred deciphers the work, it becomes clear that what he is reading is the story of devil worship and the practice of the dark arts. After two years of studying the book of magic, Maximillian appears to Alfred in a dream with a story and a warning. Maximillian tells the story of his beautiful daughter Augusta, kidnapped, raped, and almost killed by one of his slaves. When the slave was apprehended, Maximillian and his men tortured him for weeks before finally killing him. But the slave, Jean Jacques Laveau, was a powerful houngan, a Voodoo practitioner of the black arts, and his followers brought him back from the dead as a vengeful zombie after he was executed by Maximillian. Once raised, Laveau placed a curse on the Carter family, and soon all the direct descendants of the Carter family were born with hideous deformities. After years of battle with the undead, Laveau was contained within a tomb and the curse was momentarily contained. However, that is about to change, according to Maximillian, who ends his story with a dire warning of a terrible storm soon to hit the city of New Orleans, where Laveau will be released and once again unleash his fury upon the Carter family line. Maximillian then infects Alfred with a thirst for revenge that cannot be denied.

The next morning Alfred wakes up from his nightmare and finds that the city of New Orleans has been hit by Hurricane Katrina. Alfred immediately sets out for the Big Easy. As he travels through the devastated city, he ignores the suffering caused by the storm in his haste to find his blood relations and stop the zombie curse. Alfred makes his way to the French Quarter, where he finds the descendant of one of the great voodoo queens, Madame Bazin, who insists that Maximillian's tale was filled with lies. Confused, Alfred decides he will receive no help from her and goes in search of his relatives. His family, who appears to have fallen on hard times, welcomes him into their home, ending Issue No. 0. In Issue No. 1, Arthur explains his purpose to his family, who all appear to have physical or mental challenges, except for the lovely Magnolia, the doppelgänger of Maximillian's doomed daughter Augusta. The family demands he give them the book of magic, stolen from them by their Yankee cousins; Arthur puts them off, ending Issue No. 1.

Undead Evil was originally released in hard copy as a small print run by Asylum Press in July 2007 with the title *Undead Evil: Special Edition No. 0.* It was re-released digitally in July 2013 as *Undead Evil No. 1,* with changes that included an epilogue highlighting the zombies, expanded artwork, and storyline during Maximillian's narration of his daughter's defilement and his killing of Laveau. The 2013 version also includes an expanded ending in which Arthur is introduced to his family and explains his purpose in seeking them out. In the 2013 digital comic, an epilogue is included featuring two unidentified men with hunting rifles in a swampy area surrounded by zombies. They are eventually turned to zombies, and the scene shifts to the story of Alfred Carter. This was not included in the 2007 print run.

See also: Graphic Novels and Comics; Voodoo

Alicia Ahlvers

UNIVERSAL STUDIOS

Universal Studios has been synonymous with horror, more than any other major movie production and distribution studio; however, in its early history it failed to capitalize on the (Voodoo) zombie craze in the 1930s and 1940s. Bela Lugosi's three zombie films were produced by studio rivals Monogram Pictures (*Bowery at Midnight* [1942] and *Voodoo Man* [1944]) and RKO (*Zombies on Broadway* [1945]). In more recent years, the studio has distributed some of the most popular and iconic zombie, and zombie-like character-related films. These include *Phantasm II* (1988), *The People under the Stairs* (1991), *Death Becomes Her* (1992), *Army of Darkness* (1992), *Phantasm III* (1994), *Dawn of the Dead* (2004), and *Shaun of the Dead* (2004).

Universal Studios Incorporated, also known as Universal Pictures, is one of the six major movie studios. The oldest movie studio in the United States, Universal was founded in 1912 by Carl Laemmle (born Karl Lämmle, 1867–1939) and others. An early nickelodeon owner, in 1909, he founded the Yankee Film Company, which evolved into the Independent Moving Pictures Company, producing some of the first films in the early 20th century. The Universal Film Manufacturing Company was founded in 1912, and Laemmle became president; after a buy-out of his partners, Laemmle created Universal Studio to handle movie production, distribution, and exhibition venues. In 1915, Laemmle opened the largest production facility, Universal City Studios, which became the largest studio in Hollywood, for a decade. In 1945, the British entrepreneur J. Arthur Rank (born Joseph Arthur Rank, 1888–1972) bought into a merger with Universal, culminating in the studio's eventual reorganization as Universal-International. William Goetz (1903–1969), a founder of International, stopped the studio's low-budget production of horror films. By the late 1940s, Goetz was ousted for losing money, and the studio returned to low-budget films. In 2004, the controlling stake in the company was sold to General Electric, parent of NBC, resulting in the creation of the super-conglomerate NBC Universal.

Lon Chaney (born Leonidas Frank Chaney, 1883–1930) was Universal's big draw in the 1920s. The management genius of Irving Thalberg (born Irving Grant Thalberg, 1899–1936), studio chief, and animation genius of Walt Disney (born Walter Elias Disney, 1901–1966) gave the studio stability in the industry, with Disney's co-creating the character Oswald the Lucky Rabbit. However, when Disney and Thalberg left (both over money issues), Universal lost both its foothold in animation and its effective management, a consequence that lasted decades. In the 1930s, Laemmle's son (Carl Laemmle Jr. [born Julius Laemmle, 1908–1979]) began to update the studio, converting it to sound production and high-quality production. He also introduced the Universal horror line: *Dracula* (1931), *Frankenstein* (1931), *The Mummy* (1932), and *The Invisible Man* (1933). Laemmle Jr. was known for lavish spending on film projects, and his 1936 filming of *Showboat* ultimately put the studio into receivership with the Standard Capital Corporation in that year.

New president J. Cheever Cowdin (born John Cheever Cowdin, 1889–1960) instituted severe cuts in production budgets. By the early 1940s, lower-budget productions like horror pictures were the emphasis. These included *The Black Cat* (1934), Universal's biggest box office hit of the year which paired Lugosi and Boris Karloff; *Bride of Frankenstein* (1935), which starred Karloff; *The Raven* (1935), again pairing Karloff and Lugosi; *Werewolf of London* (1935); *Dracula's Daughter* (1936); *The Invisible Ray* (1936), with Karloff and Lugosi; *Night Key* (1937), a science fiction crime film with Karloff; *Son of Frankenstein* (1939), featuring Karloff as the Monster and Lugosi as Ygor; *The Invisible Man Returns* (1940); *The House of the Seven Gables* (1940), starring Vincent Price; *The Mummy's Hand* (1940); *The Invisible Woman* (1940), a horror crime comedy; *Man-Made Monster* (1941), the debut horror film for Lon Chaney Jr. (born Creighton Tull Chaney, 1906–1973) about a man immune to electricity who is experimented on to create an army of electrobiologically sustained undead zombies; *The Black Cat* (1941); *The Wolf Man* (1941), with Chaney Jr. and Lugosi; *The Ghost of Frankenstein* (1942), also with Chaney Jr. and Lugosi; *Night Monster* (1942), with Lugosi; *The Mummy's Tomb* (1942), with Chaney Jr.; *Frankenstein Meets the Wolf Man* (1943), with Chaney Jr. and Lugosi (as Frankenstein's monster); *Son of Dracula* (1943), with Chaney Jr.; *The Invisible Man's Revenge* (1944); *The Mummy's Ghost* (1944); *House of Frankenstein* (1944); *The Mummy's Curse* (1944); *House of Dracula* (1945); *House of Horrors* (1946); and *Abbott and Costello Meet Frankenstein* (1948).

See also: *Bowery at Midnight*; *Dawn of the Dead*; *Evil Dead* Series; Hammer Film Productions; Lugosi, Bela; *Mummy, The*; *Phantasm* Series; *Shaun of the Dead*; Voodoo Man; *Zombies on Broadway*

Anthony J. Fonseca

VAMPIRES AND WEREWOLVES

Vampires and werewolves have their beginnings in basically the same folklore, that of the shape-shifter creature which possesses some kind of affinity with the wolf. In addition, vampires have always been related to zombies in that they are both examples of the corporeal reanimated dead. The relationship between werewolves and zombies is a relatively new one, established in 2002 when Danny Boyle's *28 Days Later* introduced the idea of the fast, ferocious, mutated (rather than undead) zombie. The creatures in Boyle's film are more similar to the werewolf than to the vampire, in fact more similar to the werewolf than to previous iterations of the zombie, in how they interact with and dispose of human victims. Both vampires and werewolves share with zombies the mythology of passing on their inhuman conditions through a bite.

While vampires and werewolves are both mythological, or folkloric, they differ in that vampires feed on some type of human essence, usually blood (although this can vary per fiction). The term vampire became popular in the 18th century, based on European folklore, namely that of the Eastern Europe. Some of these vampires were often quite decrepit physically, resembling zombies in that they were bloated corpses. In fact, one of the elements common in European vampire is the bloated appearance, sometimes coupled with a purplish or dark color due to the recent blood feast. In some legends, they are represented as having blood leaking from their mouths and noses. John Polidori's (born John William Polidori, 1795–1821) *The Vampyre* (1819) established the modern prototype; vampires afterward would be represented as being charismatic, sophisticated, and beautiful (with some notable exceptions). If there is one vampire fiction which can claim the title of benchmark or classic, it would be Bram Stoker's *Dracula* (1897), the novel that rewrote the vampire and which all subsequent vampire texts must invoke. The vampire is related to the loop-garou, a shape-shifting creature that is a mixture of French and African Voodoo belief.

The loop-garou is common in myths of the Caribbean Islands and Louisiana and is a version of the werewolf. Werewolves, also known as lycanthropes (from the Greek words for wolf and man), like vampires, have a special relationship with animals, especially those in the *Canis lupus* family. While the vampire can shape shift into a wolf, the werewolf can shape shift into a hybrid creature. The werewolf has little in common with either the Voodoo zombie or the traditional undead zombie which follows Romero's Rules. However, it shares many common traits with the mutated, fast zombies made popular by the *28 Days Later* series, especially the tendency to rip bodies limb from limb and eat the parts (in some myths werewolves devour recently buried corpses). Reports of werewolf attacks date back at least as far as 16th-century France, and these attacks normally include murder and cannibalism, although one could argue that werewolves were an integral part of witch trials, as early as the 15th century. Werewolves are usually gendered male; however, some stories have old women as werewolves, complete with poisonous claws (poison being the usual weapon for women) and a paralyzing gaze.

The blending of the vampire and or the werewolf with the zombie is seen in some zombie fiction produced over the past half decade. For example, the undead in Richard Matheson's novella *I Am Legend* (1954) believe themselves to be vampires, as this mythology is the only frame of reference they have to explain why they have reanimated after their deaths and are allergic to sunlight and garlic. As a consequence, they try to drink the blood of the living, and many who were Christians in life fear crosses. Nevertheless, the undead are more similar to zombies in that they are filthy and mindless. The undead in Jim Mickle's film *Stake Land* (2010) are also similar to vampires in how they must be staked in order to be destroyed, yet they are also like the werewolf in their ferocity. The zombies in Garth Ennis's graphic novel series *Crossed* are more similar to werewolves as well given how the infected are extremely violent and their boil-covered countenances are transformed into a permanent snarl that is characteristic of a viscous animal.

See also: Africa; Cannibalism; *I Am Legend* (Novel); Romero's Rules; *Stake Land*; *28 Days Later* Series; Voodoo

Anthony J. Fonseca

VIDEO GAMES

Video games have been a recent foray for zombie fandom, perhaps riding the wave of zombies in visual media, which has recently altered the film industry. The creation of one major franchise, as well as the expansion and failure of other companies, has hinged on the success of their zombie-themed games. The first official mainstream zombie video game, *Zombie Zombie,* was released by ZX Spectrum. The game utilized cutting-edge 3D technology, and a player's objective was to clear out the zombies within its fictional city, using an air rifle. Despite the fact that *Zombie Zombie* had only a limited release in Europe and was never sold in the United States or converted for other platforms, it left a legacy of first-person action horror gaming, with its story and strategy laying the groundwork for all future zombie first-person video games.

The idea of zombies as video game fodder began to evolve, with the undead becoming star players and even protagonists in later games. The *Monkey Island* series, created in 1990, started featuring zombies with its second game, *LeChuck's Revenge* (1991), whose storyline includes a pirate captain who was transformed via a hex. The *Monkey Island* games were one of the first to provide a backstory for the zombies' origin. While many modern zombie games rely upon a medical or military experiment gone wrong as an origin story, the *Monkey Island* games go a more traditional route, with a Voodoo curse. In 1992, *Wolfenstein 3D* introduced the first modified zombie opponent in a video game. Here, the undead have weapons attached to their bodies, a change which upped the ante for players. The arcade version of this game was highly popular. Similarly, *House of the Dead* (1997) is a still-popular arcade shooting game where the player takes on a variety of undead denizens of a manor. Currently, one of the most popular arcade and console video games is *Mortal Kombat* (1992), a franchise that has seen many alterations and some reboots in order to maintain player interest. Main character Liu Kang was transformed into a zombie for the sequel *Mortal Kombat: Deception*. However, due to the popularity of his character as one of the original fighters, he was restored to pre-undead life in the franchise's next game. Also in 1992, LucasArts released *Zombies Ate My Neighbors*, a highly controversial game that required several tweaks before it was released in the United States and Europe. Unfortunately, the game was not as well received as anticipated and caused the company to restructure its decision making. The premise of the game is two teenagers attempt to save their neighborhood from zombies. The game was available for several platforms, including Sega Genesis and Super Nintendo.

By 2012, the most widely known zombie video game was *Resident Evil* (1996). Cross-promotional products and films have turned the video game into a franchise, beginning with a game in 1996 that was stylistically similar to other survival horror game. *Resident Evil* provided the player with opportunities for expanded play and followed a movie-like story arc. In the years after its release, the franchise has been responsible for 14 games that are currently available on numerous platforms, as well as graphic novels, books, five films, and a plethora of affiliated merchandise. It has, undoubtedly, been the most profitable zombie video game to date. *Resident Evil* also cemented the position of the PlayStation as the premiere gaming console of the time. During the same year that it was released, another game became available to arcade goers in America and Europe. *The House of the Dead,* unlike its cohort, was a streamlined shooting game. The player followed an uncontrollable path filled with the undead and shot as many as possible. More a test of shot accuracy than strategy, this game was enjoyed for its in-your-face graphics and the simulated fright of a persistent zombie onslaught. *The Typing of the Dead* (1999), an educational game designed to teach players how to type, was modeled after *The House of the Dead*.

More recently, the video game industry has endured innovative and successful as well as tarnished moments. One of the greatest disappointments for zombie game aficionados was the cancellation of George Romero's *City of the Dead*. After a year of promotional efforts and design, the video game was previewed at the 2005 E3 entertainment convention. It was not yet completed, however, when the company responsible for production, Hip Interactive, experienced significant financial losses. Also released in 2005, Stubbs the Zombie in *Rebel without a Pulse* blurred the lines between horror and comedy in video gaming. Featuring a 1950s salesman-turned zombie as the protagonist, the game was the first to have a zombie as the primary player option. The player, as Stubbs, must amass an army of undead to assist with seeking out his lost love and getting his vengeance on the retro-futuristic town where he was murdered. In 2006, zombie video games became more innovative. *Dead Rising,* modeled after the seminal zombie film *Dawn of the Dead* (1978), features a protagonist battling hordes of zombies in a shopping mall. Its sequel sets the zombies and the players in a Vegas-like landscape complete with casinos, showgirls, and strategically attached weaponry.

Left 4 Dead, released in 2008, marked another milestone in zombie video game development. This game allows players to participate in the game as a zombie. While it was not the first game to provide this option, it was the most graphically successful. Another innovation in zombie video games occurred in 2008, with the secret level being unlocked in *Call of Duty: World at War.* This level, Nazi Zombies, uses a basic zombie game premise. The player must defend a small area from an increasing horde of zombies. Due to its popularity, Treyarch released several expansions for extended play. Director George Romero is a zombie character in this game, where his nickname is The Father of All Zombies. *Plants vs. Zombies,* released in 2006 for computers and as an iPhone app, allows players to grow a garden of different plants that have defense mechanisms in order to protect their home from zombies. The game's bright colors and cheerful music, as well as the ease of play and cartoonish appearance of the zombies, have made it popular for a variety of age and gaming skill levels. These features were responsible for making it one of the highest grossing apps. One of the most popular and financially successful multiplayer online games, *World of Warcraft* (1994), features a type of zombie as one of the primary playable races. The Undead are a faction of the Horde and the product of an infection passed on by the Scourge, a nefarious group controlled by The Lich King. Players see the Undead as sympathetic characters, cursed by the games "big bad." There are entire maps within the game devoted to areas where the Scourge have tainted the landscape, and players from all factions and races, including the Undead, must work to cleanse the land. The culmination of the game's third expansion is an extensive raid on the citadel where The Lich King, an undead paladin, resides. This raid requires players to invest hundreds of hours of playtime for preparation, acquirement of gear, and strategizing as well as cooperative play. In proceeding expansions, the Undead are still struggling to cleanse their land as a dragon wreaks havoc upon the world's inhabitants.

See also: Dawn of the Dead; Left 4 Dead; Plants vs. Zombies; Resident Evil (Video Game); Romero, George; Zombies Ate My Neighbors

Celise A. Reech-Harper

VOODOO

Voodoo developed at the height of the slave trade during the 18th century. Also called vodoun, vodou, voudou, vodu, and hoodoo, it is a syncretization of Roman Catholicism and West African spiritual beliefs and is the dominant religion of Haiti, where some 90 percent of the population follows the belief system. The word Voodoo derives from a term in the Fon language of Dahomey and means spirit. Voodoo comprises a set of complex beliefs in a close relationship between one's ancestors and the spirit world. In the Voodoo belief system, Bondyè (whose name means the good god) is the being who created the world; his powers, however, are manifested through the loas, or spirits. The primary function of male (houngans) and female (mambos) Voodoo priests is the practice of benevolent magic to heal the infirm, but they also perform rituals intended to pacify the loas, cast spells, create protection devices, initiate new priests, and read dreams. Houngans and mambos may also be sorcerers, and they are called bokurs and caplatas, respectively. In addition to practicing benevolent magic, they can practice black magic, like fashioning zombies. The vast majority of priests, however, are dedicated to magic of the benevolent kind. Dancing and the accompaniment of drums, as well as, at times, the sacrifice of animals, are staples of Voodoo services, in which it is not uncommon to witness the possession of a participant's body by loas.

All scholarly descriptions and definitions of the zombie agree that a zombie's body is resurrected by unknown means. However, Haitian Voodoo zombies are people who did not die at all but in whom an artificial state of death was induced by poisoning or some evil enchantment, then afterward were buried alive, exhumed, and reclaimed by their masters. The word Voodoo, while not preferred most by cultural anthropologists and linguists, is the term generally recognized internationally. Following the publication of William Seabrook's *The Magic Island* (1929), and with Hollywood's help, the word has ever since been associated with maliciousness and the figure of the zombie. The zombie, also referred to as the zombie or jumby, is the exemplar of Voodoo's pervasiveness in mainstream culture. Films like *White Zombie* (1932), followed by *Revolt of the Zombies* (1936), *King of the Zombies* (1941), and *Revenge of the Zombies* (1943), firmly cemented the zombie among Hollywood's other creature-feature superstars like Dracula, Frankenstein's monster, The Mummy, The Creature from the Black Lagoon, and The Wolfman. The 1943 film *I Walked with a Zombie*, a zombie retelling of *Jane Eyre*, was RKO Pictures' attempt to cash in on the popularity of the horror films made by rival studio Universal. Hammer Studios' 1966 film *Plague of the Zombies* is a zombie retelling of *Dracula*.

The noticeably foreign, early screen zombies of Voodoo origins, while much evolved from their historical roots, have retained still particular features of their Haitian ancestry. An example worth considering is the Haitian belief that zombies are recognizable by the nasal speech they produce, a feature shared, too, by the Gede, or gods of death and the cemetery; generally, zombies communicate very little or not at all. Another common feature that has transcended folklore is the zombie's ravenous hunger for flesh and life. Media events in the late 1980s brought Voodoo and zombification mainstream attention. Wade Davis, an ethnobiologist, published in 1985 *The Serpent and the Rainbow,* a book centered on the Haitian zombie and the use of ethnobotanical poisons as a pharmacological origin for zombification. In 1988, Davis more fully explained his findings in a book titled *Passage of Darkness: The Ethnobiology of the Haitian Zombie.* The discovery of Clairvius Narcisse in 1981, a Haitian man who claimed to have been zombie after being drugged, buried alive, taken out of the grave, then enslaved, inspired Davis's research. The Haitian Diaspora has helped the Voodoo belief system to reach other parts of the world, particularly France, Canada, and the United States. On April 3, 2003, the government of Haiti officially recognized Voodoo as a religion.

See also: Africa; Bokur/Caplata; Davis, Wade; Haiti; Hurston, Zora Neale; *I Walked with a Zombie*; Narcisse, Clairvius; *Plague of the Zombies, The*; Seabrook, W. B.; *Undead Evil*; *White Zombie*

John Edgar Browning

VOODOO MAN

Voodoo Man is a 1944 film directed by William Beaudine (born William Washington Beaudine, 1892–1970), arguably Hollywood's all-time most prolific director, who took over for Phil Rosen (born Philip E. Rosen, 1888–1951), when he was unable to complete the project. It starred horror mainstays Bela Lugosi and John Carradine. Of the Lugosi-related Poverty Row Voodoo zombie films, *Voodoo Man* is considered the best, as the characters are sympathetic and somewhat tragic, with Lugosi playing his role—as a doctor who has lost his beloved wife—for pathos.

A filling station owner aids Dr. Richard Marlowe, a mad scientist, in capturing young women from a dark and deserted highway, using a false exit. Marlowe hopes to use his knowledge of Voodoo and the black arts on the women to transfer their life force to his zombified, dead wife. Another assistant, the simple-minded Toby, played by John Carradine, assists in the Voodoo ceremonies by playing tribal rhythms on congas. He places the women in a state of suspended animation with the goal of restoring his wife, brain dead now for two decades, to her normal self, which he succeeds in doing briefly at times. The wife is eventually resurrected but dies again when Marlowe is shot by police. The girls who had been placed in zombified trances so that their life force could be stolen recover. In a metatextual twist, the film ends when a Hollywood screenwriter Ralph Dawson tries to stop the mad doctor from stealing the life from his girlfriend and ends up penning a script based on the experience, suggesting that none other than Lugosi should play his Voodoo doctor. Other metatextual moments hint that the film was intended to be an inside joke, rather than a straightforward horror movie: Dawson is a writer working for Banner Productions, the company that produced the film, distributed by Monogram Pictures; Dawson works for a man known only as S. K., an allusion to the film's co-producer Sam Katzman (1901–1973), chief executive at Banner/Monogram; and the film references contemporary zombie movies, including *White Zombie* (1932), which starred Lugosi in a similar role. Carradine's performance plays up his character's loneliness.

The film's zombies are less scary than exploitative. Dr. Marlowe creates a legion of sexy, entranced young women who walk around blankly, or simply stand around, almost as props. The film does contain an early example of an undead zombie, Marlowe's resurrected wife. *Voodoo Man* is also noteworthy in that none of the zombies get revenge on their maker in its conclusion. Instead, Marlowe is defeated by bumbling lawmen, and all characters are returned to their normal states of life or death.

See also: Lugosi, Bela; Universal Studios; Voodoo

Anthony J. Fonseca

WALKING DEAD, THE (COMIC)

The Walking Dead is an ongoing, monthly comic book series published by Image Comics since 2003. It recounts the struggles of Deputy Sheriff Rick Grimes and other survivors of a zombie apocalypse. Robert Kirkman created and writes the black-and-white series, with the first six issues illustrated by Tony Moore (born Michael Anthony Moore, 1978–). Issues number seven to the present are penciled and inked by Charlie Adlard (born Charles Adlard, 1966–). The series has inspired a television show on The American Movie Classics and associated web episodes, along with video games, novelizations, and other merchandise. Kirkman establishes in the first volume of the series, *Days Gone Bye* (2004), his intention to craft a sprawling epic, an ongoing narrative that explores how characters would grow, develop, and change over the course of a seemingly never-ending zombie apocalypse. So far, *The Walking Dead* is indeed the longest sustained zombie narrative in existence.

Kirkman begins *The Walking Dead* like many other apocalypse narratives—with the protagonist waking in a hospital to a world turned upside down. After being shot on duty, Deputy Grimes had lain in a coma while an unspecified cause reanimated the dead and overran the country with contagious zombies. He immediately seeks out his family, a theme that recurs throughout the comic's run, and when he finds his home abandoned, he heads to Atlanta in search of his wife Lori and his son Carl. Once there, Rick meets up with not only them but also, among others, his police partner Shane, a young man named Glenn, a retiree named Dale, a young woman named Andrea, and a little girl, Sophia. The series follows the journeys of this core group of survivors as they initially try to find help and, later, simply a place to live in safety.

Aside from the zombies, the comic features a number of increasingly dangerous and malicious human antagonists. The first is Shane, who resents Rick's return because of the affair he has initiated with Lori. Carl is forced to shoot and kill Shane in order to protect his father, establishing a key theme in the series: sometimes one has to kill to stay alive. The surviving group soon leaves Atlanta, picking up others along the way, including a resourceful man named Tyreese and his daughter Julie. They spend some time at a farm owned by Hershel, a deeply religious man, and Rick eventually invites him and his family, notably his daughter Maggie, to join the larger group at an abandoned prison. Although the group believes that they are safe behind the fortified fences, Rick learns he must establish a sense of martial law to protect his people from others, such as the murderous prisoners Thomas and Dexter.

The relative peace and stability of the prison stronghold is soon challenged by the megalomaniacal leader of Woodbury, a nearby community. This psychopath, who calls himself simply The Governor, captures and tortures Rick and Michonne, a katana-wielding survivalist who joined the group at the prison. The two groups go to war over territory and supplies, and for personal vengeance, after Michonne mutilates The Governor, Rick kills the Woodbury spy Martinez, and The Governor executes Tyreese. In a violent battle at the prison, The Governor drives a tank through the fences, scatters Rick's group, and murders Lori and her newborn daughter Judith. Woodbury resident who witnesses the act is horrified and shoots and kills The Governor, but the damage is already done.

The survivors of the prison eventually reunite and continue their wanderings, soon joining a group heading for Washington D.C. led by Abraham, an army sergeant, and Eugene, a former science teacher who claims he has information about the cause of the zombie plague. As the new group heads northeast, they encounter a violent band of cannibals, who capture, dismember, and eat Dale. Rick leads his group on a rescue mission, and they dispassionately slaughter the cannibalistic hunters. Rick's dwindling group makes it to the Alexandria Free-Zone, a fortified residential community (outside Washington D.C.) established and run by Douglas Monroe, a former U.S. Congressman. After indulging in so much mistrust and violence, Rick and his team find it difficult to integrate into the community, but upon the death of Monroe in a zombie attack, Rick becomes the new leader of the Free-Zone. He establishes something of a diplomatic trade relationship with a nearby group of survivors from Hilltop Colony, led by Gregory. Both groups, however, find themselves at the mercy of Negan, a powerful warlord and the leader of a group called the Saviors. To force Rick to recognize his power and authority, Negan brutally murders Glenn, and Rick pretends to agree to Negan's terms of submission and tribute. However, Rick begins to organize an alliance with both Hilltop Colony and another oppressed community, The Kingdom. With the help of the latter group's King Ezekiel, Rick plans the overthrow of Negan.

More than any other zombie apocalypse narrative, *The Walking Dead* explores in detail what it would take to survive in a violent and lawless society. Thanks to the popularity of the narrative, many adaptations, prequels, and games based on *The Walking Dead* abound, including the television series *The Walking Dead* (2010–); the video games *The Walking Dead* (2012), *The Walking Dead: Assault* (2012), and *The Walking Dead: Survival Instinct* (2013); and three novelizations written by Kirkman and horror author Jay Bonansinga (1988–): *Rise of the Governor* (2011), *The Road to Woodbury* (2012), and *Fall of the Governor* (2013).

See also: Apocalypse; Cannibalism; Gender; Graphic Novels and Comics; *Night of the Living Dead* Series; Romero's Rules; Television; Video Games; *Walking Dead, The* (Television Series)

Kyle William Bishop

WALKING DEAD, THE (TELEVISION SERIES)

The Walking Dead (2010–) is a U.S. television serial produced by American Movie Classics (AMC). It is relatively faithful to the epic graphic novel series of the same name (2003–) by Robert Kirkman, on which it is based. The series was originally created by Frank Darabont (born Darabont Ferenc, 1959–). Like the comic, the television show chronicles the adventures of Deputy Sheriff Rick Grimes and his family and friends as they struggle to survive a global pandemic that turns dead humans into flesh-eating zombies. Rick and his companions fight the undead, malicious human enemies, and occasionally each other.

The first season of *The Walking Dead,* just six episodes, depicts Rick's journey from his hometown to Atlanta to a Centers for Disease Control and Prevention (CDC) installation. After being shot, Rick awakens from a coma in an abandoned hospital that is swarming with reanimated and violent corpses. He returns home to find his wife Lori and son Carl missing; however, he presumes they have traveled to Atlanta. After learning about the undead, called walkers, from a neighbor, Rick gathers weapons and supplies from the sheriff's station and rides for Atlanta on horseback. The city is overrun with undead, and Rick must be rescued from hundreds of ravenous zombies by a group of resourceful survivors, but he finds

In this cast poster from Season 3 of AMC's *The Walking Dead* series, Sheriff Rick Grimes (Andrew Lincoln) continues to fight to protect his friends and family from both the undead and other members of the living who would threaten their lives in this post-apocalyptic world. *The Walking Dead* has been renewed for a fifth season. (AMC/Photofest)

himself at violent odds with one of them, a racist ex-convict named Merle. The group escapes an attack, and Rick reunites with Lori and Carl, along with his resentful ex-police partner Shane, who had been sleeping with his presumably dead partner's wife. The group unites under Rick's leadership and travels to the CDC, where they encounter Dr. Jenner, who reveals that the world's governments have collapsed in the face of an insurmountable virus that is creating zombies. Jenner thinks suicide is the only solution, but before he destroys the facility, he lets Rick and his group go.

The 13-episode second season takes place primarily on Hershel Greene's farm, but it begins with the remains of Rick's group leaving the CDC. While scavenging for parts and supplies, the group must hide from a gigantic herd of zombies, and one of their members, a little girl named Sophia, disappears in the confusion. Carl is accidentally shot by Otis, a hunter, as the group searches the woods for Sophia. Otis takes Carl to Hershel for medical attention, as he was once a veterinarian, and is now the closest thing they have to a physician. Hershel reluctantly agrees to let Rick's group camp on his property while Carl recovers, and they continue to search for Sophia. Otis takes Shane into town to find medical supplies, but when they are cornered by walkers, Shane further reveals his duplicitous nature when he shoots Otis in the leg, leaving him to bait the zombies while he escapes. Glenn, another member of Rick's group, begins to fraternize with Hershel's daughter Maggie. Meanwhile, Lori discovers that she is pregnant, and Glenn learns that Hershel's locked barn is filled with reanimated family, neighbors, and even strangers, as Hershel believes that one day there will be a cure for their condition. Glenn eventually tells the group about the walkers in Hershel's barn. While Rick agrees to live on the farm on Hershel's terms, including tolerating the presence of the undead among them, Shane goes into a rage, breaking open the barn's doors and executing the zombies. To everyone's shock, Sophia staggers out of the barn as a walker, and a defeated Rick shoots her in the head. Shane becomes increasingly unstable. A walker mortally wounds Dale, who is euthanized at his request. Rick stabs and kills Shane in a fight; Shane reanimates as a walker, and Carl shoots the new zombie in the head. The gunplay at the farm attracts a herd of walkers, and zombies overwhelm the encampment. As Rick reorganizes his team, he reveals that Jenner told him that all of the living are infected with the virus and all will rise from the dead regardless of how they die. In the very last episode of the second season, a mysterious hooded figure, later revealed to be the comic book fan favorite Michonne, is introduced.

The Walking Dead's 16-episode third season sees Rick's group settle down in a prison facility while combating the megalomaniacal man called The Governor, who leads the nearby Woodbury compound. After a hard winter, Rick's team finds a prison, and they begin to exterminate the walkers inside the fences in preparation for taking over the facility. They discover five prisoners hiding in the cafeteria, and although Rick initially agrees to share the facility with them, he is uncomfortable about sharing his living space with convicts. A fight soon ensues between the two groups in which the remaining prisoners are driven from the prison. Some of these prisoners find the Woodbury compound where The Governor welcomes them after they reveal to him the existence of the place they were driven from, which contains valuable weapons and supplies. Back at the prison, another walker attack results in more deaths, while Lori dies after an emergency C-section and must be shot by Carl to keep from reanimating. One of The Governor's men captures Maggie and Glenn, part of Rick's group, while they are scavenging a nearby town for baby formula for Lori's orphaned baby. The Governor's men torture Maggie and Glenn for more information about the prison. Meanwhile, Michonne, who only recently arrived in Woodbury and distrusts The Governor, decides to leave the community. She discovers the prison and joins Rick's community, telling him that The Governor is holding two members of his group and encouraging him to lead a small team to rescue them. During the raid in which Maggie and Glenn are rescued, Michonne takes The Governor's eye, something that prompts him to lead his heavily armed people to attack the prison community in revenge. After various battles, major characters are captured and manage to escape, and The Governor, losing control of his community, leads a second assault against the prison, but Rick's group ambushes them. Afterward, The Governor pursues his own retreating forces, slaughtering almost all of them for their alleged cowardice in battle. Rick allows the survivors of the now splintered Woodbury group to join the prison community, but The Governor remains at large.

The Walking Dead explores the strains a zombie apocalypse would place on human survivors over an extended period of time. In fact, the series is more about living people than zombies, as the walking dead of the title actually refers to the struggling humans. In addition to the regular broadcast series, AMC has produced two sets of webisodes, *Torn Apart* (2011) and *Cold Storage* (2012), and aired a post-broadcast talk show called *Talking Dead* (2011–). A video game developed by Terminal Reality, *The Walking Dead: Survival Instinct* (Activision, 2013), recounts the prequel adventures of two brothers before they reach Atlanta. The show has enjoyed a record-setting viewership, with 12.4 million people watching the Season 3 finale. As a result of the series' popularity, AMC also airs *The Talking Dead*, a companion talk show, that runs immediately after the broadcast of original episodes on Sunday nights.

See also: Apocalypse; Cannibalism; Epidemics; *In the Flesh*; Romero's Rules; *Talking Dead, The*; Television; Video Games; *Walking Dead, The* (Comic)

Kyle William Bishop

WARM BODIES (FILM)

Warm Bodies is a film adaptation by Jonathan Levine of the 2011 novel of the same name by Isaac Marion. It transforms Marion's story from one that explores existentialism through the trope of the zombie into a Rom Zom Com, or romantic zombie comedy. While the novel is a loose retelling of William Shakespeare's *Romeo and Juliet*, Levine's film puts even greater emphasis on Shakespeare's text.

The film is the story of the zombie named R, played by Nicholas Hoult (1989–), and his love for the human Julie, played by Teresa Palmer (1986–), in a world where

In this zombie rewriting of *Romeo and Juliet*, the zombie R. (Nicholas Hoult) and the living girl Julie (Teresa Palmer) pursue their love in a world where contact between zombies and humans is forbidden. (Summit Entertainment/Photofest)

an unknown force has caused the dead to reanimate as zombies who operate very loosely under Romero's Rules. However, R deviates from these rules in that he is a sentient zombie who narrates the story. Still, the zombie R can no longer remember his full name, or his occupation, while living. R falls in love with a human named Julie after he sees her working with a team to scavenge prescription drugs in the ruined world outside of the fortified compound where she lives. He gets to know Julie better after he kills her boyfriend Perry, one of the mission's team members; he eats Perry's brain, thereby accessing his memories. When R sees that Julie is about to be eaten by his fellow zombies, he smears blood on her face to disguise her smell and takes her back to his space at the airport, where all of the local zombies congregate.

R and Julie are like Shakespeare's Romeo and Juliet in that they must explore their love over the objections of their families, in this case, the zombies and the humans, rather than the Montagues and the Capulets. Their relationship eventually revitalizes R, causing his heart to beat and making him lose his craving for human flesh, so that he becomes human again. R's transformation affects the other zombies as well when their hearts also start to beat, and they no longer desire human flesh. Meanwhile, the remaining humans are changed as well when they start to see the undead as afflicted humans who are worthy of their care rather than as zombies who are to be terminated with extreme prejudice.

Levine's film is relatively faithful to Marion's novel, but it does subtly change the characters. Marion's R wears a dress shirt and tie, indicating that in life he worked in an office or was some sort of low level manager. Levine's R, on the other hand, wears a hoodie, which R believes indicates that he was unemployed before he was turned into a zombie (although he cannot remember), and which also makes him seem younger, a teenager rather than a young adult. This change makes R a more believable Romeo in that his age is closer to Shakespeare's love-lorn Montague. Also, the *Romeo and Juliet* theme is better emphasized in the visual medium of film than in Marion's novel. While the dead wander among the living in the ruins of the now abandoned city, each has retreated to a relatively isolated space that is connected to his or her general way of experiencing the world. The zombies live at the airport, shuffling around the complex in a stupor in a way similar to how air travel has been represented as mind-numbing and estranging in films such as *Fight Club* (1999), where the nameless narrator loses all sense of time and even identity as he flies from airport to airport. The living, meanwhile, occupy the football stadium, a dwelling that emphasizes the vivacity induced by watching sports matches.

See also: Apocalypse; Cannibalism; Comedy; Rom Zom Com; Romero's Rules; Sentience

June Michele Pulliam

WARM BODIES (NOVEL)

Warm Bodies is an alternative fiction novel by Isaac Marion, published in 2011. It is based loosely on William Shakespeare's *Romeo and Juliet*. Set during a present-day zombie apocalypse, it is an example of the Rom Zom Com, or romantic zombie comedy subgenre, which was popularized with the 2004 film *Shaun of the Dead*. In Marion's fictional world, zombies and humans, rather than Montagues and Capulets, feud for survival: the zombie R and the human Julie fall in love. The novel is told through R's perspective, allowing readers to see how love can change a zombie and be the cure for the plague that has toppled civilization. R's zombie life is monotonous. Food has no savor, time has no meaning, and he has no feelings of affection. Following their leaders called the Boneys, or the elder zombies, the zombies bunker at the airport, planning to perpetuate their species. Stronger zombies conduct raiding parties into the city, feeding and bringing back human leftovers to the others. Zombie children attend school to learn how to take a human victim. R marries a zombie female, and the Boneys issue the new couple two children, even though R has no affection for his new wife or kids. Neither R nor his bride knows their names, since zombies have rudimentary language skills as they live a purely functional existence, and they all are part of a zombie collective where individuality is unimportant.

R meets Julie, who is part of a security detail sent out to kill zombies, during a foraging expedition. R kills Julie's boyfriend but falls in love with her after he takes a bite of the boy's brain and is privy to his memories of Julie. Smitten, R kidnaps Julie and brings her to the airport, concealing her from the other zombies while courting her. The power of language slowly returns to R, and he is suddenly able to appreciate beauty. However, the Boneys find out about their relationship and drive the two out of the enclave. R and Julie escape to the human compound controlled by her father, who similarly disapproves of their love. As the couple flees for their lives once again, Julie notices that R is losing his craving for human flesh, his complexion is less gray, and he can sometimes pass for human. When the two kiss, both are transformed: Julie's blue eyes and R's zombie gray eyes both change to a bright gold, and R's heart starts to beat anew. The couple then fights both Julie's father and the Boneys, who are more threatened by the potential changes to both zombies and humans than the potential danger. The novel ends with Julie and R's love offering a model for how both species can be changed, which will stop the apocalypse. In 2013, *Warm Bodies* was made into a movie of the same name, directed by Jonathan Levine. Marion, recording under the name Isaac Marion's Moon Colony, released a music CD called *Dead Children* in 2007; the author considers the CD a companion piece to *Warm Bodies*.

See also: Apocalypse; Cannibalism; Comedy; Existentialism; Romero's Rules; Sentience

June Michele Pulliam

WEAPONS

Weapons, or items used in the methods of killing zombies, vary greatly depending on the fictional world created by an author or director. Killing a zombie is no easy matter, in part, because the methods and weapons used depend on the type of zombie, especially considerations of whether it is a mutated and/or infected live human or one of the living dead.

Zombies created by Voodoo or other magical means are not cannibals and generally are not a danger to anyone unless they are carrying out a revenge plan for a bokur, so they usually do not have to be dispatched in an act of preemptive self-defense. This type of zombie is most commonly killed by feeding it salt, something that reminds it of its former human existence and sends it howling back to its grave. Zombies who operate by Romero's Rules, on the other hand, must be destroyed to preserve human life. These undead zombies, popularized in George Romero's *Night of the Living Dead* (1968), are most typically found in apocalyptic narratives, where the presence of the reanimated dead foretells the end of civilization as we know it. These zombies can be killed by only destroying their brains.

Moreover, zombies operating by Romero's Rules are usually cannibals who can turn the living into zombies with just one bite, so humans must kill en masse, stopping as many of them as possible in order to maximize their own chances for survival. In the fiction representing the first months of the zombie apocalypse, desperate survivors use whatever weaponry is handy to dispatch the undead. In the United States, with its high proportion of gun owners and liberal gun laws, the weapon of choice is a firearm. While handguns are readily available, however, they are not always reliable because the shooter must be in close proximity to the target to make an accurate head shot. If the shooter misses, then the zombie is close enough to attack. Rifles are more effective than handguns for killing the undead because they allow shooters to hit their targets from a long distance. If the first shot misses the target, then the shooter has time to reload and try again before the zombie gets close enough to attack. For this reason, rifles are the weapon of choice in the recent post-apocalyptic film *Fido* (2006), where even children are trained in the use of firearms to protect them from zombies, and they can earn merit badges for rifle marksmanship. Nevertheless, handguns are useful as well because they can be easily carried and aimed in case of sudden zombie attack.

In countries with strict gun laws, survivors must find other weapons to defend themselves against zombies. In the British film *Shaun of the Dead* (2004), for example, the titular protagonist uses a cricket bat to bash in the brains of zombies since in the United Kingdom, citizens are not typically armed, and few even know how to properly use a firearm. A running question in the film is whether the Winchester rifle above the bar of Shaun's favorite pub, which has been named for this weapon, is even functional, or if British law required the owner to disable the gun before displaying it. This question underscores how differently a zombie invasion would be dealt with in a nation where citizens do not typically possess firearms. When Shaun and his friends eventually learn that the rifle is loaded, their incompetent shooting is comical in contrast to American films where anyone can conventionally pick up a firearm with little training and hit a target on the first try, often while shooting in a stance that would make accuracy less likely. The scarcity of guns in the United Kingdom causes survivor to use machetes to kill zombies in the film *28 Days Later* (2002). The only people with guns are the military, and their access to weaponry makes them brutal in comparison to the civilians who must also defend themselves against zombies. In the British miniseries *In the Flesh*, the armed militia is far more brutal than the zombies that they are supposedly defending themselves from.

However, using firearms to kill zombies ceases to be a viable option in post-apocalyptic fictional universes where civilization has collapsed and there are no longer reliable means of shipping and manufacturing ammunition. As a consequence, ammunition becomes a scarce commodity and must be husbanded. The characters in the television series *The Walking Dead* (2010–) grapple with this reality. While firearms are still useful for mowing down zombie hordes, other means not requiring ammunition are preferable. These methods include shooting the zombies in the head with a cross bow (and then retrieving the arrow), bashing in the skull of the zombie, and cutting off the head with a katana. Much of the narrative is devoted to the best way of killing zombies. Shooting is not the preferred method for dispatching the undead in the universe of *The Walking Dead* since ammunition is becoming scarce, and the sound of gunshots functions like a "dinner bell" for zombies, alerting them that there are humans nearby.

In Max Brooks's novel *World War Z* (2006), struggling military units and bands of civilians also grapple with the reality of a dwindling supply of ammunition. Arthur Sinclair Jr., the U.S. wartime minister of the Department of Strategic Resources, explains how the U.S. Marines fabricated a tool they dubbed the lobotomizer. The lobotomizer is made from recycled steel from cars and resembles the fusion of a shovel and a double-headed battle axe, which is used to decapitate a zombie. When the U.S. military does use firearms to kill zombies, dwindling supplies of ammunition necessitate that soldiers learn to use their weapons for maximum efficiency. The character Todd Wainios describes how soldiers in his unit were trained to shoot in a methodical way so that every bullet hit a zombie and no ammunition was wasted. Meanwhile, people from nations where warriors traditionally carried weapons older than firearms employ them in order to dispatch zombies. For example, Japanese nationals fight zombie hordes with the katanas of their ancestors, defending the human race while reconnecting with bushido, the ancient Japanese warrior tradition. Scotsmen, meanwhile, wield claymores to kill zombies, similarly connecting with their own warrior tradition.

Finally, as the idea of a zombie apocalypse permeates popular culture, the killing of zombies is no longer limited to fiction. Companies are now marketing actual zombie-killing products. Some of these include special knives and ammunition. As of 2013, the company Frontpage offers what it describes as a zombie sac, a backpack filled with several knives and enough preserved food and a water bottle big enough for surviving two days on the road in case of a zombie apocalypse, and many manufacturers offer zombie firing range targets as well as ammunition that is designed for killing zombies.

See also: Apocalypse; Bokur/Caplata; *In the Flesh*; *Night of the Living Dead* Series; Romero, George; Romero's Rules; *Shaun of the Dead*; *28 Days Later* Series; Voodoo; *Walking Dead, The* (Television Series); *World War Z* (Novel)

June Michele Pulliam

WELLINGTON, DAVID

David Wellington (1971–) was born in Pittsburgh, Pennsylvania, home of director George Romero. Author of 10 novels as of 2013, Wellington wrote his first novel serially online in 2004, while working as a United Nations archivist. That project became the first of the *Monster Island* trilogy, *Monster Island,* published in 2006 (Wellington's site reached 40,000 hits per update, attracting the notice of an editor). The trilogy describes a post-apocalyptic world beset by the living dead, who threaten human hegemony. *Monster Nation* (2006), a prequel, and *Monster Planet* (2007), a sequel, are the other novels in the trilogy.

Scholars credit Wellington with helping protect the zombie subgenre from complete formulaic lethargy, predictable plotting and bland characterization. Some of his walking dead are leaders who are fast, strategic, and ambitious. For example, in *Monster Island,* after medical student David Fleck runs out of food while barricaded in his apartment with no hope of rescue, he arranges to reanimate without the hypoxia-induced brain death that causes most of the undead to be mindless. He hooks himself up to ventilator before committing suicide, thereby reanimating with his faculties intact. As a sentient zombie, he is a menace to the living, who he attempts to corral and keep as livestock.

Wellington's other zombie fiction includes *Plague Zone,* a serialized novel released in 2012 on the author's website, and the comic *Marvel Zombies Return: Iron Man* (2009), which was a *New York Times* best seller. The zombies of *Plague Zone* are not a result of a supernatural phenomenon; they are created by the dementia and hallucinations associated with Creutzfeldt–Jakob disease. Wellington has also published several anthologized zombie short stories: "Grvniče" (*Exotic Gothic 2,* 2008) is a shattering tale of post-war Bosnia, wherein bullet-ridden civilians emerge to return to the barn in which they were burned alive by paramilitaries. On the march, the zombie column is watched by two American film students who record all. Unusually sympathetic for a zombie narrative, "Grvniče" portrays zombies with dignity, engaging readers' sympathies for the un-living, who are after all victims. In another tale, "Atacama" (*Exotic Gothic 4,* 2012), Wellington returns to the horror trope of mummies, which he had portrayed as the zombie antagonists in the *Monster Island* trilogy, but these are 9,000-year-old Chilean mummies, not the relatively newer Egyptian mummies, and they are allies of the living. As of 2013, Wellington is also the author of *13 Bullets* (2007), *99 Coffins* (2007), *Vampire Zero* (2008), *23 Hours* (2009), *32 Fangs* (2012); and the *Frostbite* series of werewolf novels, *Frostbite* (2009), *Ravaged* (2010), and *Overwinter* (2010).

See also: Apocalypse; *Monster Island* Trilogy; Mummies; Romero, George

Danel Olson

WELLS, H. G.

H. G. Wells (born Herbert George Wells, 1866–1946) was born into the lower middle class of late Victorian society. He died a wealthy man and literary legend at the age of 78. The son of a house cleaner and professional cricketer, he desultorily apprenticed as a draper's assistant in between fitful and ultimately fruitless attempts at a formal education. An omnivorous reader with an autodidacts' intellectual curiosity, Wells wrote a biology textbook with T. H. Huxley (born Thomas Henry Huxley, 1825–1895), as well as novels and short stories of varying quality and market success until his tour de force, *The War of the Worlds* (1898), catapulted him to lasting fame as a writer of science fiction. In 1906, he ended this brief and intense affair with genre fiction with *In the Days of the Comet* (1906), and thereafter wrote realistic novels set in contemporary times. His novels *Tono-Bungay* (1909) and *Mr. Britling Sees It Through* (1916) are written in a naturalist vein and can be read today as romantic entertainments. Although Wells never directly wrote about the phenomenon of the living dead in either his voluminous fiction or nonfiction works, he did create some of the tropes encountered in zombie genre literature.

Characters in two of his earlier works, *The Time Machine* (1895) and *The Island of Dr. Moreau* (1896) prefigure the modern zombie concept. In *The Time Machine,* the Traveler realizes that *Homo sapiens* diverged into two distinct species. The troglodytic Morlocks live and toil in underground mines to seemingly provide a paradisiacal living for the addled and child-like Eloi. While technically alive, the Morlocks, like zombies, emerge from their chthonic world to cannibalize their ostensible masters of the Over World, much like the eponymous creatures in the film *C.H.U.D.* (1984). In *The Island of Dr. Moreau,* the Beast Folk are a grotesque experiment in the hybridization of animal and human anatomies. Like Frankenstein's monster, they are a mad scientist's attempt to create artificial life from amalgamated tissues, and thus occupy a liminal space between the living and the dead. Intelligent and capable of speech, the Beast Folk inevitably revert to their animal nature as the grafts of human tissue decay and "the stubborn beast flesh day by day grows back again."

The most striking and visionary example of Wells's contribution to zombie literature is encountered in chapter 23 of *The Shape of Things to Come* (1932), a fictional work that chronicles an apocalyptic war occurring between 1940 and 1970. In addition to using poison gas, mankind attempts to exterminate itself using bacteriological weaponry. One such weapon is Maculate Fever, a disease that "discolored the face and skin, produced a violent fever, cutaneous irritation, extreme mental distress, and the *uncontrollable desire to wander*" (emphasis added). Much like the undead plague in contemporary zombie film and literature, the disease spreads through air, water, and personal contact. Perpetually in motion, the infected hordes shamble into cities. The disturbing imagery of their being hunted down and shot by the terrified living resembles the battle scenes in the films of George Romero and in the novel *World War Z* (2006), by Max Brooks. However, Wells's walkers are merely peripatetic, not cannibalistic.

See also: Brooks, Max; Free Will; Romero, George; Science Fiction; *World War Z* (Novel)

Michael E. Matthews

WHITE TRASH ZOMBIE SERIES

The *White Trash Zombie* series, by Diana Rowland, falls into the genre of paranormal romance. It is remarkable for its representation of the zombie as a creature that challenges hegemonic ideas about women and poor white communities. As of 2013, the series consists of three novels: *My Life as a White Trash Zombie* (2011), *Even White Trash Zombies Get the Blues* (2012), and *White Trash Zombie Apocalypse* (2013).

The zombie, whose most defining characteristic is a lack of free will, is commonly viewed as a metaphor for chattel slavery and/or the wage slavery, especially given its Haitian origins. The zombie is typically either the mindless drone of its master, as is the case with those created by Haitian Voodoo, or a mindless creature in thrall to a single-minded drive to tear apart the living, as is the case with post George Romero zombies. Rowland's protagonist, Angel Crawford, however, is notable: as a zombie, she is neither mindless nor lacking free will, as becoming a zombie is to her advantage since the condition makes her more focused and controlled than she was before she was undead. Crawford, who identifies herself as white trash, embodies all of the stereotypes associated with poor whites before she becomes a zombie. She is a high school dropout who was once addicted to prescription pain killers and has a felony record for petty theft. She lives in South Louisiana in a trailer with her unemployed and abusive alcoholic father and works at a string of unfulfilling minimum wage jobs.

Angel's life is changed after a traffic accident, when a mysterious benefactor turns her into a zombie to save her life. Angel awakens in the hospital with little memory of the incident. Meanwhile, this same benefactor has arranged for her to get a job driving a van for the coroner's office, which gives her access to a supply of brains so that she does not have to draw attention to her new condition through killing in order to feed and maintain her physical form. In Rowland's three novels to date, the zombie Angel takes control of her life. She begins to work on getting her graduate equivalency diploma, has her alcoholic father arrested for assault after he beats her while in a drunken rage, and no longer lets romantic partners or even strangers sell her short because she is poor and has lived a less-than-perfect life.

My Life as a White Trash Zombie shows Angel struggling to learn who is killing zombies while navigating her own undead existence. *Even White Trash Zombies Get the Blues* follows Angel as she investigates a corporation that is kidnapping zombies for use in a secret military experiment. Angel must save the human race from extinction in *White Trash Zombie Apocalypse*. While the novels are full of the sort of tough, wise-cracking, profane heroines common to contemporary paranormal romance such as those found in the Sookie Stackhouse novels of Charlaine Harris (1951–), Rowland's series is unique in that her protagonist is a zombie, rather than a more glamorous monster, such as a vampire, werewolf, or fairy.

See also: Class; Haiti; Race; Rom Zom Com; Romero's Rules; Sentience; Voodoo

June Michele Pulliam

WHITE ZOMBIE

White Zombie is a 1932 American horror film directed by Victor Halperin. Bela Lugosi stars as Murder Legendre, a Voodoo master capable of turning people into zombified slaves. The plot line is straightforward: Madeline Short meets wealthy planter Charles Beaumont during her journey to Haiti to join her fiancé Neil Parker. Unknown to Short, Beaumont has fallen in love with her, and so convinces her to wed Neil at the plantation, providing Beaumont an opportunity to woo her before her nuptials. Desperate to win Madeline should his appeal fail, he meets with Legendre, who owns a sugar mill operated entirely by zombie slave labor he has created, to ask that she be placed under a zombie spell so that he can possess her. When Madeline spurns Beaumont's advances moments before her wedding, the planter surreptitiously drugs her so that she appears to die suddenly an hour after her nuptials.

Several days after her death, Legendre resurrects her and brings her to Beaumont Meanwhile, when a grieving Neil finds Madeline's tomb empty, he gets help from a local missionary, Dr. Bruner. From Bruner he learns of Legendre's activities,

A powerful bokur and the Grand High Executioner are among those that Murder Legendre has zombified in order to turn them into his own army of undead in the film *White Zombie* (1932). (United Artists/Photofest)

and the two embark on a plan to free her. Soon Beaumont realizes that possessing a zombified woman is not terribly satisfying: while he has her body, he cannot control her mind, and so he begs Legendre to change her back. Instead, Legendre zombifies him and exerts control over Madeline, attempting to make her kill Neil and Bruner, who have come to her rescue. But the female zombie proves to be more resistant than Legendre's male zombies: she seems to remember her former life, and so when she is poised to kill her husband, she is able to stop herself long enough for Legendre's plans to be thwarted. When Bruner knocks Legendre unconscious, his now-undirected zombies walk off a cliff. When Legendre recovers, Beaumont attacks him, and the two men fall to their deaths, releasing Madeline from her zombie trance.

Inspired by a Broadway play, *Zombie,* by Kenneth S. Webb (1892–1966), *White Zombie* is the first feature-length zombie film and the prototype for zombie films; it introduces many of the conventions associated with zombie fiction: blank-eyed zombies, Voodoo drums, and zombie slave labor. Filming was completed in 11 days, and the movie was marketed on Lugosi's popularity with contemporary audiences after his success in *Dracula* (1931). Most critics focused on the poor acting and incredulous story, although modern critical reception lauds the film's atmosphere. Filmed mainly at Universal Studios, it did well financially, and inspired a sequel, *Revolt of the Zombies* (1936). Despite mixed reviews, the film did much better than Halperin expected.

See also: Class; Gender; Lugosi, Bela; Race; Universal Studios; Voodoo

Anthony J. Fonseca

WORLD WAR Z (FILM)

Marc Forster's (1969–) film version of Max Brooks's 2006 novel of the same name has very little in common with the original. The film follows Gerry Lane, played by Brad Pitt (born William Bradley Pitt, 1963–), a former high-ranking United Nations official with an unspecified job, who has been persuaded to enter service once again in order to ensure that his wife and daughters are safe aboard an aircraft carrier while hordes of the undead decimate the population on land. In Brooks's novel, no one ever learns the reason why the dead have begun returning to life, whereas Forster's film explains this phenomenon as the result of a virus, something taken from Brooks's *The Zombie Survival Guide*. When humans are bitten by zombies, they die and reanimate into zombies themselves. Brooks's zombies operate loosely by Romero's Rules, except instead of being driven by the insatiable desire to consume human flesh, they are prompted to bite the uninfected living in order to transmit the virus. Lane's task is to discover a cure to this virus before it infects the entire population.

Brooks's novel relates, approximately a decade after this event, the story of World War Z, when humanity battled the living dead for survival. It verges on being a literary mash-up, an oral history based on Studs Terkel's *The Good War* but with zombies. Brooks's novel *World War Z* features various civilians, politicians, and members of the military from all over the world who relate their experiences fighting the undead (rather than the Axis powers), all to make a better world for the next generation. These accounts are compiled by Brooks, who takes the fictional role of an agent tasked with writing a report for the United Nations Postwar Commission. The interviews in *World War Z* are Brooks's notes that were deemed too subjective for inclusion in this report, which is supposed to be a dry collection of facts, so he has collected them in this book, which chronicles the human factor of the war. The zombies who nearly destroy the human race operate by Romero's Rules and so are nearly impossible to kill. As one soldier puts it, in Brooks's novel, the zombie is an enemy that cannot be shocked and awed with the U.S. modern artillery because it lacks the intellectual capacity to fear for its own safety and it keeps going until its brain is destroyed.

While Forster's film deviates wildly from Brooks's novel, the script is nevertheless faithful to the spirit of the original in how it draws upon other well-known post-apocalyptic zombie narratives, including George Romero's *Night of the Living Dead* series, as well as Danny Boyle's *28 Days Later* series, as the zombies are fast and are the result of an infectious agent. Lane, who works for the United Nations in order to secure his family's security, is reminiscent of David Wellington's protagonist DeKalb in his *Monster Island* trilogy. Forster also conveys the everyman point of view that characterizes Brooks's novel, with its narrative that is related through multiple perspectives. The film contains no well-known actors aside from Pitt, and actors are shot in harsh light, not made artificially young and beautiful with makeup. Finally, the film's conclusion also conveys Brooks's ambiguous ending. In Brooks's novel, after 10 years, the zombies have been subdued but not eradicated. In this way, the novel considers the dangers of isolation; it shows readers that collaboration is the only way that the human race will survive. Forster's film ends with Lane's finding a vaccine to protect the remaining uninfected, but this cure is not fool proof.

See also: Apocalypse; Brooks, Max; Epidemics; Mash-Ups, Literary; *Monster Island* Trilogy; *Night of the Living Dead* Series; Romero's Rules; *28 Days Later* Series; *World War Z* (Novel); *Zombie Survival Guide, The*

June Michele Pulliam

WORLD WAR Z (NOVEL)

World War Z, subtitled *An Oral History of the Zombie War*, is a mock historical chronicle published in 2006 by Max Brooks. In an alternative universe in the near future, the last survivors of a zombie apocalypse have triumphed over the living dead, whose presence toppled governments and nearly exterminated the human race. The text is unique because although Brooks's zombies operate by Romero's Rules, it differs from other post-apocalyptic zombie narratives in which humans are struggling, and often failing, to re-establish civilization. Brooks imagines a post-apocalyptic world where humans have re-established themselves as the dominant life form on the planet. Based on the 1984 book *The Good War: An Oral History of World War II*, by Studs Terkel, Brooks's novel is a collection of interviews with hundreds of people who 40 years previous to the book's fictional publication date were involved in the zombie war.

Terkel collected the stories of those with firsthand memories of World War II so that the younger generation would have a better appreciation of how their parents fought and went on to build the greatest middle class in the history of the nation. Brooks's fictionalized account of the world zombie wars is collected by its fictionalized editor for a similar purpose, so that a whole new generation can better appreciate how their elders handled the crisis precipitated when the dead began to return to life. Following the structure of Terkel's oral history, *World War Z* is formatted as a series of interviews, each subject giving a unique angle about an event that is so large and world-changing that it is impossible to sum up in one coherent narrative. Brooks, the novel's fictitious editor, writes in his introduction that *World War Z*, the "record of the greatest conflict in human history," is the outgrowth of his work for the United Nations' Postwar Commission Report, who rejected this material as too clouded by the human factor to be accommodated into the coherent narrative they sought to document the event. Brooks's resulting product is a postmodern novel that rejects the possibility of coherent narrative perspective.

In Brooks's fictional universe, only the dead infected with the blood-borne zombie virus can return to life. While the first known outbreak is traced to a village in rural China that had been relocated by the Three Gorges Dam, no one really knows about the virus' origins. Brooks's chronicle of the ensuing pandemic is a commentary on the failure of contemporary governments to care for their citizens in the aftermath of everything from 9/11 to Hurricane Katrina to losses of life savings due to corporate greed. Many bureaucrats essentially fiddle while Rome burns, such as former White House chief of staff Grover Carlson, who weakly defends the government's inaction. In the novel, unscrupulous capitalists like Breckenridge Scott trade on the panic surrounding the initial outbreak by marketing a vaccine for African rabies, which offers no protection against the zombie virus but is bought by desperate consumers who believe rumors that a strain of rabies is causing humans to turn into raving cannibals. The government, desperate to appear to be doing something about the crisis, railroads FDA approval of this ineffective vaccine, allowing Scott to make billions. And in the Battle of Yonkers, the U.S. military, weakened by lengthy wars in Iraq and Afghanistan, is routed by the living dead after the generals insist on using outdated technology to fight an enemy that "cannot be shocked and awed." After this stunning defeat, the U.S. government retreats behind the Rockies, leaving citizens east of this line to defend themselves until the government can regroup. Other world governments fare no better in the beginning.

Yet, other narratives paint a picture of altruism and human ingenuity. General Raj Singh sacrifices himself to detonate a charge that would bring down a mountain of debris to separate the living from the undead. Everyday citizens of first-world countries learn what for them had become obsolete skills, such as farming and chimney sweeping, enabling the remaining population to survive in a world where consumer goods and reliable power sources have become scarce. Kondo Tatsumi, who spent his days and nights locked away in his room surfing the internet before the war, picks up one of the samurai swords of his ancestors to defend Japan against the undead. Terry Knox remains aboard the International Space Station to keep earth's satellites in orbit so that the surviving humans might re-establish modern civilization more quickly. And Father Sergi Ryzhkov steps outside of the role given to him by the Russian Orthodox Church to euthanize bitten soldiers to lift the burden of guilt from others who might have to do the job.

The novel concludes on an optimistic note characteristic of the perspective of its American author. Some interview subjects muse on the human race's role in bringing about World War Z in the first place. One interviewee, Mrs. Miller, holds that the lack of an immediate response that made war against the undead necessary was "the fault of everyone of my generation" but is comforted that at least her cohort is now cleaning up its own mess. Another, Joe Muhammad, says of the experience that "anywhere around the world, anyone you talk to, all of us have this powerful shared experience." His words are reminiscent of the generation that survived World War II. Brooks's novel was well received by critics. The film *World War Z* was released in 2013, which does not follow the plot of Brooks's novel, yet is faithful to the spirit of the novel in that it too is a bricolage of zombie and post-apocalyptic narratives.

See also: Africa; Apocalypse; Brooks, Max; Epidemics; Romero's Rules; *World War Z* (Film)

June Michele Pulliam

XOMBIES TRILOGY

The *Xombies* trilogy is a series of darkly comic Young Adult zombie novels by Walter Greatshell. The series includes *Xombies* (2004), which was later retitled *Apocalypse Blues* (2009), *Apocalypticon* (2010), and *Apocalypso* (2011). The emphasis of the first novel sets the tone for the series. *Xombies* concentrates more on the stories of the survivors of a zombie apocalypse than on the zombies themselves. In the first book, a group of survivors escape on a nuclear sub, and most of the novel is the ongoing story of that group.

The series begins when the virus Agent X creates a zombie plague. Agent X affects only women who have begun their menstrual cycles and gets its name from the pair of X chromosomes that the virus attacks. The infected women, sometimes referred to as blue-skinned devils, are uncontrollable and extremely strong and are driven to alternately kiss or tear apart men. The male victims then come back to life, creating an army of undead, who attack and infect other males. The resulting pandemic forces a group of young adult naval personnel, submarine shipyard mechanics, and the daughter of the sub's commander into the Arctic Ocean, where they believe the xombies cannot survive. The main character, Lulu Pangloss, who is immune to the epidemic because of a genetic disorder that prevents her from menstruating, is left to contend with a world where almost all humans have been turned into murderous maniacs, even the uninfected. Only females who do not menstruate because of their ages are also immune, but they become victims of both the xombies and of surviving humans who rape and murder after the apocalypse. Because Lulu is female and of the age where the virus should have turned her into a xombie, her fellow survivors do not trust her, and many even hate her; much of the series' conflict results from these types of human interactions.

Greatshell's xombies do not follow Romero's Rules in any respect, except that they are very difficult to kill. They have bright blue skin, possess the traits generally attributed to literary werewolves in that they are fast and quick, are strong and bestial, and they can continue to attack when body parts are chopped off. In fact, even their body parts retain sentience and can continue to attack. Generally speaking, they are sentient beings, often even intelligent beings. In a nod to sexually transmitted diseases, reminiscent of the film *Lifeforce* (1985) by Tobe Hooper, the xombie virus is spread not through the usual bite but from a kiss. In homage to the series, a New York–based hip hop and heavy metal band has named itself Xombie, and its first EP, released in 2011, was titled *Xombie EP*.

See also: Epidemics; Gender; *Lifeforce*; Science Fiction; Young Adult Fiction

Anthony J. Fonseca

YOUNG ADULT FICTION

Young adult fiction, which is primarily about the development of the adolescent into an autonomous adult, sometimes features the figure of the zombie. The zombie represents our concerns about our own autonomy, whether the creature is an undead creature, a slave whose will has been effaced through Voodoo, or an existential zombie whose existence is so routine that it fails to realize to what degree its life is controlled. In young adult fiction with zombies, the creature questions the notion of an autonomous, essential self whose actions are relatively free of the influence of other intervening forces.

This concept is brilliantly illustrated in William Sleator's novel *The Boy Who Couldn't Die* (2004). Sixteen-year-old Ken's family is sufficiently wealthy that he takes for granted that he has so much ability to control his young life: his family sends him to an exclusive private school; they live in a neighborhood that is free of violent crime; and modern medicine and access to excellent health care have prevented him and his friends and family from being debilitated by treatable conditions. Ken first realizes the limits placed on his own life after his best friend dies in a plane crash, his body so badly mangled that the family could not even have an open casket funeral. As a result, Ken becomes so fearful about his own mortality that he seeks the services of Cheri Beaumont, whose ad promises freedom from death. Cheri is a bokur who takes Ken's soul through a Voodoo ceremony in order to make him into an astral zombie, someone whose body cannot be harmed or feel pain and so cannot die. But what Ken does not realize is Cheri can also call upon his spirit to do tasks such as kill her enemies or even people that he loves. While Ken sleeps, Cheri causes his soul to take on a corporeal form and kill her enemies. Ken realizes that Cheri is controlling his body in this way after he awakens from a nightmare in which he has stabbed to death a stranger in front of Cheri's apartment. The dream is so realistic that Ken awakens clutching a butcher knife from which phantom blood disappears. To be free of Cheri's influence, Ken seeks the assistance of Sabine, a teen who lives on a Caribbean island where Voodoo is practiced. As Ken and Sabine work to free him of Cheri's magic, he realizes that perhaps Sabine too is not real but an astral zombie sent by Cheri's enemies to help him defeat her. Sleator's trope of the astral zombie is illuminating as a metaphor for how free will is an illusion in that subjectivity consists of programming so deep that we do not realize how many of our actions were not freely chosen. This level of subjectivity is one of the areas of inquiry in zombie studies.

Daniel Waters's (1969–) *Generation Dead* series similarly pursues existential themes in a way that is unique to young adult fiction. In the series, American teens return to life for an unknown reason. While they lack a heartbeat and do not need food or sleep, they are otherwise indistinguishable from the living, except that they move and talk a little more slowly. Nevertheless, the living dead must organize and fight for their civil rights, which they are denied because they are no longer living. Waters's undead teens mimic the experience of American adolescents in how their difference from adults is artificially constructed. While some cognitive abilities of teens are not fully developed until they are in their 20s, they are otherwise mature and capable of handling adult responsibilities. However, the exigencies of industrialization necessitate that many teens prolong their educations and childlike dependency on their families so that they can eventually fit into a modern workplace that requires greater levels of technical skill.

Still other works of young adult zombie fiction show teens' negotiating power structures in order to become autonomous adults with the added challenges facing them in a post-apocalyptic world, where familiar institutions such as the school, the government, and even the family that would have shaped them have collapsed. This is the case in Carrie Ryan's *The Forest of Hands and Teeth* novels, Jonathan Maberry's *Benny Imura* series, Charlie Higson's (born Charles Murray Higson, 1958–) *Enemy* series of novels, and Simon Clark's stand-alone novel *Blood Crazy*. Ryan's protagonists must struggle to find their place in a world where a handful of adults have used the threat of zombies to form a repressive society, ostensibly for the protection of all, so coming of age means first understanding that there are alternatives to these repressive structures. Maberry's Benny Imura learns how to be a bounty hunter who euthanizes the zombified loved ones of clients, while becoming a man. Adults can no longer be depended upon to nurture the young in Higson's *Enemy* series and Clark's *Blood Crazy*. In Higson's *Enemy* series, everyone over 16 either dies suddenly or is afflicted with a disease covering them with boils and causing them to kill the uninfected young. *Blood Crazy* has a similar scenario, where adults are suddenly in thrall to some sort of drive that causes them to try to kill everyone over 20. In both works, teens must struggle to re-establish some sort of working civilization so that they can collaborate to survive.

Other works of young adult zombie fiction offer comic treatments of the creature, including Walter Greatshell's *Xombies* trilogy and Serena Valentino's *How to Be a Zombie*. Both of these works connect the awkwardness of adolescence to the figure of the zombie. In Greatshell's trilogy, the virus that turns people into zombies can be spread only through kissing, a nod to how frightening sexual activity can be to teens. Valentino's tongue-in-cheek guide mimics the format of self-help books written for teens, purporting to explain the mysteries of manhood or womanhood at a time in the reader's life when the changes that their bodies are going through can seem horrifying.

See also: Blood Crazy; Bokur/Caplata; *Boy Who Couldn't Die, The*; *Forest of Hands and Teeth* Trilogy; *How to Be a Zombie*; Maberry, Jonathan; Voodoo; *Xombies* Trilogy

June Michele Pulliam

ZOMBI SERIES

The *Zombi* series consists of five Italian zombie films inspired by George Romero's *Dawn of the Dead* (1978). The first film in the series, *Zombi*, is actually the Italian-release title of Romero's *Dawn of the Dead*, re-edited by Italian horror maestro Dario Argento. It features a prominent score by the band Goblin, assisted by Argento. *Zombi*'s success in Italy inspired Argento's sometime-rival Lucio Fulci to create *Zombi 2* (aka *Zombie*, 1979), titled and marketed as an authorized sequel to *Zombi*, but really a stand-alone tale.

Zombi 2 begins when a ship of the dead brings a zombie to New York. Anne, the daughter of the ship's missing owner, teams up with Peter, a reporter, to search for her father in the Caribbean. They meet a tourist couple, Brian and Susan, and all four go to an island where Dr. David Menard lives with his wife Paola. Dr. Menard has been trying to control the island's zombie infestation, which was brought on by a Voodoo curse. The zombie plague spreads by bite as in Romero's films, but Fulci's specific representation of Voodoo, accompanied by racist depictions of the local population, harkens back to Val Lewton's *I Walked with a Zombie* (1943) and Victor Halperin's *White Zombie* (1932). The curse raises the recently and long dead alike, including wormy Conquistadors, associating the infection with colonialism and evoking images of the zombie Knights of the Templar from the Spanish zombie franchise that began with *Tombs of the Blind Dead* (1972). This narrative setup allows for a series of grisly set-pieces. Most noteworthy are the early face-off between an underwater zombie who kills a shark, and the zombie who dispatches Paola by forcing a giant splinter through her eye. Peter, Anne, and Brian eventually escape the island, only for Brian to soon succumb to a zombie bite. The film ends as Peter and Anne discover that zombies have overrun New York: the final shots show zombies shuffling across the Brooklyn Bridge toward Manhattan.

Zombi 2 outperformed *Zombi* at the Italian box office, which ensured further sequels and imitations. Fulci began directing *Zombi 3* (1988), but illness caused him to pass directorial authority to Bruno Mattei and Claudio Fragasso. Although it lacks the aesthetic panache of *Zombi 2*, *Zombi 3* nevertheless deserves consideration for solidifying the zombie-as-virus theme found in Mattei's *Hell of the Living Dead* (1980), a theme later to be essential to *28 Days Later* (2002) and other recent international successes. The virus is developed by military scientists as a chemical weapon; however, eco-rebel/terrorist forces accidentally unleash it when they try to stop its development. The usual gory contest between humans and zombies ensues. Fragasso took the helm officially for *Zombie 4: After Death* (1989), which features an island setting and Voodoo curse recalling *Zombi 2*, but is otherwise

A Voodoo curse raises the recently and long dead alike in the Italian horror film *Zombie* (aka *Zombi 2*), released in 1979. (The Jerry Gross Organization/Photofest)

unrelated to the earlier films. Like *Zombie 4, Zombie 5: Killing Birds* (1988) bears the United States *Zombie* title for marketing purposes and is not a true sequel. It is notable for its Louisiana setting, Vietnam-veteran protagonist, and late-appearing zombies.

See also: Blind Dead Tetralogy; Fulci, Lucio; *I Walked with a Zombie*; Italian Cinema; Mattei, Bruno; Romero, George; *28 Days Later* Series; *White Zombie*

L. Andrew Cooper

ZOMBIE (NOVEL)

Zombie is a Bram Stoker Award–winning epistolary novel by Joyce Carol Oates (1938–), published in October of 1995. The novel's serial murderer is 31-year-old Quentin P., who is loosely modeled after serial killer Jeffrey Dahmer. Quentin P. manipulates and kills young gay men, albeit accidentally at first, in his efforts to create a perfect zombie love slave by his performing crude lobotomies with an ice pick in an attempt to rewire the brain and dispense of all free will. Unfortunately, Quentin P. is always unsuccessful, and his failures result in a series of abductions, rapes, tortures, and deaths. As the novel progresses, he attempts to hide his secret life from family, even as he escalates by transforming into an intentional murderer, cannibal, and necrophile.

The novel's style is noteworthy for its fragmented mini chapters, font-based oddities such as random capitalization, italics, and ampersands, and its crude, gratuitous line drawings, all from the point of view of a psychotic mind. Also noteworthy is that Oates creates the ultimate irony and challenges the preconceptions of how serial murderers are created: Quentin P. is the product of an academically influential family rather than a pathologically dysfunctional one. Like real-life serial killers, Quentin P. blends in, living in a Michigan university town as a career community college student, where his experimentation with medicine, drugs, and alcohol leads to his preying on the perfect victims whose disappearances are not likely to be investigated—vagrants, pickups at gay bars, and hitchhikers. The titular use of the term zombie by Oates has little to do with the concept of the reanimated dead. Rather, the novel has more in common with the trope of the Voodoo zombie, a mindless human slave created by rituals and serums. Of Oates's 50 plus novels, *Zombie* is her most notable foray into the horror genre.

See also: Cannibalism; Free Will; Gender

Anthony J. Fonseca

"ZOMBIE" (SONG)

"Zombie" is a 1994 song released by The Cranberries, from the band's album *No Need to Argue*. Normally classified as a protest song against the constant violence in Ireland, it was written by lead singer and guitarist Dolores O'Riordan (born Dolores Mary Eileen O'Riordan, 1971–), to commemorate the deaths of two boys killed in an IRA bombing. The lyrics of the song, which contains subtle, understated verses that build to a fever pitch in the chorus and ultimately to a growl with the repetition of the word zombie, followed by O'Riordan's using her tessitura for vocalizations (ironically using her head voice), satirize the retaliatory violence that has controlled Irish culture since 1916 (the Easter uprisings). The song's refrain of "what's in your head" plays with the motifs of the mindlessness of the zombie, as well as its lack of free will, with the metaphor indicates that the violence is not only senseless, but mindless, that it turns people, even children, into mindless consumers of retributive violence.

The music video, directed by Samuel Bayer (born Samuel David Bayer, 1965–), was released in late 1994, and it emphasizes the zombie metaphor even further. Filmed mostly in black and white, its scenes of guardsmen holding semi-automatic guns at waist height (a visual pun during the guitar intro) juxtaposed with children playing war with sticks and what look like machetes are set against an apocalyptic backdrop, as the landscape looks like a war zone. Interspersed within these scenes are other scenes reminiscent of George Romero's *Night of the Living Dead* (1968), such as a guard dog eating found bones, which in context, recalls the zombie eating scenes in Romero's film. In the color portions of the video, O'Riodan is covered in gold paint and made to look like Joan of Arc set against a wooden crucifix, with gold-colored cherubs outfitted with arrows and acting like sentries positioned at her feet in such a way as to look like rising flames, with stylized, bright red trees in the background.

The song peaked at number 22 on the Billboard charts in the United States, at number 14 in the United Kingdom, and number 3 in Ireland, and topped the charts in five countries: Australia, Belgium, Denmark, France, and Germany, as well reaching number 1 on the U.S. alternative chart. "Zombie" won Best Song at the 1995 Europe MTV Music Award, and The Cranberries played the song live on *Saturday Night Live* in 1995. The released single contained the full-length cut of "Zombie," which came in at 5:06, along with the B-side songs "Away" and "I Don't Need." It was also released as a seven-inch single.

See also: Night of the Living Dead Series; Romero, George

Anthony J. Fonseca

ZOMBIE ACTORS GUILD, THE

The Zombie Actors Guild is an online organization created in attempt to unionize acting extras who make their money playing zombies in film and television. The organization's creation was predicated on expectations that the sheer number of zombie movies, television shows, web series, video games, and websites would provide a large number of members. Nicknamed ZAG, it endeavors to create better working conditions and opportunities for zombie actors and stunt zombies, which its official website claims numbered nearly 120,000 in 2011. The guild was created as a response to open calls for zombie extras placed on sites such as Craigslist, as well as to health issues inimical to zombie acting such as dealing with prosthetics made of foam latex that may cause allergic reactions and injuries sustained by slipping on fake blood or other special effects makeup during crowd and chase scenes.

As one of its charges, the organization identifies and calls for boycotts of productions that are known for their exploitation of zombie actors, including a failure to remit residuals. The site also appeals to production companies to place zombie Casting Calls on its forums. The site claims to handle contracts for its members in theatrical, television, commercial, industrial, documentary, music video, and interactive/online work via iZombie, its online casting directory. The site was created for users to search the entire ZAG talent pool by a variety of keyword queries; it also researches actors to determine if they were cleared for work with its union. The Zombie Actors Guild also retains lawyers and recommends agents and acting coaches. Its Facebook site identifies current activists who lobby for zombie actors. The official site failed to catch on and ceased to post new material in 2011; however, the Facebook site for the guild continued to follow news of mistreatment of and injuries to extras serving as zombies into 2013.

See also: Hammer Film Productions; Television; Universal Studios

Anthony J. Fonseca

ZOMBIE CUCUMBER

The zombie cucumber, or *Datura stramonium,* is a plant in the Solanaceae, or night-shade family. It has been used both as an herbal remedy for asthma symptoms (in India) and as an analgesic for surgery or bone setting (in Japan). It is also a hallucinogen that is used in vision quests. It was hypothesized to also be the substance used (in combination with the poison from the puffer fish) in Haiti to produce the Voodoo zombie.

The plant itself is poisonous. A tall, coarse annual tropical plant, it is considered a weed and has a rank-smelling foliage. The zombie cucumber has large white or violet trumpet-shaped flowers and prickly fruits. Common names for the plant include thorn apple, Jamestown weed, jimson weed, jimsonweed, and apple of Peru. All parts of the plant contain dangerous levels of atropine, hyoscyamine, and scopolamine, all classified as deliriants. The plant flowers throughout the summer, and its trumpet-shaped flowers open at night, emitting a butterfly-attracting fragrance.

Datura intoxication produces delirium, hyperthermia, and photophobia for several days. In addition, amnesia is common. These symptoms occur within 30–60 minutes, and last from 24 to 48 hours. In 1985, botanist Wade Davis traveled to Haiti in search of the powder called *coupe poudre,* which he theorized was likely used to cause the death-like trance state that defines the Voodoo zombie. His findings were the basis for *The Serpent and the Rainbow* (1985) and *Passage of Darkness: The Ethnobiology of the Haitian Zombie* (1988). According to Davis, the active ingredient in *coupe poudre* was tetrodotoxin, a poison found in the puffer fish, which in minuscule doses leads to a near-death state. He also theorized that the poisoned (and presumed dead) person could then be controlled through doses of zombie cucumber. Other theories hold that poisoned victims may also be fed *Mucuna pruriens,* a plant with stinging hairs and likely hallucinogenic properties, or a paste made of atropine and scopolamine, dissociative hallucinogens that impact on the neurotransmitters and endorphins in the brain. Recent theories attempt to refute the entirety of the drug and Voodoo zombie relationship, attributing zombiism in Haitian culture to mental disability, which is ironically what W. B. Seabrook claimed decades earlier while doing research for *The Magic Island* (1929).

See also: Davis, Wade; Dementia; Haiti; Seabrook, W. B.; *Serpent and the Rainbow, The* (Book); Tetrodotoxin; Voodoo; Zombie Cucumber

Anthony J. Fonseca

ZOMBIE GIRL: THE MOVIE

Zombie Girl is a 2009 documentary shot during the filming of the 2006 micro-budget zombie film *Pathogen* by the then 12-year-old Emily Hagins (1992–). The documentary features many interviews of the cast, local indie film producers, and notable local film critics with the Austin Film Critics Association. Directed and produced by Justin Johnson (1977–) and Aaron Marshall (1978–), *Zombie Girl* follows Hagins, her mother, and her cast over their two-year-long struggle to complete *Pathogen*. Earlier, Hagins had been invited to the exclusive "Butt-Numb-A-Thon" to meet Peter Jackson (born Peter Robert Jackson, 1961–). The event was a mix of premieres, vintage classics, low-budget indie films, foreign films, blockbusters, and forgotten gems. Hagins saw her first zombie film, the low-budget Australian movie *Undead* (2003) and fell in love with the genre. She used her summer as an assistant at an indie horror movie set to study zombie films. She wrote her first zombie script by the age of 10. She refined and improved this script until at the age of 12, when she decided to begin filming *Pathogen*. *Zombie Girl* follows Hagins at this point during the filming process.

The directors had heard about Hagins's film through an online call she sent for actors, and they were so intrigued by her story they decided to document her, remaining as inconspicuous as possible, so as not to taint or distract from Hagins's experience. They are never seen or heard in the documentary, instead focusing on Hagins and the responses of the interviewees. The documentary shows that while she directs, casts, and writes the movie herself, Hagins is not without help. Her mother serves as financer, assistant, and special effects artist. It is apparent from the documentary that shooting after school and on weekends with her young cast strained the relationship between Hagins and her mother at times. But beyond just a portrayal of the Hagins family, this movie also serves as a meditation on zombie movies and the art of filmmaking: Hagins's movie *Pathogen* is an interesting blend of zombie film tropes. The zombies are slow, shuffling, undead monsters who only desire to feed on the living, a throwback to the classic undead zombie, which was a deliberate decision by Hagins. Her plot involves a mysterious nanotechnology infection that spreads through the water of Austin, Texas, and kills those who ingest it, only to later reanimate as zombies. The film focuses on a band of middle school children who try and resist the zombie hordes growing around them.

Zombie Girl is also peppered with musings on the appeal of zombie films and on the art of filmmaking that are relevant to *Pathogen*. The interviews of Hagins and the cast members also offer a unique insight of how zombie movies are viewed in our culture through the eyes of children. Many of the adult interviewees believe Hagins wanted to make a zombie movie for her first film because she liked the gore and horror of the zombie genre. Hagins states on camera that the real reason she wanted to make a zombie film is because she felt it would be easier, since all zombie movies have rules that directors must follow. *Zombie Girl: The Movie* was showcased at several film festivals in North America during 2009, including the Slamdance Film Festival and Comic-Con International Independent Film Festival, to positive reviews. The documentary did not have a release outside of the film festivals, but the DVD is available at online outlets. It includes the entire *Pathogen* film as one of its special features.

See also: Cult Film; Jackson, Peter

Braden Dauzat

ZOMBIE HAIKU

Zombie Haiku is a 2008 poetry and humor book by American writer Ryan Mecum (1975–). It describes the events of a zombie outbreak from the zombie's point of view. The book opens with a prose note written by Chris Lynch, in which he explains that he is dying. Chris writes that he has evacuated to the airport after what he calls the plague and has hidden himself in a magazine shop with someone named Barbara after the living dead have infiltrated the airport. After Barbara dies and has been reanimated, Chris escapes, locking himself in a bathroom. Chris, who was bitten while fleeing, killed the zombie, stealing its poetry journal. This note frames the content of the text.

The first few haikus are about the beauty of nature and romantic love, but those that follow describe the zombie outbreak. The writer of the journal humorously ignores warning signs on his way to work, then narrowly escapes being bitten by a zombie coworker. He is eventually bitten by several zombies and turns into a zombie himself, so he goes on an eating spree, recording his new and unusual experiences, craving and eating human flesh, and being mutilated without feeling pain. He eats his own mother, residents at a nursing home, and (with other zombies) a family trapped in a farmhouse. He eventually arrives at the airport, where zombies are huddled on the outside of a fence. A failed escape attempt by the living destroys the fence, allowing the zombies inside. The poet stalks Lynch and Barbara as they run for shelter, and his narrative ends abruptly after he confidently attacks Lynch. The book ends with another prose passage by Lynch, imploring the reader to find his wife and deliver apologies to her, along with the message that he wants to eat her.

Zombie Haiku may be better understood as a work of horror fiction than as a collection of poetry. While the vast majority of the book is written in haiku-style units, with three lines of five, seven, and five syllables, most of the poems do not stand alone. Instead, the book is a continuous narrative delivered in an unconventional format. The poems could also be called *senryu* rather than haiku because of their subject matter; they are darkly humorous or cynical reflections on human nature. In the context of the zombie genre, it is an original and interesting work, as it casts a fairly traditional zombie as protagonist. While the idea of a zombie keeping a written journal is absurd, the glimpse into the mind of a zombie is an interesting take on the genre. The descriptions are vivid, and Mecum uses dark humor liberally. However, critics note that the story lacks real conflict or emotional appeal, as the main character is focused only on eating humans and the only major human character, Lynch, makes only a very brief appearance in the story. A sequel by Mecum, *Dawn of Zombie Haiku*, was published in 2011 by HOW Books. In it, zombies invade Manhattan. The story is told through the eyes of a 10-year-old girl whose father was a great fan of zombie movies. Mecum has also published collections of vampire and werewolf *haiku*.

See also: Apocalypse; Comedy; Romero's Rules

Derek Manuel

ZOMBIE NIGHT TRILOGY

The *Zombie Night* Trilogy is a series of films by David J. Francis, a Canadian actor, director, producer, and screenwriter known for his role as Jesus in *Dracula 2000* and *Dracula II: Ascension* (2003), as well as his three zombie films: *Zombie Night* (2003), *Zombie Night 2: Awakening* (2006), and *Reel Zombies* (2008), co-directed with Mike Masters (1976–). Francis appeared as an actor in all three.

Completely financed and cowritten by Francis and his wife Amber Lynn Francis (1974–2002), *Zombie Night* is known for its violence, gore, and sexual themes, which included some nudity. In a post–World War III society after an apocalyptic nuclear exchange, zombies rise from the grave and begin eating humans, but they attack only at night. Much like many other zombie films, the action in the *Zombie Night* trilogy revolves around a group of survivors, including the main characters, a couple and their child returning from a vacation in the woods. Along with other survivors, they take shelter in an abandoned warehouse, where power struggles among them ultimately lead to their being forced into the neighboring forests, where they must fight off the undead with limited protection. *Zombie Night 2* starts in the rain forest, where a mosquito-borne virus causes a high mortality rate. The virus makes its way to Canada, where survivors are holed up in an abandoned marina. Once the zombie attacks begin, some of the survivors are forced to sacrifice their own to remain alive. The metatextual dark comedy *Reel Zombies* is a mockumentary that follows Francis and Masters as documentary directors making a film about the undead invasions of the two previous films, while finding themselves on the lookout for real zombies.

Francis's zombies follow Romero's Rules in general, including their having a need to consume human flesh. Like Romero's zombies, the undead in the *Zombie Night* trilogy look as though they have crawled from their graves in various stages of decomposition. They move slowly; in fact, they shamble along mindlessly and are easy to outmaneuver and outrun, if not for their sheer numbers and relentlessness.

See also: Apocalypse; Cannibalism; Comedy; Mockumentaries; Romero's Rules

Anthony J. Fonseca

"ZOMBIE PRINCE, THE"

"The Zombie Prince" is a short story by Kit Reed that first appeared in the collection *Zombies: The Recent Dead* (2010). Reed's zombie, named X, is dead and reanimated by Voodoo, is sentient, and has much in common with the vampire. X is one of a recent spate of sentient zombies to appear in fiction about the creature.

The story, which is related from the zombie X's perspective, begins by establishing that the zombie does not hunger for human flesh, but rather is a stealer of souls similar to the cursed mummy Bubba Ho-Tep in the film and Joe Lansdale's short story of the same name. X is also similar to Bubba Ho-Tep in that creatures like him do not remember their names and instead are all known as either X, or nothing at all. X appears to Dana Graver, who is reeling from a recent breakup, which has left her hurting. At the moment, she would do anything to make the pain go away. X is also no rotting husk of a human when he appears to Dana. Instead, he is tall and gorgeous and dressed impeccably in white. Because the undead lack the power of speech, X relates the narrative by communicating directly with Dana's mind. Because X is undead, he has no memory of his prior existence or how he came to be in this condition. X reassures the frightened Dana that he is not there to gorge on her flesh. In fact, flesh is anathema to his kind. Instead, X is more like Persephone in the underworld.

While Dana fears X, she is also attracted to his ability to make her pain go away, and so she willingly permits him to take her soul. Yet, as X takes Dana's soul, turning her into a zombie, he too is changed; he has come too close to the living. Suddenly he remembers that he is Remy L'Hereaux, who was turned into a zombie by his father-in-law, a powerful bokur who never approved of his daughter's marriage. But before Remy had died, his wife Sallie slipped a silver bracelet onto his wrist, which ties him to the living world. Thus, when he takes Dana's soul, he is now beset with the need to see his wife and young son again, while simultaneously praying that his body decomposes before he is able to locate them and confront them with the horror of what he has become.

See also: Bokur/Caplata; Existentialism; Vampires and Werewolves; Voodoo

June Michele Pulliam

ZOMBIE STRIPPERS!

Zombie Strippers! is a 2008 horror-comedy movie written and directed by Jay Lee, starring porn superstar Jenna Jameson and *Nightmare on Elms Street* film series star Robert Englund. Lee had previously written and directed the even lower budget demon-zombie film *The Slaughter* (2006). *Zombie Strippers!* is set in a near future in which George W. Bush has been elected for a fourth term. The film centers around Rhino's, an underground strip club in a small Nebraska town. The plot device is similar to that of *The Return of the Living Dead* (1985) in that a chemical virus developed by the government to reanimate slain soldiers in order to create a super military force has been accidentally released, spreading the virus to the general population. The paramilitary Z Squad is sent to kill the zombies. When one member of the squad is bitten, he seeks refuge in Rhino's. After the club's star dancer Kat (Jameson) is bitten, she continues to perform, and her aggressive, bloodthirsty shows are a huge hit with customers, although their subsequent Champagne Room visits prove fatal to them. Kat's success prompts her fellow dancers to decide whether to become zombies themselves.

The film is most notable for Jameson, a porn industry legend considered an emblem for women who turn porn careers into lucrative, long-term businesses. *Zombie Strippers!* was Jameson's first lead role in a nonpornographic film. The film sexualizes the zombie in more overt ways than traditionally seen on film, in turn subverting the notion of the objectified and victimized female stripper: it is

Kat (Jenna Jameson) beguiles the clientele of Rhino's, who do not suspect that the exotic dancer that they find so appealing is a bloodthirsty zombie who will soon feast on their flesh. (Sony Pictures Entertainment)

the violent and sadistic strippers who prove to be a big hit with the masochistic male customers. In this way, sexually aggressive women are depicted as more appealing than the traditionally appeasing exotic dancer. The humor of the film relies in part on the dramatic irony generated by the customers' expressing glee in retiring to the private rooms with the strippers, where they will inevitably be eaten. Consequently, the male customers are the butt of the joke, while the female zombie strippers are the subjects, in spite of the film's prolonged nude dance sequences.

Lee's prior film, *The Slaughter,* also demonstrates an interest in feminine monsters, focusing on the resurrection of a zombie-related female demon. *Zombie Strippers!* had a limited theatrical release in the United States in its R-rated form; the subsequent unrated DVD release includes some scenes of gore and nudity that had been cut for the theatrical release. The film was generally received poorly by the mainstream press, who criticized the low production values, bad acting, and one-joke premise. Horror blogs and less mainstream press, however, mostly welcomed the film as a fun, albeit disposable and predictable offering. The film cost $1 million to make in 18 days of shooting.

See also: Comedy; Pornography; *Return of the Living Dead* Series; Science Fiction

Laura Helen Marks

ZOMBIE STUDIES

Zombie studies is an area of academic inquiry where the trope of the zombie is used to consider upon ideas about consciousness, particularly whether free will is an illusion in that all of our wills may be subordinated by culture and/or biological forces whose workings affect us so deeply that they are not readily visible. Zombie studies have flourished in recent years alongside of the explosion of zombie fiction.

Titles such as Christopher M. Moreman (1974–) and Cory Rushton's (no date available) *Zombies Are Us: Essays on the Humanity of the Walking Dead and Zombies* (2011), Stephanie Boluk (1979–) and Wylie Lenz's (1972–) *Generation Zombie: Essays on the Living Dead in Modern Culture* (2011), Kyle William Bishop's (1973–) *American Zombie Gothic: The Rise and Fall (and Rise) of the Walking Dead in Popular Culture* (2010) and Deborah Christie (no date available), and Sarah Juliet Lauro's (no date available) *Better Off Dead: The Evolution of the Zombie as Post-Human* use psychoanalysis, Marxist theory, and Foucault's ideas about biopower to consider how the zombie reflects humans. Richard Greene (1961–) and K. Silem Moham-mad's (no date available) *Zombies Vampires and Philosophy* (2012) and Christopher Robichaud's (no date available) *The Walking Dead and Philosophy: Shotgun, Machete, Reason* (2012) consider some of these same questions, but these books are written for non-academics. Moreman and Rushton's *Race, Oppression and the Zombie: Essays on Cross-Cultural Appropriations of the Caribbean Tradition* considers the relationship of the zombie to Orientalism, racism, postcolonialism and capitalism, while Kim Paffenroth's *The Gospel of the Living Dead: George Romero's Visions of Hell on Earth* (2006) explores how George Romero's films reveal considerations about material-ism, individualism, and theology. Andrew Whelan (no date available), Ruth Walker (no date available), and Christopher Moore's *Zombies in the Academy: Living Death in Higher Education* (2013) uses the metaphor of the zombie to examine the current state of academia. Zombies, which seem to be so unlike us, are more similar than we first realized, and as a result, they can explain many unpleasant truths about ourselves and our world.

See also: Existentialism; Free Will; Romero, George

See also: Appendix B—Zombie Studies: Academic Books and Articles about Zombies

June Michele Pulliam

ZOMBIE SURVIVAL GUIDE, THE

The Zombie Survival Guide is a 2003 book by Max Brooks. It pretends to be a work of nonfiction explaining to readers how to survive when zombies following Rome-ro's Rules eventually rise from their graves and begin to menace the living. Brooks puts in writing principles of the zombie's nature as well as rules for surviving, as gleaned from numerous post-apocalyptic films, beginning with George Romero's *Night of the Living Dead* (1968).

Thus, the guide includes sections about the best type of weaponry, means of escaping an undead horde, and places to seek shelter until either reinforcements arrive or sufficient numbers of zombies have been culled to make it possible for survivors to leave the place where they have sought refuge. Brooks attributes the ability of the dead to resurrect to the Solanum virus, which can be transferred from zombie to host only via blood-borne contact. According to Brooks, the Solanum virus has existed for millennia, and he cites historic evidence of zombie outbreaks as early as antiquity that were formerly thought to be events of mass hysteria or warfare.

The Zombie Survival Guide laid the groundwork for Max Brooks's novel *World War Z,* where the human race was nearly extinguished due to a zombie pandemic that toppled governments and claimed millions of lives. *World War Z* is the story of how the human race survived the pandemic, related by dozens of narrators from all walks of life, now reflecting on their experiences a decade later. Marc Forster's film *World War Z* in many ways follows *The Zombie Survival Guide* more faithfully than it does Brooks's novel *World War Z* on which it is loosely based, particularly in the protagonist Gerry Lane's final advice to the audience to fight if they can. The introduction to *The Zombie Survival Guide* similarly reminds readers that "knowledge is only part of the fight for survival," and that it is paramount to demonstrate a will to live through fighting when the undead begin to rise.

See also: Brooks, Max; Epidemics; *Night of the Living Dead* Series; Romero's Rules; *World War Z* (Film)

June Michele Pulliam

ZOMBIE WALK

A zombie walk is an event in which large groups of participants dressed as zombies gather and shamble through the streets of various cities or towns, either as members of flash mobs or as the culminating event of more organized gatherings. The first recorded zombie walk was a publicity stunt suggested by Bryna Lovig (no date available) on August 19, 2001, to promote a midnight film-festival in Sacramento, California. It was held originally as part of The Trash Film Orgy but was resurrected on July 27, 2002; it has since become an annual event. In 2003, Thea Munster (no date available) of Toronto, Ontario, organized a fan-driven walk, and by 2003 over 200 zombies joined to march in the streets on Halloween. Munster's zombie walk, which started with seven zombies, was up to thousands by 2010.

As of 2012, there are official zombie walks in 23 countries, including Canada, the United States, England, Mexico, Ireland, and Brazil. Although there are many disputes as to the largest zombie walk thus far, various newspaper records show that nearly 5,000 zombies participated in the 2010 New Jersey Zombie Walk. Participants who chose to walk as zombies wear no set costume; thus, they are allowed to be uniquely creative in their interpretation of the zombie character. At some events, victims are planted throughout the parade route so the zombies can attack them. In some recent walks, participants dressed as soldiers or members of

Joe Wiley, in this zombie walk held on the Ashbury Park Boardwalk in New Jersey on October 5, 2013, is a typical example of participants in this phenomenon, which began as a publicity stunt in 2001 in Sacramento, California, to promote a midnight film festival. At present, zombie walks are held in 23 countries. (Associated Press)

paramilitary groups are planted along the route, leading to mock battles against the zombie horde. Occasionally zombie walks have been subject to criticism, but most complaints have been focused on the mess that zombies leave behind, given the costumes that ooze blood and other fluids as the participants shamble. There have been very few documented instances of zombies attacking or causing problems on their routes. While the first zombie walk was used to create publicity, the most popular outcome of a zombie walk is to raise money or collect donations for charity. Blood and organ donation drives are popular choices, and drives for local food banks have proven to be enormously successful. Pub crawls are also popular as part of a zombie walk, although these are more difficult to manage. A few zombie walks have even been used to make a political or philosophical statement. However most zombie walks exist to give attendees the chance to experience the sheer joy of being a zombie. Zombie walks have become incredibly popular in recent years due to the resurging popularity of zombie texts: novels, collections, film, and television series.

See also: Romero's Rules

Alicia Ahlvers

ZOMBIECORE

Zombiecore is an obscure but growing popular music subgenre, sometimes referred to as crossover thrash, related to thrash metal and grindcore. It also incorporates elements of hardcore punk. While other music genres occasionally reference zombies, performers of zombiecore, namely the bands Send More Paramedics and Zombie Apocalypse, rely entirely on zombie idiom and mythology for lyrical content and performance practice. Recurring lyrical themes include extreme descriptions of gory attacks on humans and the adversarial relationship between the living and the walking dead. Some zombiecore takes the form of an episodic retelling or elaboration on film zombies.

Send More Paramedics, arguably the creators of zombiecore, was founded in 2001 as a side project for the emo band And None of Them Knew They Were Robots in the town of Leeds, England. Taking the band name from a line of dialogue in the film *The Return of the Living Dead* (1985), its members, who go by B'Hellmouth, Medico, X Undead, and El Diablo (album credits do not identify members by name) compose songs that make liberal use of sound and music samples from the *Return of the Living Dead* franchise and the zombie films of George Romero, alluding to

X Undead, bassist for the zombiecore band Send More Paramedics, performing during the Damnation festival in the United Kingdom on October 15, 2006. (Redferns)

the same material lyrically. "The Hordes," from their first album, *A Feast for the Fallen* (2002), features the refrain "When there's no more room in Hell, the dead will walk the Earth," a line of dialogue from Romero's *Dawn of the Dead* (1978). The same album explicitly references the *Return of the Dead* trilogy, with songs titled "Resurrection Cemetery" and "The Pain of Being Dead." *A Feast for the Fallen* concludes with an untitled bonus track. Staged as a sort of radio play, it tells the story of an outbreak of zombies in the American southwest and an attempt to escape the resulting military quarantine. The band's sophomore effort, *The Hallowed and the Heathen* (2004), was more sophisticated in its production values. The first promotional video was for the single "Zombie Crew," a celebration of their live performances. The band appears in costume and makeup consistent with their role as members of the living dead. Notable on this album is "Bokor," which describes the zombie in the Voodoo tradition. Aside from this diversion, the lyrics are principally concerned with the zombie in the science fiction setting and filmic references.

In 2006, Send More Paramedics released its final full-length album, *The Awakening*. An epic, cinematic concept album set in the year 2025, it depicts an Earth overrun by a highly contagious strain of rabies. The 15 songs explore various aspects of this hypothetical zombie apocalypse, mirroring many narrative elements found in the film *28 Days Later* (2002). The opening track "Everything Is Not under Control" includes the lyric "the end is really fucking nigh," which alludes to a graffito seen in the stairwell of an abandoned church in *28 Days Later*. More subtle and sophisticated symbolism appears in "Sever," which parallels zombiism with failed or pathological romantic attachment. A bonus disc features keyboard-dominated instrumental tracks, reminiscent of the soundtracks to *Assault on Precinct 13* (1976) and *Day of the Dead* (1985). Intended to serve as a soundtrack for the imagined film, it closes with a spoken-word track, describing the spread of the zombie infection and the apocalyptic results. A promotional video for "Blood Fever" includes a distinct nod to the *Return of the Living Dead* series. The band members drink from a bowl of punch which has been accidentally polluted with 2-4-5 trioxin, a U.S. Army research chemical that is the cause of zombiism in the *Return of the Living Dead* canon. Send More Paramedics announced their dissolution in June of 2007.

Zombie Apocalypse is an American metalcore supergroup formed in 1998 by members of Shai Hulud, Shallow Water Grave, and try.fail.try. Zombie Apocalypse's first official release was an EP in 2003. Entitled *This Is a Spark of Life* and clocking in with 10 songs in just under 12 minutes, it features samples from films like *And Justice for All* (1979), *The Mosquito Coast* (1986), and *Let It Ride* (1989). The band uses the zombie idiom more obliquely. Although as songwriters the members of Zombie Apocalypse are notoriously unlikely to comment on their intent, the lyrics seem to critique capitalism, consumerism, advertising, existential psychology, and the dilemmas of freedom.

In 2005, Send More Paramedics and Zombie Apocalypse issued *Tales Told by Dead Men*, a split album wherein each band contributed one-half of the content. Zombie Apocalypse's tracks feature samples from unexpected sources, such as *George Carlin: You Are All Diseased* (1999) and *A Mighty Wind* (2003). The song lyrics are obscure, dealing with disappointment, alienation, anxiety, and aggression by turns. "Breaking Off Fingers" was made into a promotional video featuring a live performance. Send More Paramedics' tracks begin with "Intermission of the Dead," the title a nod to Romero's franchise. Their most notable track, "Zombie versus Shark," is an elaboration of a particularly memorable scene from *Zombi 2* (1979). Their track "Nothing Tastes Like This" inspired a video that is strongly reminiscent of Romero's *Day of the Dead* (1985), notably the characters Bub and Dr. Logan.

See also: Dawn of the Dead; Day of the Dead; Mockumentaries; *Night of the Living Dead* Series; Romero, George; Romero's Rules; *28 Days Later* Series

Jeff Snell

ZOMBIELAND

Zombieland, a 2009 American horror comedy directed by Ruben Fleischer (born Ruben Samuel Fleischer, 1974–), had originally been conceived of as a television pilot in 2005. It stars Woody Harrelson (born Woodrow Tracy Harrelson, 1961–), Jesse Eisenberg (born Jesse Adam Eisenberg, 1983–), Emma Stone (born Emily Jean Stone, 1988–), and Abigail Breslin (born Abigail Kathleen Breslin, 1996–). The storyline follows four survivors of a zombie apocalypse who travel across the Southwestern United States toward California, hoping to find safety. Characters have city monikers (the cities from which they originate) rather than names. Eisenberg, the film's narrator, plays Columbus, a young college student venturing home to check on his parents.

On the road he teams with Tallahassee, whose sole goal has become to find intact Twinkies. The two raid grocery and hardware stores, as well as ammunition shops, killing zombies as they stock up. At one stop, they meet Wichita and Little Rock, who claim to be sisters headed to the Pacific Playland amusement park, the place where Little Rock remembers being happiest in the pre-apocalyptic world. The two women are also con artists and have no difficulty robbing Columbus and Tallahassee. The four cross paths on the road afterward, and in a Mexican standoff, Columbus convinces the two groups to travel together for safety. The four reach Hollywood and bunker down at a mansion owned by comic actor Bill Murray (born William James Murray, 1950–), where they find Murray (playing himself) alive. In the film's best comic moment, Columbus kills Murray after mistaking him

One of the living runs from her ravenous undead pursuer in the comic horror film *Zombieland* (2009). (Photofest/Columbia Pictures)

for a zombie. The four continue their journey, finally arriving at Pacific Playland, where they face off against a mob of zombies. Columbus discovers he can be brave, and Tallahassee finally finds Twinkies. The group defeats the zombie mob and ride off together. *Zombieland* is also an example of a Rom Zom Com, a contraction for a romantic zombie comedy, in that the plot also involves a romance. In this case, the geeky Columbus, who before the zombie apocalypse was not terribly appealing to girls, ends up with the girl of his dreams, Wichita, someone who would not have considered him as a potential love interest before the collapse of civilization took away most of the men that she would consider dating.

The zombies in the film more or less follow Romero's Rules, although they are capable of running and moving very quickly. Designed by Tony Gardner (1965–) of the music video "Thriller" fame, the zombies are characterized by tousled hair, bloody faces, yellowish teeth, wild eyes, and ragged clothing; one nude female zombie chases a human in the opening credits. The zombie design was intended to walk the tightrope between horror and comedy. The filming was done digitally, sometimes using handheld cameras, and the theme park scenes were filmed in Valdosta, Georgia's Wild Adventures Water and Theme Park, with a constructed haunted house façade. The other trademark of the film is its breaking of the fourth wall, even down to its credits and the recurring appearance of text for Columbus's ongoing Rules for Survival, which recounts the unwritten code to surviving a zombie apocalypse as represented in previous zombie films. Text is always computerized but three-dimensional, and in the opening credits, characters actually knock letters over as they run to escape zombies or fall from heights. Critics gave the film positive reviews, and it was a huge commercial success. Made between February and April 2009 by Columbia Pictures for an estimated $23.5 million, it grossed $24.7 million in its opening weekend. By year's end, *Zombieland* grossed $75.6 million.

See also: Apocalypse; Comedy; Epidemics; Existentialism; Rom Zom Com; Romero's Rules

Anthony J. Fonseca

ZOMBIES ATE MY NEIGHBORS

Zombies Ate My Neighbors is a video game that has achieved cult status. It was developed by Lucas Arts and published by Komani in 1993 for the Super Nintendo (SNES) and Sega Genesis consoles. It was re-released in 2009 as a downloadable Virtual Console title for Nintendo's Wii and Wii U systems. The game, originally titled *Monsters!,* allows the player either to choose between teenage protagonists Zeke and Julie or engage in two-player cooperative play. Players must rescue at least one of Zeke's and Julie's neighbors from the zombies and other horror movie-inspired monsters released by mad scientist Dr. Tongue in order to complete each of the 48 levels. This top-down (three-quarter overhead view) action game features primarily projectile-based combat with different weapons varyingly effective against different enemies.

The relatively fast-moving zombies dig their way out of the ground, consistently spawning, and move around with arms outstretched. A player's score at the end of a level is based on the number and type of neighbors (e.g., overweight dads in undershirts, cheerleaders, family dogs) rescued. Players must find them scattered throughout the maze-based level maps, set in a variety of horror-movie-appropriate locations, while avoiding or killing the monsters. The protagonists can temporarily gain special abilities, such as drinking a potion that turns the character into a powerful werewolf. The game requires a degree of resource and ammunition management to complete, which is typical of later zombie/horror games as well.

The game was featured in one of the earlier cases of public anxiety over video game violence. Its release occurred in the same year that *Night Trap* was condemned in U.S. Senate hearings for featuring full-motion video scenes of women, occasionally in nightgowns, being grabbed by enemies, and the game was eventually pulled from the market. In keeping with Nintendo's family-friendly branding, the SNES version had all blood removed (or turned purple) and crucifixes rendered to look more like plus signs. Australia and some European countries asked for further censorship, also reflected in different cover art and a name change to simply *Zombies*. Despite its being drawn into the debate on violence, the hallmark of the game was its humorous tone. For example, levels feature tongue-in-cheek titles like "Evening of the Undead" and "Seven Meals for Seven Zombies," and players can use backyard trampolines to jump over hedge boundaries in suburban levels. Most importantly, the game features nontraditional, do-it-yourself weaponry such as silverware, dishes, soda-can grenades, fire extinguishers, and inflatable clown decoys. This has led to associations with the *Dead Rising* games, which feature similar weapon mechanics.

Zombies Ate My Neighbors garnered overwhelmingly positive critical reviews upon release, and its cult fan following increased over time. A sequel, *Ghoul Patrol* (*GP*), was released in 1994. This was an unrelated game outsourced to development studio Motion Pixel and reworked to feature the same protagonists. The sequel, showcasing a darker tone and real guns, was less successful, and the franchise ended. *GP* became a Virtual Console title in 2010. The original game remains popular, and as of 2013, a horror-comedy film based on *Zombies Ate My Neighbors* was in development, though at an unknown stage.

See also: Comedy; *Dead Rising*; Ghoul; Romero's Rules; Video Games

John R. Ziegler

ZOMBIES ON BROADWAY

Zombies on Broadway was a zombie comedy released in 1945 in the United Kingdom by British Lion Films as *Loonies on Broadway*. An Radio-Keith-Orpheum (RKO) Pictures production, it was directed by Gordon Douglas and released in the United States on May 1. The film starred Alan Carney (born David Boughal, 1909–1973) and Wally Brown (1904–1961), RKO's answer to Abbott and Costello, as well as

Bela Lugosi. It turned a profit for RKO. The film is a parody of RKO's *I Walked with a Zombie* (1943); in fact, one of the zombies seen rising from his coffin during a Voodoo ceremony is played by the actor who also played a zombie in that film.

The premise of the film prefigures *The Producers* (1968) in that it involves two Broadway press agents, Jerry Miles and Mike Strager, who find themselves in dire need of a hit show, causing them to create an outlandish scheme. Miles and Strager, caught trying to pawn off a fake zombie as a headliner act, are threatened by their ex-gangster boss, Ace, that they will join the living dead if they fail to produce a real zombie at the club's opening. The two bumblers run away, but a couple of henchmen force them to search for an actual zombie, and the setting of the film then switches to the Caribbean. They travel to San Sebastian, a fictionalized version of the island featured in *I Walked with a Zombie*. To their aid comes Jean la Danse, a cabaret singer who desperately wants to leave San Sebastian, and she agrees to help the two find a zombie in exchange for safe passage. Through her, they are led to zombie expert and bokur Professor Paul Renault, who has already captured la Danse using one of his zombie slaves. While Renault prepares the dancer to become his next slave, Miles and Strager investigate, and they accidentally manage to save her when they create enough of a ruckus to set off Renault's guard dogs, an act which prevents him from giving the zombie serum to his intended victim, who is then moved into a temporary hiding place. La Danse escapes, but Strager is injected with the serum and becomes zombified, under Renault's spell. Renault is attacked by one of his own zombies and is apparently killed. The three return to New York with the new zombie act. Unfortunately, Strager recovers from his trance, but la Dance acts quickly and injects the serum into Ace, who is then placed on stage as a bona fide zombie.

See also: Bokur/Caplata; Comedy; *I Walked with a Zombie*; Lugosi, Bela; Universal Studios; Voodoo

Anthony J. Fonseca

ZONE ONE (NOVEL)

Zone One is a 2011 novel by Colson Whitehead (1969–) that takes place in a post-apocalyptic, not-too-distant future where a virus has reanimated the dead, who operate by Romero's Rules. The zone of this *New York Times* best seller is an area of New York City that the military is supposed to sweep clean of zombies in order to ready it for human resettlement. In this world, any changes ushered in by the zombie apocalypse are only temporary.

The protagonist, nicknamed Mark Spitz (we never learn his real name) because he cannot swim, is part of a platoon of soldiers given the detail of helping to sweep Zone One. The government and the corporations that control it plan to resettle citizens to re-establish confidence in the government's ability to maintain order. Much like post-Katrina New Orleans, the planned resettlement would not be the diverse collection of people who inhabited the area previously. Instead, it will be a

Thomas Kinkaid (1958–), Celebration, United S. A. version of diversity. The newly swept city will be populated by mostly wealthy inhabitants, with a smattering of poor and middle class people thrown in for diversity's sake—and to provide valuable services to the wealthy. To this end, the soldiers sweeping Zone One are strictly ordered to not destroy property and are enjoined to dispose of trash properly, so that it will not take the construction and sanitation crews as long to make the area habitable.

Thus, when the reader first meets Spitz and his comrades de guerre, they must drag down many flights of stairs the zombies they have euthanized, rather than toss them to the ground below. The disposal method ordered by the commanding officers is not only labor-intensive, but it is also dangerous. The zombie corpses must be dragged down the stairs in body bags to protect the soldiers from being splattered by bodily fluids, which can infect them. Even putting the zombies in body bags is no protection against this hazard if the cheap material of which they are made rips. Moreover, to placate the government, corporations are financing the cleanup of Zone One, and soldiers are strictly punished if they appropriate food or clothing they might find, a rule designed to protect private property, as the prime directive of the government is property ownership. *Zone One* is a "literary" zombie novel, written by an author who is not known as a writer of genre fiction, which gave the material some respectability among mainstream reviewers. It also challenges the assumptions of the post-apocalyptic vision of so much zombie fiction, showing us glimpses of a world that might not offer the hoped-for change that sweeps away past inequalities; rather, more horrifyingly, Whitehead depicts a new world that simply replicates the same tired model: the majority of the population continues to be exploited by the 1 percent.

See also: Apocalypse; Epidemics; Romero's Rules; Science Fiction

June Michele Pulliam

ZUVEMBIE

Zuvembie are undead creatures that first make their appearance in Robert E. Howard's (born Robert Ervin Howard, 1906–1936) posthumously published story, "Pigeons from Hell" (*Weird Tales,* 1938). Howard claims to have based this story on the old West Texas legends his grandmother told him. Set in an old, deserted Southern plantation, the story, arguably Howard's best-known foray into the horror genre, involves two New Englanders, Branner and Griswell, who travel into the Deep South to spend a night at a deserted manor house.

That night, Griswell witnesses a hypnotized Branner going upstairs, only to return an animated corpse with his head split by an axe. Branner threatens Griswell, who retreats to Sheriff Buckner. They return to the murder, and because of the mansion's reputation, Buckner believes Griswell's tale, particularly since the Blassenvilles, a family from the West Indies, once lived there. The ensuing investigation involves their interviewing an old Voodoo priest, who informs them of the abusive

Celia Blassenville. Celia victimized her mulatto servant. He also tells the men of the creatures known as zuvembie, or female zombies. The two men return to the mansion to face and kill the zuvembie, which turns out to be the abusive socialite Celia, who had been turned into a zuvembie by her maid.

"Pigeons from Hell" is considered both horror and Southern Gothic, as the investigation leads to the discovery that zuvembie Celia has been living in the mansion with the decaying corpses of her relatives. In addition, the titular ghostly pigeons that fly up from the rafters in various scenes are thought to be the souls of the Blassenvilles, released from hell. Unlike previous manifestations of the Voodoo zombie character, Howard's is not simply an entranced human with empty eyes. Zuvembie Celia has claw-like hands, with black talons. She also possesses the power to hypnotize victims, placing them in a dream state to be commanded. In addition, Howard's creation murders its victims, usually with a hatchet to the skull, so that it can feast on their blood, prefiguring two traits associated with Romero's Rules: the ability to create more zombies from victims and the desire to devour victims. Howard's zuvembie is inarticulate and does not need food, and it can command owls, bats, snakes, pigeons, and werewolves. It can be killed by lead or iron only.

"Pigeons from Hell" was adapted into an episode of the television anthology series *Thriller,* aired on June 6, 1961. Authoritative versions of Howard's stories were collected by Del Rey in 2008, and in 2009 "Pigeons from Hell" was made into a graphic novel of the same name by Joe R. Lansdale.

Due to the Comics Code Authority's prevention of the use of the word zombie until 1989, Marvel Comics used Howard's word, zuvembie, starting with *Avengers #152* (October 1976), retiring the term in 1989, although it was used in 1997 in DC's *Wonder Woman Annual #6.* Howard is best known for his *Conan the Barbarian* series and is regarded as the father of the sword and sorcery subgenre.

See also: Cannibalism; Class; Graphic Novels and Comics; Lansdale, Joe R.; Race; Romero's Rules; Television; Voodoo

Anthony J. Fonseca

Appendix A: Chronology of Zombie Films, 1920–2014

Year	Title	Director
1920	*The Cabinet of Dr. Caligari*	Robert Wiene
1932	*White Zombie*	Victor Halperin
1936	*Ouanga*	George Terwilliger
1936	*Revolt of the Zombies*	Victor Halperin
1940	*The Ghost Breakers*	George Marshall
1941	*King of the Zombies*	Jean Yarbrough
1942	*Bowery at Midnight*	Wallace Fox
1943	*I Walked with a Zombie*	Jacques Tourneur
1943	*Revenge of the Zombies*	Steve Sekely
1945	*Zombies on Broadway*	Gordon Dines and Gordon M. Douglas
1946	*The Face of Marble*	William Beaudine
1946	*Valley of the Zombies*	Philip Ford
1952	*Zombies of the Stratosphere*	Fred C. Brannon
1957	*Bury Me Alive*	Charles Marquis Warren
1957	*Zombies of Mora Tau*	Edward L. Cahn
1959	*Invisible Invaders*	Edward L. Cahn
1959	*Plan 9 from Outer Space*	Ed Wood
1959	*Teenage Zombies*	Jerry Warren
1959	*Zombie in a Haunted House (Gu wu jiang shi)*	Evan Yang
1961	*The Dead One (El Muerto)*	Barry Mahon
1961	*Doctor Blood's Coffin*	Sidney J. Furie
1962	*Santo Contra los Zombis (Invasion of the Zombies)*	Benito Alazraki
1962	*Tales of Terror (Edgar Allan Poe's Tales of Terror)*	Roger Corman
1964	*The Horror of Party Beach*	Del Tenney
1964	*I Eat Your Skin (Zombies)*	Del Tenney

Year	Title	Director
1964	*The Incredibly Strange Creatures Who Stopped Living and Became Mixed-Up Zombies*	Ray Dennis Steckler
1964	*The Last Man on Earth (L'ultimo uomo della Terra)*	Ubaldo Ragona
1965	*Terror-Creatures from the Grave*	Massimo Pupillo
1966	*The Plague of the Zombies*	John Gilling
1968	*The Astro-Zombies*	Ted V. Mikels
1968	*Mad Doctor of Blood Island*	Eddie Romero and Gerardo de León
1968	*Night of the Living Dead*	George A. Romero
1968	*The Zombie Walks (Im Banne des Unheimlichen)*	Alfred Vohrer
1971	*Escape*	John Llewellyn Moxey
1972	*Baron Blood*	Mario Bava
1972	*Blood of Ghastly Horror*	Al Adamson
1972	*Children Shouldn't Play with Dead Things*	Bob Clark
1972	*Dead of Night*	Bob Clark
1972	*Messiah of Evil*	Willard Huyck and Gloria Katz
1972	*Tombs of the Blind Dead*	Amando de Ossorio
1973	*The Crazies*	George A. Romero
1973	*Curse of the Living Dead (Les Démoniaques)*	Jean Rollin
1973	*The Hanging Woman*	José Luis Merino
1973	*The Hidan of Maukbeiang jow*	Lee Jones
1973	*Horror Express*	Eugenio Martín
1973	*House of the Living Dead*	Ray Austin
1973	*Return of the Blind Dead*	Amando de Ossorio
1973	*Vengeance of the Zombies*	León Klimovsky
1973	*A Virgin among the Living Dead*	Jesús Franco
1974	*Corpse Eaters*	Donald R. Passmore and Klaus Vetter
1974	*Garden of the Dead*	John Hayes
1974	*The Ghost Galleon*	Amando de Ossorio
1974	*The House of Seven Corpses*	Paul Harrison
1974	*Let Sleeping Corpses Lie*	Jorge Grau
1974	*Nightmare Circus*	Alan Rudolph
1974	*Sugar Hill*	Paul Maslansky
1975	*Night of the Seagulls*	Amando de Ossorio
1976	*Panic (Bakterion)*	Tonino Ricci

Year	Title	Director
1976	*Revenge of the Zombies (Gou hun jiang tou)*	Ho Meng Hua
1977	*The Child*	Robert Voskanian
1977	*Rabid*	David Cronenberg
1977	*Return of the Chinese Boxer*	Jimmy Wang Yu
1977	*Shock Waves*	Ken Wiederhorn
1978	*Dawn of the Dead*	George A. Romero
1978	*Pesticide*	Jean Rollin
1979	*Zombi 2*	Lucio Fulci
1980	*Alien Dead*	Fred Olen Ray
1980	*Bloodeaters*	Charles McCrann
1980	*The Children*	Max Kalmanowicz
1980	*City of the Living Dead*	Lucio Fulci
1980	*Erotic Nights of the Living Dead*	Joe D'Amato
1980	*Hell of the Living Dead*	Bruno Mattei
1980	*Nightmare City*	Umberto Lenzi
1980	*Zombie Holocaust (Zombi Holocaust)*	Marino Girolami
1981	*The Beyond*	Lucio Fulci
1981	*Burial Ground: The Nights of Terror*	Andrea Bianchi
1981	*Dawn of the Mummy*	Frank Agrama
1981	*Dead and Buried*	Gary Sherman
1981	*The Evil Dead*	Sam Raimi
1981	*The House by the Cemetery*	Lucio Fulci
1981	*Kiss Daddy Goodbye*	Patrick Regan
1981	*Night of the Wehrmacht Zombies*	Joel M. Reed
1981	*Zombie Lake*	Jean Rollin
1982	*The Curse of the Screaming Dead*	Tony Malanowski
1982	*I Was a Zombie for the F.B.I.*	Marius Penczner
1982	*Kung Fu Zombie (Wu long tian shi zhao ji gui)*	Yi-Jung Hua
1982	*The Living Dead Girl (La Morte^ Vivante)*	Jean Rollin
1982	*The Treasure of the Living Dead (La tumba de los muertos vivientes)*	Jesús Franco
1983	*Grave of the Living Dead*	Jesús Franco
1983	*Hysterical*	Chris Bearde
1983	*Mausoleum*	Michael Dugan
1983	*One Dark Night*	Tom McLoughlin

Year	Title	Director
1983	*Wilczyca*	Marek Piestrak
1984	*Bloodsuckers from Outer Space*	Glen Coburn
1984	*Night of the Comet*	Thom Eberhardt
1984	*Surf II*	Randall Badat
1984	*Zombie Island Massacre*	John N. Carter
1985	*Attack of the Beast Creatures*	Michael Stanley
1985	*Day of the Dead*	George A. Romero
1985	*Hard Rock Zombies*	Krishna Shah
1985	*Mansion of the Living Dead*	Jesús Franco
1985	*Re-Animator*	Stuart Gordon
1985	*The Return of the Living Dead*	Dan O'Bannon
1986	*Goremet: Zombie Chef from Hell*	Don Swan
1986	*Night of the Creeps*	Fred Dekker
1986	*Raiders of the Living Dead*	Samuel M. Sherman
1986	*The Rape After*	Ho Meng Hua and Moon-Tong Lau
1986	*The Supernaturals*	Armand Mastroianni
1986	*Zombie Brigade*	Carmelo Musca and Barrie Pattison
1986	*Zombie Nightmare*	Jack Bravman
1986	*Zombiethon (Zombie Thon)*	Ken Dixon
1987	*Creepshow 2*	Michael Gornick
1987	*Evil Dead II*	Sam Raimi
1987	*I Was a Teenage Zombie*	John Elias Michalakis
1987	*Killing Spree*	Tim Ritter
1987	*Prince of Darkness*	John Carpenter
1987	*Redneck Zombies*	Pericles Lewnes
1987	*Revenge of the Living Dead Girls*	Pierre B. Reinhard
1987	*The Video Dead*	Robert Scott
1987	*Zombie Death House*	John Saxon
1987	*Zombie High*	Ron Link
1987	*Zombie vs. Ninja*	Godfrey Ho and Joseph Lai
1988	*Dead Heat*	Mark Goldblatt
1988	*The Dead Next Door*	J. R. Bookwalter
1988	*FleshEater*	Bill Hinzman
1988	*Flesh Eating Mothers*	James Aviles Martin
1988	*Return of the Living Dead Part II*	Ken Wiederhorn
1988	*The Serpent and the Rainbow*	Wes Craven

Year	Title	Director
1988	*Summer among the Zombies*	Nobuhiko Obayashi
1988	*Waxwork*	Anthony Hickox
1988	*Zombi III (Zombie Flesh Eaters 2)*	Lucio Fulci and Bruno Mattei
1988	*Zombie Vampire (Robo Vampire)*	Godfrey Ho
1989	*Zombie 4: After Death*	Claudio Fragasso
1988	*Zombie 5*	Jesús Franco
1989	*The Aliens and Kong Kong Zombie*	Seung-ho Ahn
1989	*Beverly Hills Bodysnatchers*	Jonathan Mostow
1989	*Bride of Re-Animator*	Brian Yuzna
1989	*C.H.U.D. II: Bud the C.H.U.D.*	David Irving
1989	*Curse of the Zombie*	Hao Lee
1989	*The Dead Pit*	Brett Leonard
1989	*Hellgate*	William A. Levey
1989	*Night Life*	David Acomba
1989	*Pet Sematary*	Mary Lambert
1989	*Spirit vs. Zombie (Jiang shi da nao xi men ding)*	Feng Pang
1989	*The Vineyard (Curse of the Zombies)*	James Hong
1989	*Working Stiffs*	Michael Legge
1989	*Zombie Rampage*	Todd Sheets
1990	*The Boneyard*	James Cummins
1990	*Dead Men Don't Die*	Malcolm Marmorstein
1990	*Frankenhooker*	Frank Henenlotter
1990	*Linnea Quigley's Horror Workout*	Kenneth J. Hall
1990	*Night of the Living Dead*	Tom Savini
1991	*Black Demons (Dèmoni 3)*	Umberto Lenzi
1991	*Chopper Chicks in Zombietown*	Dan Hoskins
1991	*Nudist Colony of the Dead*	Mark Pirro
1991	*The Zombie Army!*	Betty Stapleford
1991	*Zombie Cop*	J. R. Bookwalter
1991	*Zombie '90: Extreme Pestilence*	Andreas Schnaas
1992	*Army of Darkness*	Sam Raimi
1992	*Braindead (Dead Alive)*	Peter Jackson
1992	*Dead Is Dead*	Mike Stanley
1992	*Pet Sematary Two (Pet Sematary II)*	Mary Lambert
1992	*Urban Scumbags vs. Countryside Zombies*	Patrick Hollmann and Sebastian Panneck

Year	Title	Director
1992	*Waxwork II: Lost in Time*	Anthony Hickox
1992	*Zombie Rampage 2*	Todd Sheets
1993	*Ed and His Dead Mother*	Jonathan Wacks
1993	*Ghost Brigade*	George Hickenlooper
1993	*My Boyfriend's Back*	Bob Balaban
1993	*Ozone*	J. R. Bookwalter
1993	*Return of the Living Dead 3*	Brian Yuzna
1993	*Space Zombie Bingo*	George Ormrod
1993	*Zombie Bloodbath*	Todd Sheets
1994	*Cemetery Man (Dellamorte Dellamore)*	Michele Soavi
1994	*Shatter Dead*	Scooter McCrae
1995	*Death Metal Zombies*	Todd Jason Cook
1995	*Legion of the Night*	Matt Jaissle
1995	*Zombie Bloodbath 2: Rage of the Undead*	Todd Sheets
1995	*Zombie Holocaust (Female Mercenaries on Zombie Island)*	Gary Whitson
1996	*Living a Zombie Dream*	Todd Reynolds
1996	*Uncle Sam*	William Lustig
1997	*Back from the Dead*	Craig Godfrey
1997	*The Necro Files*	Matt Jaissle
1997	*Plaga Zombie*	Pablo Parés and Hernán Sáez
1997	*Premutos: Lord of the Living Dead*	Olaf Ittenbach
1997	*Zombie Ninja Gangbangers*	Jeff Centauri
1998	*Attack of the Flesh Devouring Space Worms from Outer Space*	Mike A. Martinez
1998	*Bio Zombie (Sun faa sau si)*	Wilson Yip
1998	*Laughing Dead*	Patrick Gleason
1998	*Zombie Cult Massacre*	Jeff Dunn
1998	*Zombie Toxin*	Thomas J. Moose
1999	*Hollywood Mortuary*	Ron Ford
1999	*Hot Wax Zombies on Wheels*	Michael Roush
1999	*I Zombie: The Chronicles of Pain*	Andrew Parkinson
1999	*Night of the Living Dead: 30th Anniversary Edition*	John A. Russo
1999	*Raw Zombie 11*	Jared Saverino
1999	*Untot (Undead Unleashed)*	Martin Erling

Year	Title	Director
1999	*Zombie! vs. Mardi Gras*	Will Frank and Karl DeMolay
2000	*The Dead Hate the Living!*	Dave Parker
2000	*Flesh Freaks*	Conall Pendergast
2000	*Meat Market*	Brian Clement
2000	*Prison of the Dead*	David DeCoteau
2000	*Teenage Zombie House Massacre*	Jared Bulls
2000	*Versus (Vasasu)*	Ryuhei Kitamura
2000	*Wild Zero*	Tetsuro Takeuchi
2000	*Zombie Bloodbath 3: Zombie Armageddon*	Todd Sheets
2000	*Zombie Snake (Hebi Onna: Snake Woman)*	Atsushi Shimizu
2001	*All You Zombie*	Sebastian Kutzli
2001	*Biohazardous*	Michael J. Hein
2001	*Children of the Living Dead*	Tor Ramsey
2001	*Ghosts of Mars*	John Carpenter
2001	*Meat Market 2*	Brian Clement
2001	*Mulva: Zombie Ass Kicker!*	Chris Seaver
2001	*Plaga Zombie*	Pablo Parés and Hernán Sáez
2001	*The Resurrection Game*	Mike Watt
2001	*Ritual (Tales from the Crypt Presents: Revelation)*	Avi Nesher
2001	*Route 666*	William Wesley
2001	*Stacy*	Naoyuki Tomomatsu
2001	*The Zombie Chronicles*	Brad Sykes
2002	*Dead/Undead*	Daniel Casey and Mark T. Elliott
2002	*Death Factory*	Brad Sykes
2002	*Deathwatch*	Michael J. Bassett
2002	*The Last Days of Humanity*	Peter Dubiel
2002	*Mark Of The Astro Zombies*	Ted V. Mikels
2002	*Necropolis Awakened*	Garrett White
2002	*Resident Evil*	Paul W. S. Anderson
2002	*28 Days Later*	Danny Boyle
2002	*Walk Like a Zombie (Jombi-cheoreom georeobwa)*	Yoon Young-ho
2002	*Zombie Campout*	Joshua D. Smith
2002	*Zombie Ferox*	Jonathon Ash

Year	Title	Director
2003	*Battlefield Baseball (Jigoku Kōshien)*	Yudai Yamaguchi
2003	*Beyond Re-Animator*	Brian Yuzna
2003	*Blood of the Beast*	Georg Koszulinski
2003	*The Bog Creatures*	J. Christian Ingvordsen
2003	*Boot Hill Blind Dead*	Chris Mackey and Alana Smithe
2003	*Corpses Are Forever*	Jose Prendes
2003	*Daddy Kiss Me*	Michael P. DiPaolo
2003	*Dead Clowns*	Steve Sessions
2003	*Exhumed*	Brian Clement
2003	*The Ghouls (Cannibal Dead)*	Chad Ferrin
2003	*Gory Gory Hallelujah*	Sue Corcoran
2003	*House of the Dead*	Uwe Boll
2003	*I'll See You in My Dreams*	Miguel Ángel Vivas
2003	*The Mental Dead*	Adam Deyoe
2003	*The Necro Files 2*	Ron Carlo
2003	*Noctem*	Jens Wolf
2003	*Operation: Nazi Zombies (Maplewoods)*	David B. Stewart III
2003	*The Revolting Dead*	Michael Su
2003	*Undead*	Michael Spierig and Peter Spierig
2003	*Wiseguys vs. Zombies*	Adam Minarovich
2003	*Zombie Night*	David J. Francis
2003	*Zombiegeddon*	Chris Watson
2003	*Zombiegore*	Maarten van Druten
2004	*Angry and Moist: An Undead Chronicle*	James Raynor
2004	*Bad Friend*	Dustin Austen and Johan Lindsay
2004	*Bone Sickness*	Brian Paulin
2004	*Choking Hazard*	Marek Dobes
2004	*Corpses*	Rolfe Kanefsky
2004	*Curse of the Maya*	David Heavener
2004	*Dawn of the Dead*	Zack Snyder
2004	*Dead and Breakfast*	Matthew Leutwyler
2004	*Dead Meat*	Conor McMahon
2004	*Death Valley: The Revenge of Bloody Bill*	Byron Werner
2004	*Feeding the Masses*	Richard Griffin
2004	*Ghost Lake*	Jay Woelfel

Year	Title	Director
2004	*Graveyard Alive: A Zombie Nurse in Love*	Elza Kephart
2004	*Hide and Creep*	Chuck Hartsell and Chance Shirley
2004	*Hunting Creatures*	Andreas Pape
2004	*Lord of the Undead*	Timo Rose
2004	*Oh! My Zombie Mermaid (Â! Ikkenya puroresu)*	Naoki Kubo
2004	*Punk Rock Zombie Kung Fu Catfight*	Peter Bernard
2004	*Resident Evil: Apocalypse*	Alexander Witt
2004	*Rotten Shaolin Zombies*	Blaine Wasylkiw
2004	*SARS Wars: The Bangkok Zombie Crisis*	Taweewat Wantha
2004	*Shaolin vs. Evil Dead (Shao lin jiang shi)*	Douglas Kung
2004	*Shaun of the Dead*	Edgar Wright
2004	*Tele-Zombie*	Lory-Michael Ringuette
2004	*They Came Back*	Robin Campillo
2004	*Vampires vs. Zombies*	Vince D'Amato
2004	*Zombie Graveyard*	Jonathon Ash
2004	*Zombie Honeymoon*	David Gebroe
2004	*Zombie King and the Legion of Doom (Zombie Beach Party)*	Stacey Case
2004	*Zombie Nation*	Ulli Lommel
2004	*Zombie Planet*	George Bonilla
2005	*All Souls Day*	Jeremy Kasten
2005	*Beneath Still Waters*	Brian Yuzna
2005	*Boy Eats Girl*	Stephen Bradley
2005	*Bubba's Chili Parlor*	Joey Evans
2005	*Day of the Dead 2: Contagium*	Ana Clavell and James Glenn Dudelson
2005	*Day X*	Jason Hack
2005	*Dead at the Box Office*	Shawn Stutler
2005	*Dead Creek*	Edward Boe
2005	*Dead Life*	William Victor Schotten
2005	*Dead Men Walking*	Peter Mervis
2005	*Dead Serious*	Joe Sullivan
2005	*Dead Summer*	Eddie Benevich
2005	*Die Zombiejäger*	Jonas Wolcher
2005	*Doom*	Andrzej Bartkowiak

Year	Title	Director
2005	*The Drunken Dead Guy*	John Greff
2005	*Fragile*	Jaume Balagueró
2005	*The Graveyard of Death*	Jonathon Ash
2005	*Hood of the Living Dead*	Eduardo Quiroz and Jose Quiroz
2005	*House of the Dead 2*	Michael Hurst
2005	*Land of the Dead*	George A. Romero
2005	*Legion of the Dead*	Paul Bales
2005	*Livelihood*	Ryan Graham
2005	*Mortuary*	Tobe Hooper
2005	*Pleasures of the Damned*	Mark Leake
2005	*Pot Zombies*	Justin Powers
2005	*Raiders of the Damned*	Milko Davis
2005	*Return of the Living Dead: Necropolis*	Ellory Elkayem
2005	*Return of the Living Dead: Rave to the Grave*	Ellory Elkayem
2005	*Rise of the Undead*	Jason Horton and Shannon Hubbell
2005	*The Roost*	Ti West
2005	*Severed: Forest of the Dead*	Carl Bessai
2005	*The Stink of Flesh*	Scott Phillips
2005	*Swamp Zombies*	Len Kabasinski
2005	*Tokyo Zombie*	Sakichi Sato
2005	*Z: A Zombie Musical*	John McLean
2005	*Zombie Planet 2: Adam's Revenge*	George Bonilla
2005	*Zombiez*	Zachary Winston Snygg
2006	*After Sundown*	Christopher Abram
2006	*Automaton Transfusion*	Steven C. Miller
2006	*Black Sheep*	Jonathan King
2006	*City of Rott*	Frank Sudol
2006	*Dead and Deader*	Patrick Dinhut
2006	*Dead in the Water*	Marc Buhmann
2006	*The Dead Live*	Darrin Patterson
2006	*Die and Let Live*	Justin Channell
2006	*Doomed to Consume*	Jason Stephenson
2006	*Electric Zombies*	John Specht
2006	*Enter the Zombie*	Ben Mathus
2006	*Fido*	Andrew Currie

Year	Title	Director
2006	*Forbidden Siren (Sairen)*	Yukihiko Tsutsumi
2006	*Gangs of the Dead*	Duane Stinnett
2006	*Last Rites of the Dead*	Marc Fratto
2006	*Meat Market 3*	Brian Clement
2006	*Mulberry Street*	Jim Mickle
2006	*Night of the Dead: Leben Tod*	Eric Forsberg
2006	*Night of the Living Dead 3D*	Jeff Broadstreet
2006	*Pathogen*	Emily Hagins
2006	*The Plague (Clive Barker's The Plague)*	Hal Masonberg
2006	*Poultrygeist: Night of the Chicken Dead*	Lloyd Kaufman
2006	*The Quick and the Undead*	Gerald Nott
2006	*Shadow: Dead Riot*	Derek Wan
2006	*The Slaughter*	Jay Lee
2006	*Slither*	James Gunn
2006	*Special Dead*	Thomas L. Phillips and Sean Simmons
2006	*Stoned Dead*	Ray Etheridge
2006	*They Must Eat*	Tommy Brunswick
2006	*War of the Dead*	Sean Cisterna
2006	*War of the Living Dead*	David A. Prior
2006	*War of the Zombies*	Giuseppe Vari
2006	*Wicked Little Things*	J. S. Cardone
2006	*Zombie Commando*	The Outtake Team
2006	*The Zombie Diaries (Zombie Diaries)*	Michael Bartlett and Kevin Gates
2006	*Zombie Night 2: Awakening*	David J. Francis
2006	*Zombie Outbreak*	Sarah N. Stennett
2006	*Zombie Self-Defense Force*	Naoyuki Tomomatsu
2006	*Zombie Wars*	David A. Prior
2006	*Zombies Anonymous*	Marc Fratto
2006	*Zombies by Design*	Dave Wascavage
2006	*ZombieWestern: It Came from the West*	Tor Fruergaard
2007	*American Zombie*	Grace Lee
2007	*Awaken the Dead*	Jeff Brookshire
2007	*Beneath the Surface*	Blake Reigle
2007	*Black Swarm (Night of the Drones)*	David Winning

Year	Title	Director
2007	*Brain Blockers*	Lincoln Kupchak
2007	*Brain Dead*	Kevin Tenney
2007	*Days of Darkness*	Jake Kennedy
2007	*Dead and Gone*	Yossi Sasson
2007	*Dead Heist*	Bo Webb
2007	*Dead Noon*	Andrew Weist
2007	*Doomed*	Michael Su
2007	*Evil Keg*	Allen Wilbanks
2007	*Flight of the Living Dead: Outbreak on a Plane*	Scott Thomas
2007	*Fog²- Revenge of the Executed*	Oliver Krekel
2007	*Forever Dead*	Christine Parker
2007	*Ghost Zombie (Yûrei zonbi)*	Koji Shiraishi
2007	*I Am Legend*	Francis Lawrence
2007	*I Am Omega*	Griff Furst
2007	*The Mad*	John Kalangis
2007	*Motocross Zombies from Hell*	Gary Robert
2007	*Otto or Up with Dead People*	Bruce LaBruce
2007	*Planet Terror*	Robert Rodriguez
2007	*The Rage*	Robert Kurtzman
2007	*[REC]*	Jaume Balagueró and Paco Plaza
2007	*Resident Evil: Extinction*	Russell Mulcahy
2007	*Rise of the Dead*	William Wedig
2007	*Risen*	Damon Crump
2007	*Shaolin vs. Evil Dead: Ultimate Power*	Douglas Kung
2007	*Street Team Massacre*	Adam Deyoe and Eric Gosselin
2007	*28 Weeks Later*	Juan Carlos Fresnadillo
2007	*Undead or Alive*	Glasgow Phillips
2007	*Undead Pool (Attack Girls Swim Team vs the Unliving Dead)*	Kôji Kawano
2007	*Undead Ted*	Daniel Knight
2007	*Urban Decay*	Harry Basil
2007	*Zibahkhana (Hell's Ground)*	Omar Khan
2007	*Zombie Cheerleader Camp*	Jon Fabris
2007	*Zombie Farm*	B. Luciano Barsuglia
2007	*Zombie Hunters*	Peter Maris

Year	Title	Director
2007	*Zombie Town*	Damon Lemay
2007	*Zombies Gone Wild*	Gary Robert
2007	*Zombies: The Beginning*	Bruno Mattei
2007	*Zombies! Zombies! Zombies!*	Jason M. Murphy
2008	*Army of the Dead*	Joseph Conti
2008	*Colin*	Marc Price
2008	*Dance of the Dead*	Gregg Bishop
2008	*Day of the Dead*	Steve Miner
2008	*Dead Country*	Andrew Merkelbach
2008	*The Dead Outside*	Kerry Anne Mullaney
2008	*Dead Space: Downfall*	Chuck Patton
2008	*Deadgirl*	Marcel Sarmiento and Gadi Harel
2008	*Deep River: The Island*	Ben Bachelder
2008	*Descendents*	Jorge Olguín
2008	*Diary of the Dead*	George A. Romero
2008	*Evilution*	Chris Conlee
2008	*Fast Zombies with Guns*	Bennie Woodell
2008	*Flick*	David Howard
2008	*Grave Mistake*	Shawn Darling
2008	*House of the Damned*	Sean Weathers
2008	*I Sell the Dead*	Glenn McQuaid
2008	*Insanitarium*	Jeff Buhler
2008	*King Zombie (Yau chat guen see um leun nei)*	Cub Chin
2008	*Last of the Living*	Logan McMillan
2008	*Make-Out with Violence*	Deagol Brother
2008	*Mud Zombies (Mangue Negro)*	Rodrigo Aragão
2008	*Mutant Vampire Zombies from the 'Hood!*	Thunder Levin
2008	*Ninjas vs. Zombies*	Justin Timpane
2008	*O.C. Babes and the Slasher of Zombietown*	Creep Creepersin
2008	*Onechanbara: Zombie Bikini Squad*	Yôhei Fukuda
2008	*Outpost*	Steve Barker
2008	*Pig Hunt*	James Isaac
2008	*Plaguers*	Brad Sykes
2008	*Plague Town*	David Gregory

Year	Title	Director
2008	*Pontypool*	Bruce McDonald
2008	*Quarantine*	John Erick Dowdle
2008	*Reel Zombies*	David J. Francis
2008	*Resident Evil: Degeneration (Biohazard: Degeneration)*	Makoto Kamiya
2008	*RetarDEAD*	Rick Popko and Dan West
2008	*Sabbath*	William Victor Schotten
2008	*Samurai Zombie*	Kurando Mitsutake
2008	*Sexykiller*	Paco Cabeza
2008	*Slime City Massacre*	Greg Lamberson
2008	*Stag Night of the Dead*	Neil Jones
2008	*Trailer Park of Terror*	Steven Goldmann
2008	*Uniform SurviGirl I (Uniform Sabaigaru)*	Hiroshi Kaneko
2008	*Uniform SurviGirl II (Seifuku sabaigâru II)*	Hiroshi Kaneko
2008	*The Vanguard*	Matthew Hope
2008	*Virus Undead*	Wolf Wolff and Ohmuti
2008	*Zombie Apocalypse Now! (Un Cazador de zombis)*	Germán Magariños
2008	*Zombie Strippers!*	Jay Lee
2009	*Against the Dark*	Richard Crudo
2009	*Alice Jacobs Is Dead*	Alex Horwitz
2009	*Autumn*	Steven Rumbelow
2009	*Bio Dead*	Stephen J. Hadden
2009	*Blood Creek*	Joel Schumacher
2009	*Blood Moon Rising*	Brian Skiba
2009	*The Bloodfest Club*	Oscar Madrid
2009	*The Brass Ring*	William Victor Schotten
2009	*Broken Springs*	Neeley Lawson
2009	*The Crypt*	Craig McMahon
2009	*Dark Floors*	Pete Riski
2009	*Dead Air*	Corbin Bernsen
2009	*Dead Moon Rising*	Mark E. Poole
2009	*Dead Snow*	Tommy Wirkola
2009	*The Dead Undead*	Matthew R. Anderson and Edward Conna
2009	*The Dead . . . Will Rise!*	Jordan L. Salkil

Year	Title	Director
2009	*Doghouse*	Jake West
2009	*Drive-In Horrorshow*	Michael Neel
2009	*Eat Me! (The Eaters)*	Katie Carman
2009	*Edges of Darkness*	Jason Horton and Blaine Cade
2009	*Evil: In the Time of Heroes*	Yorgos Noussias
2009	*George's Intervention*	J. T. Seaton
2009	*The Horde (La Horde)*	Yannick Dahan and Benjamin Rocher
2009	*The Living Corpse (The Corpse)*	Justin Paul Ritter
2009	*Mutants*	David Morlet
2009	*Night of the Living Dead: Reanimated*	Mike Schneider
2009	*Platoon of the Dead*	John Bowker
2009	*Pushin' Up Daisies*	Patrick Franklin
2009	*[REC]²*	Jaume Balagueró and PacoPlaza
2009	*Redneck Carnage*	Johnno Zee
2009	*The Revenant*	D. Kerry Prior
2009	*Sick and the Dead*	Jordy Dickens and BrocktonMcKinney
2009	*Silent Night, Zombie Night*	Sean Cain
2009	*The Sky Has Fallen*	Doug Roos
2009	*Survival of the Dead*	George A. Romero
2009	*Tormented*	Jon Wright
2009	*Urban Scumbags vs. Countryside Zombies Reanimated*	Maxim Matthew
2009	*ZMD: Zombies of Mass Destruction*	Kevin Hamedani
2009	*Zombie Allegiance*	Tony Nunes
2009	*Zombie Dearest*	David Kemker
2009	*Zombie Farm (La granja de los zombies)*	Ricardo Islas
2009	*Zombies of the Night*	Stuart Brennan
2009	*Zombie Reanimation*	Jochen Taubert and Thomas Kercmar
2009	*Zombie Women of Satan*	Steve O'Brien and Warren Speed
2009	*Zombieland*	Ruben Fleischer
2010	*Astro Zombies M3: Cloned*	Ted V. Mikels
2010	*Atom the Amazing Zombie Killer*	Richard Taylor and Zack Beins
2010	*Atomic Brain Invasion*	Richard Griffin
2010	*Attack of the Vegan Zombies*	Jim Townsend
2010	*Beverly Lane*	Joshua Hull

Year	Title	Director
2010	*Beyond the Grave (Porto dos Mortos)*	Davi de Oliveira Pinheiro
2010	*Big Tits Zombie (Big Tits Dragon: Hot Spring Zombie vs. Stripper 5)*	Takao Nakano
2010	*Biophage*	Mark A. Rapp
2010	*Bounty*	Kevin Kangas
2010	*The Crazies*	Breck Eisner
2010	*The Dead*	Howard J. Ford and Jonathan Ford
2010	*Dead Past*	Daniel Flügger
2010	*Devil's Playground*	Mark McQueen
2010	*Dug Up*	Dustin Rikert
2010	*Gatekeeper: Unlock Your Worst Fears*	Jimmy Weber
2010	*Hell Driver (Nihon bundan: Heru doraibâ)*	Yoshihiro Nishimura
2010	*Highschool of the Dead*	Tetsuro Araki
2010	*Horrorween*	Joe Estevez
2010	*I Walked with a Zombie*	Adam Marcus
2010	*L.A. Zombie (Gay of the Dead)*	Bruce LaBruce
2010	*The Legend of Zombie Road 3D*	Howard Smith and Ethan Terra
2010	*Necro Wars*	Robert Conway
2010	*Night of the Living Dead: Origins 3D*	Zebediah de Soto
2010	*Night of the Living Heads*	George A. Taramas and Michael Gruosso
2010	*Nightmare Alley*	Laurence Holloway and Scarlet Fry
2010	*The Pack*	Frank Richard
2010	*Project Nine (Project 9)*	Dan Sullivan
2010	*Rammbock: Berlin Undead*	Marvin Kren
2010	*Resident Evil: Afterlife*	Paul W. S. Anderson
2010	*Slices of Life*	Anthony G. Sumner
2010	*They Walk*	Charles House II
2010	*Unrated: The Movie*	Andreas Schnaas and Timo Rose
2010	*Zombie Abomination*	Thomas Berdinski
2010	*Zombie Apocalypse*	Ryan Thompson
2010	*Zombie Atrocity*	Thomas Berdinski
2010	*Zombie Driftwood*	Bob Carruthers
2010	*Zombie Massacre*	Uwe Boll
2010	*Zombie Roadkill*	David Green
2010	*Zombie Undead*	Rhys Davies

Year	Title	Director
2010	*Zomblies*	David M. Reynolds
2010	*Zombrex: Dead Rising Sun*	Keiji Inafune
2011	*Bloodlust Zombies*	Dan Lantz
2011	*Bong of the Dead*	Thomas Newman
2011	*The Cabin in the Woods*	Drew Goddard
2011	*Caustic Zombies*	Johnny Daggers
2011	*Dylan Dog: Dead of Night*	Kevin Munroe
2011	*Eaters*	Luca Boni and Marco Ristori
2011	*Exit Humanity*	John Geddes
2011	*Fading of the Cries*	Brian A. Metcalf
2011	*First Platoon*	Chris Gabriel
2011	*Harold's Going Stiff*	Keith Wright
2011	*Humans Versus Zombies*	Brian T. Jaynes
2011	*Juan of the Dead (Juan de los Muertos)*	Alejandro Brugués
2011	*Ninja Zombies*	Noah Cooper
2011	*Pirates of the Caribbean: On Stranger Tides*	Rob Marshall
2011	*Pop Punk Zombies*	Steve Dayton
2011	*Post Mortem America 2021*	Cameron Scott
2011	*Quarantine 2: Terminal*	John Erick Dowdle
2011	*Remains (Steve Niles' Remains)*	Colin Theys
2011	*Rise of the Damned*	Michael Bafaro
2011	*Schoolgirl Apocalypse*	John S. Cairns
2011	*Stripperland*	Sean Skelding
2011	*Virulents*	John Moore
2011	*War of the Dead (Stone's War)*	Marko Makilaakso
2011	*Zombie Apocalypse*	Nick Lyon
2011	*Zombie Apocalypse: Redemption*	Ryan Thompson
2011	*The Zombie Diaries 2*	Michael Bartlett and Kevin Gates
2011	*Zombie Doomsday*	Tom Townsend
2012	*Abraham Lincoln vs. Zombies*	Richard Schenkman
2012	*The Battery*	Jeremy Gardner
2012	*BFF Zombie*	Fedor Steer
2012	*Celluloid Bloodbath*	Jim Monaco and James F. Murray Jr.
2012	*Cockneys vs Zombies*	Matthias Hoene
2012	*Dead Season*	Adam Deyoe

Year	Title	Director
2012	*Decay*	Luke Thompson
2012	*The Eschatrilogy: Book of the Dead*	Damian Morter
2012	*A Little Bit Zombie*	Casey Walker
2012	*Long Live the Dead*	Richard Poche
2012	*Night of the Living Dead 3D: Re-Animation*	Jeff Broadstreet
2012	*ParaNorman*	Sam Fell and Chris Butler
2012	*Parasitic*	Tim Martin
2012	*[REC]³: Génesis*	Paco Plaza
2012	*Resident Evil: Damnation*	Makoto Kamiya
2012	*Resident Evil: Retribution*	Paul W. S. Anderson
2012	*Rise of the Zombies*	Nick Lyon
2012	*Zombies vs. Strippers*	Alex Nicolaou
2012	*The Zombinator*	Sergio Myers
2013	*The Amazing Adventures of the Living Corpse*	Justin Paul Ritter
2013	*Bath Salt Zombies*	Dustin Mills
2013	*Evil Dead*	Fede Alvarez
2013	*Go Goa Gone*	Krishna D. K. and Raj Nidimoru
2013	*The Harvard Zombie Massacre*	Warren Zide
2013	*I Am Dead*	John Taylor
2013	*Percy Jackson: Sea of Monsters*	Thor Freudenthal
2013	*Warm Bodies*	Jonathan Levine
2013	*World War Z*	Marc Forster

Appendix B: Zombie Studies: Academic Books and Articles about Zombies

Balaji, Murali. *Thinking Dead: What the Zombie Apocalypse Means.* Lanham, MD: Lexington Books, 2013

Bishop, Kyle William. *American Zombie Gothic: The Rise and Fall (and Rise) of the Walking Dead in Popular Culture.* Jefferson, NC: McFarland, 2010.

Bishop, Kyle William. "The Idle Proletariat: *Dawn of the Dead*, Consumer Ideology, and the Loss of Productive Labor." *The Journal of Popular Culture* 43.2 (2010): 234–248.

Boluk, Stephanie, and Wylie Lenz. *Generation Zombie: Essays on the Living Dead in Modern Culture.* Jefferson, NC: McFarland, 2011.

Boluk, Stephanie, and Wylie Lenz. "Infection, Media, and Capitalism: From Early Modern Plagues to Postmodern Zombies." *Journal for Early Modern Cultural Studies* 10.2 (2010): 126–147.

Christie, Deborah, and Sarah Juliet Lauro. *Better Off Dead: The Evolution of the Zombie as Post-Human.* New York: Fordham University Press, 2011.

Comaroff, Jean, and John Comaroff. "Alien-Nation: Zombies, Immigrants, and Millennial Capitalism." *South Atlantic Quarterly* 101.4 (2002): 779–805.

McAlister, Elizabeth. "Slaves, Cannibals, and Infected Hyper-Whites: The Race and Religion of Zombies." *Anthropological Quarterly* 85.2 (2012): 457–486.

McIntosh, Shawn, and Marc Leverette. *Zombie Culture: Autopsies of the Living Dead.* Lanham, MD: Scarecrow Press, 2008.

Miller, Cynthia J., and A. Bowdoin Van Riper, eds. *Undead in the West: Vampires, Zombies, Mummies, and Ghosts on the Cinematic Frontier.* Lanham, MD: Scarecrow Press, 2012.

Moreman, Christopher, and Cory Rushton, eds. *Race, Oppression and the Zombie: Essays on Cross-Cultural Appropriations of the Caribbean Tradition.* Jefferson, NC: McFarland, 2011.

Moreman, Christopher, and Cory Rushton, eds. *Zombies Are Us: Essays on the Humanity of the Walking Dead and Zombies.* Jefferson, NC: McFarland, 2011.

Paffenroth, Kim. *The Gospel of the Living Dead: George Romero's Visions of Hell on Earth.* Waco, TX: Baylor University Press, 2006.

Paffenroth, Kim, and John W. Morehead, eds. *The Undead and Theology.* Eugene, OR: Pickwick Publications, 2012.

Pulliam, June. "Our Zombies, Ourselves: Exiting the Foucauldian Universe in George A. Romero's *Land of the Dead*." *Journal of the Fantastic in the Arts* 20.1 (2009): 42–56.

Pulliam, June. " 'We're Them and They're Us': Zombies, Evil and Moral Agency in American Culture." In *Evil in American Culture*, edited by Sharon Packer. Westport, CT: Greenwood, 2014.

Robichaud, Christopher, ed. *The Walking Dead and Philosophy: Zombie, Shotgun, Reason.* New York: Wiley, 2012.

Rutherford, Jennifer. *Zombies.* New York: Routledge, 2013.

Sidorsky, David. "Post Mortems of the Sixties: Deep Structure Specters and Walking Zombies." *Partisan Review* 69.2 (2002): 240–54.

Smith, Robert. *Braaaiiinnnsss!: From Academics to Zombies*. Ottawa: University of Ottawa Press, 2011.

Waller, Gregory A. *The Living and the Undead: From Stoker's Dracula to Romero's Dawn of the Dead*. Urbana: University of Illinois Press, 1986.

Wetmore, Kevin J. *Back from the Dead: Remakes of the Romero Zombie Films as Markers of Their Times*. Jefferson, NC: McFarland, 2011.

Wolf, Michael P. "Could I Just Be a Very Epistemically Responsible Zombie?" *Southwest Philosophy Review: The Journal of the Southwestern Philosophical Society* 25.2 (2009): 69–72.

Yuen, Wayne. *The Walking Dead and Philosophy*. Chicago: Open Court Press, 2012.

Further Reading

Allmer, Patricia, Emily Brick, and D. Huxley, eds. *European Nightmares: Horror Cinema in Europe since 1946*. New York: Columbia University Press, 2012.

Andrae, Thomas. *Carl Barks and the Disney Comic Book: Unmasking the Myth of Modernity*. Jackson: University Press of Mississippi, 2006.

Badley, Linda. *Film, Horror, and the Body Fantastic*. Westport, CT: Greenwood Press, 1995.

Bansak, Edmund G. *Fearing the Dark: The Val Lewton Career*. Jefferson, NC: McFarland, 1995.

Barber, Paul. *Vampires, Burial, and Death: Folklore and Reality*. New Haven, CT: Yale University Press, 1988.

Beard, William. *The Artist as Monster: The Cinema of David Cronenberg*. Toronto: University of Toronto Press, 2001.

Beresford, Matthew. *From Demons to Dracula: The Creation of the Modern Vampire Myth*. London: Reaktion, 2008.

Betrock, Alan. *The I Was a Teenage Juvenile Delinquent Rock "n" Roll Horror Beach Party Movie Book: A Complete Guide to the Teen Exploitation Film, 1954–1969*. New York: St. Martin's Press, 1986.

Bettelheim, Adriel. *Aging in America, A-Z*. Washington, DC: CQ Press, 2001.

Bloom, Clive. *The "'Occult" Experience and the New Criticism: Daemonism, Sexuality, and the Hidden in Literature*. Sussex: Harvester Press, 1987.

Bloom, Harold, ed. *Cormac McCarthy: Bloom's Modern Critical Views*. New York: Infobase Publishing, 2009.

Bodart, Joni Richards. *They Suck, They Bite, They Eat, They Kill: The Psychological Meaning of Supernatural Monsters in Young Adult Fiction*. Lanham, MD: Scarecrow, 2012.

Bondanella, Peter. *A History of Italian Cinema*. New York: Continuum, 2009.

Boyle, Danny, and Brent Dunham. *Danny Boyle: Interviews*. Jackson: University Press of Mississippi, 2011.

Brown, Eric S., and H. G. Wells. *The War of the Worlds: Plus Blood, Guts and Zombies*. New York: Gallery, 2009.

Brown, Jennifer. *Cannibalism in Literature and Film*. New York: Palgrave MacMillan, 2012.

Brunas, Michael, John Brunas, and Tom Weaver. *Universal Horrors: The Studio's Classic Films, 1931–1946*. Jefferson, NC: McFarland, 1990.

Brunetta, Gian Piero. *The History of Italian Cinema: A Guide to Italian film from Its Origins to the Twenty-First Century*. Trans. Jeremy Parzen. Princeton, NJ: Princeton University Press, 2009.

Burrows, David J., Frederick R. Lapides, and John T. Shawcross. *Myths and Motifs in Literature*. New York: Free Press, 1973.

Bussey, George Moir, ed. *The Thousand and One Nights*. Trans. Edward Forster. New York: Carleton, 1872.

Butler, Judith. *Gender Trouble: Feminism and the Subversion of Identity*. New York: Routledge, 1990.

Cannon, P. H. *H. P. Lovecraft*. Boston: Twayne Publishers, 1989.

Cardin, Matt, ed. *Mummies around the World: An Encyclopedia of Mummies in History, Religion, and Popular Culture*. Santa Barbara, CA: ABC-CLIO, 2014.

Carroll, Noel. 1990. *The Philosophy of Horror, or Paradoxes of the Heart*. New York: Routledge, 1990.

Cerasini, Marc A., and Charles E. Hoffman. *Robert E. Howard*. Mercer Island, WA: Starmont House, Inc., 1987.

Chambers, Cullen. *Back to One, the Movie Extras Guidebook: How to Make Good Money as a Background Actor in Film and TV*. 19th ed. Hollywood, CA: Back to One Publications, 2006.

Chan, Leo Tak-hung. *The Discourse on Foxes and Ghosts: Ji Yun and Eighteenth-Century Literati Storytelling*. Honolulu: University of Hawaii Press, 1998.

Chapman, James. *License to Thrill: A Cultural History of the James Bond Films*. New York: Columbia University Press, 2000.

Chodorow, Nancy. *The Reproduction of Mothering: Psychoanalysis and the Sociology of Gender*. Berkeley: University of California Press, 1978.

Clover, Carol J. *Men, Women and Chainsaws: Gender in the Modern Horror Film*. London: BFI, 1992.

Colbert, David. *The Magical Worlds of Harry Potter*. Revised ed. New York: Berkley Trade, 2008.

Cooper, L. Andrew. *Dario Argento*. Champaign: University of Illinois Press, 2012.

Courlander, Harold. *The Drum and the Hoe: Life and Lore of the Haitian People*. Berkeley: University of California Press, 1960.

Cremer, Robert. *Lugosi: The Man behind the Cape*. Chicago: H. Regnery Co., 1976.

Cronin, Gloria L. *Critical Essays on Zora Neale Hurston*. New York: G. K. Hall, 1998.

Crouse, Richard. *The 100 Best Movies You've Never Seen*. Toronto: ECW, 2003.

Dailey, Stephanie. *Myths from Mesopotamia: Creation, the Flood, Gilgamesh, and Others*. Revised ed. Oxford: Oxford University Press, 2008.

Daniel, Tim, and Robert Kirkman. *The Walking Dead Survivors' Guide*. Image Comics: Orange, 2011.

Davis, Wade. *The Serpent and the Rainbow*. New York: Simon and Shuster, 1985.

Day, Jasmine. *The Mummy's Curse: Mummymania in the English-speaking World*. New York: Routledge, 2006.

Dayan, Colin. *Haiti, History and the Gods*. Berkeley: University of California Press, 1998.

De Camp, L Sprague. *Lovecraft: A Biography*. Garden City, NY: Doubleday, 1975.

Dendle, Peter. *The Zombie Movie Encyclopedia*. Jefferson, NC: McFarland, 2001.

Dendle, Peter. *The Zombie Movie Encyclopedia: 2000–2010*. Jefferson, NC: McFarland, 2012.

Deren, Maya. *Divine Horsemen: The Living Gods of Haiti*. Kingston, NY: McPherson, 1983.

Desmangles, Leslie G. *The Faces of the Gods: Vodou and Roman Catholicism in Haiti*. Chapel Hill: University of North Carolina Press, 1992.

Douglas, David. *The Atlas of Lost Cults and Mystery Religions*. London: Godsfield, 2009.

Duriez, Colin. *Field Guide to Harry Potter*. Downers Grove, IL: IVP Books, 2007.

Edwards, Kathryn A. *Werewolves, Witches, and Wandering Spirits: Traditional Belief and Folklore in Early Modern Europe*. Kirksville, MO: Truman State University Press, 2002.

Eisner, Lotte H. *The Haunted Screen: Expressionism in the German Cinema and the Influence of Max Reinhardt*. London: Thames and Hudson, 1969.

Eller, Jonathan R. *Becoming Ray Bradbury*. Champaign: University of Illinois Press, 2011.

Eller, Jonathan R., and William F. Touponce. *Ray Bradbury: The Life of Fiction*. Kent, OH: Kent State UP, 2004.

Ellis-Davidson, Hilda Roderick. *The Road to Hell: A Study of the Conception of the Dead in Old Norse Literature*, Kindle edition. Idunnas Press, 2011.

Fallows, Tom, and Curtis Owen. *George A. Romero*. Harpenden, UK: Pocket Essentials. 2008.

Fields, R. Douglas. *The Other Brain: From Dementia to Schizophrenia, How New Discoveries about the Brain Are Revolutionizing Medicine and Science*. New York: Simon and Schuster, 2010.

Fujiwara, Chris. *Jacques Tourner: The Cinema of Nightfall*. Jefferson, NC: McFarland, 1998.

Gagne, Paul R. *The Zombies That Ate Pittsburgh: The Films of George A. Romero*. New York: Dodd, 1987.

George, Andrew. *The Epic of Gilgamesh*. New York: Penguin, 2003.

George, Nelson. *Thriller: The Musical Life of Michael Jackson*. New York: De Capo, 2010.

Goldsmith, Arnold L. *The Golem Remembered, 1909–1980: Variations of a Jewish Legend*. Detroit: Wayne State University Press, 1981.

Gordon, Bruce, and Peter Marshall. *The Place of the Dead: Death and Remembrance in Late Medieval and Early Modern Europe*. Cambridge, UK; New York: Cambridge University Press, 2000.

Grams, Martin. *The Twilight Zone: Unlocking the Door to a Television Classic*. Churchville, MD: OTR Publishing, 2008.

Grant, Michael. *The Modern Fantastic: The Films of David Cronenberg*. Westport, CT: Praeger, 2000.

Greene, Richard, and Silem K. Mohammad, eds. *The Undead and Philosophy: Chicken Soup for the Undead Soul*. Chicago: Open Court Press, 2006.

Greene, Richard, and Silem K. Mohammad, eds. *Zombies, Vampires and Philosophy: New Life for the Undead*. Chicago: Open Court Press, 2010.

Gresh, Lois H., and Robert E Weinberg. *The Science of James Bond: From Bullets to Bowler Hats to Boat Jumps, the Real Technology Behind 007's Fabulous Films*. Hoboken, NJ: Wiley and Sons, 2006.

Guran, Paula, and Neil Gaiman, eds. *Zombies: The Recent Dead*. Rockville, MD: Prime Books, 2010.

Gwinn, Beth, and Stan Wiater. *Dark Dreamers: Facing the Masters of Fear*. Baltimore: Cemetery Dance Publications, 2001.

Haining, Peter. *Cannibal Killers*. London: Magpie Books, 2008.

Hallenbeck, Bruce G. *Comedy-Horror Films: A Chronological History, 1914–2008*. Jefferson, NC: McFarland, 2009.

Hantke, Steffen, ed. *American Horror Film: The Genre at the Turn of the Millennium*. Jackson: University Press of Mississippi, 2010.

Harris, Laurie Lanzen. *Characters in 20th-Century Literature*. Detroit: Gale Research, 1990.

Hearn, Marcus. *Hammer Glamour*. London: Titan, 2009.

Helford, Elyce Rae. *Fantasy Girls: Gender in the New Universe of Science Fiction and Fantasy Television*. Lanham, MD: Rowman and Littlefield, 2000.

Herron, Don. *The Dark Barbarian: The Writings of Robert E. Howard, a Critical Anthology*. Westport, CT: Greenwood, 1984.

Herskovits, Melville J. *Dahomey, an Ancient West African Kingdom*. Evanston, IL: Northwestern University Press, 1967.

Hofstadter, Douglas R., and Daniel C. Dennett. *The Mind's I: Fantasies and Reflections on Self and Soul*. New York: Basic Books, 1981.

Hogarth, David. *Documentary Television in Canada: From National Public Service to Global Marketplace*. Montreal; Ithaca, NY: McGill-Queen's University Press, 2002.

Holm, John. *Pidgins and Creoles*, Cambridge: Cambridge University Press, 1989.

Hoolboom, Michael. *Inside the Pleasure Dome: Fringe Film in Canada*. Toronto: Coach House Books, 2001.

Hoppenstand, Gary. *Stephen King*. Pasadena, CA: Salem Press, 2011.

Hortelano, Lorenzo J. Torres. *Directory of World Cinema: Spain*. Bristol, UK; Chicago: Intellect, 2011.

Hurston, Zora Neale. *Tell My Horse: Voodoo and Life in Haiti and Jamaica*. Philadelphia: J. B. Lippincott, 1938.

Hurston, Zora Neale. *Voodoo Gods: An Inquiry into Native Myths and Magic in Jamaica and Haiti*. London: J.M. Dent and Sons, ltd, 1939.

Hutchings, Peter. *Hammer and Beyond: the British Horror Film*. Manchester, UK: Manchester University Press, 1993.

Hutchisson, James M. *Poe*. Jackson: University Press of Mississippi, 2005.

Huxley, Francis. *The Invisibles: Voodoo Gods in Haiti*. New York: McGraw-Hill 1969.

Ireland, W. M. *Remarks on the Medical Properties of the Stramonium: Being a Series of Facts and Observations Made for the Purpose of Ascertaining the Qualities and Effects of That Valuable Plant*. New York: James Eastburn, 1817.

James, C. L. R. *The Black Jacobins: Toussaint L'ouverture and the San Domingo Revolution*. New York: Vintage Books, 1963.

Jancovich, Mark, Antonio Lázaro Reboli, Julian Stringer, and Andrew Willis, eds. *Defining Cult Movies: The Cultural Politics of Oppositional Taste*. New York: Palgrave, 2003.

Joshi, S. T. *H. P. Lovecraft: Four Decades of Criticism*. Athens: Ohio University Press, 1980.

Joshi, S. T. *A Subtler Magick: The Writings and Philosophy of H. P. Lovecraft*. San Bernardino, CA: Borgo Press, 1996.

Kane, Paul, and Marie O'Regan. *Voices in the Dark: Interviews with Horror Writers, Directors and Actors*. Jefferson, NC: McFarland, 2011.

Kaplan, Matt. *Medusa's Gaze and Vampire's Bite: The Science of Monsters*. New York: Scribner, 2012.

Kay, Glenn. *Zombie Movies: The Ultimate Guide*. Chicago: Chicago Review Press, 2008.

Kendrick, James. *Film Violence: History, Ideology, Genre*. London; New York: Wallflower, 2009.

Kenemore, Scott, and Adam Wallenta. *Zombies vs. Nazis: A Lost History of the Walking Dead*. New York: Skyhorse, 2011.

Kennedy, J. Gerald. *Poe, Death, and the Life of Writing*. New Haven, CT: Yale University Press, 1987.

King, Stephen, Tim Underwood, and Chuck Miller. *Bare Bones: Conversations on Terror with Stephen King*. New York: McGraw-Hill, 1988.

Kirkland, Douglas. *The Making of Thriller: 4 Days, 1983*. New York: Hachette, 2010.

Konow, David. *Reel Terror: The Scary, Bloody, Gory, Hundred-Year History of Classic Horror Films*. New York: St. Martin's Griffin, 2012.

Koven, Mikel. *La Dolce Morte: Vernacular Cinema and the Italian Giallo Film*. Lanham, MD: Scarecrow Press, 2006.

Kracauer, Siegfried. *From Caligari to Hitler: A Psychological History of the German Film*. Leonardo Quaresima, ed. Princeton, NJ: Princeton Classic Editions, 2004.

Kronzek, Allan Zola, and Elizabeth Kronzek. *The Sorcerer's Companion: A Guide to the Magical World of Harry Potter*. New York: Broadway Books, 2001.

Landis, John. *Monsters in the Movies: 100 Years of Cinematic Nightmares*. New York: DK, 2011.

Laraque, Paul, and Jack Hirschman, eds. *Open Gate: An Anthology of Haitian-Creole Poetry*. Creole and English Edition. Seattle: Curbstone Press, 2001.

Lecouteux, Claude. *The Return of the Dead: Ghosts, Ancestors, and the Transparent Veil of the Pagan Mind*. Rochester, VT: Inner Traditions, 2009.

Lennig, Arthur. *The Immortal Count: The Life and Films of Bela Lugosi*. Lexington: University Press of Kentucky, 2003.

Leonard, Frances McNeely, Ramona Cearley, and Joe Holley. *Conversations with Texas Writers*. Austin: University of Texas Press, 2005.

Lerner, Neil, ed. *Music in the Horror Film: Listening to Fear*. New York: Routledge, 2009.

Lowder, James, ed. *Triumph of the Walking Dead: Robert Kirkman's Zombie Epic on Page and Screen*. Dallas: Benbella Books, 2011.

MacKenzie, Norman I, and Jeanne MacKenzie. *H. G. Wells: A Biography*. New York: Simon and Schuster, 1973.

Marshall, Wendy L. *William Beaudine: From Silents to Television*. Lanham, MD: Scarecrow Press, 2005.

Mason, Herbert. *Gilgamesh: A Verse Narrative*. New York: Penguin, 1972.

Mathijs, Ernest, and Xavier Mendik, eds. *The Cult Film Reader*. New York: Open University Press, 2009.

McCarty, John. *The Fearmakers: The Screen's Directorial Masters of Suspense and Terror*. New York: St. Martin's Press, 1994.

McCarty, John. *The Sleaze Merchants: Adventures in Exploitation Filmmaking*. New York: St. Martin's Griffin, 1995.

McCarthy, Michael. *Modern Mythmakers: Interviews with Horror, Science Fiction and Fantasy Writers and Filmmakers*. Jefferson, NC: McFarland, 2008.

Meikle, Denis. *A History of Horrors: The Rise and Fall of the House of Hammer*. Lanham, MD: Scarecrow, 1996.

Métraux, Alfred. *Voodoo in Haiti*. New York: Schocken Books, 1972.

Milano, Roy, Bela Lugosi, and Jennifer Osborne. *Monsters: A Celebration of the Classics from Universal Studios*. New York: Del Rey Books, 2006.

Miller, Cynthia J., and A. Bowdoin Van Riper, eds. *Undead in the West: Vampires, Zombies, Mummies, and Ghosts on the Cinematic Frontier*. Lanham, MD: Scarecrow Press, 2012.

Milne, Carly, ed. *Naked Ambition: How Women Are Changing Pornography*. New York: Carroll & Graf, 2005.

Muir, John Kenneth. *Eaten Alive at a Chainsaw Massacre: The Films of Tobe Hooper*. Jefferson, NC: McFarland, 2002.

Muir, John Kenneth. *Terror Television: American Series, 1970–1999*. Jefferson, NC: McFarland, 2001.

Muir, John Kenneth. *The Unseen Force: The Films of Sam Raimi*. New York: Applause Theatre and Cinema, 2004.

Muir, John Kenneth. *Wes Craven: The Art of Horror*. Jefferson, NC: McFarland, 1998.

Nelson, Victoria. *Gothicka: Vampire Heroes, Human Gods, and the New Supernatural*. Cambridge, MA: Harvard University Press, 2012.

Paszylk, Bartlomiej. *The Pleasure and Pain of Cult Horror Films: An Historical Survey*. Jefferson, NC: McFarland, 2009.

Paul, Louis. *Italian Horror Film Directors*. Jefferson, NC: McFarland, 2005.

Paul, William. *Laughing, Screaming: Modern Hollywood Horror and Comedy*. New York: Columbia UP, 1994.

Pryor, Ian. *Peter Jackson: From Prince of Splatter to Lord of the Rings*. New York: St. Martin's, 2004.

Reino, Joseph. *Stephen King: The First Decade, Carrie to Pet Sematary*. Boston: Twayne, 1988.

Rhodes, Gary Don. *The Films of Joseph H. Lewis.* Detroit: Wayne State University Press, 2012.

Rhodes, Gary Don. *Lugosi: His Life in Films, on Stage, and in the Hearts of Horror Lovers.* Jefferson, NC: McFarland, 1997.

Robb, Brian J. *Screams and Nightmares: The Films of Wes Craven.* Woodstock, NY: Overlook Press, 1998.

Rozenberg, Yehudah Yudl. *The Golem and the Wondrous Deeds of the Maharal of Prague.* New Haven, CT: Yale University Press, 2007.

Rubin, Steven Jay. *The Complete James Bond Movie Encyclopedia.* Chicago: Contemporary Books, 2003.

Ruditis, Paul. *The Walking Dead Chronicles: The Official Companion Book.* New York: Abrams, 2011.

Russell, Jamie. *Book of the Dead: The Complete History of Zombie Cinema.* Surrey, UK: FAB Press, 2007.

Saint Nicholas, Michael. *An Actor's Guide, Your First Year in Hollywood.* New York: Allworth Press, 2000.

Salisbury, Mark, and Alan Hedgcock. *Behind the Mask: The Secrets of Hollywood's Monster Makers.* London: Titan, 1994.

Sandars, N. K., Trans. *The Epic of Gilgamesh: An English Version, with an Introduction.* New York: Penguin, 1972.

Savini, Tom. *Grande Illusions: A Learn-By-Example Guide to the Art and Technique of Special Make-Up Effects from the Films of Tom Savini.* Pittsburgh: Imagine, 1983.

Schultes, Richard Evans, Albert Hofmann, and Christian Rätsch. *Plants of the Gods: Their Sacred, Healing, and Hallucinogenic Powers.* Rochester, VT: Healing Arts Press, 2001.

Shreffler, Philip A. *The H. P. Lovecraft Companion.* Westport, CT: Greenwood Press, 1977.

Sibley, Brian. *Peter Jackson: A Film-Maker's Journey.* London: Harper Collins Entertainment, 2006.

Silver, Alain, and James Ursini. *The Horror Film Reader.* New York: Limelight Editions, 2000.

Simek, Rudolf. *Dictionary of Northern Mythology.* Suffolk, VA: D. S. Brewer, 1996.

Smith, Don G. *H. G. Wells on Film: The Utopian Nightmare.* Jefferson, NC: McFarland, 2002.

Sproston-North, Wendy E. *The Lazarus Story within the Johannine Tradition.* Sheffield, UK: Sheffield Academic Press, 2001.

Steiger, Brad. *Real Zombies, the Living Dead, and Creatures of the Apocalypse.* Canton, MI: Visible Ink Press, 2010.

Taraborrelli, J. Randy. *Michael Jackson: The Magic, the Madness, the Whole Story, 1958–2009.* New York: Grand Central, 2009.

Taylor, Richard P. *Death and the Afterlife: A Cultural Encyclopedia.* Santa Barbara, CA: ABC-CLIO, 2000.

Telotte, J. P., ed. *The Cult Film Experience: Beyond all Reason.* Austin: University of Texas Press, 1991.

Tibbets, John C. *The Gothic Imagination: Conversations on Fantasy, Horror, and Science Fiction in the Media.* New York: Palgrave, 2011.

Timpone, Anthony. *Men, Makeup, and Monsters: Hollywood's Masters of Illusion and FX.* New York: St. Martin's Griffin, 1996.

Thomson, Douglass H., Jack G. Voller, and Frederick S. Frank, eds. *Gothic Writers: A Critical and Bibliographical Guide.* Westport, CT: Greenwood, 2002.

Turner, George E, and Michael H. Price. *Forgotten Horrors: Early Talkie Chillers from Poverty Row.* South Brunswick, NJ: A. S. Barnes, 1979.

Walsh, Lynda. *Sins against Science: The Scientific Media Hoaxes of Poe, Twain, and Others.* Albany: State University of New York Press, 2006.

Walton, Priscilla L. *Our Cannibals, Ourselves.* Urbana: University of Illinois Press, 2004.

Wand, Kelly. *Voodoo: Fact or Fiction.* San Diego, CA: Greenhaven Press, 2004.

Warren, Bill. *The Evil Dead Companion.* New York: St. Martin's Griffin, 2001.

Warren, Bill. *Set Visits: Interviews with 32 Horror and Science Fiction Filmmakers.* Jefferson, NC: McFarland, 1997.

Weaver, Tom. *Double Feature Creature Attack: A Monster Merger of Two More Volumes of Classic Interviews.* Jefferson, NC: McFarland, 2003.

Weiner, Robert G., and John Cline, eds. *Cinema Inferno: Celluloid Explosions from the Cultural Margins.* Lanham, MD: Scarecrow Press, 2010.

Whalley, Lawrence. *The Aging Brain.* New York: Columbia University Press, 2001.

Williams, Tony. *The Cinema of George A. Romero: Knight of the Living Dead.* New York: Wallflower, 2003.

Williams, Tony: *George A. Romero: Interviews (Conversations with Filmmakers Series).* Jackson: University Press of Mississippi, 2011.

Wilkinson, Simon A. *Hollywood Horror from the Director's Chair: Six Filmmakers in the Franchise of Fear.* Jefferson, NC: McFarland, 2008.

Winter, Douglas E. *Faces of Fear: Encounters with the Creators of Modern Horror.* New York: Berkley, 1985.

Wooley, John. *Wes Craven: The Man and His Nightmares.* Hoboken, NJ: Wiley, 2011.

Wright, Bradford. *Comic Book Nation: The Transformation of Youth Culture in America.* Baltimore: Johns Hopkins University Press, 2003.

Wright, Handel Kashope, Michael Singh, and Richard Race, eds. *Precarious International Multicultural Education: Hegemony, Dissent and Rising Alternatives.* Rotterdam, The Netherlands: Sense Publishers, 2012.

Zicree, Marc Scott. *The Twilight Zone Companion.* New York: Bantam, 1982.

About the Editors and Contributors

THE EDITORS

At the tender age of eight, **June Michele Pulliam** was permitted to stay up by herself and watch George Romero's *Night of the Living Dead*. She was so traumatized by the experience that she now teaches courses on horror fiction at Louisiana State University. Additionally, Pulliam has authored (with Anthony Fonseca) three volumes of *Hooked on Horror* and *Read On . . . Horror,* as well as several articles about zombies, Stephenie Meyer's *Twilight Saga*, Roald Dahl and teen female lycanthropes in young adult fiction. She is also the editor of *Dead Reckonings: A Review Magazine for the Horror Field*. She makes her home in Baton Rouge, Louisiana, in a creaky old house with several feline familiars who variously thwart and assist her writing deadlines.

Anthony J. (Tony) Fonseca is the library director of Alumnae Library, Elms College, Massachusetts. He has authored (with June Michele Pulliam) three volumes of *Hooked on Horror* and *Read On . . . Horror,* and is coeditor of *Dead Reckonings: A Review Magazine for the Horror Field*. He has also published articles/chapters on doppelgängers, psychics, horror readership, vampire music, female vampires in film, bhangra-beat music, patron-driven acquisitions, and information literacy. He is currently working on articles on horror film music, Robert Aickman, and *The Boondocks*.

THE CONTRIBUTORS

Alicia Ahlvers is currently a Kansas City Public Library branch manager. She has served on the American Library Association's (ALA's) RUSA CODES Notable Books Council and the ALA RUSA CODES Reading List Book Award committee where she helped select the best books in various genres. Alicia also works at the University of Missouri, Kansas City, as a weekend reference librarian where, during finals week, she frequently encounters the walking dead. She "almost" appeared in a budget zombie film, but her lack of dead white eyes thwarted her bid for a Hollywood zombie career. When not working, she can be found on Twitter perfecting her Zombie Apocalypse Plan with her friends and followers.

Titus Belgard has degrees in history and English from Louisiana College in Pineville, Louisiana, and holds an MLIS from the University of Southern Mississippi. He has been on staff of the James C. Bolton Library at LSU-Alexandria since 2004. Prior to that, he was a clerk, curator, and manager of the Marksville State Historic Site (a 2,000-year-old Native American mound museum). Belgard lives in

Pineville, Louisiana, where he is an active member of Emmanuel Baptist Church in Alexandria, Louisiana. He has had several book reviews published in *Louisiana Libraries* and *Codex*.

Kyle William Bishop is an associate professor of American literature and film studies at Southern Utah University. He has published a variety of articles on Gothic literature, horror cinema, and science fiction texts, including *Night of the Living Dead, Fight Club, Buffy the Vampire Slayer, Dawn of the Dead, Zombieland, The Birds,* and *The Walking Dead*. His first book, *American Zombie Gothic: The Rise and Fall (and Rise) of the Walking Dead in Popular Culture,* explores the cultural history of the zombie figure and is available from McFarland Publishers.

Richard Bleiler is the humanities librarian at the University of Connecticut's Homer Babbidge Library.

John Edgar Browning is Arthur A. Schomburg Fellow and PhD student (American Studies) in the Department of Transnational Studies and adjunct faculty member in the Department of English at SUNY-Buffalo. He has contracted or co-written a number of books and articles on horror cinema, *Dracula,* vampires, and Bram Stoker, most recently with *Speaking of Monsters: A Teratological Anthology* (with Caroline J. S. Picart) and *The Forgotten Writings of Bram Stoker,* both from Palgrave Macmillan.

Robert Butterfield is a musician and music instructor. His longtime interest in the literary arts resulted in his going back to school late in life and receiving a degree in creative writing from Louisiana State University. While there, he had the opportunity to write reviews for *Necropsy,* an online quarterly review of horror literature. He is the author of a self-published novel, *Van Ark*.

Deborah G. Christie earned her PhD from Fordham University in 2005 and is currently an English Professor with E.C.P.I. University in Virginia Beach, Virginia. She is coeditor of *The Journal of Supernatural Studies* and is on the editorial board for the *Journal of Monsters and the Monstrous*. In her research and writing, she takes a cultural studies approach to constructions of monstrosity and its associated tropes of exclusion and suppression. Forthcoming projects include articles on *The Walking Dead, Nosferatu, Vampire Diaries,* and a book project titled *Death Is Not the End: How the Un-Dead Complicate Nature and Humanist Philosophy*.

Margo Collins is a visiting assistant professor of English at DeVry University. She holds a PhD in Eighteenth-Century British literature from the University of North Texas and in recent years has focused on Gothic literature and popular culture.

L. Andrew Cooper teaches film at the University of Louisville. His first book, *Gothic Realities* (2010), traces links between horror fiction and horrific realities from the 18th century forward. His second, *Dario Argento* (2012), treats the maestro's films as rhetorical challenges to cinematic norms. Cooper also coedited the popular college textbook *Monsters* and wrote the novels *Burning the Middle Ground* (2012), about supernatural mind control in the South, and *Descending Lines* (2013), in which a couple uses ghastly means to save their child. He received his PhD from Princeton University in 2005.

David E. Cowen is a sixth-generation Texan and a resident of Houston and a licensed trial attorney. David is the author of a book of poetry, *Sixth and Adams* (2001), and has published in online and hard copy journals in the United States, Great Britain, and Australia. One of his poems was featured in the Canadian Broadcasting Company *Radio's Outfront* program 9/11 tribute. His recent publications include an essay in *This I Believe: On Motherhood* (2012) published by the This I Believe Foundation; a book review in *CineAction Magazine,* Canada's leading film magazine; and a book review to be published in *Screem Magazine's* October 2013 edition. David's short story "Goth Thing" is in the fifth volume of the award-winning anthology series *Exotic Gothic,* edited by Danel Olson, published by PS Publishing.

Braden Dauzat is an undergraduate English student at Louisiana State University. Born in Texas, he quickly traded in his cowboy boots for Mardi Gras beads and Voodoo. With a love of all things frightful and fantastic, starting at an early age, he has consistently embarrassed and humiliated his family and friends with his passion for the two. This includes cosplay, taking Halloween a little too seriously, loud and heated debates in inappropriate areas, and the general attitude that there is no such thing as discussing the fantastic and grotesque too much.

Kevin Dole once entertained fantasies of becoming a distinguished scholar of supernatural horror fiction. Lacking the masochistic rigor necessary for grad school, he became instead a regular guy who happens to know a lot about Algernon Blackwood, Thomas Ligotti, and zombies. He lives in the eerie and immanent fog of northern California.

Jason Dupuy earned his doctorate from Louisiana State University in 2010. He is an assistant professor of English at River Parishes Community College in Sorrento, Louisiana, and lives in Baton Rouge with his wife, whom he finally convinced to watch *Dawn of the Dead.*

For nearly two decades, **Will Hires** has worked mostly in academic libraries as a reference librarian and currently is also serving as liaison to the science, technology, engineering and mathematics disciplines at Howard University in Washington, DC. He has also served, on two campuses, as scholarly communications librarian and coordinator of efforts to increase campus-wide awareness and understanding of scholarly publishing, open access, and institutional repositories. A former member of the Special Libraries Association, he is currently active in the American Library Association and the Association of College and Research Libraries and serves on several committees. He has an undergraduate degree in electrical engineering, MLIS degree, and a doctorate in business organization and information technology management.

Leah Larson earned a PhD in medieval literature from the University of Louisiana at Lafayette, where she enjoyed studying Icelandic sagas in Old Norse. She is professor of English at Our Lady of the Lake University in San Antonio, Texas, where she directs the English graduate and undergraduate programs. She has developed and taught a wide range of classes, including Dark Romanticism, Social Issues in Victorian Literature, Reading Medieval Women, and Literature and the Earth. This semester she is teaching a class on Shakespeare and a graduate seminar on Post-Apocalyptic Literature. Her research interests include horror, especially the films of Kiyoshi Kurosawa, and the many variations of the Robin Hood legend, and she has published and presented numerous conference papers on both topics. Her leisure interests include European travel, gardening, lazing on the beach, and herding cats.

Derek Manuel lives in muggy, muddy Central Louisiana, where the ground is often so wet and soft that one could easily crawl right out of it. His days involve muttering strange and powerful incantations in broken Latin to a robed figure with a disapproving countenance. He also possesses a BS in Biology, which is not particularly helpful in understanding and discussing zombies. In his spare time, he reads, watches, and listens to horror, science fiction, and fantasy, and occasionally writes humor and genre fiction. He has also been a grocery store clerk, a blogger, superstitious, arachnophobic, an excessive coffee drinker, an unimpressive guitarist, and a podcaster.

Laura Helen Marks holds a PhD in English and Women's and Gender Studies from Louisiana State University. Her research concerns film, gender, genre, and sexual representation, specifically pornographic genre and rhetoric. Her current work focuses on hardcore film adaptations of Victorian literature, and the various ways pornography makes use of "the Victorian" as a canvas on which to construct erotic appeal. She is currently enjoying revising her dissertation, *Erotic Transgressions: Pornographic Uses of the Victorian,* into a book.

Michael E. Matthews is currently associate professor and head of Serials, Media, and Interlibrary Loan at Northwestern State University of Louisiana. He is a steadfast member of the academic establishment who fondly remembers his carefree youth as a graveyard-shift stock clerk who once bowled seven strikes with a frozen Pilgrim's Pride chicken to the astonishment, and lasting admiration, of his fellow Delchamps employees. In between writing gigs and the budgetary pressures of his day job, Michael enjoys reading about neoliberalism, governmentality, and methods of self-emancipation in our postmodern world. He lives with his wife and child in a location inaccessible to everyone and everything, even Google Earth, so do not even bother trying.

Ben McCorkle is an associate professor of English and Writing Program administrator at the Ohio State University at Marion, where he teaches courses on composition, the history and theory of rhetoric, and digital media production. He is the author of the book *Rhetorical Delivery as Technological Discourse: A Cross-Historical Study,* published by Southern Illinois University Press and has published essays in various journals and edited collections, including *Computers and Composition Online, Rhetoric Society Quarterly,* and *Composition Studies.*

Matthew McEver is a student in the Master of Fine Arts in Creative Writing Program at Converse College in Spartanburg, South Carolina. His primary research interests include Southern Gothic and Grotesque, Literature of the American West, Gallows Humor, and Violence in Literature. He currently lives in northeast Georgia.

Robert Morrish is the former editor of *Cemetery Dance* magazine and *The Scream Factory* magazine, and has edited or coedited several anthologies, including *October Dreams* (winner of the International Horror Guild award). He has been the lead horror reviewer for *Publishers Weekly* and has had reviews and articles appear in publications such as *The San Francisco Chronicle, The Los Angeles Daily News, Weird Tales, Rue Morgue, Cinefantastique,* and *Rod Serling's Twilight Zone Magazine.* Robert is currently a columnist for three horror-focused magazines: *Cemetery Dance, Dark Discoveries,* and *Beware the Dark,* and he maintains a website, TwilightRidge.net, devoted to the horror small press. He also writes short fiction on occasion, and his stories have appeared in more than two dozen anthologies, including *The UFO Files, At Ease with the Dead, Shocklines,* and all seven volumes of the *Shivers* series.

Since 2007, **Danel Olson** has debuted new stories by some of the contributors and writers discussed in *The Encyclopedia of the Zombie* (including David Cowen, David Wellington, and Simon Clark),in his original fiction series *Exotic Gothic*. A winner of the Shirley Jackson Award and two-time World Fantasy Award nominee, the five *Exotic Gothic* volumes (from Ash-Tree Press and also PS Publishing) form the text in Olson's Horror, Ghost and Gothic course at Lone Star College in Houston. He is also the editor of *21st Century Gothic: Great Gothic Novels since 2000* (Scarecrow), *The Exorcist: Studies in the Horror Film* (Centipede), and forthcoming studies on *The Shining, The Devil's Backbone,* and *Pan's Labyrinth* (all from Centipede).

Solimar Otero is associate professor of English and a folklorist at Louisiana State University. Her research centers on gender, sexuality, Afro-Caribbean spirituality, and Yoruba traditional religion in folklore, literature, and ethnography. She is the author of *Afro-Cuban Diasporas in the Atlantic World* (University of Rochester Press in 2010). She is also the coeditor of *Yemoja: Gender, Sexuality, and Creativity in Latina/o and Afro-Atlantic Diasporas* (SUNY Press, 2013). Dr. Otero is the recipient of a Ruth Landes Memorial Research Fund grant (2013); a fellowship at the Harvard Divinity School's Women's Studies in Religion Program, (2009 to 2010); and a Fulbright award (2001). She is currently working on a volume that explores interorality in Afro-Cuban religious cultures and writing. Her work has also appeared in *Western Folklore, Africa Today, The Black Scholar, Atlantic Studies, Phoebe,* and *The American Journal of Psychoanalysis.*

Jacob Peoples is a biological sciences senior at Louisiana State University. He hails from Houma, Louisiana, and plans to attend medical school to become a cardiologist and eventually return to serve his hometown. He enjoys playing golf, reading autobiographies, and watching movies. He is also a huge football fan, who can be found either in Tiger Stadium or watching the Saints on fall weekends. His greatest hope is to never grow up, only older.

John Llewellyn Probert reviews films at his House of Mortal Cinema site (www.johnlprobert.blogspot.co.uk). He is the author of five short story collections so far, including *The Faculty of Terror,* which won the Children of the Night award, its sequel The *Catacombs of Fear* (both available from Gray Friar Press), *Coffin Nails* (Ash Tree Press), and *Wicked Delights* from Atomic Fez. His book *The Nine Deaths* *of Dr Valentine* has been shortlisted for this year's British Fantasy Award for best novella. He is married to the writer Thana Niveau and lives in the United Kingdom.

Walter Rankin has taught culture, language, and literature courses at George-town, George Washington, Hampton, and George Mason Universities, and he has published extensively on literary, film, and pedagogical topics. He is the author of *Grimm Pictures: Fairy Tale Archetypes in Eight Horror and Suspense Films* (2007, McFarland Publishers) and is working on his second book that looks at images of Nazis in both American and German propaganda films from World War II to modern-day references in popular culture. He currently serves as the interim dean for the School of Continuing Studies at Georgetown University.

Celise A. Reech-Harper lives in DeRidder, Louisiana, where she is the associate director of Public Services for the Beauregard Parish Public Library. She has advanced degrees in English and Information Science from Northwestern State University and the University of Tennessee. She is intensely interested in the ever-changing manifestations of cultural fears within horror fiction and cinema. Celise blames her mother for her love of reading and research. She also enjoys watching suspense-horror films with her husband, John, and two feline companions: Thor and Percy.

Tracy Stephenson Shaffer is associate professor in the Department of Communication Studies at Louisiana State University (LSU) where she teaches courses in performance and film. She is coauthor of *Performance Studies: The Interpretation of Aesthetic Texts* and has published essays in *Text and Performance Quarterly, Theatre Annual, Cultural Studies < = > Critical Methodologies,* and *Liminalities: A Journal of Performance Studies.* She has a chapter devoted to Alexandre Aja in the upcoming *Global Fear: International Horror Directors.* She also serves as producing director of the HopKins Black Box, an experimental laboratory theater on LSU's campus, where she also directs original work. In 2009, she created and directed *Nonfiction Zombie,* an ensemble performance that considered the zombie's recent rise in popularity as a useful metaphor and critique of contemporary life.

Jeff Snell was born in the heart of the military industrial complex before the release *of Star Wars Episode IV,* but after the assassination of Martin Luther King Jr. He learned to play baseball on a mountaintop in Tennessee and kissed his first girlfriend in a suburb of New Orleans. Today, he makes his home in Louisiana with a lovely wife and their retinue of dogs and cats. He has collected a respectable cache of weapons and supplies in preparation for the inevitable apocalypse. He sits transfixed in mesmerized delight and really hopes you are getting this.

Hank Wagner lives in northwestern New Jersey with his wife and four daughters. A respected critic and interviewer, his work has appeared in numerous genre publications such as *Mystery Scene, Cemetery Dance, Hellnotes, Horror Garage, Nova Express* and *Crimespree.* He has contributed articles to *Supernatural Literature of the World: An Encyclopedia, Icons of Horror: An Encyclopedia of Our Worst Nightmares,* and *The Encyclopedia of the Vampire.* Wagner is a coauthor of *The Complete Stephen*

King Universe and *Prince of Stories: A Guide to the Many Worlds of Neil Gaiman.* His also coedited *Thrillers: 100 Must Reads,* a 2011 Edgar, Anthony, and Macavity award finalist, with David Morrell.

Antoinette F. Winstead received a BFA in film and television production from New York University and an MFA. in film from Columbia University. She is currently a professor of Mass Communications, Drama, and English at Our Lady of the Lake University in San Antonio, Texas, where she serves as Program Chair of Mass Communications and Drama and teaches courses in screenwriting, film studies, and production. Her research interest range from the effects of genocide and war on film production in small African nations to the heroic journey in science fiction and horror texts (literary and filmic).

Jerome Winter is the associate editor of *Los Angeles Review Book's* SF page, and is a PhD candidate studying science fiction and contemporary American literature at the University of California, Riverside. His articles, reviews, and interviews have appeared in *Science Fiction Studies, The Oxford Handbook of Science Fiction,* and *The Eaton Journal of Archival Research.*

John R. Ziegler is currently director of the Writing Center at Concordia College, New York and teaches in the English Department at LaGuardia Community College, City University of New York. He has published on Shakespeare and heavy metal, representations of early modern Irish clothing, and court masques in early modern plays. On the more contemporary side, he has essays forthcoming about the boundaries of selfhood in the video games *Prototype* and *Prototype 2* and nonnormative family groups in *The Walking Dead* comics and television series.

Index

Note: Page numbers in **boldface** reflect main entries in the book.